THE BLUE GUIDES

Austria
Belgium and Luxembourg
Channel Islands
China*
Corsica
Crete
Cyprus
Egypt
England
France
Germany
Greece
Holland
Hungary*
Ireland
Northern Italy
Southern Italy
Morocco
Portugal
Scotland
Sicily
Spain
Switzerland
Turkey: Bursa to Antakya
Wales
Yugoslavia

Boston and Cambridge
Florence
Istanbul
Jerusalem
London
Moscow and Leningrad
New York
Oxford and Cambridge
Paris and Versailles
Rome and Environs
Venice

Cathedrals and Abbeys of England and Wales
Literary Britain and Ireland
Museums and Galleries of London
Victorian Architecture in Britain

in preparation

Aerial view of the Île de la Cité

BLUE GUIDE

PARIS

AND VERSAILLES

Ian Robertson

Maps and plans by John Flower

A & C Black
London

W W Norton
New York

Seventh Edition 1989

Published by A & C Black (Publishers) Limited
35 Bedford Row, London, WC1R 4JH

Published in the United States of America by
WW Norton & Company, Incorporated
500 Fifth Avenue, New York, NY 10110

Published simultaneously in Canada by
Penguin Books Canada Limited
2801 John Street, Markham, Ontario LR3 1B4

ISBN 0–7136–3032–9

A CIP catalogue record for this book
is available from the British Library.

ISBN 0-393-30484-1 USA

Printed and bound in Great Britain by
Hazell Watson & Viney Limited
Member of BPCC plc
Aylesbury Bucks

Ian Robertson was born in Tokyo and educated in England. After
spending several years in publishing and bookselling in London, he
began working on *Blue Guides* when he was commissioned to rewrite
Blue Guide Spain in 1970. He has since revised the Blue Guides to
Ireland, France, Paris, Portugal and Switzerland, as well as writing
Blue Guide Austria and *Blue Guide Cyprus*. He has also written
introductions to reprints of Richard Ford's *Handbook for Travellers in
Spain*, Joseph Baretti's *Journey from London to Genoa* and Gleig's
The Subaltern.

PREFACE

'To visit Paris at random is a most foolish and dangerous thing' wrote Thomas Cook in 'The Excursionist', and the same warning advice still applies.

This *Seventh Edition* of the *Blue Guide* incorporates numerous revisions and additions, for several important changes have taken place in the French capital and its immediate surroundings since the publication in 1985 of the previous edition. The section on Practical Information and amenities has been up-dated. It retains a summary Historical Introduction to Paris in relation to French history in general, which will, it is hoped, provide the chronological framework necessary for a better understanding of her past.

With the publication early in 1988 of the second edition of *Blue Guide France*, which covers in detail the Île-de-France, previously included in Blue Guide Paris and Environs (the title of the last three editions), it has been decided to change the title of this new edition to Paris and Versailles, on which it now concentrates. It does, however, also contain full descriptions of St.-Denis, Vincennes, Écouen, Sceaux, Malmaison, and St.-Germain-en-Laye, and condensed descriptions of the Musée Condé at Chantilly, Senlis, and the Château at Fontainebleau, as they are often visited in day trips from central Paris.

An entirely new Blue Guide to *Corsica* was added to the series in 1987. Both this, and the guide to France, now provide the traveller with wide-ranging yet compact descriptions of their landscapes and monuments, the very diversity of which should satisfy the demands of the most energetic and enthusiastic tourist.

Some of the cultural associations between Paris and Great Britain included in previous editions, which may have been of comparatively slight importance, have been substituted by others of more interest (such as those referred to on p 207–8), but the Editor would much appreciate receiving additional information from readers concerning other associations (apart from the 'Queen Elizabeth slept here' variety), which might be incorporated in future editions.

The 32 urban routes are described for sightseeing on foot, almost always the most convenient and enjoyable way of getting about, while some of the nearest *métro* stations are also indicated along each route. Visitors to Paris are warned that, because of the sheer scale of many of her monuments, and the extensive sweep of many of her vistas, it is only too easy to underestimate distances, and one should not attempt too much sightseeing in a day. Indeed, the *Musée du Louvre* alone deserves and physically demands several visits.

The publication of this edition coincides with an era of continuing uncertainty in which a number of the major museums of Paris are still undergoing radical reorganisation, as with the *Musée du Louvre* itself, where whole departments are being moved around and certain sections are likely to be closed entirely for long periods of time, while others may well be shut temporarily for partial re-arrangement. The museums will attempt to keep a proportion of their collections on view during this period of upheaval, but in certain cases the Editor has little alternative but to list a selection of important works which may be seen *somewhere* in the building rather than specify their precise whereabouts, an unsatisfactory situation which it is hoped will be improved by the time the next edition of this Guide is published. Among the more drastic changes which have taken place recently has been the transference of the Impressionists in the *Jeu de Paume* to the

new *Musée d'Orsay*, in the reconstructed *Gare d'Orsay*, which also
houses a number of subsidiary collections which had been temporarily accommodated in the *Palais de Tokyo* and elsewhere. Among
other collections recently inaugurated are those devoted to the
Islamic arts in the *Institut du Monde Arabe*. The *Cité des Sciences
et de l'Industrie* has likewise opened its doors at *La Villette*.

Successive Présidents, ambitious to leave their mark on French
culture, continue to inaugurate prestigious monuments, some of
which may redound to their creuit. Among projects still under way
are the redevelopment of *Bercy*, the construction of an opera-house
at the Pl. de la Bastille, the restoration and reorganisation of the
Grand Louvre, with its controversial pyramidal entrance, and the
completion of the complex of *La Défense*.

Although endeavouring to keep abreast of all the most recent
changes and rearrangements, inevitably the latest facts are not
always forthcoming, and getting advance information accurate
enough to print is virtually impossible.

Travellers returning to Paris after a period of years will find many
changes, not all for the good. Certainly the cleaning of façades
(even if only the façades in some cases) has improved its general
appearance, and indeed, in spite of aggressive traffic flowing along
the quais of the Seine (unobtrusively underground at some
stretches), much of the centre still retains its immense charm. One
continues to be diverted by the gushing runnels of water cleansing
the gutters, although the more fastidious will continue to complain,
not unreasonably, of the unedifying state in which the canine
population of Paris chooses to leave the adjacent *trottoirs*.

The transformation of the area occupied by the old *Halles* has
been virtually completed, but many have suffered from agoraphobia after visiting the commercial *Forum* now filling the immense
'trou', but at least one now has a better view of both *St.-Eustache*
and the nearby *Bourse du Commerce*, which is some compensation.
Meanwhile many familiar horizons have been broken by the
erection of vast blocks of buildings, perhaps the most injudiciously
placed—apart from the *Centre Beaubourg*—being the *Tour Montparnasse*, which, dominating the surrounding area, has also irrepa-
rably affected the cityscape. Nevertheless, much of the modern
architecture of Paris is of a high standard, and while certain squalid
outlying districts are being transformed out of all recognition,
others of considerable architectural interest—such as the *Marais*—
continue to be tastefully restored. Unfortunately the view of many
monuments is spoiled by shoals of blatantly parked coaches, but
there is still a great deal to see not far off the beaten track.

A wide range of accommodation is available in the area covered,
lists of which, together with those of a range of restaurants, are
readily obtainable free of charge from the French National Tourist
Offices.

The practice of 'starring' the highlights has been continued, even
if the system is subjective and inconsistent, for such asterisks do
help the hurried traveller to pick out those things which the general
consensus of opinion (modified occasionally by the Editor's personal prejudice, admittedly) considers should not be missed. (It has
been suggested that he might also include 'daggers' to indicate
what would be better avoided, if possible.) In certain cases a
museum has been starred, rather than individual objects among
those described, when the standard of its contents is remarkably
high.

Selection remains the touchstone by which guide-books are judged, and it is hoped that this edition will provide a balanced account of most aspects of a great city and its immediate surroundings without neglecting any that might appeal to the intelligent resident or visitor, and without being so exhaustive as to leave him no opportunity of discovering additional pleasures for himself; and yet, in the words of Richard Ford (author of the famous 'Hand-Book for Spain' of 1845): '...how often does the wearied traveller rejoice when no more is to be "done"; and how does he thank the faithful pioneer, who, by having himself toiled to see some "local lion", has saved others the tiresome task, by his assurance that it is not worth the time or trouble'.

Most of the revisions—the amount of alteration varying from very minor corrections to the addition of considerable new matter—have been made from personal observation on the spot during recent walks and tours made in the service of this edition, but not every locality in Paris can be visited for each edition of so comprehensive a guide. Its preparation has depended largely on the Editor alone, and certain unintentional omissions are inevitable, since Paris offers an 'embarras de richesses' that can never be encompassed in a single volume. The readers' co-operation is therefore solicited. Any constructive suggestions for the improvement of future editions will be welcomed and acknowledged by the Editor, who alone is responsible for all inexactitudes, shortcomings, inconsistencies, and solecisms.

Its street-atlas, maps, and plans have been corrected; the cartography has again been undertaken by *John Flower.*

In addition to those providing facilities and material assistance, or offering information and advice, who were listed at this point in the previous edition, the following must be mentioned: *Marie-France Brault* at the Caisse Nationale des Monuments Historiques; *Mlle Baron* (Musée du Louvre); *Annick Bouret* (La Villette); *Véronique Moreaux* (Cité des Science et de l'Industrie); *Mirelle Gebrecht* (Musée du Prieuré, St.-Germain-en-Laye); *Mme Berger* (Musée des Antiquités Nationales, St.-Germain-en-Laye); *Véronique Janneau* (Union des Arts Décoratifs); *Beatrix Saule* (Château de Versailles); *Magdalena Pfeiffer* (Château de Maisons); *Isabelle d'Andlau* (Musée Marmottan); *Claire Ferras* (Direction des Musées de France); *Sylvie Poujade* (Réunion des Musées Nationaux et Direction des Musées de France); *Alan Watson* Établissement Public du Grand Louvre; *Michèle Andrieux* (Maison de la France, Paris); *Nicolle Roques* and *Nathalie Paul* (Office de Tourisme de Paris); *Patrick Vittet-Philippe* (French Embassy, London).

The Editor must again record his appreciation of the generous hospitality he has enjoyed both chez Boyars in London, and chez Peyronnet and chez Amar in Paris and Versailles respectively, and at the Hôtel Latitude St.-Germain; while Paul Langridge and Gemma Davies have given all essential support and practical assistance. My wife has continued, tirelessly, to accompany me on most of my perambulations in Paris and excursions in its vicinity.

Just before this edition went to press, it was learnt that the *Musée Jacquemart-André* had closed and that the *Musée Cognacq-Jay* has also closed, temporarily, prior to moving to new premises.

The publishers would like to thank Caisse Nationale des Monuments Historiques, Heather Waddell, and the Cité des Sciences et de l'Industrie, for permission to reproduce the illustrations in this guide.

A NOTE ON BLUE GUIDES

The Blue Guide series began in 1918 when Muirhead Guide-Books Limited published 'Blue Guide London and its Environs'. Finlay and James Muirhead already had extensive experience of guide-book publishing: before the First World War they had been the editors of the English editions of the German Baedekers, and by 1915 they had acquired the copyright of most of the famous 'Red' Handbooks from John Murray.

An agreement made with the French publishing house Hachette et Cie in 1917 led to the translation of Muirhead's London Guide, which became the first 'Guide Bleu'—Hachette had previously published the blue-covered 'Guides Joanne'. Subsequently, Hachette's 'Guide Bleu Paris et ses Environs' was adapted and published in London by Muirhead. The collaboration between the two publishing houses continued until 1933.

In 1931 Ernest Benn Limited took over the Blue Guides, appointing Russell Muirhead, Finlay Muirhead's son, editor in 1934. The Muirheads' connection with Blue Guides ended in 1963 when Stuart Rossiter, who had been working on the Guides since 1954, became house editor, revising and compiling several of the books himself.

The Blue Guides are now published by A & C Black, who acquired Ernest Benn in 1984, so continuing the tradition of guide-book publishing which began in 1826 with 'Black's Economical Tourist of Scotland'. The Blue Guide series continues to grow: there are now more than 30 titles in print with revised editions appearing regularly and many new Blue Guides in preparation.

'Blue Guides' is a registered trademark.

EXPLANATIONS

Type. The main routes are described in large type. Smaller type is used for deviations, for historical and preliminary paragraphs, and for descriptions of greater detail or less importance.

Asterisks indicate points of special interest or excellence: two 'stars' are used sparingly.

Street Numbering. In Paris, in streets parallel to the river, the houses are numbered from E to W; in those at right-angles to the Seine, from the end nearest the river.

The **Population** figures given (in round figures) are based on those of the census of 1982, or revisions of them.

Anglicisation. For the sake of consistency, place-names and the names of kings, etc. have retained their French form.

Abbreviations. In addition to generally accepted and self-explanatory forms, the following occur in this guide:

Av. = Avenue
C = Century
Blvd = Boulevard
m = metres
N.-D. = Notre-Dame, Our Lady
Pl. = Place, or Plan
R = Room
Rte = Route
St.- or Ste.- = Saint

The sign ◇ immediately after certain monuments and buildings indicates that the *Caisse Nationale des Monuments Historiques* is responsible for them; see p 172.

CONTENTS

12 CONTENTS

HISTORICAL INTRODUCTION

The foundations of modern France may be said to date from the passage of the Alps by the Romans in 121 BC and the establishment of the province (Latin provincia; modern Provence) of Gallia Narbonensis. Important remains such as the Pont du Gard, and the theatres and amphitheatres at Nîmes, Arles and Orange are still extant. But the whole of France as we now know it did not become subject to Rome until after Julius Caesar's decisive defeat of Vercingetorix at Alésia in 52 BC. In the previous year Caesar had first mentioned—under the name of Lutetia—the fortified capital of the Parisii, an insignificant Gallic tribe, confined on islands in the Seine, which he nominated as the rendez-vous of deputies from conquered Gaul.

In spite of occasional local revolts, Rome gradually imposed her government, roads, speech, and culture on Gaul. By c AD 250 the country had become partially Christianised, St. Dionysius (Denis) being its first bishop, but within a few years began the first of a series of Barbarian invasions. In 292 Paris became a base of the Emperor Constantius Chlorus, although it was not until 360 that the name was applied to the river-port. Barbarian mercenaries (among them Visigoths and Burgundians) were employed to defend the frontiers of the Empire in its decline, but they wearied of their alliance with the degenerate Gallo-Romans, and after the repulse of Attila and his Huns at the Catalaunian Fields (451) became virtually masters of the land, the most powerful tribe being the Salian Franks under their leader Merovius.

Merovius's grandson Clovis I (481–511) defeated Syagrius (the Roman governor of Soissons) in 486, and the Alemanni at Tolbiac in 496, after which he adopted the Christian religion, and in the following year Paris opened her gates to him (traditionally on the advice of Ste. Geneviève), although he did not make it his official capital until 508. According to Frankish custom, the kingdom was divided on his death between his three sons into Austrasia (between the Meuse and the Rhine), Neustria (the territory to the NW, from the Meuse to the Loire), and Burgundy (to the S), and although the Merovingians remained in control, the dynasty was weakened by internecine warfare during the next two centuries.

Eminent among the Merovingians was Chilperic I (king of Neustria from 561–84) and Dagobert (king of Austrasia from 622 and of all France from 628 until his death in 638). Paris remained the political centre of conflicting Frankish interests, its growing population overflowing to form suburbs around monasteries situated on both banks of the river; but after the death of Dagobert, who refounded the abbey of St.-Denis, most of the power passed into the hands of the 'maires du Palais', one of whom, Charles Martel (714–41), an Austrasian, was to defeat at Poitiers in 732 the invading Moors, who had overrun Spain during the previous two decades. In 751 Pepin, Martel's son, deposed Childéric III, the last of the Merovingians, and founded a new dynasty.

Carolingians
Pepin, le Bref   (751–68)
Charlemagne   (768–814)
Louis, le Débonnaire   (814–40)
Charles, le Chauve   (840–77)
Louis II, Le Bègue   (877–79)

Louis III, and Carloman   (879–82)
Carloman   (882–84)
Charles, le Gros   (884–87)
Count Eudes   (887–98)
Charles, le Simple   (898–922)
Louis IV, d'Outremer   (936–54)
Lothaire   (954–86)
Louis V, le Fainéant   (986–87)

Although Pepin resided occasionally at Paris, his son Charlemagne, in alliance with the Pope, extended his dominion over Germany and Italy, and was crowned 'Emperor of the West', or 'Holy Roman Emperor'. He moved the seat of government from France to Aix-la-Chapelle. Not only a great ruler, Charlemagne also presided over a remarkable revival of learning and education. However, the system of dividing territories on the death of kings was to cause the eventual disintegration of the empire, and in 843, by the Treaty of Verdun, those areas which were to form modern France were transferred to his grandson Charles 'le Chauve' (the Bald). Further division ensued, and France became little more than a collection of independent feudal states controlled by dukes and counts.

The situation was further disturbed by the invasion of Scandinavian or Norse pirates. By 912 the Vikings had settled in Rouen and had carved out the duchy of Normandy for themselves, having in 885 besieged and pillaged Paris itself from their encampment (possibly on the present site of the Louvre). The Cité had been successfully defended by Eudes, Duc de France and comte de Paris, who in 888 deposed Charles 'le Gros', but the Carolingian dynasty continued to stagger on for another hundred years. It was to be a century of disunity for France, distinguished politically by the growth of Norman power, and religiously by the foundation in 910 of a Benedictine abbey at Cluny, later to gain fame and influence.

Capetians
Hugues Capet   (987–96)
Robert, le Pieux   (996–1031)
Henri I   (1031–60)
Philippe I   (1060–1108)
Louis VI, le Gros   (1108–37)
Louis VII, le Jeune   (1137–80)
Philippe Auguste   (1180–1223)
Louis VIII, le Lion   (1223–26)
Louis IX, St. Louis   (1226–70)
Philippe III, le Hardi   (1270–85)
Philippe IV, le Bel   (1285–1314)
Louis X, le Hutin   (1314–16)
Jean I   (1316; died 4 days old)
Philippe V, le Long   (1316–22)
Charles IV, le Bel   (1322–28)

Hugues Capet was elected by the nobles at Senlis in preference to any more incapable Carolingians, and he and his successors proceeded to make Paris the base of a centralising policy by which they might control the disunited country. But this policy frequently brought them into conflict with independent spirits, one of whom, William, duke of Normandy, in 1066 invaded and conquered England. Paris grew steadily in size and importance, particularly on the North Bank, and during the reign of Louis VI, if not earlier, a second town wall was thrown up. The 'Hanse Parisienne', a league of merchants, was established, marking the foundation of the municipality.

The marriage in 1152 of the future Henry II of England to Eleanor of Aquitaine (the divorced wife of Louis VII), whose dowry brought Henry about one-third of France, was to cause a power struggle between the two countries which lasted three centuries. Meanwhile, in 1095 Urban II preached the First Crusade at Clermont; in 1198 the Abbey of Cîteaux was founded; in 1115 Clairvaux was founded by St. Bernard, who in 1146 was to preach the Second Crusade at Vézelay. In 1163 the foundation-stone of Notre-Dame was laid (and some years later Philippe Auguste built the fortress of the Louvre). This religious enthusiasm was in part the reason for the Jews in France being expelled in 1182. The cathedral schools of Paris (at which Guillaume de Champeaux and Abélard had taught) were united to form one University, which was granted its first statutes by Pope Innocent III in 1208. This was established on the Left Bank of the Seine, where the growing student population settled; the Right Bank became the centre of commerce, industry, and administration. Some streets were paved; the two ancient wooden bridges were replaced by ones of stone; and the city was enclosed by an extensive line of fortifications.

In the political field Philippe Auguste won back a large part of the lost provinces (Normandy and Anjou), having inflicted a heavy defeat on the allies of John of England at Bouvines in 1214; and the bloody Albigensian Crusade of 1209–13 eventually restored Languedoc to French rule.

During the long reign of Louis IX, the Hospice des Quinze-Vingts and the theological college of the Sorbonne were founded, the latter to become a dominant influence in the University. The Palais de la Cité was rebuilt (parts of which, notably the Ste.-Chapelle, still exist), and the office of Provost was reformed; statutes were drawn up for the many guilds, which were to remain in force until the Revolution. Louis, canonised in 1297, was a great crusader, and eventually lost his life at Tunis. He was succeeded by Philippe III, Philippe IV, and Louis X, respectively. With the death of Charles IV in 1328 the direct branch of the Capetian dynasty became extinct.

House of Valois
Philippe VI   (1328–50)
Jean II, le Bon   (1350–64)
Charles V, le Sage   (1364–80)
Charles VI, le Bien-Aimé   (1380–1422)
Charles VII, le Victorieux   (1422–61)
Louis XI   (1461–83)
Charles VIII, l'Affable   (1483–98)
Louis XII, le Père du Peuple   (1498–1515)
François I   (1515–47)
Henri II   (1547–59)
François II   (1559–60)
Charles IX   (1560–74)
Henri III   (1574–89)

The claim of Philippe de Valois to the throne was disputed by Edward III of England, who invaded France, precipitating the Hundred Years War (1337–1453). He routed the French army at Crécy (1346) and inflicted a further defeat on Jean II at Poitiers in 1356. The ravages and depredations of both French and English soldiery roused the peasants (the Jacquerie) and the burgesses to revolt. In Paris, Étienne

Marcel (Maire du Palais and provost of the merchants) took advantage of the situation to increase the influence of the municipality, but he offended public opinion by attempting to hand over the city to Charles of Navarre, and was assassinated in 1358. Two years later, by the Treaty of Brétigny, England renounced her claims, but soon after desultory warfare between the two countries broke out again, and continued until the French had won back a large part of their lost territory, largely due to the tactics of Du Guesclin.

Charles V was able to bring back some order to the kingdom. He built the fortress of the Bastille, but anarchy returned during the following reign, when his weak-minded son Charles VI provoked the citizens of Paris—at that time numbering some 280,000—by excessive taxation. Although the resulting revolt of the 'Maillotins' was bloodily suppressed, the king became the pawn of rival regents, and for the next 40 years France suffered from dissensions between the aristocratic party, the Armagnacs, and the Burgundians, the popular party (Jean II had made his fourth son, Jean sans Pèur, Duke of Burgundy).

Seizing the opportunity, Henry V of England invaded France, and supported by the Burgundians, defeated a French force at Agincourt (1415). By the Treaty of Troyes (1420) he received the hand of Catherine, Charles VI's daughter, together with the right of succession to the throne. But in 1422 Henry died at Vincennes, only seven weeks before the death of Charles VI. Charles VII, by himself no match for the English and Burgundians, found a champion in Jeanne d'Arc (Joan of Arc; 1412–31). But the English continued to control Paris, until 1436. In 1429 John, Duke of Bedford repelled an assault led by Joan, who, after a brilliant campaign, defeated the English at Orléans in May of that year. Captured at Compiègne by the Burgundians in 1430, she was handed over to the English, and condemned as a heretic by a court of ecclesiastics, was burned at the stake in Rouen. But the successful revolt she had inspired continued, and by 1453 only Calais remained of the once extensive English possessions in France. A vivid account of conditions prevailing in Paris during the years 1405–49 is given in the anonymously compiled 'Journal d'un Bourgeois de Paris'. The poet Villon was born here in 1431.

With the reign of Louis XI the change from a medieval social system to the modern state was accelerated. A brilliant and unscrupulous politician (and relieved of the menace of England, then occupied with the domestic 'War of the Roses'), he proceeded to crush the great feudal lordships which encroached on his territory, the most threatening being that of Charles the Bold ('le Téméraire') of Burgundy. The Peace of Péronne (1468) gave the Burgundians a momentary advantage, but Louis managed to alienate Charles' English allies by the Treaty of Picquigny (1475). After Charles's death before the walls of Nancy in 1477, Louis soon overwhelmed his lesser adversaries, and brought Arras, the Franche-Comté, Anjou, and Maine into direct allegiance to the crown. In 1469/70 the first printing-press in France was set up in the Sorbonne; and in 1484 the first meeting of the Estates-General was convened at Tours, near which, in the Loire valley, several châteaux were being rebuilt as royal residences.

The following half century was principally occupied with indecisive campaigns in Italy, the only tangible result of which—particularly during the reign of *François I*—was the establishment in France of the cultural concepts of the Italian Renaissance. Among the more important literary figures of the period were Marot, Rabelais, Du Bellay, and Ronsard—the last two being members of the circle known as La Pléïade.

Charles VIII and Louis XII were successive husbands of Anne de Bretagne, whose dowry, the important duchy of Brittany, was formally united to France in 1532 on the death of her daughter, wife of François I. The reign of Henri II saw the acquisition by France of the Three Bishoprics (Metz, Toul, and Verdun), while Calais fell to the Duc de Guise in 1558. In 1559 Henri II concluded the treaty of Cateau-Cambrésis with Felipe II of Spain, thus ending the Italian wars. In 1564 an edict fixed the beginning of the year as 1 January, inaugurating the 'new style' of dating.

The short reign of François II, who while still dauphin (aged ten) had married Mary Stuart, Queen of Scots, was followed by that of his brother Charles IX. At the instigation of Catherine de Médicis (1519–89), his bigoted and domineering mother, Charles signed the order for the massacre of protestant Huguenots on the Eve of St. Bartholomew (23 August 1572). (Catherine was mother also of Henri III, and of Marguerite de Valois, the first wife of Henri of Navarre.) From 1560 until the promulgation of the Edict of Nantes in 1598, the country was ravaged, sporadically, by the Religious Wars of the League (La Ligue). In 1589 the ultra-Catholic Henri, Duc de Guise, was murdered at Blois by Henri III, against whom he had been an overt rebel. The king himself was assassinated at St.-Cloud the following year.

House of Bourbon

Henri IV, le Grand   (1589–1610)
Louis XIII, le Juste   (1610–43)
Louis XIV, 'le Roi Soleil'   (1643–1715)
Louis XV, le Bien-Aimé   (1715–74)
Louis XVI   (1774–92)
Louis XVII   (never reigned)
Louis XVIII   (1814–24)
Charles X   (1824–30)

The parents of Henri IV (of Navarre) were Jeanne d'Albret (daughter of Marguerite of Navarre) and Antoine de Bourbon, of the Bourbon branch of the Capetian dynasty, descending from Robert of Clermont, sixth son of Louis IX. A Protestant, Henri eventually defeated the Catholics at Ivry (1590), but was unable to enter the besieged capital until 1594, after he had ostensibly abjured his faith with (it is said) the cynical remark that 'Paris vaut bien une messe'. Despite his conversion, he granted Protestants freedom of worship, by the Edict of Nantes. Among the many who joined in the general recognition of Henri as the legitimate heir to the throne was Montaigne, whose 'Essays' were published in part in 1580.

Peace established, Henri set about enlarging the palaces of the Louvre and the Tuileries, planned several squares including the Place Royale, and completed the Pont Neuf. However, with his assassination by Ravaillac in 1610, religious restlessness returned, and the admirable reforms and economies instituted by Sully, his able minister, were brought to nothing by the extravagant favourites of young Louis XIII (whose mother, Marie de Médicis Henri had married in 1600 after his divorce from Marguerite de Valois. On Henri's death, Marie became Regent, but in 1624 Card. Richelieu (1585–1642) took over the reins of government. His main aim was the establishment of absolute royal power in France, and of French supremacy in Europe. He suppressed all Protestant influence in politics, capturing their stronghold, La Rochelle, in 1628. Anyone defying Richelieu suffered severe penalties, and numerous fortresses throughout the country were dismantled in the process of repression. The cardinal then turned his attention to the House of Habsburg, which under the Emperor Charles V had been encroaching on the frontiers of France, and, in alliance with Gustavus Adolphus of Sweden, Richelieu involved France in the Thirty Years' War. The campaigns of the Grand Condé (1621–86; a member of a collateral branch of the Bourbons) resulted in the temporary acquisition of Picardy, Alsace, and Roussillon.

In 1635 and 1640 respectively, the 'Académie Française' and the 'Imprimerie Royal' were founded; a fifth wall was erected around Paris, where several new quarters arose, such as the Pré-aux-Clercs (Faubourg St.-Germain), the Île-St.-Louis, and the Marais, which became a favourite residence of the nobility. Marie de Médicis built the Palais du Luxembourg; Anne of Austria, consort of the king since 1614, founded the church of Vâl-de-Grace in thanksgiving for the birth of a son (later Louis XIV) in 1638; and Richelieu built for himself the Palais-Cardinal, later the Palais-Royal.

Richelieu had been succeeded meanwhile by Card. Mazarin (1602–61), who carried on his predecessor's policies. Although France was assured of the possession of Alsace and the Three Bishoprics by the Treaty of Westphalia in 1648, the expenses of campaigning were crippling. Civil war broke out, known as 'La Fronde', from which no one—the insurgents, Mazarin, Condé, or Marshal Turenne (1611–75)—emerged with much credit. During the Fronde, Condé (who had defeated the Spaniards at Recroi in 1643), allied himself with Spain (who had not subscribed to the Treaty of Westphalia), but Turenne's victory at the Battle of the Dunes (1658) forced Spain to accept the Treaty of the Pyrenees the following year.

On Mazarin's death in 1661 Louis XIV, who had succeeded as a minor in 1643, decided to govern alone, duped by the conviction that 'L'État c'est moi'. The nobility were reduced to being ineffectual courtiers, and the king selected his ministers from the *haute bourgeoisie*, some, such as Colbert (1619–83), being very able. He then launched a series of costly wars of self-aggrandisement, which although they eventually increased the territory of France—its frontiers fortified by Vauban (1633–1707)—were to bring his long reign to a disastrous close. At the same time his indulgence in such extravagant projects as the building of a palace fit for the 'Roi Soleil' at Versailles (extended by Hardouin-Mansart, with gardens laid out by Le Nôtre, and its lavish decoration supervised by Le Brun), where Louis had chosen to transfer his court in 1672, further beggared the country. At Versailles were gathered most of the great artists of this and succeeding epochs, while among composers Lully (from 1652 until his death in 1687), Couperin, and (in the following reign) Rameau, provided music to entertain the court.

In Paris, which had now grown to a metropolis containing some 500,000 inhabitants and 25,000 houses, boulevards were laid out on the lines of Étienne Marcel's wall. The Hôtel des Invalides was founded in 1671. The University quarters were incorporated within the city, which had become one of the cultural centres of Europe—Corneille, Racine, Molière, La Fontaine, Boileau, and Pascal (the latter associated with the activities of the reforming Jansenists of Port-Royal) making their home there—while the salons of Mme de Rambouillet and Mme de Sablé, among others, had become the influential intellectual rendez-vous of such figures as La Rochefoucauld, the Scudérys, and Bossuet. Meanwhile, in 1685, Louis had revoked the Edict of Nantes, which again imposed Catholicism on the country.

The king's preoccupation with 'La Gloire' involved him first in the rapid campaign of 1667–68, which secured the possession of several towns in Flanders; while the Dutch War of 1672–78 ended in the Peace of Nijmegen and the absorption of the Franche-Comté. Less successful were the campaigns against the League of Augsburg (or the Grand Alliance; 1686–97), and of the war of the Spanish Succession (1701–13), in which French forces suffered repeatedly at the hands of Marlborough and Prince Eugène (at Blenheim in 1704; Ramillies in 1706; Oudenaarde in 1708; and Malplaquet in 1709), although Marshal Villars won a victory at Denain (1712) after the withdrawal of the English from the war.

'If greatness of soul consists in a love of pageantry, an ostentation of fastidious pomp, a prodigality of expense, an affectation of munificence, an insolence of ambition, and a haughty reserve of deportment; Lewis certainly deserved the appellation of Great. Qualities which are really heroic, we shall not find in the composition of his character.' Such was Smollett's condemnation. Life at court during the latter part of the reign and subsequent regency (under Philippe, duc d'Orléans; 1715–23) is brilliantly recorded in the 'Mémoires' of the Duc de Saint-Simon. Several bad harvests (particularly in 1726, 1739 and 1740) decimated the peasantry—who formed four-fifths of the population of 20,000,000 in 1700—but colonial trade improved, and merchants thrived in such provincial centres as Bordeaux, Nantes, and Marseille.

The marriage in 1725 of Louis XV to Maria, daughter of Stanislas Leczinski (the deposed king of Poland) drew France into the War of the Polish Succession (1733), and further ruinous wars followed, including that of the Austrian Succession (in which Louis was allied with Frederick the Great of Prussia in opposition to England and Holland, who supported the cause of Maria Theresa, Empress of Austria). In spite of Saxe's brilliant victory at Fontenoy (1745) the French gained little, while the English improved their position as a maritime power, and Prussia likewise gained in strength. The Seven Years' War (1756–63), in which France was allied to Austria, was disastrous for France, and saw the loss of flourishing colonies in India, North America, and the West Indies. By 1788 the cost of these wars had created a situation whereby three-quarters of the State expenditure was being spent on reducing the national debt and on defence.

Nevertheless, grandiose buildings continued to be erected in Paris, such as the Panthéon, and the Palais-Bourbon; but a sixth wall, raised as a customs-barrier by the powerful and rapacious farmers-general of taxes, only fostered further discontent ('Le mur murant Paris rend Paris murmurant'). In spite of the general degradation of his court, and the corruption and negligence rife among his administrators, the reign of Louis XV was made illustrious by some of the great names in French literature: Voltaire, Rousseau, Montesquieu, Marivaux, the Encyclopédistes (Diderot, Condillac, Helvetius, d'Alembert, et al), who frequented the fashionable salons of the Marquise de Lambert, Mme de Tencin, Mme du Deffand, Mlle Lespinasse, Mme Geoffrin, or Baron d'Holbach, and others of lesser influence. But many of the philosophers vehemently attacked both the establishment and the clergy, and their ideas undoubtedly helped to sow the seeds of revolution. At the same time the expulsion of the Jesuits in 1764, after years of struggle with the Jansenists, removed one of the pillars of the Ancien Régime.

On his succession Louis XVI found the populace critical of his predecessor's extravagance and lack of military success, but was too weak to cope with the interminable financial crises (in spite of the reforms initiated by Turgot from 1774, and of Necker from 1777). Economic problems were precipitated by bad harvests, particularly in 1787–88, when there were grain riots in many French towns, including Paris and Grenoble. These crises inspired reforms, which, if accepted, would have adversely affected the privileged estates ('Les Privilégiés')—the upper ranks of the clergy (the First Estate), and the majority of the nobility (the Second Estate)—who therefore rejected them. Louis' foreign policy, which supported the American colonies in their struggle for independence from England, was not only financially disastrous, but indirectly did much to disseminate democratic ideals.

In an attempt to reform methods of taxation—for Les Privilégiés held innumerable hereditary rights by which they avoided paying taxes, yet levied them to their own advantage—the king convoked an assembly of the États généraux. The 1165 deputies elected met at Versailles on 5 May 1789, for the first time since 1614. The first political act of the Third Estate, the Non-Privilégiés (which numbered almost 600) was the creation of a National Assembly (17 June), which, meeting separately in the Jeu de Paume on the 20th, swore not to disband until a constitution had been given to the country which would limit royal autocracy and guarantee liberty, equality, and fraternity. Three days later Mirabeau defied the king: 'Nous sommes ici par la volonté du peuple et ... on ne nous arrachera que par la force des baïonnettes'; and on the 9 July, reinforced by many of the clergy and a minority of the nobility, the renamed Assemblée constituante set to work to frame such a constitution. But two days later Necker, who had promised further financial reforms, was dismissed by the king, and it was feared that this gratuitous act would be followed by the dissolution of the Assembly.

The **Revolution**. The citizens of Paris—and also in the provinces at Dijon, Rennes, Lyon, Nantes, and Le Havre—were provoked into a more open rebellion, culminating in the storming of the Bastille on 14 July; but while the next few months saw numerous reforms, there was little political or economic stability, and tensions heightened. In an attempt to avoid bankruptcy, church lands were nationalised, which produced some opposition. Many of the nobility—a class shortly, but temporarily, to be abolished—sought asylum abroad. The king and his unpopular consort, Marie-Antoinette, were virtually prisoners in the Tuileries; they attempted to flee the country, but were arrested (at Varennes in June 1791) and brought back to Paris. On 1 October 1791 a new Legislative Assembly was formed, which in the following April declared war on Austria to forestall foreign intervention. The Assembly was at first swayed by the moderate Girondins, but the following year the extreme Jacobins under Danton, Robespierre, and Marat, seized power, and, as the National Convention, meeting on 20 September (the day on which the victory of Valmy turned the tide of war in France's favour), established the Republic.

On 21 January 1793 Louis XVI was executed in the Place de la Révolution, an act followed by the setting-up in March of the dictatorial Committee of Public Safety, which, suspicious of the moderate party, ruthlessly suppressed all suspected of royalist sympathies. The guillotine was in constant action. In July Marat was assassinated, and even the Dantonists found themselves to be a moderating force, opposed to the even more bloodthirsty Hébertists.

But Robespierre, chief architect of the Reign of Terror, brooked no rivals, and early in 1794 both Hébert and Danton were guillotined. However, after further weeks of ferocious intimidation, the reaction came, and on 27 July (9 Thermidor; see below), Robespierre's own head fell.

A **Republican Calendar**, the object of which was to make a break with Christian tradition, was instituted during the autumn of 1793, the mathematician Romme being responsible for its chronology. It was to remain in force until January 1806, when France officially reverted to the Gregorian Calendar (introduced in 1582). It was antedated, as it was considered that the first year (An I) had begun at the autumnal equinox (22 September) of 1792, to coincide with the proclamation of

Detail of a popular print showing the Bastille in the process of demolition, after its capture by revolutionaries on 14 July 1789

the Republic. The year was divided into 12 months of 30 days each; each month being sub-divided into three periods of ten days or décades; and 5 days ('sansculottides') were added at the end of each year (6 in leap years) to be observed as national festivals.

The days were named in numerical order: *primidi, duodi, tridi, quartidi, quintidi, sextidi, septidi, octidi, nonidi, and décadi* (the day of rest). More poetic names, devised by Fabre d'Églantine, were given to the months: *Vendémaire, Brumaire*, and *Frimaire* being the autumn months of vintage, fog, and frost; *Nivôse, Pluviôse*, and *Ventôse* the winter months of snow, rain, and wind; *Germinal, Floréal*, and *Prairial*, the spring months of seed-time, flowers, and meadows; while *Messidor, Thermidor*, and *Fructidor* were the summer months of harvest, heat, and fruit.

By 1795 the Girondins were again in control, although the Royalists continued to make determined efforts to change the course of events, particularly in the Vendée, where they were eventually suppressed by Hoche. On the 28 October 1795 a Directory of five members assumed power. One of the five was Barras, to whom the young Corsican general, Napoléon Bonaparte (1769–1821), owed his promotion as general of the Interior. During the next four years French republican armies under Bonaparte won notable successes abroad, especially in campaigns against the Austrians (whom he was to crush at Marengo on 14 June, 1800). Returning to Paris after his failure to destroy the British fleet at the Battle of the Nile, Bonaparte found the tyrannical Directory generally detested, and with the help of the army and of Siéyès, established the Consulate by a coup d'étât on 9–10 November 1799. Bonaparte became First Consul, assisted by Siéyès and Roger Ducos. A new constitution awarded him the consulate for life, but such was his personal ambition that he declared himself 'Emperor of the French', and was crowned Napoléon I in Notre-Dame by Pope Pius VII (18 May 1804). A Civil Code, largely retaining the liberal laws of the Revolution, was laid down. Paris was embellished with monuments and bridges, as befitted the capital of an expanding empire, and was further enriched by the spoils of conquest.

First Empire. Faced by a new coalition of England, Austria, and Russia, Napoléon shattered the last two at Austerlitz in 1805, and imposed on them the humiliating Peace of Pressburg, but his fleet had been virtually destroyed at Trafalgar only six weeks earlier. In the following year Prussian armies were cowed at Jena and Auerstadt, and a further campaign against Russia was ended by the Treaty of Tilsit, which brought temporary peace to the Czar. Austria attempted to renew the struggle, but suffered disastrous defeats at Essling and Wagram. The subsequent Peace of Vienna (1809) marked perhaps the apogee of the emperor's power.

Meanwhile, his brother Joseph had been imposed on the Spaniards, whose guerrilla methods of carrying on the war in the Peninsula were to cause a continual drain on Napoléon's reserves of power. England sent out two expeditionary forces to assist the incapable Spaniards, and under Wellington they inflicted a series of defeats on the French, among them Salamanca, and culminating in the battles of Vitoria (1813), and—on French territory—Toulouse.

Napoléon himself had just returned from the suicidal invasion of Russia, where the 'Grande Armée' although successful at Borodino, was virtually annihilated at the crossing of the Beresina by 'Generals January and February'. The Prussians, having recovered from their previous defeats, were able to retaliate at Leipzig (October 1813), and also entered France. Paris itself surrendered to the Allies (31 March 1814) after skirmishing on the heights of Montmartre. The emperor abdicated at Fontainebleau, and retired to the island of Elba.

The Bourbons were restored, but the Treaty of Paris (30 May 1814) cut down the empire to size. During 'the Hundred Days' (26 March–24 June 1815), Napoléon made a desperate attempt to regain absolute power, having claimed at Grenoble (en route to Paris from Elba) that he had come to deliver France from 'the insolence of the nobility, the pretensions of the priests, and the yoke of foreign powers'. His defeat at Waterloo (18 June), and subsequent banishment to St. Helena, where he died in 1821, enabled the king—Louis XVIII—to resume his precarious throne, which he was only able to retain by repressive measures: the University was supervised by the clergy. The reign of his successor, Charles X, under whom were passed the reactionary Ordinances of St.-Cloud, suppressing the liberty of the press and reducing the electorate to the landed classes, only proved that the bigoted Bourbons could 'learn nothing and forget nothing'. The 'July Revolution' of 1830 lost him his throne.

House of Orléans. Louis-Philippe (1830–48; son of Philippe-Égalité d'Orléans of the Revolution) was chosen as head of the 'July Monarchy', and the upper-middle class, who had striven for power since 1789, now achieved it. Most of the urban populace, however, still lived in pestilential conditions: some 19,000 Parisians of a total of about 900,000 died in an outbreak of cholera in 1832. The total population of France was then about 32,500,000. The only other towns of any size were Lyon and Marseille, with about 115,000 each, and Bordeaux and Rouen with about 90,000 each. France was still essentially a country dominated by agriculture and by a rural population.

The king devoted himself, with perhaps more energy than taste, to the further embellishment of the capital, and many pretentious buildings date from this period. Gas lighting had been first installed there in 1829. In 1840 the body of Napoléon was transferred with much pomp to its last resting-place under the Dôme des Invalides. The city was surrounded by a ring of fortifications in 1841–45, but these could not defend the 'citizen-king' against the mass of his people. Socialist ideas were spreading, but the conservative policy of Guizot opposed any reforms, and in the 'February Revolution' of 1848 Louis-Philippe was overthrown. In June 1848, during the brief military dictatorship of Gén. Cavaignac, some 4000 workmen were killed, another 1500 shot, and 11,000 imprisoned or deported to Algeria. In the elections which followed, which introduced universal male suffrage, the electorate leapt from 250,000 to 9,000,000. Among famous literary figures during the first half of the century were Balzac, Chateaubriand, Hugo, George Sand, Stendhal, Flaubert, Gautier, and Sainte-Beuve.

A Second Republic was set up by the provisional government, and Louis Napoléon (Bonaparte's undistinguished and indolent, but shrewd and cynical nephew, who as pretender had already made two abortive attempts to regain the throne), was elected Prince-President by almost 75 per cent of those who voted; but such was the sentimental prevalence of the idea of Empire, that in December 1851 a coup d'état (involving the temporary imprisonment of some 30,000 in opposition) led to his election as the Emperor Napoléon III some months later, thus inaugurating the Second Empire.

Having adopted the clever but misleading motto of 'L'Empire c'est la paix', he proceeded to embroil the country in a succession of wars, firstly in the Crimea (1854–56), and then in Italy, which he undertook to deliver from Austrian oppression, afterwards unchivalrously demanding Savoy and Nice in recompense. Meanwhile he continued the expedient policy of his predecessor, by clearing the mass of congested, evil-smelling, and tortuous lanes of old Paris, which had so favoured the erection of barricades in 1830 and 1848. In their place Baron Haussmann laid out a number of broad boulevards which are still characteristic of much of the centre, while from 1861 Garnier's Opera-house, representative of the expansive taste of the time, was being built, and the Bois de Boulogne and the Bois de Vincennes were transformed into public parks.

But these peaceful projects were halted abruptly in 1870 when Napoléon III declared war on Prussia. The inglorious campaign ended with the capitulation of Sedan, where the emperor was taken prisoner and deposed. He died in exile at Chislehurst (England) in 1873.

Third Republic
Presidents in office:
1871–73   Adolphe Thiers
1873–79   Maréchal MacMahon
1879–87   Jules Grévy
1887–94   Sadi Carnot
1894–95   Jean Casimir-Périer
1895–99   Félix Faure
1899–1906   Émile Loubet
1906–13   Armand Fallières
1913–20   Raymond Poincaré
1920   Paul Deschanel
1920–24   Alexandre Millerand
1924–31   Gaston Doumergue
1931–32   Paul Doumer
1932–40   Albert Lebrun

Gambetta and Thiers were largely instrumental in forming the Third Republic, which had been proclaimed (4 September 1870) while German troops advanced on Paris, which was invested on 19 September, its defenders commanded by Trochu. After a four-month siege and much suffering and famine, Paris capitulated on 28 January 1871. At this time the fortified enceinte of Paris, was rather more than 21 miles (almost 34km) long, and had 67 entrances or gates. A circle of 17 detached fortresses were built at strategic points beyond this boundary wall. The Louvre had been turned into an armament workshop, the Gare d'Orléans (now Austerlitz) into a balloon factory, and the Gare de Lyon into a cannon-foundry; but the army was ill-prepared. Order was not re-established until the Communard Insurrection, which then broke out (18 March–29 May), had been crushed at the cost of pitched battles in the streets, in which 3–4000 Communards were killed, and the destruction of parts of the Tuileries and other public buildings such as the Hôtel de Ville. Retaliatory measures included the summary execution of 20,000–25,000 Parisians, including women, mostly of the working classes; and the deportation of a further 4–5000. Thiers, who was ultimately responsible for these mass killings, was then declared Président. An amnesty bill, introduced by Gambetta, was not adopted until 1880.

By September 1873 the last occupying troops had gone, but France was left to pay a heavy war indemnity, and lost the provinces of Alsace and Lorraine. Various political crises, embittered by the reprehensible 'Dreyfus affair' (1894–1906), coloured much of the period up to the outbreak of the First World War. An 'Entente

Cordiale' between Britain and France was established in 1904, putting an end to colonial rivalry, and paving the way to future co-operation. In 1903 the 'Loi sur les Associations' was passed, and in 1905 the Church was separated from the State, both essential measures to counteract the pernicious influence the ecclesiastics and religious orders still had on education. During these decades building continued apace, even if much of it was of a meretricious nature. The 'Grand Palais' and 'Petit Palais', a new Hôtel de Ville, the Gare d'Orsay, the Eiffel Tower, and the basilica of Sacré-Coeur exemplify the taste of an age, differing facets of which were well described by Zola, and later by Proust. In 1910 extensive areas of Paris were inundated by the flooding of the Seine.

War with Germany broke out on 3 August 1914. French troops were dramatically reinforced at the Marne by some 11,000 men rushed to the front in Parisian taxis: citizens had the satisfaction of hearing the din of battle gradually recede, and little damage was done to the capital by air raids or long-range bombardment. But although Paris was saved from another occupation, ten departments were overrun, and the attrition of three long years of trench warfare followed. In 1916, with the Battle of the Somme, and the French stand at Verdun, the tide began to turn against Germany. On 11 November 1918 an armistice was signed. The provinces lost to France through the Treaty of Versailles in 1871 were restored, although Clemenceau, the 'Tiger', France's Prime Minister, wanted more. Nothing, however, could compensate for the staggering loss of life during the war years. For every ten Frenchmen aged between 20 and 45, two had been killed—a total of over 1,300,000. Slowly the country recovered her strength, even if politically she showed little initiative. In Paris, Thiers' fortifications were demolished in 1919–24, affording an opportunity to lay out a new ring of boulevards. A number of new edifices were erected for the Exhibition of 1937, including the Musées d'Art Moderne and the Palais de Chaillot. Meanwhile France's defensive policies were concretely expressed in the construction of a costly and supposedly impregnable barrier along the German frontier—the Maginot Line (named after a minister of war)—which was immediately side-stepped by invading armoured divisions at the outbreak of the Second World War (September 1939), underlining the sagacity of the French high command.

Demoralised French forces, in no state to resist, and not capable of mounting a successful counter-attack, ostensibly capitulated to the triumphant Reich, while a high proportion of the British army was able to re-cross the Channel from Dunkerque (27 May–4 June, 1940) in a fleet of open boats sent to its rescue. The Germans proceeded to occupy the northern half of the country and the Atlantic coast, overrunning the rest of France after 11 November 1942. For the rest of the war, the underground Resistance Movement did what it could to thwart the collaborating policies of the 'Vichy Government' presided over by the octogenarian Marshal Pétain, hero of Verdun, and Pierre Laval, among others.

Meanwhile, a provisional government had been set up in London by Gén. Charles de Gaulle (1890–1970), and Free French forces co-operated in the liberation of France. Allied troops disembarking in Normandy and in the South of France (on 6 June and 15 August, 1944, respectively) converged on Paris, which was free by late August. But an armistice with Germany was not signed until 8 May 1945. The occupying troops were, after a fierce campaign, driven from French soil, and France was able to participate in the victory celebrations.

In October 1946 the **Fourth Republic** was proclaimed, of which Vincent Auriol (1947–54), and René Coty (1954–58) were presidents. Women now had the vote, and proportional representation was adopted. Slowly, despite many changes in government and despite defeat in Indo-China and revolt in Algeria, the country was restored to economic prosperity after the physical and moral devastation of war. In 1957 a Common Market (EEC) was established, in which France, West Germany, Italy, and the Benelux countries were founder members.

Fifth Republic
1958–69   Charles de Gaulle
1969–74   Georges Pompidou
1974–81   Valéry Giscard d'Estaing
1981–   François Mitterrand

In 1958 de Gaulle prepared a new constitution, which was approved by a referendum, and the general was elected the first president of the new republic by universal direct suffrage, for a period of seven years. The powers of the head of state were considerably—some would say inordinately—increased: he nominates the prime minister, who in turn recommends the members of the government; he can make laws and refer decisions of major importance to popular vote by referendum; in extreme cases he has the power to dismiss the National Assembly.

In 1962 Algerian independence was proclaimed, and a remarkable number of Algerians can still be seen in the industrial towns of France. In 1965 de Gaulle was returned to power with enthusiasm, but with a reduced majority. In May 1968 a serious 'Student Revolution' took place in Paris, which precipitated overdue educational reforms. The following year de Gaulle was succeeded by Pompidou, who died in office in 1974. His successor was Giscard d'Estaing, whose somewhat cavalier attitude to the mass of his countrymen produced a reaction, and a swing to the Left, with Mitterrand moving into the Élysée. But, like the Bourbons, the Socialist regime appears also to have 'learnt nothing and forgotten nothing'. Mitterrand immediately alienated many of his supporters by the inclusion of Communist ministers in the government, a devious manoeuvre which in turn provoked reaction. In spite of instituting changes in the electoral system in an attempt to retain socialist control, they lost the election of March 1986, when Jacques Chirac, who had been the right-wing *maire* of Paris since 1977 (when the title was changed from that of Préfet de la Seine) became Prime Minister, inaugurating what was called a period of 'cohabitation' with the socialist President, who in 1988 was re-elected, and the Socialist party returned to power.

Glossary of Architectural and Allied Terms

ACAJOU, mahogany

ARC-BOUTANT, flying buttress

ARCHIVOLT, the series of mouldings which form the ensemble of an arch

ARDOISES, slates

AUTEL, altar

BOISERIES, decorative woodwork

CAISSONS, EN, coffered

CARREFOUR, crossroads

CARRELAGES, floor tiles

CASERNE, barracks

CHEVET, exterior of an apse; also ABSIDE

COLONNETTE, little column for a vaulting shaft

CONTREFORTS, buttresses

CORBELS, wooden or stone projections supporting a beam or parapet, and often elaborately carved.

DESSUS DE PORTE, a painting above a door

DONJON, keep

DOUVES, moat; wet or dry

ÉBÉNISTE, cabinet-maker

ÉGLISE, church

ÉMAIL, enamel

ESCALIER, staircase, *à vis*, spiral

FLÈCHE, spire

HÔTEL, mansion

HÔTEL DE VILLE, town hall, also MAIRIE

HÔTEL-DIEU, principal hospital in many towns

JEU DE PAUME, a real tennis-court

JUBÉ, rood-screen

MANSARDE, roof of which each face has two slopes, the lower steeper than the upper, named after the architect François Mansart (1598–1666)

NACRE, mother of pearl

NARTHEX, an ante-nave, porch or vestibule to a church or basilica

NEF, nave

OEIL-DE-BOEUF, small circular, sometimes oval, window (bull's eye)

PIÈCE D'EAU, an expanse of water, usually ornamental

PORTE-COCHÈRE, carriage gateway

POUTRES, curved rib in Gothic vaults springing from the same point as the intersecting diagonal rib, and rising to the end of the ridge-rib

TYMPANUM, space, often decorated, between door lintel and arch

VERMEIL, silver-gilt

VITRAIL, stained-glass window

VOUSSOIRES, wedge-shaped stones used in constructing arches or vaults

Select Bibliography

General and Topographical: *Pierre Couperie*, Paris through the Ages (an illustrated historical atlas of urbanism and architecture); *Jacques Hillairet*, Connaissance du Vieux Paris; *Henri Bidou*, Paris (1939); *John Russell*, Paris; *Theodore Zeldin*, The French.

Historical: *Alain Decaux* and *André Castelot*, Dictionnaire d'Histoire de France PERRIN; *Saint-Simon*, Historical Memoirs (trans. and ed. Lucy Norton); *John Lough*, France Observed in the 17C by British travellers, and France on the Eve of Revolution: British travellers' Observations 1763–1788; *Arthur Young*, Travels in France; *Harold Nicolson*, The Age of Reason (1700–1789); *Theodore Zeldin*, France, 1848–1945; *J. Ardagh*, France Today; *R.D. Anderson*, France 1870–1914; *Alistair Horne*, The Fall of Paris; *J. Huizinga*, The Waning of the Middle Ages; and several studies by *Richard Cobb*, notably, The People's Army.

Literary: *Paul Harvey* and *J.E. Heseltine*, The Oxford Companion to French Literature; *D.G. Charlton* (Ed.), France: a Companion to French Studies; *J.M.H. Reid*, The Concise Dictionary of French Literature; *P.E. Charvet* (Ed.), A Literary History of France (6 Vols.).

Art and Architecture: *Anthony Blunt*, Art and Architecture in France, 1500–1700; *W. G. Kalnein* and *M. Levey*, Art and Architecture of the 18C in France; *Vivian Rowe*, Royal Châteaux of Paris; *Ian Dunlop*, Versailles, Royal Palaces of France, and The Cathedral's Crusade; *Allan Braham*, The Architecture of the French Enlightenment; *Joan Evans*, Art in Medieval France; *Pierre Lavedan*, French Architecture; *Otto von Simson*, The Gothic Cathedral; *Michel Gallet*, Paris Domestic Architecture of the 18C; *David Thomson*, Renaissance Paris. *John Milner*'s The Studios of Paris (in the late 19C), recently published, appeared too late for the Editor to incorporate any of its detailed information in this edition of the Guide. *Lawrence Gowing*, Paintings in the Louvre.

Maps

For Paris and its immediate surroundings the following are recommended to supplement the Atlas section at the end of this Guide.

Michelin, Plan de Paris (No. 10, at 1:10,000), also available with street references as No. 12. Perhaps more convenient when walking, and now containing métro and bus maps is their *Paris Atlas* (No. 11), which also includes a list of names, addresses, and telephone numbers of organisations likely to be useful to visitors. Nos 10, 11 and 12 show the position of underground car-parks and 24-hour petrol stations. Other maps published annually by *Michelin* are *Outskirts of Paris* (No. 101, at 1:50,000), *Environs of Paris* (No. 196, at 1:100,000), *Paris Region* (No. 237, at 1:200,000). Map No. 170 covers the same area as No. 196, but concentrates on Sport and open-air recreation. The same company also publishes a new series (18, 20, 22 and 24) of the *suburbs of Paris* (with street indexes). Recently published is their Map 9, Paris Transports.

The *Institut Géographique National* (IGN) map of the *Environs de Paris* (No. 90, at 1:100,000) may be preferred by some to the Michelin map of the same area as it gives a better indication of contour and the general lie of the land. Paris is covered in more detail in their *Serie Orange* (No. 2314 at 1:50,000), and two in their *Serie Bleue* (No. 2314 est, and ouest, at 1:25,000). The environs of Paris are covered by four sheets of their *Série Verte* at 1:100,000, Maps Nos 8, 9, 20, and 21. Also of use are the IGN map of *Région d'Île de France: patrimoine artistique* at 1:150,000, w..ich will help with the pin-pointing of monuments, and, covering a more extensive area, No. 103 in their *Série Rouge* (Carte de l'Environnement Culturel et Touristique) at 1:250,000. IGN also produce an excellent series of *Forest Maps* at 1:25,000: Nos 401 (Fontainebleau), 404 (Chantilly), and 419 (St.-Germain-en-Laye) cover the wooded areas described in this Guide.

For planning one's route to Paris, or on from Paris, Michelin's No. 236 for the area between the Channel ports and Paris, is recommended, and also *France-Grandes Routes* (No. 989), or the IGN *France-Routes: autoroutes* (No. 901), both at 1:1,000,000. Also now available are the Michelin *Motoring Atlas France* at 1:200,000, and their hardback *Road Altas France*. Collins publish a *Road Atlas France* at 1:250,000, based on IGN maps.

It is always advisable to have the latest editions of maps, which can normally be found at Edward Stanford Ltd, 12–14 Long Acre, London WC2, or McCarta Ltd, 122 King's Cross Road, London WC1X 9DS, and at most good booksellers in the UK or France. The London offices of the Michelin Tyre Co. Ltd are at Davy House, Lyon Road, Harrow, Middx, HA1 2DQ. In Paris the offices of Pneu Michelin are at 46 Av. de Breteuil, S of the Invalides. IGN's Paris address is 107 Rue La Boétie (the Champs-Élysées end of the street; Métro. Franklin Roosevelt).

PRACTICAL INFORMATION

Formalities and Currency

Passports are necessary for all British and American travellers entering France. British passports, valid for ten years, are issued at the Passport Office, Clive House, Petty France, London SW1, and from certain provincial offices, or may be obtained for an additional fee through any travel agent. British Visitors' Passports (valid one year), available from Post Offices in the UK, are also accepted. Normally no visa is required for British or American visitors, although in 1986, as a temporary measure, they were obligatory for non-EEC nationals. Should any foreigner intend to remain in France for more than three months, he should apply in advance to the nearest French Consulate, or if already in France, to the Préfecture de Police (Service des Étrangers) in Paris (7 Blvd du Palais, 4e). Procedures are at present in the process of revision.

British subjects seeking employment in France should write to the Consular Section of the Embassy (see below), but it should be emphasised that it is not an employment agency, nor can they help to find accommodation. They will advise on the procedure to be followed, according to the status of the person concerned under the EEC regulations.

Custom House. Except for travellers by air, who have to pass customs at the airport of arrival, or those travelling on international expresses, where their luggage is examined in the train, luggage is still liable to be scrutinised at the frontier, or ports of departure and disembarkation. Provided that dutiable articles are declared, bona-fide travellers will find the French customs authorities (*douaniers*) courteous and reasonable.

It is well to check in advance with French Consulates or Tourist Offices before starting out as to the latest regulations with regard to the importation of firearms, whether sporting or otherwise.

Embassies and Consulates, etc. British Embassy, 35 Rue du Faubourg St.-Honoré, 8e; the Consulate is at 2 Cité du Retiro, a turning N off the same street a short distance E, just beyond the Rue d'Anjou. British Chamber of Commerce, 6 Rue Halévy, 9e; British Council, 9 Rue De Constantine, 7e.

American Embassy, 2 Av. Gabriel, 8e (just N of the Pl. de la Concorde); Canadian Embassy, 35 Av. Montaigne, 8e; Australian Embassy, 4 Rue Jean Rey, 15e; New Zealand Embassy, 7ter Rue Léonard-de-Vinci, 16e; Irish Embassy, 4 Rue Rude, 16e.

Security. No objects of any value should be left inside parked cars. In general, it is advisable to deposit any valuables with the manager of one's hotel, against receipt. Women should beware of bag-snatchers. Note that any parcels or luggage left about and apparently abandoned may be destroyed by the authorities. Normally, however, with a reasonable amount of circumspection, the tourist will find his property respected.

Currency Regulations. There is no restriction on the amount of sterling the traveller may take out of Great Britain. However, it is advisable to check in advance at a bank the latest regulations with regard to the export or re-export of money from France; proof in the form of a 'declaration of entry' may be required if the sum involved is in excess of 5000 francs.

Money. The monetary unit is the *franc*, subdivided into 100 *centimes*. Bank notes of 20, 50, 100, 200 and 500 francs are in circulation, and there are also coins of 5, 10, 20 and 50 centimes, 1 franc, 2 francs, 5 francs, 10 francs and 100 francs.

Branches of most French **Banks** are open from 9.00 to 16.30 from Monday to Friday; most branches close on Saturday morning, but central branches of the principal banks may have a 'bureau de change' open from 9.00 to 12.00. Banks are likely to shut at noon on days preceding public holidays. At the Gare de Nord and Gare de Lyon the 'bureaux de change' are open daily from 6.30 to 22.00 or 23.00; that at the Gare Montparnasse, from 9.00 to 19.00. Those at the international airports operate a daily service from 6.00 to 23.00.

Larger hotels will also accept and exchange travellers' cheques, but they will give a lower rate of exchange than banks. It is advisable to obtain a sufficient supply of French currency for incidental expenses before leaving home, particularly if arriving in France during a weekend. It is also usually worthwhile to 'shop around', for different banks give different rates of exchange.

Approaches to Paris and Transport in Paris

Paris may be reached from Great Britain by a variety of ways, and a car is not essential if only Paris and its immediate surroundings are to be visited. Most important towns, railway termini, and airports provide car-hire facilities.

There are a number of rapid rail services from London to Paris, while the quickest but least interesting means of transit is by air: see below.

Travel Agents. General information may be obtained from the *French Government Tourist Office*, 178 Piccadilly, London W1V 0AL and in the United States at 610 Fifth Av., New York, with branches at 645 N Michigan Av. Chicago; 9401 Wilshire Blvd, Beverly Hills; 360 Post Street, San Francisco, and 2050 Stemmons Freeway, Dallas; their Canadian office is at 1981 Av. McGill College, Montreal, with a branch at 1 Dundas Street W, Toronto.

Any accredited member of the Association of British Travel Agents will sell tickets and book accommodation. As some once-reliable firms appear to concentrate on 'groups', the individual private traveller is advised to contact one of the many good but smaller organisations offering a personal service. Some agents impose an additional charge when booking open-dated return air tickets not originally issued by themselves, and it is preferable to visit the individual airline's offices in such cases.

Rail and Ferry Services. Numerous and frequent Passenger, Car, and Coach Ferry services are operated by British and French Railways, etc. and for the latest information on services, inquiries should be made to the Sealink Travel Centre, Victoria Station, London SW1. Hovercraft services may be erratic in adverse weather conditions but the crossing is considerably quicker.

The **Channel Tunnel**. In February 1986 the *Channel Tunnel Treaty* was signed by representatives of the British and French governments, committing them to go ahead with the long gestating project of constructing a tunnel below the Strait of Dover/Pas de Calais. Of the several projects submitted, that of a twin-bored rail and shuttle tunnel was chosen. The immense project is being carried out under the direction of the Channel Tunnel Group Ltd in conjunction with France Manche SA, and it is expected that the tunnel will be completed and the rail link in operation by 1993.

The terminal in England will be at *Cheriton*, just W of Folkestone, directly approached by the M20; the French terminal will be near *Coqnelles*, some 5km SW of Calais, with a link road to the A26.

Further information with regard to its progress will be included in the next edition of this Guide.

British Rail Europe provide tickets, sleeping-berth tickets, seat reservations, etc. on Continental as well as British Rail services. The offices of French Railways Ltd, (SNCF, or Société Nationale des Chemins de Fer Française) adjacent to the French Tourist Office in Piccadilly, are helpful, but do not actually sell tickets. Both can provide the prospective traveller with full details of the variety of services available, together with their cost.

The Paris office of British Rail is at 12 Blvd de la Madeleine, 9e.

For railway stations in Paris, see p 34.

To avoid considerable inconvenience and irritation on train journeys, travellers are advised to check their tickets closely at the point of issue, particularly as to their validity (including the return trip), and should make sure that the 'global' charge has been made, including all possible supplements, etc.

There are several regular **Bus** or **Coach services** from the UK to Paris, and details may be obtained from Victoria Coach Station, London SW1, British Rail Travel Centres, and travel agents.

Service on board some passenger **Ferries** has deteriorated, more attention being given to the selling of 'bingo' tickets than to the comfort of passengers, who are frequently treated like cattle. Those finding conditions unacceptable should complain without compunction to the purser while on board, and on their return by writing to higher authorities (such as the European Rail Traffic Manager, Euston House, Eversholt Street, London NW1).

Motorists driving to Paris will save much trouble by joining the *Automobile Association* (Fanum House, Basingstoke, Hants RG21 2EA), the *Royal Automobile Club* (83 Pall Mall, London SW1), or the *Royal Scottish Automobile Club* (17 Rutland Sq., Edinburgh). The *American Automobile Association* is at 8111 Gatehouse Road, Falls Church, Virginia 22042. These organisations will provide any necessary documents, as well as information about rules of the road abroad, restrictions regarding caravans and trailers, and arrangements regarding delivery of spare parts, insurance, etc. Motorists who are not the owners of their vehicle should possess the owner's permit for its use abroad. The use of safety-belts is compulsory in France. Children under ten may not travel in the front seats (unless the car has no back seat). Both the AA and RAC have offices in Paris, the former c/o the *Touring Club de France*, 6–8 Rue Firmin Gillot, 15e; the latter at 8 Pl. Vendôme. The insurance facilities offered by *Europ Assistance* should be taken advantage of.

The area between the French Channel ports and Paris is described in detail in *Blue Guide France*.

By Road, the most rapid approach to Paris from Calais or Boulogne is the A1 autoroute (on which there are tolls—*péages*—to pay), joined by the A26, entered NW of *St.-Omer*, which runs S of and approx. parallel to the N43 between *St-Omer* and *Béthune*. Those disembarking at **Dunkerque** join the A1 at Lille, by following the A25, but it may be preferable to join the A26 just W of St.-Omer, reached by taking the D928 not far S of Dunkerque.

There are of course a variety of alternative roads, the most frequented being the N1 from **Calais** to **Boulogne**, bypassing Montreuil, and traversing Abbeville, then following the D901 to Beauvais, also bypassed, and there regaining the N1 for Paris. Alternative routes from Abbeville are the continuation of the N1 via Amiens and Breteuil to Beauvais; or from Amiens on the D934 to meet the A1 motorway 108km N of Paris; or bearing SE from Breteuil via Clermont to either Chantilly or Senlis (see Rte 39) for Paris.

Travellers disembarking at **Dieppe** may follow either the D915 via Gournay-en-Bray and the N31 to Beauvais, also bypassed, or continue on the D915 via Gisors and Pontoise, both of which may now be bypassed. Another route from Dieppe is the N27 driving S to Rouen, following the N14 SE past Magny-en-Vexin to Paris (or the slower N15 S of the Seine via Vernon and Mantes; or alternatively joining the A13 autoroute S of Rouen for Paris. The A13 may also be approached from **Le Havre** via the Pont de Tancarville, or via Rouen.

It is as well to have a good idea of exactly where in Paris one is making for, and to familiarise oneself as to which exit (*sortie*) to aim for prior to entering the *Ceinture* or *Blvd Périphérique*. Exits are usually well indicated some distance in advance, but care must be taken to be in position to make one's exit well before bearing off the motorway.

Parking is restricted in central Paris, and use should be made of its underground parks (but see *Security*, above). While traffic wardens are not always in evidence, it will be noticed that a meter system is in operation. In some streets tickets are obtained from machines and must then be placed behind the windscreen. Certain areas in which one may see a number of cars parked may not necessarily be permissible sites, and the police, if feeling officious, may either fine one or have the car towed away. Ill-parked foreign cars are removed as ruthlessly as native ones, and may take hours to recover from the '*fourrière*' or pound, and at a considerable charge; there will be a heavy fine to pay in addition. Alternatively, a clamp or *sabot* may be attached to a wheel. In either case, the owner should apply to the nearest *gendarme* or *Commissariat de Police*.

Regular **Air Services** between England and France are maintained by *Air France* working in conjunction with *British Airways*. Full information regarding flights from London and other cities in the UK may be obtained from British Airways, 75 Regent Street, London W1, and from Air France, 158 New Bond Street, W1. There are also daily flights from Gatwick with British Caledonian (215 Piccadilly, W1, and 29A Royal Exchange, Threadneedle Street EC3).

There are regular international flights from most European capitals and larger cities to Paris, and direct services from New York, and Montreal, etc., and from many other non-European countries, apart from those provided by Charter companies.

British Airways have Paris offices at 91 Av. des Champs-Élysées and 34 Av. de l'Opéra; Air France offices are at 119 Av. des Champs-Élysées; and British Caledonian at 5 Rue de la Paix, 2e.

Internal or domestic services are maintained by *Air Inter*, 232 Rue de Rivoli, Paris 1er, and branches.

Paris is served by two international airports: *Charles de Gaulle* (near the village of Roissy-en-France, 23km NE of the capital), comprising two separate terminals; and *Orly* (South and West), 14km S of the city.

Charles de Gaulle is linked by a RER train service with the Gare du Nord and Denfert-Rochereau; Orly with the Gare d'Austerlitz and Les Invalides. They are also connected by an Air France bus service leaving each terminal every 20 minutes between 6.00 and 23.00.

A frequent and regular bus service is also provided between Charles de Gaulle, via Porte Maillot, to Étoile; and between Orly and the town terminal of Les Invalides. They run during the same period, and also operate later at night to meet scheduled flights, even if delayed.

Taxis can be found at the airports and car-hire firms have offices there.

Railway termini in Paris. The main stations, all on Métro lines, have most of the facilities required by the traveller, including left-luggage offices (*consigne*) or lockers, trolleys, information bureaux, etc. Some, such as Gare d'Austerlitz and Gare du Nord, are also connected by regular bus services.

The main stations of the SNCF, which provide a remarkably efficient service, are:

Gare d'Austerlitz (Pl. 15; 6–8), serving the Région Sud-Ouest (Tours, Bordeaux, Toulouse, Bayonne, the Pyrenees, Madrid, etc.).
Gare de l'Est (Pl. 9; 3) for the Région Est (Reims, Metz, Strasbourg, Frankfurt, Bâle, Zürich, etc.).
Gare de Lyon (Pl. 15; 6) for the Région Sud-Est (Lyon, Dijon, Provence, Côte d'Azur, Italy, etc.), including the *Trains à Grande Vitesse* or TGV.
Gare Montparnasse (Pl. 12; 8), terminus for the Région Ouest (Brittany, La Rochelle, etc.) and, in future, for the TGV to the SW of France.
Gare du Nord (Pl. 9; 3) for the Région Nord (Lille, Brussels, Amsterdam, Cologne, Hamburg, etc., and also for boat-trains to Boulogne, Calais, and Dunkerque).
Gare St.-Lazare (Pl. 7; 4), another terminus of the Région Ouest (Normandy lines, Rouen, and boat-trains from Dieppe, Le Havre, Cherbourg, etc.).

Note. French Railways do not have ticket control at platform barriers. Passengers purchasing a ticket in France must punch-and-date-stamp (or *composter*) their ticket in an orange-red-coloured machine at the platform entrance before boarding the train. Those failing to do so are liable to pay a supplementary fee/fine to the inspector. This procedure does not apply to tickets purchased outside France.

A telephone information service in English is available at (Paris) 45820841.

Public Transport in Paris. Buses (*autobus*) and the underground railway (*Métro*) in Paris are controlled by the RATP (Régie Autonome des Transports Parisiens), with offices at 53 bis Quai des Grands-Augustins (just S of the Pont Neuf, with a branch in the Pl. de la Madeleine (on the E side of the church). For enquiries, call 43461414 (English spoken).They issue useful maps of the Métro and bus systems (including lines of the RER: see below), and also a leaflet giving details of various summer excursions. (The *Michelin* Map No. 9 (Paris Transports) is handy.)

RATP also sell a 2, 4, or 7-day *Paris-Sésame ticket* (available at the main railway stations, at some 70 of the more important Métro stations, from the Tourist Office at 127 Av. des Champs-Élysées and from several suburban stations; also from French Railways in London), allowing unlimited travel on the RATP system; this can be useful and comparatively cheap if used constantly. The yellow weekly ticket is known as a *coupon hebdomadaire jaune*. Visitors staying more than a few days should consider purchasing a *Carte Orange* (available at any Métro station), for which a passport-size photograph is required.

Another convenient method is to buy a *carnet* of ten tickets at any booking office of the Métro. First and second-class tickets are available: second class compartments are usually perfectly satisfactory, although usually more crowded. Tickets, which operate a turnstile, should be retained until the end of the journey.

The **Métro** (*Métropolitan*) provides a rapid means of transport throughout Paris, and its modernisation continues. The most convenient Métro stations are listed at the beginning of each route described in this Guide. Trains glide silently on rubber wheels through impressively clean stations, which lie approx. 500m apart. Platforms at the Louvre station are decorated with casts from the collections of the museum; at Varenne are casts from the adjacent Musée Rodin. The service, from 5.30 in the morning until approx. 1.30 at night, is normally frequent and regular. As in most large cities, women should avoid travelling alone late at night, and all travellers should beware of bag-snatchers and pickpockets. The fare is the same for any distance on the main inner network, including all necessary changes, making long journeys reasonably inexpensive in comparison to the shorter distances covered—and certainly cheaper than the London 'Underground'.

The first line of the Métro was opened in 1900, and certain stations, notably the Bois de Boulogne entrance of Porte Dauphine, retain their 'art nouveau' decoration. The various lines are called by the names of the terminal stations: e.g. Ligne 1, Château de Vincennes–Pont de Neuilly. The direction in which the train is running is indicated by a sign naming the terminal station. Trains keep to the right. At interchange stations, the passages leading to the line concerned are clearly indicated by an orange-lighted sign marked *Correspondance*, followed by the name of the terminal stations of the connecting line. Certain changes necessitate an inordinately long walk.

The fast exterior lines of the *RER* (*Réseau Express Régional*) have recently been extended. Line **A** runs W to E across Paris from *St.-Germain-en-Laye* to *Boissy St.-Léger* or *Torcy* (connected to the Métro at Étoile, Auber, Châtelet-Les Halles, Gare de Lyon, and Nation). The transverse line **B** leads S from Châtelet-Les Halles to Sceaux and Robinson, and to St.-Rémy-lès-Chevreuse (the latter connected to the Métro at Châtelet and Denfert-Rochereau). It leads N from Châtelet-Les Halles via the Gare du Nord, to the airport of Roissy-Charles de Gaulle, or Mitry-Claye.

A third line (**C**), running S of the Seine, connects St.-Quentin-en-Yvelines and Versailles-Rive-Gauche with Orly, on the line to Massy-Palaiseau, and to other suburban lines, and is connected to the Métro at Javel, Champ-de-Mars, Invalides, Musée d'Orsay (Solférino), St.-Michel, and Gare d'Austerlitz. Those making the excursion to Versailles will find this a convenient means of transport, but should make sure that they are on the correct branch line. Line B is useful if visiting *Sceaux*.

The otherwise inclusive Métro ticket is valid on these three lines within Central Paris but if travelling further afield a separate one must be bought at the interchange stations, which have elaborate automatic ticket machines.

Buses. Bus-stops, which are all 'request stops' (*arrêt facultatif*), are indicated by small placards showing the numbers of the routes and their destinations. Depending on the length of the journey, one, two, or more tickets of the *carnet* will be required, the tickets for buses and the Métro being interchangeable. Buses therefore are generally more expensive than the Métro; ask the driver-conductor if in doubt as to the fare.

Owing to the large number of one-way streets, buses do not necessarily return along the same route that they follow to their destination, and this can lead to confusion.

Smoking is forbidden on both buses and the Métro. Where possible, avoid the use of public transport during 8.00–9.00, and during 17.30–19.30, when the rush-hour is at its height. In some areas traffic is also heavy between 12.00 and 14.00.

River Trips. *Les Bateaux-Mouches* (Pont de l'Alma) and *Les Bateaux-Parisiennes* (Pont d'Iéna or Pont Neuf) run trips along the Seine both during the day and after dark, which can offer some unusual and attractive low-level vistas as the launch emerges from beneath the numerous bridges. (The importance of the river in the growth and planning of Paris is, perhaps, made more apparent by taking a leisurely walk, between the Pont d'Iéna and the Pont de Sully, along the Quais. Unfortunately, these are less attractive than they once were since traffic has been diverted along the water's edge.)

Taxis will be seen cruising or waiting at a rank, marked 'Tête de Station', and with a telephone. Visitors making regular use of taxis should make a note of the telephone number of the nearest rank.

Some taxi-drivers expect a tip of 10 per cent in addition to the charge on the meter. Rates are displayed inside the vehicle. Note that the night tariff (between 22.00 and 6.00) is considerably higher than the day. There is an additional charge for luggage placed in the boot, and—unaccountably—taxis waiting (or merely arriving at a queue) at a railway terminus, are also allowed to charge extra.

Parisian taxi-drivers have gained a reputation for truculence and rapacity but usually their bark is worse than their bite. Female taxi-drivers are escorted by their Alsatians. Any complaints should be addressed to the *Service des Taxis de la Préfecture de Police*, 36 Rue des Morillons, 15e.

Topography of Paris

Paris, the capital of France, lies on both banks of the Seine, near the centre of the so-called Paris Basin. Its height above sea-level varies from 25 to 130m, and its distance from the sea is 150km (or over 320km by the windings of the river). The Seine, the third in length of the four great rivers of France, enters the capital some 500km from its source, and describes a curved course through the city, at the same time forming two islands, the *Île St.-Louis* and the larger *Île de la Cité*.

Much of the attraction of Paris stems from the way the river, with its numerous bridges, has been used to unite rather than divide the northern or Right Bank (*Rive Droite*) and the southern or Left Bank (*Rive Gauche*); indeed, the two are much more nearly of equal importance than the N and S banks of the Thames. Unlike London, Paris was bounded by a definite line of ramparts, which, although they have long been demolished and their sites built upon, served to contain the population, denser than in any other European city (recently over 21,800 inhab. per square kilometre), and enclosed an area of 7800 hectares. The line of the 19C defensive walls can be imagined by following the exterior Blvd Périphérique, and certain forts still remain some distance beyond, although largely engulfed by suburbs (*banlieues*).

The total municipal population of Paris, according to the census of 1982, was—in round figures—2,189,000, while the total population of France was approx. 54,257,000. (A century earlier the figures were 2,269,000 for Paris and 39,238,000 for France.) Some 20 per cent of the population of Paris is made up of foreigners, many from the poorer nations of Europe, but also including large numbers of Algerians, Tunisians, Moroccans, and others from Black Africa, as confirmed by recent demographic surveys, which this edition of the Guide will not attempt to detail, but those interested in such figures are advised to contact that useful and helpful organisation, the *Institut National de la Statistique et des Études Économiques* (INSEE), its head offices at 18 Blvd Adolphe Pinard, 14e, and with its centre for the Île-de-France in Tour Gamma A, 195 Rue de Bercy, Paris 12e (easily approached from the level of the Gare de Lyon).

With the growth of Paris, the old department of the Seine was by a decree which took effect in 1968, subdivided into four new departments: Ville-de-Paris (75; again with a *Maire*); Hauts-de-Seine (92; préfecture Nanterre); Seine-St.-Denis (93; préfecture Bobigny); and Val-de-Marne (94; préfecture Créteil). The old department of Seine-et-Oise was similarly divided into three: Val-d'Oise (95; préfecture Cergy-Pontoise); Yvelines (78; préfecture Versailles); and Essonne (91; préfecture Évry). At the same time the department of Seine-et-Marne (77; préfecture Melun) was incorporated to make up the District de la Région Parisienne, now known as La Région d'Île-de-France.

The topography of Paris can perhaps be best understood by taking Pl. de la Concorde (Pl. 7;7) as a focal point, although historically the Pl. du Parvis-Notre-Dame (from which kilometric distances in France are measured) might be more appropriate. Here (and elsewhere) we can appreciate the artistic town-planning of the past, which deliberately allowed vistas from one bank of the river to extend to the far bank. These great perspectives are one of the most memorable features of Paris.

Turning to the NW, we can discern the Arc de Triomphe (and La Défense beyond), at the far end of the Av. des Champs-Élysées: in the opposite direction, the immense bulk of the Louvre beyond the gardens of the Tuileries. This is flanked, to the N, by the Rue de Rivoli, which with its continuation, the Rue St.-Antoine, leads to the Pl. de la Bastille; and further E, by the Rue du Faubourg St.-Antoine, to the Pl. de la Nation, and Vincennes beyond. It is perhaps this transverse road axis, which, more than the river, cuts Paris into two almost equal parts.

The **Arrondissements**. These municipal districts, of which there are twenty in central Paris, each with its Maire and *Mairie*, or town hall, are important administrative and topographical entities, and their names and numbers convey far more than that of a municipal borough or postal district in London, and the visitor should make himself familiar with the situation of some of them: see plan on pp 4–5 of Atlas.

As in London, certain areas are known more familiarly by their unofficial titles. Their numeration follows a spiral working out clockwise from the centre. When addressing correspondence to Paris the arrondissements should be written as 75001, 75002, etc. rather than 1er, 2e., etc., the prefix 75 indicating the department.

1er; Louvre: the W half of the Cité, the Louvre, Pl. Vendôme, Palais-Royal and St.-Eustache.

2e; Bourse: containing also the Bibliothèque Nationale.

3e; Temple: comprising the N half of the Marais, the Temple, and Archives.

4e; Hôtel de Ville: includes the E half of the Cité, with Notre-Dame, the Île St.-Louis, and the Centre Pompidou, and the S part of the Marais, with the Pl. des Vosges, and is bounded by the Pl. de la Bastille to the E.

5e; Panthéon: the 'Quartier Latin', with the Sorbonne, Panthéon, Val-de-Grâce, and Jardin des Plantes.

6e; Luxembourg: with St.-Germain-des-Prés, St.-Sulpice, and the Palais du Luxembourg.

7e; Palais-Bourbon: comprising the Faubourg St.-Germain, the Musée d'Orsay, Les Invalides, the École Militaire, and bounded to the W by the Eiffel Tower.

8e; Élysée: with the Pl. de la Concorde, the Madeleine, the Champs-Élysées, and Faubourg St.-Honoré, and including the Parc Monceau to the N, and containing the Av. George-V to the W.

9e; Opéra: reaching up to the Blvd de Clichy and Pl. Pigalle.

10e; Enclos St.-Laurent: with the Gares du Nord, and de l'Est, and Hôpital St.-Louis.

11e; Popincourt: the area NE of the Pl. de la Bastille, and reaching to Pl. de la Nation.

12e; Reuilly: the area SE of the Pl. de la Bastille, including the Gare de Lyon and Bercy.

13e; Gobelins: the area S of the Gare d'Austerlitz, including the Gobelins, and Pl. d'Italie.

14e; Observatoire: including the Cimetière de Montparnasse, Parc de Montsouris, and Cité Universitaire.

15e; Vaugirard: the area SW of the Tour Montparnasse and Av. de Suffren.

16e; Passy: between the Seine and Bois de Boulogne, its N half crossed by the Avenues Foch, Victor-Hugo, and Kléber, radiating from the Étoile, and containing the districts of Chaillot, Passy, and Auteuil.

17e; Batignolles Monceau: the area NW of the Étoile.

18e; Butte Montmartre: the area NE of the Pl. de Clichy, and reaching as far E as the Rue d'Aubervilliers.

19e; Buttes-Chaumont: and including La Villette.

20e; Ménilmontant: including Père Lachaise.

It must be admitted that few of the *banlieues* of Paris merit the attention of the visitor, unless he is interested in *Urbanisme*. Whatever one may feel about the vast schemes of *aménagement* and *rénovation* taking place in all areas, proceeding on a scale resulting too often in huge windswept spaces between ugly horizontal and/or vertical boxes, the efforts of the road engineers have clearly been successful.

Employment of Time

A good deal of Paris may be seen in a week by the energetic traveller, but this will allow only a superficial glance at some few treasures of its museums. With the information given on pp 45–8 the visitor will be able to plan his or her campaign, and should have no difficulty, using the index and Atlas section, in choosing and following an itinerary of their own. The arrangement of routes has been designed to assist the less experienced traveller to explore the city systematically.

A list of convenient Métro stations is given at the beginning of most routes: see also Atlas, pp 4–5.

For those with the time and curiosity, an interesting general view of parts of Paris may be had, for the price of a single ticket, by taking the Métro at the *Étoile* (for example, or indeed anywhere on Ligne 6), direction *Nation*; there changing onto Ligne 2, direction *Porte Dauphine* (two stops beyond *Étoile*). In this way, because much of the journey is made overground rather than under, one can get a glimpse of certain areas which one would not otherwise have any particular reason for visiting. The journey can of course be made in the reverse direction.

For those spending only a short time in central Paris it is perhaps advisable to visit first the Cité Rtes 1–2, before crossing to the Left Bank, where one might concentrate on the 'Quartier Latin' (including the *Musée de Cluny*) and the Faubourg St.-Germain (including the *Musée d'Orsay*, if only for the Impressionists; Rte 9); nor should the *Invalides* be overlooked (Rte 11).

Crossing to the Right Bank, one may follow Rte 13 (taking in the *Musée des Arts Décoratifs*) to the *Louvre*, the contents of which are described in Rte 16. One may combine Rte 17 with a view of the *Madeleine* and the *Opéra*, but of more interest is the *Marais* (Rte 21; including the *Pl. des Vosges* and the *Musée Carnavalet*), while at least the *Musée d'Art Moderne* at the *Centre Pompidou* should be seen (Rte 20). It must be emphasised, however, that this recommended itinerary will only provide an imperfect view of the capital, and each visitor will have his or her own priorities. The excursion to the *Château of Versailles*, at least, should be made (see Rte 34), and—depending on one's preferences—either the *Musée Condé* at *Chantilly*, or the *Château de Fontainebleau*; see Rtes 39 and 40.

Hotels and Restaurants

Hotels of every class, size, and price abound in Paris, but it is prudent to book rooms in advance either directly or through a travel agency, for they are often full during the tourist season, particularly at Easter and during the course of Exhibitions, Trade Fairs, etc. Branches of the *Office de Tourisme de Paris* (see p 43) will endeavour to make on-the-spot bookings, which are automatically cancelled if not taken up within 1½ hours. They can also provide an up-to-date *Guide des Hôtels* for Paris and region. Among other useful lists is that published by *Michelin*, entitled *Paris et sa banlieue: Hôtels et Restaurants*, which includes the better-known and well-equipped hotels by arrondissements.

The latest edition of the annual publications of *Michelin*, *Kléber*, *Gault-Millau*, the *Logis de France*, or the *Guide des Relais Routiers* are useful in the selection of accommodation and restaurants to suite the individual's taste and purse. Local Syndicats d'Initiatives can also provide a brochure listing hotels in their area. It is wise, during certain seasons, to book in advance if a weekend excursion is planned.

The availability of accommodation is *not* indicated in this Guide, there being a wide range of every category in the area described. For hotels for the disabled, see p 43.

All Hotels are officially classified, and their grading is shown by stars, depending on their amenities and the type of hotel, from 4-stars 'L' (Luxury) to 1-star (plain but comfortable). Hot and cold running water will be found in all bedrooms, but only a proportion of hotels in the 1-, 2-, and even 3-star categories have rooms with a private bath and WC en suite, although many more will provide a shower and bidet. Similarly, many hotels have no restaurant, although almost all will provide a continental breakfast: but see below.

Charges vary, of course, according to the grade of hotel and the time of year, being at their highest from mid June to mid September. In most hotels (especially when quoting 'en pension' terms) 15 per cent is now added to the bill for 'service'—whether provided or not—and certainly when the bill is marked 'service et taxes compris' (s.t.c.) no additional gratuity is expected.

Most of the more expensive hotels in Paris are situated in the 1st, 6–10th, and 16–17th arrondissements. Large hotels outside the centre are used by groups and those attending Trade Fairs but are inconvenient for the tourist. It is important to check the hotel's location and room price when booking, particularly in view of the fact that many appear to be geared to the 'expense-account' visitor.

Restaurants of every kind and category are plentiful in Paris, and have likewise been officially graded to indicate that they adhere to certain criteria. Although the prices tend to be comparatively high, very often (but by no means always) one will obtain better value for money than in some other countries who do not take the ritual and etiquette of eating so seriously, and who are prepared to accept lower standards.

At most restaurants the day's set menu, 'à prix fixe', is available, with a certain choice of dishes, and at a much lower price than 'à la carte', even if somewhat unimaginative in the more modest establishments; and this is displayed, with prices, at the entrance, and should be perused in advance. Frequently there is more than one selected menu to choose from, apart from the recommended 'plat du jour', even if the cheapest is so uninspired that the client is thus obliged to take one at a higher price.

The **wine**, either *rouge*, *blanc*, or *rosé*, in bottles or carafes, is usually very fair at most restaurants, while many can provide a liberal choice of superior wines at relatively high prices. When dining *à la carte*, the traveller should not allow the suggestions of the waiter, however plausible, to add more dishes to the menu than he really wants, for the slightest additions (of vegetables, for example) can easily swell the bill by a disproportionate amount. The bill (*l'addition*), which should be carefully scrutinised, should be in writing; the gratuity is now usually included in the price of a set menu; this is not so if one has chosen à la carte, but any misunderstanding can be avoided by asking *Le service est-il compris?*. If no gratuity has been included, the waiter may be rewarded with some 10 per cent of the bill, according to the quality of service: less where a considerable proportion of the total is for a single bottle.

There are, of course, a number of French gastronomic guides (see above) listing a great range of eating-places in Paris and elsewhere, among them the better-known 'de luxe' restaurants where French cookery *should* reach its perfection—at a price which few can afford—but it must be admitted that the traveller without inside knowledge will often have better value for his money at the less pretentious establishments.

Unfortunately there is a tendency, particularly in areas frequented by tourists rather than by a regular clientele, to serve stereotyped meals of a mediocre quality for the prices charged. Some restaurants, which can easily be avoided, also assume that piped music is conducive to a better appetite. Many restaurants are closed on Sundays, and during August. It is advisable to book a table in advance at the better-known or more fashionable restaurants.

Galerie Vivienne (Heather Waddell)

The many **Cafés** of Paris—there were said to be as many as 300 as early as 1715 (although the custom of drinking coffee had only been introduced by the Turkish ambassador, Soliman-Aga, in 1667; but see p 68)—are more numerous in the larger streets and squares of Paris, and in many cases tables and chairs are set out on the adjacent pavement (known as the *terrasse*)—or behind a glazed conservatory/observatory—where the customer may spend an entertaining hour watching the passers-by. The *café* or *café crème* is usually very good, but tea-making is still a perfunctory performance. A 'Continental breakfast' (*petit déjeuner*) may be obtained in the mornings at many cafés, with fresh rolls, *croissants*, or *brioches*, and butter, with coffee or—less frequently—chocolate.

The usual order for a small beer is a *demi*; draught beer is *à la pression*. It is cheaper to stand at the bar; prices are automatically raised if one subsequently takes a seat. The waiter should not be paid after each drink, but just prior to leaving. Travellers are warned that the prices charged at some pretentious cafés or patisseries are quite exorbitant, and it is always as well to check before ordering, to avoid an unpleasant shock.

Postal and Other Services

Most **Post Offices**, indicated by the sign **PTT** (prounounced Pay Tay Tay), are open from 8.00 to 19.00 on weekdays, and until 12.00 on Saturdays. The main Post Office in Paris is at the Hôtel des Postes, 52 Rue du Louvre, 1er, which provides a 24-hour service in some departments, while that at 71 Av. des Champs-Elysées, 8e, is open from 8.00 until 23.00. English is spoken at both branches. The main post office is the destination of all letters, etc. marked merely 'Poste Restante, Paris', without any arrondissement number being given. When this has been added, the head post office in the appropriate district should be visited. Correspondence marked 'poste restante' may be addressed to any post office, and is handed to the addressee on proof of identity (passport preferable). Letters may be sent registered (*recommandé*) for a small fee, and are likewise not delivered without proof of identity.

Telegrams in English may be telephoned to 42332111. There are *Telex* offices at 7 Rue Feydeau and 9 Pl. de la Bourse, both 2e. Telex messages may be telephoned to 42471212.

Letter-boxes are painted yellow. Postage-stamps (*timbres*) are on sale at all post offices and most tobacconists.

Among other services, that of the *pneumatiques* has been replaced by that of *Post-Express*, with a 5kg weight limit, which should deliver the letter or packet within two hours within Paris itself.

Telephones. Public call-boxes may be found at most post offices, métro stations, cafés, restaurants, and at some bus stops (taxiphones). With patience and sufficient small change, one should have little difficulty in making the right connection. Paris is in STD communication with the British Isles, and most of Europe, etc. Reversed-charge calls ('PVC') are accepted. Some call-boxes only take *jetons*, which have to be bought. Note that the charge for calls made from hotels may be as much as 40 per cent higher than for those made from public telephone boxes. When calling abroad, one must wait after dialling the prefix 19 (international) for a change in the dialling tone before continuing.

The normal tariff applies from 8.00–18.00 on weekdays, and until 14.00 on Saturdays. It is 30 per cent less between 18.00–21.30 Monday–Friday; 50 per cent less between 6.00–8.00, and 21.30–23.00 Monday–Friday, 6.00–8.00, and 14.00–23.00 on Saturday, and 6.00–23.00 on Sunday. The charge is 50 per cent less between 23.00–8.00 daily (or rather, nightly); these reductions only apply within France.

If telephoning the UK from France, dial 44 after the tone change, and then the area code (but omit the zero) and number required. A list of essential telephone numbers (bank, insurance company, family, etc.) including area codes should be carried abroad with one as a precautionary measure. When calling the provinces from Paris, the prefix 16 is first dialled, followed after a change of tone, by a 2-figure department code, and then the 6-figure number. (Both the department and 6-figure number are required when dialling from one department to another or within a department.) Telephone-boxes displaying a 'bell' sign may be dialled to. For directory enquiries, dial 12; for operator, 13; telegrams, 14; police, 17; and fire, 18.

Information Bureaux. The *Office de Tourisme de Paris*, with its headquarters at 127 Av. des Champs-Élysées, open daily from 9.00 to 22.00 (until 20.00 in winter, and until 18.00 or 20.00 on Sunday), has a patient and helpful English-speaking staff, who will endeavour to answer most general queries concerning Paris and the environs (apart from giving information on the rest of France). Otherwise known as *Le Bureau Central d'Accueil* ('Welcome' reception office), it has subsidiary branches at the Gare d'Austerlitz, Gare de l'Est, Gare du Nord, Gare de Lyon, and in summer at the Tour Eiffel.

A more central office near the Louvre may be opened in the not too distant future, which may supersede the municipal office in the N vestibule of the *Hôtel de Ville*, 29 Rue de Rivoli, 4e.

For a comparatively small charge, depending on the category of hotel, they will book accommodation in Paris, and from the head office, by telex, in the provinces. They will supply visitors with leaflets giving information about temporary exhibitions, entertainment, inexpensive restaurants, swimming pools, etc.

Most towns in the environs of Paris have a *Syndicat d'Initiative*.

Medical Services. Hospitals with English-speaking staff: the *British Hospital (Hertford)*, 48 Rue de Villiers, NW of the Porte de Champerret, with an entirely new wing; and the *American Hospital*, 63 Blvd Victor-Hugo, Neuilly. In an emergency, dial 17 for the *Police*, and 15 for SAMU (Service Aide Médicale d'Urgence).

The *Pharmacie Anglaise* is at 62 Av. des Champs-Élysées, 8e; other chemists (indicated by a green cross) open daily are the *Pharmacie des Arts*, 106 Blvd du Montparnasse, 14e; *Pharmacie Mozart*, 14 Av. Mozart, 16e; and the *Pharmacie du Départ*, 3 Rue du Départ, 14e.

The Disabled. The French are to be commended for their consideration for the disabled, who will find 'Access in Paris' useful. This booklet is available from 'The Paris Survey Project', 68b Castlebar Road, Ealing, London W5. Helpful advice can also be given by the Central Council for the Disabled, 34 Eccleston Sq., SW1.

Lost Property Office. Articles lost on the Métro or in buses (in which case they are held for claiming for the first 48 hrs at the terminus of the route concerned), in the street, theatres or cinemas, etc., should be enquired for at the *Bureau des Objets Perdus*, 36 Rue des Morillons, 15e (open Mondays–Fridays, 8.30–17.00 and on Thursdays until 20.00 except July–August); the nearest Métro is *Convention*. The telephone number is 48283236. Property lost on trains, at stations, on planes and at airports should be reclaimed at the Lost Property office of the terminus or airport in question.

Museums, Collections, and Monuments

A table giving hours of admission etc. is printed below, but it should be noted that the times shown are liable to be changed without warning. As a general rule, the National Museums are closed on Tuesdays, and the Municipal Museums are closed on Mondays. Some museums are closed on public holidays (jours fériès), and it is wise to check in advance. The convenience of guardians rather than of the interested visitor being the governing factor, most museums—with some enlightened exceptions—still open late and close early, and may be shut between the sacred hours of 12.00–14.00 (sometimes 15.00). This also applies in the case of some churches and other monuments. In many cases the admission fee is reduced on Sundays, when in a few cases entry may be free (but they may also be uncomfortably crowded, as are the Centre Pompidou and Musée d'Orsay most of the time). All national museums are free on Wednesdays.

Musées et Monuments Carte. A card permitting direct entry to some 60 museums and monuments in Paris and environs may be obtained at many museums and métro stations. This is available for 1 or 3 or 5 consecutive days.

Lecture tours are organised by several bodies; those promoted by the *Caisse Nationale des Monuments Historiques* (who also publish a number of informative guides, and edit a magazine entitled *Monuments historiques*) are listed in a bi-monthly brochure entitled *Musées, Monuments historiques, Expositions, Visites Conféferences in Paris and the l'Île de France*, obtainable from the Hôtel de Sully, 62 Rue St.-Antoine, 3e; the Bureau d'Action Culturelle de la Direction des Musées de France, Palais du Louvre, 34 Quai du Louvre, 1er; and Tourist Offices, etc.

A list of such guided visits may also be found in some newspapers. No advance application is normally necessary: the visitor merely goes to the place indicated at the time stated, and pays a fee. The group is conducted by a competent official French-speaking guide-lecturer; guided tours by English-speaking lecturers may be arranged.

It may be remarked that visitors coming from countries where they are used to entering museums free of charge may sometimes baulk at paying the fee imposed. In fact, in many cases, the charge is in no way disproportionate to the size and quality of the collections to be seen, an increasing number of which are being reformed and displayed with imagination and taste. Unfortunately this is not always so, and the same charge can apply to museums and monuments whose curators appear to remain unconcerned as to whether they are giving value for money, and who are insensitive to the comparative excellence of other collections.

It may also be mentioned that although considerable work seems to have gone into the preparation and production of lavishly illustrated catalogues, selling at high prices, of temporary exhibitions, few of the important museums—perhaps because so many of them are undergoing drastic reorganisation—publish good general catalogues or inventories of their permanent collections of use to the interested visitor, for whom the few *Publications scientifiques* available are both too detailed and highly priced, and who find the slighter booklets too superficial. There are signs of improvement, with the publication by the *Editions de la Réunion des musées nationaux* of illustrated summary catalogues of the paintings in the Musée du Louvre, issued in five volumes—but also expensive. A list of catalogues in print by this organisation is available from the bookstalls of any of the national museums.

Hours of Admission to the principal Museums, Collections, and Monuments

With the exception of the *Musée Rodin* and *Musée Picasso*, this list does not include collections devoted to individual artists or sculptors, for which see Index. The more important are indicated by bold type. Some museums will not allow entry some 45 minutes before closing time—even in mid-morning, prior to their lunchtime closure. Sections of some museums may be closed at times other than those indicated; some will remain open later during summer months. Many are closed on Bank Holidays (*jours fériés*).

Arabe, Institut du Monde Quai St.-Bernard, 5e.	13.00–20.00; closed Monday
Art Moderne de la Ville de Paris 11 Av. du Prés.-Wilson, 16e	10.00–17.30; 10.00–20.30 on Wednesdays; closed Monday
Arts Africains et Océaniens 293 Av. Daumesnil, 12e	9.45–12.00; 13.30–17.20 closed Tuesday
Arts Décoratifs 107 Rue de Rivoli, 1er	12.30–18.00 Wednesday– Saturday; 11.00–18.00 Sunday; closed Monday and Tuesday
Arts de la Mode 109 Rue de Rivoli, 1er	12.30–18.00 Wednesday– Saturday; 11.00–18.00 Sunday; closed Monday and Tuesday
Arts et Traditions Populaires 6 Av. du Mahatma-Gandhi (Bois de Boulogne)	10.00–17.15; closed Tuesday
Beaubourg: see **Pompidou**	
Cabinet des Médailles, *Bibliothéque Nationale* 58 Rue de Richelieu, 2e	13.00–17.00; closed Sunday
Carnavalet 23 Rue de Sévigné, 3e	10.00–17.40; closed Monday
Cernuschi 7 Av. Velasquez, 8e	10.00–17.40; closed Monday
Chasse 60 Rue des Archives, 3e	10.00–12.30; 13.30–17.30; closed Tuesdays
Cinema Palais de Chaillot, 16e	10.00–17.30; closed Tuesday
Cluny 6 Pl. Paul-Painlevé, 5e	9.45–12.30; 14.00–17.15 closed Tuesday

Cognacq-Jay 23 Blvd des Capucines, 2e	(temporarily closed)
Conciergerie 1 Quai de l'Horloge, 4e	10.00–17.00 or 18.00
Gobelins 42 Av. de Gobelins, 13e	14.15 Tuesdays–Thursdays (Guided visit)
Guimet 6 Pl. d'Iéna, 16e	9.45–12.00; 13.30–17.15; closed Tuesday
Hôtel de Soubise *(Archives Nationales)* 60 Rue des Francs-Bourgeois, 3e	14.00–17.00; closed Tuesday
Homme, Musée de l' Palais de Chaillot, 16e	9.45–17.15; closed Tuesday
Instrumental 14 Rue de Madrid, 8e	(in the process of moving to the Cité de la Musique at La Villette)
Invalides, Les (Musée de l'Armée) Esplanade des Invalides, 7e and	10.00–17.00/18.00
Plans-Reliefs Esplanade des Invalides, 7e	10.00–18.00
Jacquemart-André 158 Blvd Haussmann, 8e	(temporarily closed)
Jardin des Plantes (Histoire Naturelle) 57 Rue Cuvier, 5e	Closed Tuesday, but zoo open daily 9.00–17.00/18.00
Legion d'Honneur 2 Rue de Bellechasse, 7e	14.00–17.00; closed Monday
Louvre, Musée du Palais du Louvre, 1er	9.45–17.00/18.30; closed Tuesday
Marine Palais de Chaillot, 16e	10.00–18.00; closed Tuesday
Marmottan 2 Rue Louis-Boilly, 16e	10.00–17.30; closed Monday
Mode et du Costume, La Palais Galliéra, 10 Av. Pièrre-1er de Serbie, 16e	10.00–17.40; closed Monday
Monuments Français Palais de Chaillot, 16e	9.45–12.30; 14.00–17.15; closed Tuesday
Nissim de Camondo 63 Rue de Monceau, 8e	10.00–12.00; 14.00–17.00; closed Monday and Tuesday
Notre-Dame, Crypte *Archéologique*	10.00–17.00 or 18.00
Orangerie Pl. de la Concorde, 1er	9.45–17.15; closed Tuesday
Orsay, Musée d' 1 Rue de Bellechasse, 7e	10.30–18.00; 9.00–18.00 Sunday; 10.30–21.45 Thursday; closed Monday
Panthéon Pl. du Panthéon, 5e	10.00–12.00; 14.00–17.00/18.00

Petit Palais Av. Winston Churchill, 8e	10.00–17.40; closed Monday
Photographie, Centre *National de la* Palais de Tokyo, 13 Av. Prés. -Wilson, 16e	10.00–17.00
Picasso 5 Rue de Torigny, 3e	9.15–17.15; 9.15–22.00 Wednesday; closed Tuesday
Pompidou, Centre (CNAC) 4e	12.00–22.00; 10.00–22.00 Saturday and Sunday; closed Tuesday
Postal museum 34 Blvd Vaugirard, 15e	10.00–17.00; closed Sunday
Publicité (posters) 18 Rue de Paradis, 10e	12.00–18.00; closed Tuesday
Rodin, Musée 77 Rue de Varenne, 7e	10.00–17.00/17.45; closed Tuesday
Sainte-Chapelle Blvd du Palais, 4e	10.00–17.00/18.00
Sciences et de l'Industrie (La Villette) 30 Av. Corentin-Cariou, 19e	10.00–18.00 Tuesday, Wednesday, Friday; 12.00–21.00 Thursday; 12.00–20.00 Saturday, Sunday; closed Monday
Serrure, La (locksmiths) 1 Rue de la Perle, 3e	10.00–12.00; 14.00–17.00; closed Monday and Tuesday
Techniques (Science museum) 270 Rue St.-Martin, 3e	13.00–17.30; 10.00–17.15 on Sunday; closed Monday
Vincennes, Château de	10.00–17.00/18.00

Environs of Paris

Chantilly (Musée Condé)	10.00–18.00; closed Tuesday
Écouen, Château de (Musée de la Renaissance)	9.45–12.30; 14.00–17.15; closed Tuesday
Fontainebleau, Château de Petits Appartements	9.30–12.30; 14.00–17.00; closed Tuesday, Saturday and Sunday
Maisons, Château de	9.00–12.00; 14.00–17.00; closed Tuesday and Sunday morning
Malmaison and *Bois-Préau*	10.00–12.30; 13.30–17.00/17.30; closed Tuesday
St. Denis, Basilique de	10.00–16.00/18.00
St.-Denis, Musée d'Art	10.00–17.30; 14.00–18.30 on Sunday; closed Tuesday
Musée des Antiquités **Nationales,** St-Germain-en-Laye	9.45–12.00; 13.30–17.15; closed Tuesday
Preiuré 2 bis Rue Maurice-Denis, St.-Germain-en-Laye	10.00–17.30/18.30; closed Monday and Tuesday

Sceaux, Château de (Musée de l'Île de France)	14.00–18.00 Monday and Friday; 10.00–12.00; 14.00–18.00 Wednesday, Thursday, Saturday and Sunday; closed Tuesday
Sèvres, Céramique de	10.00–12.00; 13.30–17.15; closed Tuesday
Versailles, Château de	9.45–17.30; closed Monday
Grand Trianon	9.45–12.00, 14.00–17.30; closed Monday
Petit Trianon	14.00–17.30; closed Monday

Although this table includes many of the principal attractions of Paris and environs, it by no means exhausts the list of things to see or the heights to which one can ascend (such as the terrace of the Arc de Triomphe, the Tour Montparnasse, or Tour Eiffel). The visitor is reminded of the following additional points of interest, to mention a few only which deserve a visit, details of which will be found in the text: the Arènes de Lutèce; Palais-Royal; Palais Luxembourg; Palais de Justice; the Hôpital St.-Louis, and Hôpital de la Salpêtrière; École Militaire; and the churches of La Madeleine, Val-de-Grâce, St.-Eustache, St.-Étienne-du-Mont, St.-Germain-l'Auxerrois, St.-Germain-des-Près, St.-Roch, St.-Médard, St.-Séverin, St.-Sulpice, Ste.-Ursule de la Sorbonne; the cemeteries of Père Lachaise, Montmartre, Montparnasse, and Picpus; the Pl. Vendôme and Pl. des Vosges, without listing individually the numerous hôtels of the Marais and the Faubourg St.-Germain.

The cemeteries are normally open from 7.30 to 18.00 in summer, and from 8.00 to 17.00 in winter; that of Picpus is open during the afternoon only.

A torch, and a pair of binoculars, will be found useful equipment when exploring the recesses of churches and cathedrals, and perusing the details of capitals and stained-glass windows, etc.

Entertainment

Topical information about theatres, cinemas, cabarets, night clubs, 'manifestations', 'sporting' events, fairs, exhibitions, etc., are advertised in the Press, or may be found in any of the magazines and 'guides' devoted to What's On, available from most tourist offices, agents, and kiosks.

Theatres. The National, or State-subsidised, theatres are the *Comédie-Française*, Pl. André-Malraux, 1er; the *Théâtre de France* (de l'Odéon), Pl. Paul-Claudel, 6e; *Théâtre National Populaire* (TNP), Palais de Chaillot, 16e; *Théâtre de l'Est Parisien* (TEP), 17 Rue Malte-Brun, 20e; *Théâtre de la Ville* and *Théâtre Musical de Paris* (TMP), the latter devoted to ballet, and concerts (see below), both in the Pl. du Châtelet, 4e; and the 'Théâtre Lyrique', better known as the *Opéra*, Pl. de l'Opéra, 9e. The once-famous *Opéra-Comique* is now used as an experimental theatre. The new opera-house on the E side of the Pl. de la Bastille is expected to be inaugurated a year or so after 1989.

Some smaller establishments, *Music Halls, Chansonniers*, etc., also survive, often devoted to revues of no very refined nature. Many specialise in political satire, for there are targets in plenty (cf. 'Le Canard Enchainé', a periodical wittier than most), but these can only be appreciated by those with a fairly thorough knowledge of the language and the latest *argot*.

Few Cabarets leave much to the imagination, although some purport to offer 'artistic performances', and attempt to provide something to suit all tastes in their entertainment, from the exotic (or simply *érotique*) to the grossly vulgar; but the curious visitor is warned that the announcement of *entrée libre* (free admission) to any of these *boîtes*, night-clubs, and other 'tourist traps' simply means that the price of admission is added to the already exorbitant charge for *consommations* which he is expected to order. The obscure world of 'dancings', Cafés-théâtres, discothéques, and what not, lies outside the scope of this Guide.

Cinemas of all types, many of the larger converted to show various films in the same building, abound—Paris claims to contain 500—and most of them run continuously from 12.00. Many of them are devoted to 'porno', in a variety of shades of 'bleu'. Programmes normally change on Wednesdays. Prices charged in the better-known cinemas are high, and yet ushers still expect a tip, although the practice is progressively ignored. The same applies in theatres.

Many theatres close for some weeks in the summer, and on one evening a week, usually Monday or Tuesday. *Smoking is forbidden*. Note that tickets bought through an agency will cost as much as 25 per cent more than at the box-office of the theatre concerned, usually open between 11.00 and 18.30 or 19.00.

Concerts take place at the *Théâtre des Champs-Élysées*, 15 Av. Montaigne; the restored *Théâtre Musical de Paris*, Pl. du Châtelet; *Salle Gaveau*, 45 Rue La Boétie; *Salle Pleyel*, 252 Rue du Faubourg-St.-Honoré; *Salle Cortot*, 78 Rue Cardinet; the *Palais de Chaillot*, Pl. du Trocadero; the *Maison de l'ORTF* (or 'de la Radio'), 116 Av. du Président-Kennedy; at the *Palais des Congrès*, Porte Maillot, and elsewhere.

Church Music and *Organ Recitals* can be heard at Notre-Dame, St.-Eustache, St.-Germain-des-Prés, St.-Louis des Invalides, St.-Séverin, St.-Sulpice, St.-Roch, St.-Clotilde, St.-Étienne-du-Mont, and the Madeleine, among other churches, and any special concerts are usually well advertised.

Art Exhibitions. Although smaller shows devoted to individual artists can be seen at any number of galleries and art-dealers' shops, many of them in the 6e arrondissement, the more important temporary exhibitions are held in the Grand Palais, Petit-Palais, Musée d'Orsay, Palais de Tokyo, Musée des Arts Décoratifs, etc., while the Centre National d'Art et de Culture Georges Pompidou (CNAC, or Centre Beaubourg) is now an important focus of exhibitions of modern art, 'pop' and otherwise, etc.

A useful guide to the art world of Paris is the *Paris Art Guide* by Fiona Dunlop (Art Guide Publications, A & C Black).

General Information

Directories. Almost any address may be turned up in 'Le Bottin' (the *Annuaire-Almanach du Commerce et de l'Industrie Didot-Bottin*), which may be consulted at post offices, hotels, restaurants, shops, etc., where a notice may be displayed: 'Ici on consulte le Bottin'. Residential and official addresses may be found also in the 'Bottin Mondain'. *Le Bottin* was initiated in 1819 by Sébastien Bottin (1764–1853), who took over an earlier *Almanach du Commerce* founded in 1798. At Bottin's death it merged with the *Annuaire général du commerce* published by Didot. Although a somewhat ponderous example of Gallic methodology, it can be useful on occasions.

Climate. The main characteristic of the **weather** in Paris is changeability, particularly in the winter and spring, although long periods of fine weather occur each year. Perhaps because of its long wide boulevards, which sometimes act as wind tunnels, the wind is more noticeable than in London, and bitterly cold blasts can be experienced in some quarters during certain seasons, and it can remain cold until well after Easter. Its mean temperature is 11·6°C; only for a few days a year does it become oppressively hot (30°C). The average number of days a year on which the temperature falls below freezing-point is about 35; the number of days of snowfall has averaged 15 in recent decades. In spring and autumn, although the days are shorter, the weather is better adapted for the active sightseer, for in summer (June–August) Paris is packed with tourists. In August the city is deserted by a high proportion of its regular residents, and many theatres, libraries, and even restaurants, are closed.

Language. The visitor who knows no language but English can usually get along without too much trouble in Paris, although he will probably pay in cash for his ignorance. Any *attempt* to speak some French is always appreciated.

Manners. Forms of politeness in France are still less casual than in some other countries, and there is more handshaking at meeting and parting. It is also polite to use 'Monsieur', 'Madame', or 'Mademoiselle' as a form of address (without the surname) even after some acquaintance, but such standing on ceremony is becoming progressively relaxed in most circles.

Public Holidays. 1 January (*Jour de l'An*; gifts—*étrennes*—exchanged); Easter Monday; Whit Monday (*Pentecôte*); Ascension Day; 1 May (with Lily of the Valley sold in the streets); 8 May (commemorating the end of the war in Europe); 14 July (Fête Nationale; Bastille Day); 15 August (*Assomption*); 1 November (*Toussaint*; All Saints' Day); 11 November (Armistice Day); and 25 December (*Noël*; Christmas).

Shopping, and **Markets**. Many of the smartest and most expensive shops are to be found in the 1er, 6e, 8e, and 16e arrondissements, particularly in the area of the Rue du Faubourg-St.-Honoré, but in fact good shops and department stores (among which are *Les Galeries Lafayette* and *Au Printemps*, at 40 and 69 Blvd Haussmann respectively) can be found in most districts of central Paris, and their prices are usually less extravagant. Many of the antique shops and *brocanteurs* (second-hand dealers) are to be found in the 6e, while the so-called *Village Suisse* (shut Tuesday–Wednesday; W of the École Militaire), and the extensive *Marché aux Puces* (open Saturday–Monday; a few minutes walk N of the Porte de Clignancourt Métro), sometimes produce rare bargains among the bric-à-brac. A recent—but more expensive—attraction is the *Louvre des Antiquaires*, between the Palais du Louvre and Palais-Royal.

Auctions are held regularly at the rebuilt *Salle Drouot*, 6 Rue Rossini, 9e. Nearby, in the Rue Drouot and further S in the arcades of the Palais-Royal, are the haunts of philatelists; while an open-air *Stamp Market* is held at weekends and Thursday mornings at the

The central dome at Galeries Lafayette, 1898 (Heather Waddell)

junction of the Av. de Marigny and Av. Gabriel. Other colourful markets are devoted to *flowers*: in the Pl. Louis-Lépine (not far E of the Conciergerie), on the E side of the Madeleine, at the Pl. des Ternes,

A Gallo-Roman bronze figure (grasping baguette?) from the
Musée des Antiquités Nationales, St.-Germain-en-Laye

and Pl. de la République. On Sundays the flowers of the Pl. Louis-
Lépine give way to a *Bird* Market, while opposite, on the Quai de la
Mégisserie, is a *Pet* Market (not Sunday).

On the N side of the Pl. de la Madeleine some superbly displayed
food shops may be seen, although less sumptuous establishments will
tempt the eye and palate throughout Paris; indeed, one of the great
pleasures of wandering about the city is the quality and display of the
merchandise seen in many of the smaller shops selling cheese,
pâtisserie, or *charcuterie*.

Food markets not too far from the centre may be visited in the Rue
de Montorgueil (leading N from Les Halles Métro); the Rue Mouffetard, 5e; Rue des Martyrs, 9e; Rue de Lévis (NE of the Parc de

Monceau); Rue Cler, 7e; and Rue Buci (just N of the Odéon Métro); and there are of course many others. Food shopping on a Sunday morning at one of the street markets of Paris is almost always an agreeable occupation.

Bookshops and Libraries. Bookshops continue to proliferate throughout central Paris, but differ widely in the range of books stocked, and in the quality of their service. English newspapers and magazines can be found at a price at many kiosks near the centre. A selection of books in English is provided by *Brentano* (37 Av. de l'Opéra), *Galignani* (224 Rue de Rivoli: near the Tuileries Métro), *W.H.Smith* (248 Rue de Rivoli; also with a teashop), among others.

The Library of the *British Institute* is at 9 Rue du Constantine, on the E side of the Esplanade des Invalides. There is an *American Library* at 10 Rue de Gén. Camou, 7e.

Working Hours, etc. It will be found that in France work starts earlier than in the UK, and generally meals are also begun at an earlier hour. Although there is a movement towards the 'English' weekend, most food shops are open on Sunday mornings, and remain open later on weekday evenings; but they are likely to be shut on Mondays.

Sports. General information about a variety of sporting events, sporting facilities, addresses of tennis-clubs, squash-courts, golf-courses, swimming-pools, etc. in Paris and environs, may be obtained from the *Office de Tourisme de Paris*, 127 Av. des Champs-Élysées, and its branches, and from the *Direction de la Jeunesse et des Sports*, 17 Blvd Morland, 4e.

They can also advise on the capacities of the French sporting federations to assist the visitor, who is recommended to apply well in advance to the offices of his own home club or sporting organisation, which may well be able to give more practical information. *Michelin* Map No. 170 concentrates on sports and open-air recreations in the vicinity of Paris.

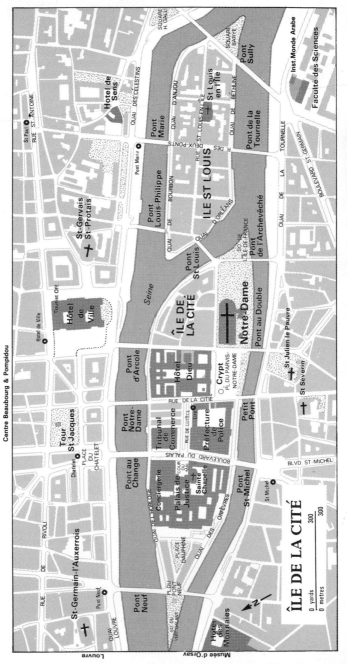

ÎLE DE LA CITÉ

THE CITÉ AND THE ÎLE-ST-LOUIS

1 The Île de la Cité
The Conciergerie; Ste. Chapelle

MÉTROS: Cité, St.-Michel, Pont-Neuf, Châtelet.

The **Île de la Cité** (Pl. 14; 2–4 and opposite), the earliest inhabited part of Paris, lies in the river like a ship, the 'Pointe' as its prow and *Notre-Dame* as its poop, moored to the banks by numerous bridges: the freighted vessel on a sea argent, which has always figured in the arms of Paris, with the device 'fluctuat nec mergitur' (tossed but not engulfed), is indeed appropriate. The Cité was the site of the original Gallic settlement of Lutèce or Lutetia Parisiorum, and after the destruction of the later Roman city on the Left Bank, became the site of Frankish Paris.

It remained the royal, legal, and ecclesiastical centre long after the town had extended onto both river-banks, and—for the visitor with little time—even a brief tour of the Cité will give a good idea of its importance in the historical development of Paris.

The Cité derives its importance from its situation at the crossroads of two natural routes across northern France. The Capetian kings were the great builders of the Cité, and it remained little changed from 1300 to the Second Empire, when Haussmann, after massive demolition, left it more or less with its present appearance.

From the QUAI DU LOUVRE the picturesque **Pont-Neuf** crosses the W extremity of the island. It is, in spite of its name, the oldest existing bridge in Paris, begun by *Baptiste du Cerceau*, completed in 1607, and several times repaired since. It was also the first to be built without houses lining each side, and with pavements. This 'Pointe de la Cité' is occupied by the SQ. DU VERT-GALANT, so-called in allusion to the amorous adventures of Henri IV, a statue of whom, by *Lemot* (1818), stands adjacent, replacing another, by Giambologna and Tacca, which stood here from 1635 to 1792.

E of the Pont-Neuf, entered by the Rue Henri-Robert, is the **Pl. Dauphine*, retaining two rows of houses, some dating from the reign of Louis XIII, but many have been altered since. Unfortunately the E wing of the triangle was demolished in 1874 to provide an unmerited view of Louis Duc's W façade of the *Palais de Justice* (1857–68; see below).

During the 17th and 18C the PL. DU PONT-NEUF and the bridge swarmed with pedlars and mountebanks. Tabarin set up his 'théâtre' in the Pl. Dauphine. Here, too, was the original site of the *Samaritaine*, one of the earliest hydraulic pumps, constructed by a Fleming for Henri IV to supply water for the royal palaces of the Louvre and Tuileries. It derived its name from a figure of the Good Samaritan on the fountain.

Other bridges connecting the Cité to the Right Bank of the Seine are the *Pont au Change* (1858–59), replacing a stone bridge dating from 1639 lined with moneylenders' shops; the *Pont Notre-Dame*, rebuilt in 1913 on the site of the main Roman Bridge; and beyond is the *Pont d'Arcole* (1855), named after a youth killed in 1830 leading insurgents against the Hôtel de Ville.

To the S, the Cité is connected to the Left Bank by the *Pont St.-Michel*, rebuilt several times since the late 14C (last in 1857), affording a fine view of the façade of *Notre-Dame*. Beyond is the *Petit Pont* (1853), on the site of another Roman bridge. Until 1782 it was defended at the S end by the *Petit Châtelet*, the successor of the Tour de Bois, which in 886 held Norman marauders at bay. From the W front of Notre-Dame, the *Pont-au-Double* (1882) replaced a mid 17C bridge, for crossing which the toll of a diminutive coin known as a 'double' was charged; while from the E extremity of the Cité, near the site of the archbishop's palace (pulled down in 1831), is the *Pont de l'Archevêché* (1828), providing a good view of the apse, with its profusion of flying buttresses.

Following the QUAI DE L'HORLOGE (N of the *Palais de Justice*), and entered just beyond twin towers (see below), is one of the world's famous prisons, the ***CONCIERGERIE** ◇ , occupying part of the lower floor of the Palais, and originally the residence of the 'Concierge', chief executive of the Parlement.

Its historical associations are numerous. In 1418 the Comte d'Armagnac was massacred here with many of his partisans by the hired assassins of the Duc de Bourgogne. The Marquise de Brinvilliers, the poisoner, was held here. During the Revolution, Marie-Antoinette, Bailly, Malesherbes, Mme Élisabeth, Mme Roland, Mme du Barry, Camille Desmoulins, Charlotte Corday, Danton, André Chénier, and Robespierre passed their last days in the Conciergerie. 288 prisoners perished here in the massacres of September 1792. Later prisoners were Georges Cadoudal (died 1804) the Chouan leader, Marshal Ney, Mérimée (for a fortnight in 1852), and the Duc d'Orléans (1890).

The *Salle des Gardes*, a handsome vaulted room of the 14C (restored 1877), where visitors await the guide, contains two stairs (no admission) ascending (right) to the *Tour de César*, where François Ravaillac, the murderer of Henri IV, was imprisoned (1610); the other leads to the *Tour d'Argent*, which served as a prison for Robert François Damiens, who attempted to kill Louis XV (1757). The spiral staircase in the right-hand corner as we leave the room was climbed by Marie-Antoinette and some 2275 other prisoners on their way from their cells to the Tribunal (see below).

The impressive four-aisled Gothic *Salle des Gens-d'Armes* (restored in 1868–80), was the original 'Salle des Pas-Perdus', said to be so called because the victims of the Revolution walked through it on their way to the Cour du Mai and execution; the name has since been transferred to the hall above (and to the waiting-rooms of other public buildings accommodating French functionaries).

Near the far end, to the left, a curious open spiral stair leads to the so-called *Cuisines de St.-Louis* (14C), also vaulted, and with four huge fireplaces. Returning to the first bay, we turn left past a grille flanking the Rue de Paris, reserved for the *pailleux* (prisoners who slept on straw, being unable to bribe their gaolers). We next enter the diminutive *Galerie des Prisonniers*, the windows of which look out onto the *Cour des Femmes* where the female prisoners took exercise, and also the scene of the massacres of September 1792. A railing which still exists divided off a section for men. To the left in the Galerie des Prisonniers was the cell where the condemned had their hair shorn and awaited the departure of the tumbril for the guillotine. At the end is the iron wicket which was the only entrance to the prison in Revolutionary times.

At the opposite end of this gallery is the original door (but in a different position) of Marie-Antoinette's cell, where the queen remained from 2 August to 16 October 1793. Adjacent, and now communicating with it, is Robespierre's cell.

Staircase in the interior of the Conciergerie

Next comes the *Chapel* (with a gallery for the prisoners) where the Girondins were incarcerated. It now displays a collection of souvenirs, including a blade of the guillotine, a crucifix said to have been found in Marie-Antoinette's cell, orders for arrest, etc.

On leaving the Conciergerie, we turn right into the BLVD DU PALAIS passing the *Cour du Mai*, on the E side of the Palais de Justice, named after the maypole set up here annually by the 'Basoche' or society of law clerks.

The **Palais de Justice**, a huge block of buildings occupying the whole width of the island, also includes within its precincts the *Ste.-Chapelle* (see below), which, with the four towers on the N side, are the oldest surviving portions.

The site of the Palais de Justice was occupied as early as the Roman period by a palace, which was a residence of Julian the Apostate, proclaimed emperor here in 360. The Merovingian kings divided their time between the Thermes and this Palais de la Cité, which was inside the walls, when not in the country. Louis VI died in the palace in 1137; Louis VII in 1180; and in 1193 Philippe Auguste was married here to Ingeborg of Denmark. Louis IX altered the palace and built the *Ste.-Chapelle*. From 1431 it was occupied entirely by the *Parlement*, who had previously only shared it with the king, but it was not until the Revolution that it acquired its present function.

Here, in the 16th Chambre Correctionelle, took place the trials of Flaubert's 'Madame Bovary' and Baudelaire's 'Les Fleurs du Mal' (29 January, and 20 August 1857, respectively).

The main buildings, of the 18C, were greatly enlarged in 1857–68 and again in 1911–14. The 14C *Tour de l'Horloge*, at the NE corner, with a clock copied from the original dial designed c 1585 by Germain Pilon, was virtually rebuilt in 1852. The upper part of the N façade was also rebuilt in the style of the original 14C work by Enguerrand de Marigny. The domed *Galerie Marchande*, dominating the Cour du Mai, is embellished with sculptures by Pajou.

The more interesting part of these law courts may be entered directly from the Boulevard just N of the Cour du Mai, by stairs ascending to the *Salle de Pas-Perdus. This magnificent hall, which replaced the great hall of the medieval palace (where in 1431 the coronation banquet of Henry VI of England was celebrated), was rebuilt in 1622 by *Salomon de Brosse*, and restored in 1878 after being burned by the Communards. At the far end of the room, divided in two by a row of arches, and to the right, is the entrance to the *Première Chambre Civile*, formerly the *Grand'Chambre* or *Chambre Dorée* (restored in the style of Louis XII), perhaps originally the bedroom of Louis IX. Later it was used by the *Parlement*, in contempt of which Louis XIV here coined his famous epigram 'L'État, c'est moi'. The Revolutionary Tribunal, with Fouquier-Tinville as public prosecutor, sat here in 1793 (see *Conciergerie*, above).

A vaulted gateway leads from the *Cour du Mai* to the *Cour de la Ste.-Chapelle*.

The *SAINTE CHAPELLE ◊ was built in 1243–48 by Louis IX as a shrine for miscellaneous relics, among them those purporting to be the Crown of Thorns and fragments of the True Cross, etc. The building is ascribed to *Pierre de Montreuil* (cf. St.-Denis, and St.-Germain-en-Laye), and is remarkable for the impression of lightness it conveys. It was often the scene of royal marriages, and Richard II of England was betrothed here in 1396 to Isabelle of France. It was 'restored' in 1837–57 by *Duban, Lassus* (who reconstructed a leaden flèche in the 15C style; the fifth on this site), and *Viollet-le-Duc*.

36m long, 17m wide, and 42·50m high, the building gives an impression of great height in proportion to its length and breadth. It consists in fact of two superimposed chapels, the lower for servants and retainers, the upper reserved for the royal family and court. The lofty windows of the upper chapel, an innovation, are surmounted by delicately sculptured gables and a graceful balustrade. The leaden roof is modern. The portal consists of two porches, one above the other; the statues are 19C restorations.

The interior of the *Chapelle Basse*, with carved oak bosses, and 40 columns sustaining the upper chapel, is darkened by the decoration of *Émile Boeswillwald* (1815–96), who attempted to reproduce its medieval paintwork. There are a number of 14–15C tombstones in the pavement.

A spiral staircase ascends to the *Chapelle Haute* (20·50m high),

The Sainte Chapelle

certainly one of the outstanding achievements of the Middle Ages; but sadly in need of cleaning. With the walls stripped of its 19C painting and gilding, the simple lines of its architecture would be seen to better advantage; its *Stained-Glass* (restored 1845) would glow more luminously.

The 86 panels from the Apocalypse in the large rose-window were a gift of Charles VIII. The first window on the right depicts the Legend of the Cross and the removal of the relics. The other windows in the nave and apse depict scenes from the Old and New Testaments. Beneath the windows on either side runs a blind arcade; of the apostles against the pillars, the 4th, 5th, and 6th on the left, and the 3rd, 4th, and 5th on the right, are original.
The two deep recesses under the windows of the 3rd bay were the seats reserved for the royal family. In the centre of the restored arcade across the apse is a wooden canopy beneath which the relics used to be exhibited on Good Friday; those few surviving the Revolution are in the treasury of Notre-Dame.
Exit by the second spiral stair.

To the S, at 36 QUAI DES ORFÈVRES, is a *Museum of Police History*, with a room devoted to the part they played in the Resistance, and Liberation of Paris.

Opposite the Cour du Mai, the Rue de Lutèce leads between (right) the *Préfecture de Police* and (left) the domed *Tribunal de Commerce* (by *Bailly*; 1860–65), behind which the *Marché aux Fleurs* offers a colourful contrast. A Bird Market is held here on Sundays.

2   Notre-Dame

MÉTRO: Cité.

On the E side of the Rue de la Cité, we turn right and then left into the PL. DU PARVIS NOTRE-DAME, a space which Haussmann increased sixfold by his demolitions. To the left is the *Hôtel-Dieu*, rebuilt here in 1868–78 to the N of its original site. The first hospital was founded here by St. Landry, Bp of Paris, c 660.

John Northleigh, writing in 1702, refers to it then accommodating 4000 men: 'tended and looked after by the Religious of the Order of St.-Augustine, young perfect Nuns, and for the generality very comely Women, whom they venture among Men when infirm, though perhaps sometimes too far; for one of our infirm Irish-men was grown on a sudden so lusty, that he made a shift to run away with one of the pretty Tenders'.
The ecclesiastical authorities tried heretics on the *Parvis* here, where the condemned knelt before execution to acknowledge their sin and beg absolution. In 1314 Jacques de Molay, grand master of the Templars, summoned to repeat his confession publicly and accept sentence of imprisonment, unexpectedly protested the innocence of his Order, and was hustled off to the stake.

Near the W end of the Parvis is the entrance to the ***Crypte Archéologique** ◊ , displaying architectural remains of all ages of the Cité's past uncovered in 1965 when the area was being excavated for the construction of the adjacent underground car-park. The site is exceptionally well exhibited, and dioramas and models explain the growth of the district prior to the ravaging fire of 1772. Sections are illuminated by press-button lighting, and explanatory notes are printed both in French and English.

The path we first follow leads above the foundations of the *Gallo-Roman rampart* (late 3C), a section of which is later seen. Further to the E, beyond the excavated area, lie the foundations of the W end of the Merovingian cathedral of St.-Étienne (6C). After passing display cases of artefacts uncovered here, we follow the foundations of the demolished Hospice des Enfants-Trouvés and other medieval buildings once flanking the Rue Neuve Notre-Dame, some (to the right as we approach the exit) as early as the 2C, and (left) relics of hypocausts, etc.

Notre-Dame from the South, a photograph taken in 1842, before its restoration

To the E rises ***NOTRE-DAME**** (Pl.14;4), the exterior of which has been cleaned. Although ranking after some others in beauty, archaeologically and historically it is one of the most interesting of the Gothic cathedrals of France. Commenced when Gothic art was beginning to throw off the traditions of the Romanesque style, Notre-Dame was completed in the 13C, so that it is possible to follow the gradual progress of the new style until its decadence in the 14C.

Road distances in France are calculated from its W door.

The idea of replacing the cathedral of St.-Étienne (founded by Childebert in 528: see above) and that of Notre-Dame, further E, by a single building, on a much larger scale, was due to Maurice de Sully, Bp of Paris (died 1196). The old Notre-Dame replaced a Roman temple of Jupiter more or less on the site of the present cathedral, the foundation stone of which was laid by Pope Alexander III in 1163. The choir was finished by 1182, except for the roof; the nave was added in 1208; and the W front and its towers c 1225–50. A series of chapels was added: in the nave (1235–50) and apse (by *Pierre de Chelles* and *Jean Ravy*; 1296–1330). The side porches were begun in 1258; the crossings of the transept were built by *Jean de Chelles* and *Pierre de Montreuil* (1250–67).

The School of Music at Notre-Dame was influential during the late 12th and 13Cs.

Henry VI of England was crowned king of France (by Henry Beaufort, Bp of Winchester, and son of John of Gaunt) in the cathedral choir in 1431, at the age of ten. Here too were celebrated the marriages of James V of Scotland and Madeleine of France (daughter of François I, on 1 January 1537), François II to Mary Stuart (1558), Henri of Navarre (later Henri IV) to Marguerite de Valois (1572), and Charles I of England (by proxy) to Henrietta Maria (1625).

Until the end of the 17C Notre-Dame had preserved intact its appearance of the 14C, but the reigns of Louis XIV and Louis XV brought deplorable alterations, particularly in the destruction of tombs and stained glass. Many sculptures and treasures were destroyed during the Revolution, when an opera-singer, Mlle Maillard, was enthroned here as the Goddess of Reason. In 1804, Napoléon I and Joséphine were crowned here by Pius VII; Napoléon III and Eugénie de Montijo were married here in 1853. In 1845 a thorough 'restoration' was begun under the direction of Lassus (died 1857) and Viollet-le-Duc. It narrowly escaped serious damage in 1871, for piled chairs were ready to be set ablaze by the Communards, when they received orders to evacuate the church.

On 26 August 1944 the thanksgiving service following Gén. de Gaulle's entry into liberated Paris was interrupted by sniping from internal and external galleries. Notre-Dame continues to be the scene of ceremonial functions, state funerals, etc.

Exterior. The *W front consists of three distinct storeys. The central *Porte du Jugement*, ruined by Soufflot in 1771, has a 19C Christ on the pier, and in the tympanum, the Last Judgment, restored by Viollet-le-Duc; only the upper tier of sculptures is ancient.

The *Porte de la Vierge* (left) contains a restored Virgin on the pier; three kings and three prophets, and the Resurrection of the Virgin, in the lower part of the tympanum; above is the Coronation of the Virgin.

The sculptures of the *Porte de Ste.-Anne* (right) are mostly of 1165–75, designed for a narrower portal, with additions of c 1240. On the pier is St. Marcellus (19C); above, scenes from the life of St. Anne and the Virgin, and the Virgin in Majesty, with Louis VII (right) and Maurice de Sully (left). The two side doors retain their medieval wrought-iron hinges.

Above the portals is the *Gallery of the Tree of Jesse* (reconstructed by Viollet-le-Duc), its statues destroyed in 1793 because the Parisians assumed that they were of kings of France (cf. Musée de Cluny). The magnificent rose-window, 9·6m in diameter, is flanked by double windows within arches. Higher still is an open arcade.

The *Towers*, originally intended to be surmounted by spires, offer extensive views; entrance in the N tower. In the S tower hangs the great bell, recast in 1686 and weighing 13 tonnes; Victor Hugo's bell-ringer, Quasimodo, may be remembered. The *Chimières* (gargoyles), grotesque figures of devils, birds, and beasts, were redesigned by Viollet-le-Duc.

The side façades and apse likewise consist of three distinct and receding storeys; the bold flying buttresses of the latter, by Jean Ravy, are also admired for their elegance. The S porch, according to a Latin inscription at the base, was begun in 1257 (1258 new style) under the direction of Jean de Chelles. The story of St. Stephen, as depicted in the tympanum, and the medallions of student life, are original. The N porch, of the same period, retains an original statue of the Virgin, and in the tympanum, the story of Theophilus. Just to the E of this porch is the graceful *Porte Rouge*, probably by Pierre de Montreuil. To the left, below the windows of the choir chapels, are seven 14C bas-reliefs. The *Flèche* (90m above the ground), a lead-covered oak structure, was rebuilt by Viollet-le-Duc in 1859–60, the original having destroyed in the 18C.

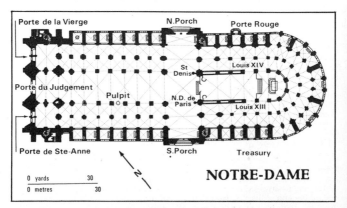

West front of Notre-Dame

The best view of the **Interior** is obtained from beneath the *Organ* (1733, by Cliquot; rebuilt in 1868 by Cavaillé-Coll, and electrified in the 1960s), at the W end. The cathedral (130m long, 48m wide, and 35m high) consists of a nave of ten bays of great purity of design, flanked by double aisles continued round the choir (of five bays). 37 chapels surround the whole. A vaulted gallery overlooks the nave; the windows above were altered in the 13C. The vaulting is supported by 75 piers, surmounted by bold yet graceful capitals. New glass, with an abstract design, was placed in the nave in 1963–64. Of the three *Rose-windows*, retaining their original 13C glass, the N is the best preserved and finest.

At the crossing, 'Notre-Dame de Paris', a 14C figure, stands against the SE pillar; against the NE pillar is St. Denis, by N. Coustou. Seven paintings (by Charles Le Brun, Sébastien Bourdon, and others), presented by the Goldsmiths' Guild of Paris in 1634–51, hang in the side-chapels of the nave.

The *Choir*, modified in 1708–25 by Louis XIV in fulfilment of his father's vow of 1638, attracted Viollet-le-Duc's 'restoring' hand.

The Descent of Christ into Limbo (13C), Notre-Dame

Seventy-eight of the original 114 *Stalls* remain, adorned with
bas-reliefs from the designs of Jules Degoullons (1711–15). Canopied
archiepiscopal stalls stand at either end. The bronze angels (1712–13)
against the apse-pillars escaped the Revolutionary melting-pot.

In front of the high-altar Geoffrey Plantagenet, fourth son of Henry II
of England, was buried in 1186, having died suddenly while in Paris.
Behind Viollet-le-Duc's altar is a Pietà by Nicolas Coustou, with a base
sculptured by Girardon, part of the 'Voeu de Louis XIII'. The statue of
Louis XIII (S) is also by Coustou; that of Louis XIV (N) is by Coysevox.

In the first four bays of the choir may be seen the remains of the screen which,
until the 18C, extended round the whole apse; the expressive bas-reliefs on the
exterior, finished in 1351, were unfortunately restored and repainted by
Viollet-le-Duc. In the blind arches below are listed some of the eminent people
buried in the church.

The *Ambulatory* contains the tombs of 18–19C prelates. Behind the high altar is the tomb-statue of Bp Matiffas de Bucy (died 1304). In the 2nd chapel S of the central chapel is the theatrical tomb, by Pigalle, of the Comte d'Harcourt (died 1769); here also are the restored tomb-statues of Jean Jouvenel des Ursins and his wife (died 1431, 1451).

On the S side of the ambulatory is the entrance to the *Sacristy*, now containing the *Treasury*, a somewhat indifferent collection of ecclesiastical plate, reliquaries, and cult objects.

In the Rue du Cloître Notre-Dame, adjacent to the N tower of the cathedral, stood (until 1748) the chapel of *St.-Jean-le-Rond*, on the steps of which the natural son of Mme de Tencin (1682–1749) was found exposed. Baptised Jean-le-Rond, he grew up to become famous under the name d'Alembert (1717–83). At No. 10 is the *Musée Notre-Dame de Paris*, with collections relating to the history of the cathedral.

The Rue Massillon turns N into the Rue Chanoinesse: on the site of a house at the junction, the poet Joachim du Bellay died in 1560; opposite died the famous anatomist M.-F.-X. Bichat (1711–1802). Parallel to the N (at No. 19 Rue des Ursins; but no admission) part of the nave is preserved of the *Chapelle St.-Aignan* (1115–18), where mass was said in secret in 1789–91. Nicolas Boileau (1636–1711) died nearby in a house destroyed when the SQ. DE L'ARCHEVÊCHÉ was laid out.

In the SQ. DE L'ÎLE-DE-FRANCE, at the extreme E end of the Cité, is a *Memorial* to some 200,000 Frenchmen deported to German concentration camps during the 1939–45 war.

3   The Île-St.-Louis

MÉTRO: Cité, Pont-Marie, Sully-Morland.

The **Île St.-Louis** is reached from the Île de la Cité by crossing the *Pont St.-Louis* (dating from 1614, but replaced in 1969). Still a comparatively quiet backwater, although in danger of exploitation, it was formerly two islets, and was not built over until the 17C, when as an annexe of the Marais to the N, it became the site of a number of imposing mansions. It is connected to the N bank by the *Pont Louis-Philippe* (rebuilt 1862); beyond stands the *Pont Marie* (1635; named after its builder), crossing to the QUAI DES CÉLESTINS. Further E, the island is crossed obliquely by the *Pont de Sully* (1876), at the N end of which, beyond the SQ. H.-GALLI, stands the striking *Hôtel Fieubet* (see Rte 19).

On the S side of the island the *Pont de la Tournelle* (built of wood in 1369; rebuilt in 1654, and again in 1928) crosses from the Rue des Deux-Ponts (in which Restif de la Bretonne once lodged) to the QUAI DE LA TOURNELLE.

To the SE is the new *Institut du Monde Arabe* (see Rte 5), and the adjacent *Science Faculty Building*, with its tower, built on the site of the old *Halles aux Vins*.

In the transverse Rue St.-Louis-en-l'Île is the *Hôtel Chenizot* (No. 51, with a balcony), of 1730, residence of Teresa Cabarrus (later Mme Tallien) in 1788–93. No. 21, the richly decorated church of **St.-Louis-en-l'Île**, was begun by Le Vau in 1664 and finished in 1726 by Jacques Doucet. The tower and curious openwork spire were added in 1765. The ornamental stone-carving in the interior was executed under the direction of J.-B. de Champaigne (died 1681; buried in the church). It contains six Nottingham alabasters from the same series as those in St.-Leu-St.-Gilles.

At No. 12 in this street lived Philippe Lebon (1769–1804), who first introduced into France the principle of lighting by gas (1799). Between Nos 9 and 7 is an arch of the *Hôtel de Bretonvilliers*, finished by Jean I du Cerceau in 1640. Fénelon (1651–1715) lived at No. 3. No. 2 is the **Hôtel Lambert**, by Le Vau (c 1650), once a residence of Voltaire and Mme du Châtelet, and from 1842 the home of the Czartoryski family and a centre of Polish life in Paris.

On the NE side of the island, in the QUAI D'ANJOU, No. 3 belonged to Le Vau; No. 9 was the home of Honoré Daumier (1808–79) from 1846. The **Hôtel de Lauzun** or *de Pimodan* (No. 17; 1657), by Le Vau, was the residence in 1682–84 of the Duc de Lauzun, commander of the French contingent at the Battle of the Boyne, who resided here with 'la Grande Mademoiselle'.

Baudelaire lived on the third floor in 1845, and Gautier had apartments here in 1848, where meetings of the Club des Haschichins took place. The artists responsible for its splendid decoration were Le Brun, Le Sueur, Patel, and Sébastien Bourdon. Admission Saturday and Sunday 10.00–17.40; at other times apply to the Municipal Tourist Office, Hôtel de Ville (tel. 42765404.

Ford Madox Ford's 'Transatlantic Reviewed' was published from No. 29 on the quai.

Further W, Nos 13 and 15 QUAI DE BOURBON were the *Hôtel Le Charron* (17C), with a delightful courtyard; while No. 11 was owned by Philippe de Champaigne. No. 1 was the *Franc-Pinot*, an inn kept during the Revolution by the father of Cécile Renault, who had attempted to murder Robespierre.

Turning S, in the QUAI D'ORLÉANS, No. 6 is the *Musée Adam Mickiewicz*, with an important Polish library, and souvenirs of the poet (1798–1855), and also of Chopin.—Further E, in the QUAI DE BÉTHUNE, is the mansion of Armand, Duc de Richelieu, great-nephew of the cardinal (Nos 16–18).

At the eastern extremity of the island is the triangular SQ. BARYE.

THE SOUTH OR LEFT BANK:
LA RIVE GAUCHE

4 The 'Quartier Latin'
St. Séverin; St.-Nicholas-du-Chardonnet;
St.-Étienne-du-Mont; Panthéon;
the Sorbonne

MÉTROS: St.-Michel, Maubert-Mutualité, Card. Lemoine,
Luxembourg.

This area, on the S bank of the Seine opposite the *Île de la Cité* (see Rte 1) derives
its present name (conferred by Rabelais) from the language spoken by the early
students. It grew up with Abélard's removal in c 1200 from the school attached to
Notre-Dame to the Montagne Ste.-Geneviève. Originally known as the *Université*, it has remained to a large extent the learned quarter of Paris, and still
contains the main educational and scientific institutions. This district occupies
the site of Roman *Lutetia*.
  In the mid 19C the BLVD ST.-GERMAIN was driven E through the old streets, and
many ancient buildings were swept away. In 1968 its paving-blocks were found
to be useful missiles during the 'student revolution'. Cafés and bookshops
abound, and the students appear to spend more time in the former than in the
various faculty buildings. In 1922 a 'Cité Universitaire' was founded in the 14th
arrondissement, to the S (see Rte 7).

From the PL. ST.-MICHEL (Pl. 14;4), linked to the Cité by the *Pont
St.-Michel*, and with the *Fontaine St.-Michel* at its S end, erected by
Davioud in 1860, and incorporating a memorial of the Resistance of
1944, the busy BLVD ST.-MICHEL (popularly known as the 'Boul Mich')
leads S to the *Carrefour de l'Observatoire*, in part following the
Roman Via Inferior (see pp 73 and 84).

It was laid out by Haussmann as a direct continuation of the *Blvd de Strasbourg*
and the *Blvd de Sébastopol*, and shortly crosses the *Blvd St.-Germain*, running
roughly parallel to the Seine. Almost the only interest of these main thoroughfares lies in their animation; the architectural and historical character of the
Quartier is found in the side-streets.

Immediately to the E of the Pl. St.-Michel, in a still decrepit corner of
Old Paris, diverges the Rue de la Huchette (the 'Narrow Street' of
Elliot Paul), off which run the Rue Xavier-Privas and Rue du
Chat-qui-Pêche, an alley named after an old shop-sign. Théophile de
Viau composed his 'Parnasse Satirique' at No. 1 Rue de la Huchette,
and at No. 8 (or 10) Napoléon lodged in 1795; here also is the
diminutive *Théâtre de la Huchette*.
  Diverging right along the Rue de la Harpe, and taking the first
turning left, brings us to *ST.-SÉVERIN, rebuilt in the 13–16C on the
site of an oratory of the time of Childebert I, where Foulque of
Neuilly-sur-Marne preached the Fourth Crusade (c 1199).

The lower part of the W front and the W bays of the nave date from the early 13C;
the outer S aisle was added c 1350, the outer N aisle and the E part of the church
were in construction in 1450–96, the chapels in 1500–20. The main W portal, of
the early 13C, was brought piecemeal from St.-Pierre-aux-Boeufs in the Cité in
1837. The upper two storeys date from the 15C. On the left is a tower of the 13C,
completed in 1487, with a door which was once the main entrance; the
tympanum dates from 1853, but in the frame is a 15C inscription: 'Bonnes gens

qui par cy passés, Priez Dieu pour les trespassés'. To the left of the tower, a niche holds a statue of St. Séverin.

The INTERIOR impresses by the breadth of its double ambulatory. The most striking details are the ribs of the vaulting and the choir triforium, which approach English Perpendicular in style. The apse was partially classicised in the 17C at the expense of Mlle de Montpensier. In the nave, the first three bays contain late-14C glass from St.-Germain-des-Prés, but much restored; from the fourth bay on the glass is mid-15C. One of the subjects on the S side of the nave is the murder of Thomas Becket, while the W rose-window contains a Tree of Jesse (c 1500) masked by an organ of 1745.

To the S of the choir are the 15C galleries of the graveyard, beneath which the first operation for the stone was successfully carried out in 1474.

On the far side of the Rue St.-Jacques diverges the Rue Galande, one of the oldest existing streets in Paris (14C), with, on No. 42, a carved representation of the life of St. Julian.

The church of **St.-Julien-le-Pauvre** (right) rebuilt c 1170–1230 and used in the 13–16C as a university church and in 1655–1877 by the old Hôtel-Dieu for various secular purposes, has since 1889 been occupied by Melchites (Greek Catholics subject to papal authority). The present W front was built in 1651. Note the foliated capitals within; an iconostasis obscures the E end.

A good *View of Notre-Dame* may be had from the SQ. RENÉ-VIVIANI, just to the N.

From the NE side of this square runs the Rue de la Bûcherie, where No. 13 was occupied by the École de Médecine from 1483 to 1775, with a rotunda built in 1745 by the Danish doctor Jacques-Bénigne Winslow. Restif de la Bretonne (1734–1806) died at No. 16 (previously No. 27).

Edward Browne, visiting Paris in 1664, refers to a 'Coffe house' in this street, kept by an Englishman named Wilson, and it appears that the institution may have been introduced to Paris prior to 1669, when a Turkish envoy is said to have made the drink fashionable.

S of the Sq. René-Viviani is the Rue du Fouarre (named after the 'straw' on which the students sat), the centre of four 14C schools of the University, and referred to by Dante, who is supposed to have attended lectures here.—The Rue Lagrange leads SE to meet the Blvd St.-Germain at the PL. MAUBERT ('la Maub'), where Étienne Dolet (1509–46) was burnt as a heretic. Crébillon *fils* (1707–77) was born here.

The ancient Rue de Bièvre runs NE, just E of the Pl. Maubert, in which Dante is said to have written part of the 'Divina Commedia'.—To the W is the Rue des Anglais, infested by English students in medieval times.

A short distance along the Rue Monge, leading SE, is (left) **St.-Nicolas-du-Chardonnet** ('of the thistle-field'), a Renaissance church built mostly in 1656–1709; the clumsy tower (1625) is a relic of an earlier edifice. Some of the statues and stucco work are by Nicolas Legendre.

The dark interior contains, in the 1st chapel on the right, *Corot's* study for the Baptism of Christ; the 2nd chapel on the right of the choir, beyond the transept, contains a monument by *Girardon* of Bignon, the jurist (died 1656). In the 8th chapel (round the apse) is the tomb of Le Brun's mother, by Tuby and Collignon, designed by *Le*

Brun in the theatrical style of Bernini; against the window is a monument of Le Brun (died 1690) and his widow, by *Coysevox*. Note the 18C organ-case. A Crucifixion by *Brueghel the Younger* is preserved in the Sacristy.

Diverging left along the Rue St.-Victor, we pass (left) the Rue de Poissy, where at No. 24 are the remains of the 14C refectory of the ancient *Collège des Bernardines*; it was occupied by firemen from 1844 to 1970.

At the far end of this street, where it meets the QUAI DE LA TOURNELLE, stands the 17C *Hôtel de Nesmond* (Nos 55–57), restored, and now accommodating the offices of *La Demeure Historique*.

This association of proprietors of privately-owned historic residences throughout France, founded in 1924, is devoted to promoting a public interest in this aspect of their architectural and cultural patrimony. They publish a map showing the situation of c 330 châteaux, indicating hours of admission, etc.

At No. 47 in the quai is the former convent of the 'Miramiones' or Filles Ste.-Geneviève, founded by Mme de Miramion (died 1696), now accommodating a small *Museum* devoted to the Hospitals of Paris. No. 15 is *La Tour d'Argent*, a famous restaurant, which gained its gastronomic reputation in the Second Empire, built on the site of an earlier tavern dating from 1582.

On the right is the interesting church of *ST.-ÉTIENNE-DU-MONT* (Pl. 14;6), showing the transition from the Gothic to the Renaissance style.

It was almost continuously in construction from 1492 to 1586. Marguerite de Valois laid the foundation stone of the portal in 1610 and even this preserves certain Gothic motifs. The tower, begun in 1492, was completed in 1628. The N side, with its picturesque porch, dates from 1630–32.
It replaced an earlier parish church dependent upon and entered through the abbey church of *Ste.-Geneviève* (see above). During the Revolution, it became the 'Temple of Filial Piety'.

The INTERIOR has lofty columns, a wide ambulatory, and ribbed vaulting with pendent keystones. Its originality lies in the balustrade which runs along the supporting pillars of the nave and choir. The beautiful fretted *Rood Screen*, built in 1525–35, is a masterpiece of design and carving (the date 1605 on the side refers only to the door to the spiral staircases by which it is ascended). The organ-case by Jean Buron dates from 1631–32; the pulpit of 1651 is the work of Germain Pilon, with sculptures designed by Laurent de la Hire. The *Stained-glass* ranges in date from c 1550 to c 1600; the oldest windows are those in the apse.

Between the 6th and 7th chapels in the S aisle a tablet commemorates the Jacobins, an order of preaching friars established in the Rue St.-Jacques in 1218. Above the 1st chapel in the choir is an ex-voto to St. Geneviève, with the provost and merchants of Paris, by *François de Troy* (1726), while higher, to the right, is a similar painting by *Largillierre*, of 1696. On either side of the chapel are the epitaphs of Pascal and Racine (by Boileau), whose graves are at the entrance to the *Lady Chapel*. Also buried in the church are Charles Rollin (1661–1741), the historian, and, the artist Eustache Le Sueur (1616–55). The next chapel S of the choir contains the copper-gilt shrine of St. Geneviève (1853). Within is a fragment of her tomb; her remains were burned by the mob in the Pl. de Grève in 1801.

From the next bay runs a corridor, at the end of which (right) is the Presbytery, built in 1742 for Louis d'Orléans (son of the Regent), who died here in 1752. On the left is the *Charnier*, or gallery of the

The West front of St.-Étienne-du-Mont

graveyard, with 12 superb *Windows* of 1605–09; note one depicting the Mystic Wine-press. Most of them are after the designs of Léonard Gautier.

To the W of the PL.-STE.-GENEVIÈVE (Pl. 14;6) rises the grandiose bulk of the **PANTHÉON** ◇ , situated on the 'Mont de Paris', the highest point on the Left Bank (60m) and the legendary burial-place of Geneviève (5C), a *pucelle* of Nanterre, later regarded as the patron saint of Paris.

In 1744, lying ill at Metz, Louis XV vowed that if he recovered, he would replace the former church, and the present building was begun 20 years later, although not completed until 1789. Its architect, Soufflot, died of anxiety, it is said, owing to criticism that subsidence of the walls (noticeable near the choir) would occur because their foundations had been laid on clay pits dug by Roman potters.

In 1791, after the death of Mirabeau, the Constituent Assembly decided that the church should be used as a Panthéon or burial-place for distinguished citizens, and the pediment was inscribed with the words 'Aux Grands Hommes la Patrie reconnaissante'. From the Restoration to 1831 and from 1851 to 1885 it was again used as a church, but on the occasion of Victor Hugo's interment it reverted to the name and purpose decreed in 1791.

An imposing building, the **Panthéon** is built in the shape of a Greek cross, 110m long, 82m wide, and 83m high to the top of the majestic *Dome*. The pediment above the portico of Corinthian columns is a masterpiece of *David d'Angers*, representing France between Liberty and History, distributing laurels to famous men. Forty-two windows were walled up during the Revolution.

The INTERIOR is of slight interest. Coldly Classical, it is adorned with paintings, among which are some pallid works by Puvis de Chavannes, while in the transepts are monuments by Landowski. The colossal group of the Convention, at the E end, is by Sicard.

The *Dome*, supported by four piers united by arches, contains three distinct cupolas, of which the first is open in the centre to reveal the second, with a fresco by *Gros*. By the first pillar (right) is a monument to Rousseau by *Bartholomé*: on the left, another to Diderot and the Encyclopaedists by *Terroir*. Other tablets commemorate Antoine de Saint-Exupéry (1900–44) and Henri-Louis Bergson (1859–1941). Within the dome, in 1852, the physicist Léon Foucault gave the first public demonstration of his pendulum experiment proving the rotation of the Earth.

Conducted tours of the **Crypt** (entrance in the NE corner) may be made, first passing a shrine containing the heart of *Gambetta* (1838–82). Among the tombs are those of *Rousseau* (died 1778; and transferred here in 1794); *Voltaire* (died 1778; transferred 1791), with a statue attributed to Houdon; and *Jacques-Germain Soufflot* (1714–80), the architect. Of men whose remains have been reinterred in the vaults, the most eminent are *Victor Hugo* (1802–85) and *Émile Zola* (1840–1902); *Marcelin Berthelot* (1827–1907), the chemist; *Jean Jaurès* (1859–assassinated 1914), the socialist politician; *Louis Braille* (1809–52), benefactor of the blind; the explorer *Bougainville* (1729–1811; from St.-Pierre-de-Montmartre), and *Jean Moulin* (1899–1944), the Resistance hero. *Mirabeau* and *Marat* were interred here with great state, but their remains were soon cast out with ignominy: the former now rests in the cemetery of Ste.-Catherine, the latter in the graveyard of St.-Étienne-du-Mont. *Jean Monnet* (1888–1979), the 'Father of Europé, was buried in the Panthéon in November 1988.

At No. 32 in the Rue du Card.-Lemoine, the next main street running S, stood the *Collège des Bons-Enfants*, where Vincent de Paul founded his congregation of mission-priests.—Further S, No. 49 is the *Hôtel Le Brun*, built by Boffrand for the artist in 1700, and later occupied by Watteau and by Buffon.

Ascending SW at the junction of the Rue du Card.-Lemoine with the Rue Monge, we approach the Rue Clovis, where a section of Philippe Auguste's perimeter *Wall* may be seen.

No. 65 Rue du Card.-Lemoine, the *Institution Ste.-Geneviève*, was the **Scots College** (*Collège des Écossais*; apply to the concierge), re-founded in 1662 by Robert Barclay. George Buchanan graduated in 1528 at the earlier Scots College, founded in 1326. He remained teaching in Paris until 1534, again in 1544–7, and in 1553.

The *Chapel*, on the first floor, contains the tomb of Frances Jennings, Duchess of Tyrconnel (died 1730), the spirited elder sister of Sarah, Duchess of Marlborough; a memorial erected to James II (who bequeathed his brain to the college) by James Drummond, Duke of Perth, with a long Latin epigraph; and the tomb of Sir Patrick Menteith, who died in 1675 in the service of Louis XIV.

Blaise Pascal (1623–62) died on the site of No. 67.

No. 5 Rue Descartes, crossing the Rue Clovis, is the entrance to the influential **École Polytechnique**, founded by Monge in 1794 for the training of artillery and engineer officers, transferred in 1805 to the buildings of the *Collège de Navarre*, and greatly extended in 1929–35.

Founded in 1304 by Jeanne de Navarre, queen of Philippe le Bel, the Collège de Navarre numbered among its pupils Gerson, Ramus, Henri III, Henri IV, Henri de Guise, Richelieu, Bossuet, Condorcet, and André Chénier. The *Collège de Boncourt* (No. 21), taken over by the Collège de Navarre in the 17C, had earlier contained perhaps the first theatre in Paris. In 1792 Giovanni Battista Piranesi's sons established their engraving works in the college.

At No. 34 Rue Montagne-Ste.-Geneviève, further down the hill, are remains of the *Collège des Trente-Trois*, founded in 1633 by Claude Bernard, friend and follower of Vincent de Paul, and named after its 33 scholarships (one for each year of Christ's life).

At No. 23 Rue Clovis is the entrance to the *Lycée Henri-IV*. The Tower (restored) has a Romanesque base and two Gothic upper storeys (14–15C) and is a relic of the church (demolished 1802) of the Abbaye Ste.-Geneviève.

Practically all the conventual buildings were rebuilt in the 18C, but the former refectory (now the chapel), is an over-restored 13C building, and the kitchens are also medieval. The fact that the abbey came under papal jurisdiction, not that of the Bishop of Paris, influenced Abélard's choice of this area.

Bernardin de Saint-Pierre lived from 1781 to 1786 at No. 4 Rue Rollin, where he wrote 'Paul et Virginie'. The street is named after Charles Rollin (1661–1741; the uncritical historian), who died at No. 8; Descartes lived at No. 14 in 1644–48. Mérimée (1803–70) was born at No. 7 Carré de Ste.-Geneviève, which was adjacent.

In the NW corner of the PL. DU PANTHÉON was the *École de Droit*, begun by Soufflot in 1771, subsequently enlarged and now known as Universities I and II: see below. Opposite is the *Mairie of the 5th Arrondissement* (1844–50), built in the same style.

The **Bibliothèque Ste.-Geneviève**, on the N side of the Place, originated in the library of the famous Abbey of Ste.-Geneviève. The present building, also of 1844–50, by Labrouste, is on the site of the *Collège de Montaigu*, founded in 1314, where Loyola, Erasmus, and Calvin were students. It was also known as the *Hôtel des Haricots*, as it was presumed that beans were the staple fare of its inmates. It was in later years a prison.

The library contains c 700,000 vols (nearly 4000 MSS.) and over 30,000 prints and engravings (including 10,000 portraits). Rooms are devoted to Scandinavian literature (c 90,000 vols) and the *Bibliothèque Jacques Doucet*, comprising c 8000 vols of late 19th and 20C French authors, including MSS. of Rimbaud, Verlaine, Baudelaire, Gide, and Valéry. Among the illuminated MSS. which are occasionally exhibited, are an English Bible, copied by Manerius in the 12C; the Chronicles of St.-Denis (late 13C); several MSS. of the Carolingian period; the 'De Proprietatibus Rerum' of Barthélemy l'Anglais (Catalan translation of the 15C); and 'La Cité de Dieu' of St. Augustine (late 15C). The building also contains a number of busts by Coysevox, J.-J. Caffieri, Lemoyne, and Houdon.

On the right of the Library, in the Rue Valette, are the remains of the *Collège Fortet* (No. 21), dating from 1397, where Calvin was a student in 1531.

Further downhill to the right, in the Rue des Carmes, is *St.-Ephrem*, a Syrian Catholic church, formerly the chapel (1760) of a community of Irish priests, who established themselves in the 17C buildings of the *Collège des Lombards*.

To the left of the Library, on the right in the Rue Cujas, is the *Collège Ste.-Barbe*, founded in 1460, the oldest existing public educational establishment in France, at which Francisco Xavier was a scholar. The Law Faculty Library has been built on part of the grounds.

Descending W from the Panthéon towards the *Luxembourg Gardens* is the wide Rue Soufflot, where (right) at No. 14 a tablet commemorates the site of the Dominican or Jacobin convent (1217–1790) where Albertus Magnus and Thomas Aquinas taught.

The Rue St.-Jacques, which we first cross, an important thoroughfare in medieval times, following the course of the Roman road—the Via Superior—from Lutetia to Orléans, formed part of the pilgrim route to Santiago de Compostela, and so attracted many convents. The S section is described on p 84.

Turning right along the Rue St.-Jacques, we pass (right) the *Lycée Louis-le-Grand*, formerly the Jesuit *Collège de Clermont*, founded in 1560 and rebuilt in 1887–96. Molière, Voltaire, Robespierre, Desmoulins, Delacroix, and Hugo studied here.

We next pass the **Collège de France**, with its entrance in the Pl. Marcelin-Berthelot (Pl. 14; 4–6). In the courtyard, with its graceful portico, is a statue of Guillaume Budé (Budaeus; 1468–1540). It was founded by François I in 1530 under Budé's influence, to spread humanism and counteract the narrow scholasticism of the Sorbonne. It was independent of the University, and its teaching was free and public. The present building was begun in 1610, completed by Chalgrin c 1778, and since enlarged. During work in 1894 traces were found of Gallo-Roman baths.

In a garden on the NE side of the college is a monument to the 'Pléïade', the 16C poetical coterie (notably Du Bellay and Ronsard) which originated in a vanished college near this site (the Collège Coqueret; founded in 1418, but surviving only until 1643). Other members of the group, formed in 1549, were Antoine de Baïf, Rémy Belleau, Jodelle, Pontus de Tyard, and Jean Dorat (who took the place of Jacques Peletier).

To the W of the Collège de France stands the **SORBONNE**, founded as a modest theological college in 1253 by Robert de Sorbon (1201–74), chaplain to Louis IX. It was rebuilt at Richelieu's expense by Jacques Lemercier in 1629, but, with the exception of the church, the present buildings date from 1885–1901.

The *University of Paris*, which disputes with Bologna the title of the oldest university in Europe, arose in the first decade of the 12C out of the schools of dialectic attached to Notre-Dame. (Josse de Londres is said to have endowed the College des Dix-Huit in 1180.) Transferred by Abélard to the Montagne Ste.-Geneviève, the university obtained its first statutes in 1208, and these served as the model for Oxford and Cambridge and other universities of northern Europe. By the 16C it comprised no fewer than 40 separate colleges. In 1550 John Dee, the mathematician and astrologer, lectured on Euclid at the Collège de Reims, the first ever to do so in Paris. In 1577 James Crichton (1560–83) 'The Admirable Crichton', is said to have disputed on scientific questions in 12 languages at the University.

Before the end of the 13C the Sorbonne had become synonymous with the faculty of theology, overshadowing the rest of the University and possessing the power of conferring degrees, and was distinguished for its religious rancour, supporting the condemnation of Joan of Arc, justifying the massacre of St. Bartholomew, and refusing its recognition of Henri IV. Nevertheless in 1469 it was responsible for the introduction of printing into France, by allowing Ulrich Gering and his companions to set up their presses within its precincts.

Marlowe refers to its 'blockish Sorbonests'; in 1713 it was visited by George Berkeley, who was present at a disputation there, 'which indeed had much of the French fire in it'. Later in the 18C it attacked the 'philosophes', and in 1792 was itself suppressed. It was refounded by Napoléon, and in 1821 became the official headquarters of the University of Paris. The student 'revolution' of May 1968 eventually had the effect of instigating overdue reforms in the university system, and in 1970 the University of Paris was replaced by the formation of thirteen autonomous universities in the region. The Sorbonne accommodates Universities III and IV.

The ponderous buildings, which still house the *University Library* of 700,000 volumes, the *Académie de Paris*, and minor learned institutions, include the *Grand Amphithéâtre* (the main lecture hall, containing *Puvis de Chavannes'* mural, 'Le Bois sacré'), which may be visited on application at the main entrance in the Rue des Écoles.

Apply here also to visit *Ste.-Ursule de la Sorbonne**, facing the PL. DE LA SORBONNE founded in the 13C and rebuilt by Lemercier in 1635–59 at the expense of Richelieu. The dramatic *Tomb* of the great cardinal (1585–1642) was designed by Le Brun and sculptured by Girardon (1694); it had particularly impressed Philip Thicknesse when he saw it in 1775, as it did Arthur Young in 1787. The *Dome* was the first example of a true dome in Paris.

5   Musée de Cluny

MÉTROS: Maubert-Mutualité, Odéon, St.-Michel.

Opposite the entrance to the Sorbonne is the SQUARE PAUL-PAINLEVÉ (Pl. 14;3–4; with a statue of Montaigne by Landowski). It is flanked to the N by the *Hôtel de Cluny**, built at the end of the 15C on the site of Roman ruins, known as the *Palais des Thermes*, and one of the finest extant examples of medieval French domestic architecture. It houses the **MUSÉE DE CLUNY**, devoted to the arts and crafts of the Middle Ages, and one of the most rewarding to visit of the museums of Paris. The entrance is in the right-hand corner of the courtyard, beyond an archway surmounted by the Amboise arms.

The property was bought in 1340 by Pierre de Chalus, Abbot of Cluny in Burgundy, and the mansion was built c 1490 by Abbot Jacques d'Amboise as the town house of the abbots, although rarely occupied by them. In 1515 it became the residence of Mary Tudor (1496–1533), daughter of Henry VII and later widow of Louis XII. She was known as 'La Reine Blanche' from the white mourning worn by her as queen-dowager of France. James V of Scotland was lodged here in 1537 before his wedding with Madeleine, daughter of François I. Later occupants were the Card. de Lorraine, Claude de Guise, Mazarin, and the papal nuncios (1600–81).

In the 18C the tower was used as an observatory by the astronomer Messier. At the Revolution the mansion became national property, but in 1833 it was bought by *Alexandre Du Sommerard* (1771–1842) and filled with the treasures which he spent his lifetime collecting. These were bought by the State and supplemented by many new acquisitions, during the long curatorship of his son, Edmond Du Sommerard (died 1889), and since.

GROUND FLOOR. **R1** is devoted to the accessories of medieval costume, such as buckles, clasps, ornamental trinkets etc.; shoes— one *à la poulaine*, with a pointed toe (late 14C); and metal and leather caskets, etc. Outstanding in this and the next four rooms are the collection of *Tapestries*, mostly 15C, although that of The Resurrection is early 14C. Among them are The Concert; The Miracle of St. Quentin; Vintage Scenes and the set of six scenes illustrating the activities of a noble household of c 1500, entitled 'La Vie seigneuriale' in **RR4** and **6**. Also remarkable are the carved Head of Jeanne of Toulouse (c 1280) in **R2**; the textiles and embroidery in **R3**, some Coptic or Byzantine, others of French, Italian, English, and Spanish origin, including examples of Hispano-Moresque fabrics. **RR5** and **6** are devoted to carpentry and woodwork, and display an interesting series of misericords (from St.-Lucien, Beauvais) and a chest-front on which jousting scenes are depicted.

In the corridor (**R7**) adjoining R5 are a number of Nottingham alabasters, and a charming statue of St. Ursula sheltering some of her eleven thousand companions.—A room to the right accommodates sculptural fragments from the central portal of Notre-Dame, and mutilated heads from the Tree of Jesse gallery from the cathedral, recently discovered, and at present in the adjacent Thermae.—The fine collection of medieval sculpture in **R8** (left) will probably be moved elsewhere in the building.

Among outstanding works are statues of the Magdalen from Brussels, said to be a portrait of Mary of Burgundy, daughter of Charles the Bold; the seated Virgin reading to the Child, from the lower Rhine; the group with the Virgin swooning, carved at Burgos in the Dutch style; a marble Virgin, from Le Breuil (Marne); and the painted Pietà from Tarascon (mid 15C), and a number of carved altarpieces.—**R9** contains four mutilated statues of the Apostles from the Ste. Chapelle (1243–48), carved capitals, some of Catalan workmanship; carved altarpieces, and further examples of wood and stone statuary; and ivory oliphants.—Earlier capitals, some of the 7C from St.-Denis, and from St.-Germain-des-Prés (mid 11C) are displayed in **R10**, together with a number of tombstones and a fine 7C sarcophagus.

Below is the *Frigidarium* of the Gallo-Roman baths, remarkable in that it still preserves its vault, unique in France. The room (20m by 11·5m and 14m in height) with the *Piscina* probably on the N side, is all that remains in its entirety of the baths of the building. It was probably erected during the reign of Caracalla (212–17): slight ruins are extant of its *Tepidarium* and *Caldarium*. Here is displayed the museum's collection of Gallo-Roman sculpture.

Returning through R10, we ascend to the FIRST FLOOR and enter **R11**, circular in shape, in which are displayed the series of six exquisite *millefleurs* tapestries known as **La Dame à la Licorne** (or Unicorn), probably woven in the southern Netherlands for Jean Le Viste between 1484 and 1500: the arms of the family—gules, a band azur with three crescents argent—being frequently seen. They had long hung in the Château of Boussac, and were first brought to public notice by both Mérimée (when Inspector of Historical Monuments) and George Sand, and were eventually acquired by the museum in 1883.

They illustrate the Senses, and their disposition is the same as when originally hung: to the right, *Sight*, in which the unicorn gazes into the mirror held before him by the Lady; and *Hearing*, in which the Lady plays a portative organ: to the left, *Touch*, in which the Lady gently grasps the horn of the unicorn; and *Smell*, in which a monkey sniffs a flower, while the Lady weaves a garland: beyond is *Taste*, with the Lady feeding both the monkey and a parakeet from a bowl of sweetmeats; while further to the right the Lady stands before a tent-like pavilion, while returning jewels to a casket held by her maid, a gesture said to indicate 'Free Choice', and the non-submission to the senses; the top of the pavilion is embroidered with the motto 'A mon seul désir'.

One of the six late 15C 'millefleurs' tapestries depicting
'La Dame à la Licorne', and said to represent the non-submission
of the five Senses shown in the other tapestries

R12 contains a collection of Enamels, including late Roman and Byzantine examples; others from the Rhineland and Meuse region, including a mid 12C altarpiece from Stavelot; remarkable *Collections of Limoges enamel-ware from the late 12C to 14C, among them a number of reliquaries, chalices, pyxes, shrines, plaques, croziers, and crucifixes of outstanding workmanship; and a Brussels tapestry of the legend of Augustus and the Sibyl (early 16C).—**R13** and **14** are devoted to jewellery, including gold torques, bracelets, buckles, and fibulas; ornamented belts; two rock-crystal lionheads (5C; probably once decorating a Consular chair), found on the banks of the Rhine; Part of the Treasure of Gurrazar (Toledo), Visigothic votive crowns with their pendant crosses, dating from the late 7C, and discovered in 1858; the Treasure of Colmar (early 14C coins and jewellery found in a wall of the Rue des Juifs, Colmar, in 1853); the Golden Rose given by Pope Clement V to the prince-Bishop of Basle (early 14C); a silver-gilt and coral statue of Daphne (by Wenzel Jamnitzer, Nüremburg; mid 16C); the Reliquary of St. Anne (1472; by Hans Greiff); a collection of cameos, intaglios and glyptics; Merovingian and Gallo-Roman jewellery; Processional Crosses, including one from Barcelona (14C) and another from Siena (mid 15C); the Reliquary of the Ste.-Chapelle, made to the order of Louis IX; and the Tapestry of the Prodigal Son (early 16C).

In the corridor (**R15**) are displayed a variety of medieval artefacts, among them domestic utensils; mirrors; riding accessories; game-boards; stamps, dies, and seals; and writing equipment.—An adjacent room will later display more Goldsmiths' and Silversmiths' work.—To the right is **R16** containing examples of stained glass, including panels from St.-Denis (1144), Troyes (c 1200), and medallions from the Ste.-Chapelle (mid 13C); and **R17**, devoted to ceramics, including a fine collection of Hispano-Moresque ware, and other examples of lustreware from Manises (Valencia); and a 17C German Organ.

Returning through R16 we turn right into **R18**, containing the reassembled *Choir-stalls from the abbey of St.-Lucien at Beauvais (1492–1500), some misericords from which are shown in R5.—**R19** displays the gold *Altar-frontal from Basle cathedral (c 1015), made for the Emperor Heinrich II; a collection of Byzantine and Consular Ivories, including a large figure of *Ariadne (c 500); a richly mounted reliquary-casket; a 15C Italian Bust-reliquary, etc.

Adjacent is the ***Chapel** (**R20**), a masterpiece of Flamboyant vaulting from a central pillar, with a filigree of delicate moulding between the main ribs. Above the Oriel window are 15C sculptures, with the Father blessing His dying Son, and angels with the instruments of the Passion, etc. Also notable are the recumbent funeral effigy (copper on wood) of Blanche of Champagne (died 1283), from the abbey of La Joie, near Hennebont (Morbihan); and the first part of a set of tapestries depicting the Life of St. Stephen, woven for Jean Baillet, Bp of Auxerre c 1490: the series is continued in the adjoining rooms.

From R18, we turn left into **R21**, devoted to metalwork, largely of copper and bronze, including an eagle-lectern (1383); measures and weights; 'aquamaniles'; cauldrons, candlesticks, and other implements. **R22** Iron work, with fine examples of grilles (12C); a metal-plated chest; bolts, locks and keys; a small selection of arms and armour, spurs, and knives; shields and targes or bucklers; coffers, etc. **R23** contains articles of pewter, tin, and lead, including a collection of medallions, pilgrims' badges (and their moulds); guild counters, toys, etc. **R24**, with an imposing Jewish Tabernacle of the Law (1471), and other items of medieval furniture, etc.

Most of the later objects, from the era of the Renaissance, but part of the collections of this museum, are now to be seen at **Écouen**: see Rte 37.

6 The Institute du Monde Arabe; the Jardin des Plantes; the Gobelins; St.-Médard

MÉTROS: Monge, Gare d'Austerlitz, St.-Marcel, Gobelins, Censier-Daubenton.

At the E end of the Rue des Écoles (conveniently approached from Métros Maubert Mutualité or Cardinal Lemoine) rises the extensive new utilitarian block of buildings, and obtrusive tower, housing departments of the *Faculty of Science* (Universities V and VI; see p 74), to the N of which the Rue des Fossés-St.-Bernard descends towards the Seine at the Pont Sully. At No. 5 in this street are displayed the mineralogical collections of the university.

Here, until their transfer to Bercy, stood the huge bonded warehouses of the Halles aux Vins, itself on the site of the *Abbaye de St.-Victor*. This had been dispersed in 1790: here Thomas Becket and Abélard resided, and in its library Rabelais studied.

The **Institut du Monde Arabe** was inaugurated in the autumn of 1987 at 23 Quai St. Bernard. It was founded in 1980 in an attempt to further cultural and scientific relations between France and some 20 Arab countries. The building covers an area of $7250m^2$, and rises to a height of 32m. The public parts of the Institute include a Library and documentation centre, Museum, and temporary exhibition room. A curious feature of the exterior of the S façade are the shutters of the windows, the size of which can be regulated by photo-electric cells reacting to the sun's intensity, while a spiral of white marble is visible in the Book Tower.

The *Library* occupies three floors and an area of $1076m^2$; the *Museum* comprises $2800m^2$ with an addition $700m^2$ for temporary exhibitions. A proportion of the material in the museum has come from the Arab-Islamic collections of the Musée du Louvre, the Musée des Arts Africains et Océaniens, and from the Union Central des Arts Décoratifs.

Between the QUAI ST.-BERNARD and the Seine, among riverside gardens, extends the *Musée de Sculpture en Plein Air* (Pl. 15;5), set up in 1980, in which some 40 characteristic examples of contemporary 'sculpture', fabrications, etc., are exhibited. Few are notable; the most noticeable is Nicolas Schöffer's gyrating metallic tower, with its struts and discs, while among earlier works are some by Brancusi, and Zadkine.

Bearing S from the Rue Jussieu, we ascend the Rue Linné, off which the Rue des Arènes climbs right to the relics of the 2–3C amphitheatre of Roman Paris, only discovered in 1869 and fully excavated since 1883. The **Arènes de Lutèce** are now surrounded by the gardens of the SQ. CAPITAN named after Dr Capitan, who restored the ruins in 1917–18.

At the junction of the Rue Linné with its continuation, the Rue Geoffroy-St.-Hilaire, stands the *Fontaine Cuvier* (1840), and the NW entrance to the **JARDIN DES PLANTES** (previously known, until 1793, as the *Jardin du Roi*), officially the *Musée National d'Histoire Naturelle* (Pl. 15;7), 28 hectares in area, and combining the attractions of a menagerie, botanical gardens, and natural history galleries. Its collections of wild and herbaceous plants are unrivalled, and in May and June the peonies make a magnificent show. The *Library* contains a remarkable collection of botanical MSS., including the *Vélins du Roi*, illustrated by Nicolas Robert (1614–85) and others; also works by Redouté, etc.

The *Gardens, Menagerie, Aquarium*, and *Vivarium*. are open daily 7.00–20.30, and until dusk in winter. The *Jardin d'Hiver* and the *Zoological Galleries* are open from 13.30 to 17.00 daily, except Tuesday; the *Jardin Alpin* is closed from October to April.

There are other entrances in the Rue Geoffroy-St.-Hilaire, and in the semicircular PL. VALHUBERT to the E opposite the *Gare d'Austerlitz*. The nearest Métro stations are Jussieu, Monge, Censier-Daubenton, and Gare d'Austerlitz.

Founded in 1626 under Louis XIII as a 'physic garden' for medicinal herbs by the royal physician Guy de la Brosse, the garden was first opened to the public in 1650. In 1647–51 its keeper was William Davidson, a Scotsman. Its present importance is mainly due to the great naturalist *Buffon* (1707–88), who was superintendent from 1739, and greatly enlarged the grounds. In 1793 it was reorganised by the Convention under its present official title, and provided with twelve professorships. The animals from the royal collection at Versailles were brought to form the nucleus of a menagerie during Bernardin de Saint-Pierre's brief directorship. In 1792, Richard Twiss was told by the director that the names of some plants had been changed: 'We will not have any aristocratic plants!'

Many distinguished French naturalists have taught and studied here, and are commemorated by monuments in the garden or nearby. A statue of Lamarck (1744–1829) faces the E entrance. Among other scientists associated with the Jardin des Plantes are Geoffroy Saint-Hilaire (1772–1844), Louis Daubenton (1706–99; who did the honours when visited by Joseph Townsend in 1786), Joseph de Tournefort (1656–1708) and Bernard de Jussieu (1690–1777).

Entering from the NW we pass (left) the *Maison de Chevreul* (named after the centenarian chemist) and the *Maison de Cuvier*, where Georges Cuvier (1769–1832), zoologist and paleontologist, gave Saturday evening receptions during the 1820s and 30s, attended by Mérimée, Stendhal, and Delacroix, among others. Here also are the Administrative Building, in a mansion of 1785, and the Amphithéâtre or lecture hall, of 1788 (restored). The Menagerie occupies most of the N side of the gardens. It is said that many of its earlier occupants were killed in 1870–71 to feed besieged Parisians during the Franco-Prussian War.

On the right of the entrance is the *Butte*, a hillock with a maze, and with the first cedar of Lebanon (from Kew Gardens) to be planted in France (by Jussieu, in 1734), and on the summit, a *belvedere*. The sundial here bears the inscription 'Horas non numero nisi serenas': I only count the sunny hours. In the centre are the *Jardin d'Hiver* and *Jardin Alpin*.

Along the S side of the gardens are ranged the *Zoological Galleries*, in the N vestibule of which is the tomb of Guy de la Brosse (died 1641); the *Mineralogical Galleries*, with the *Library* (c 700,000 vols and 2500 MSS.) and *Buffon's House*, occupied by him from 1773 to his death; the *Botanical Gallery*; and *Paleontological Gallery*. To the S, on the far side of the Rue Buffon, is an Annexe to the museum.

To the W of the Rue Geoffroy-St.-Hilaire is a green-tiled *Mosque*, complete with minaret, which has stood there since 1925.

Slightly further W (in the Rue Puits-de-l'Ermite) was the site of the *Prison de Ste.-Pélagie*, where Joséphine, the future empress, and Mme du Barry, were confined during the Revolution, and where Mme Roland (1754–93) wrote her memoirs.

Not far to the S, we reach the BLVD ST.-MARCEL, near which point was the *Cimetière Ste.-Catherine*, where the bodies of Mirabeau and other revolutionaries were reburied after being ejected from the Panthéon. This thoroughfare leads NE to meet the BLVD DE L'HÔPITAL.

To the right of this latter junction stands the huge *****Hôpital de la Salpêtrière** (Pl. 15;8), founded in 1656 as a home for aged or insane women, on the site of a gunpowder factory.

In 1684 a criminal wing was built, in which 'Manon Lescaut' and Mme de la Motte were gaoled, and which was notorious for its filth and vice. A house of correction for wayward wives and young girls was later added, and in 1790 there were said to be 8000 females living there including, according to Townsend, 7000 foundlings and about 900 prostitutes (of the 28,000 then on the lists of the police). Part of the building contained political prisoners during the Revolution, and some of the worst massacres of September 1792 took place here.

The main building, by Le Vau and Le Muet, dates from 1657–63; the domed **Church of St.-Louis**, built in 1670–77, is by Libéral Bruant. Statues by Étex were added after 1832. As a whole, it is a notable example of the austere magnificence of the architecture of the period, and may be compared in many ways to the Invalides.

Dr Charcot (1825–93), the hypnotist, is commemorated by a monument to the left of the gateway; his consulting-room, laboratory and library have been preserved intact.

Adjacent to the S is the *Hôpital de la Pitié*, transferred in 1911 from the Rue Lacépède, where it had been founded by Marie de Médicis in 1612.

To the NE is the **Gare d'Austerlitz**, the main railway terminus for Tours, Bordeaux, Bayonne, Toulouse, etc.; see Pl. 15;6. Between 1870 and 1871, the station, then known as the Gare d'Orléans, was turned into a balloon factory under the management of Eugene Godard. Some 65 manned balloons left Paris during the siege, carrying letters and dispatches. One was blown as far afield as Norway!

The BLVD ST.-MARCEL diverges SW to meet the Av. des Gobelins, beyond which it divides to be continued by the BLVD ARAGO (leading due W to the Pl. Denfert-Rochereau), and the BLVD DE PORT-ROYAL (eventually meeting the Blvd du Montparnasse).

A short distance S of this junction stands (right) **La Manufacture Nationale des Gobelins ◇** (Pl. 14; 8; admission Wednesday–Friday afternoons only; guided tour), the famous tapestry factory which has been a state institution for over three hundred years, and still retains some of its 17C buildings.

The original manufactory at Fontainebleau was moved to Paris by Henri II. Suspended during the 16C Religious Wars, the industry was revived by Henri IV and installed in 1601 in the buildings of the Gobelins, named after Jean Gobelin (died 1476), head of a family of dyers who made their reputation with the discovery of a scarlet dye, and who had set up their dye-works here on the banks of the Bièvre in 1443. In 1662, under Colbert, the royal carpet factory of the *Savonnerie*, started in 1604 in the galleries of the Louvre, and subsequently moved to a 'savonnerie' (soap-factory) at Chaillot, was placed under the same management (it transferred its workshops to the Gobelins' factory in 1826). In 1667 Louis XIV added the royal furniture factory, and Charles Le Brun and then Pierre Mignard (in 1690) were appointed as directors. The Beauvais tapestry workshops, destroyed in 1940, have also been transferred here.

On the left are two workshops, separated by a staircase. The tapestry is woven on high-warp looms, several of which date from the time of Louis XIV. The weaver works on the reverse side of the tapestry, having the painting which he is copying behind him and reflected in mirrors. The average amount of tapestry that a weaver can produce in a day is 15cm^2.

In the former Chapel hang two tapestries specially made for it. The tour crosses the Rue Berbier-du-Mets, behind the factory, which now covers the non-calcareous waters of the Bièvre, which used to flow between the dye-works and workshops. A new building contains workshops for the weaving of carpets, where the original methods are still followed.

Adjacent are the buildings of the *Mobilier National* (or National Furniture Store), and beyond them, where stood the allotments of tapestry workers, is the SQ. RENÉ-LE-GALL (with the hunting lodge of M. de Julienne, the patron of Watteau).

The Av. des Gobelins ends to the S at the PL. D'ITALIE, the hub of seven important thoroughfares, on the N side of which is the *Mairie of the 13th Arrondissement*.

Turning N down the Av. des Gobelins, we soon reach picturesque **St.-Médard** (Pl. 14;8), dedicated to the 'St. Swithin' of France. The nave and W front are of the late 15C; the choir, in construction from 1550 to 1632, was 'classicised' in 1784, when the Lady Chapel was added. Sacked by the Huguenots in 1561, not much of the 16C glass survives. The churchyard, now a garden, was notorious for the hysterical orgies of the Jansenist fanatics, or *convulsionnaires*, at the tomb of the Abbé Pâris (died 1727).

The narrow, shabby, and busy Rue Mouffetard (an ancient thoroughfare now closed to traffic at its lower end) climbs N from the front of the church through a squalid district (but with a good street market) past (left) the Rue de l'Arbalète, where at No. 3 Auguste Rodin was born in 1840. Eventually we pass (right) the PL. DE LA CONTRESCARPE, where No. 1 has a tablet commemorating the 'Cabaret de la Pomme-de-Pin', immortalised by Rabelais and the 'Pléiade'. There was another cabaret of the same name in the Rue de la Cité.

We shortly enter the Rue Descartes, at No. 39 in which Paul Verlaine (1844–96) died, before reaching the Rue Clovis, see Rte 4.

Also in this district, but slightly to the W, and best approached by the Rue d'Ulm (leading S from the Panthéon), is the Maronite church of *N.-D. du Liban* (No. 17). The *Collége des Irlandais*, founded in 1578 by John Lee, and re-founded in 1687 by English Catholics as a seminary, stands at the corner of the adjacent Rue des Irlandais.

At No. 29 Rue Lhomond, leading SE, with an 18C façade seen from the Rue Amyot, Mme du Barry and Juliette Drouet were educated in the *Couvent de Ste.-Aure*.—A short distance beyond, at the *École de Physique et de Chimie industrielles*, in the Rue Pierre-Brossolette, Pierre and Marie Curie did their experimental work in 1883–1905.

At No. 45 Rue d'Ulm is the *École Normale Supérieure*, established in 1794 for the training of teachers, and sited here since 1843. Pasteur worked in laboratories here between 1864 and 1888. Among its pupils were Taine, Bergson, Péguy, Romain Rolland, Giraudoux, Jules Romains, Jean Jaurès, and Éduard Herriot.

7   Val-de-Grâce; Observatoire; Montparnasse

MÉTROS: Luxembourg, Port-Royal, Denfert-Rochereau, Cité-Universitaire, Vavin, Montparnasse-Bienvenue.

Turning S from the Rue Soufflot along the Rue St.-Jacques (Pl. 13;8; see p 73) we pass No. 195, the *Institut Océanographique*, and No. 218, which occupies the site of the house of Jean de Meung, part-author of the 'Roman de la Rose' (c 1300).

On the right is **St.-Jacques-du-Haut-Pas**, a plain classical building (1630–88), replacing an earlier chapel, and the favourite church of the Jansenists. It was completed in 1712 with the help of the Duchesse de Longueville (1619–79; who is buried here), together with Jean

Duvergier de Hauranne (1581–1643), the prominent Jansenist, and Jean-Dominique Cassini (1625–1712), the astronomer.

No. 254, at the corner of the Rue de l'Abbé-de-l'Épée, is the *Institut National des Sourds-Muets*, a Deaf and Dumb Asylum founded by the Abbé de l'Épée (1712–89) about 1760 and taken over by the State in 1790; the building, once the Oratorian seminary of St.-Magloire, was reconstructed in 1823. In the courtyard is a statue of the Abbé by Félix Martin, a deaf and dumb sculptor (1789).

Further on, at No. 269 (left) is the **Schola Cantorum** (visitors admitted), a free conservatoire of singing and music established in 1894 by three pupils of César Franck, including Vincent d'Indy. Among composers who studied there were Albéniz, de Falla, Granados, Roussel, Satie, and Turina. Among directors in recent years has been the distinguished composer and musicologist Daniel Lesur.

The buildings (1674) are those of the English Benedictine monastery of St. Edmund, founded in France in 1615, and established on this site from 1640 to 1818. The salon and staircase are good examples of the Louis XIV style; the lower part of the chapel is now a concert hall; the *chapelle ardente*, where James II's body lay in state, may also be seen.

What was left of the corpse of James II (died 1701), and those of his daughter Louise Maria-Theresa (1692–1712), and the Duke of Berwick (1670–1734), his son by Arabella Churchill, were also buried here. At the Revolution their remains were either dispersed, or possibly hidden in the catacombs, which were once accessible from the house. The last burial here was that of Berwick's second son Charles (died 1787). In 1775 Dr Johnson was a guest here.

At No. 284 (left), the door between columns at the end of the courtyard was once the entrance to the distinguished Carmelite convent to which Louise de la Vallière, mistress of Louis XIV, retired in 1674. Another relic of the convent is a crypt beneath No. 25 Rue Henri-Barbusse, to the W.

The street widens (at Nos 277–279) opposite the impressive front of the *VAL-DE-GRÂCE* (Pl. 13;8), since 1790 a military hospital, and from 1624 the house of the Benedictine nuns of Val-Profond, whose patroness was N.-D. du Val-de-Grâce. The present more extensive buildings were erected by Anne of Austria in thanksgiving for the birth of Louis XIV in 1638 (she had been married 22 years without issue), and the first stone of the new works was laid by the young king in 1645. In the courtyard is a bronze statue of Napoléon's surgeon, Baron Larrey (1766–1842), by David d'Angers.

François Mansart was succeeded as architect before 1649 by Jacques Lemercier, and after 1654 the buildings were finished by Le Muet and Le Duc, the church being completed in 1667. The remains (often only their hearts) of royal personages interred here, including Anne of Austria, Marie-Thérèse (wife of Louis XIV), La Grande Mademoiselle, and the Regent Philippe II d'Orléans, were dispersed at the Revolution. The Army Medical School was added in 1850.

The façade of the church (by Mansart) is a notable example of the Jesuit style, and the lead and gilt *Dome* (by Le Duc) is one of the finest in France. The sculptures within are by François and Michel Anguier, Pierre Sarazin, and others. The high-altar, with its six huge twisted marble columns, is inspired by Bernini's *baldacchino* or canopy over the Saint's tomb in St. Peter's, Rome; the sculptured Nativity on it is a copy of Anguier's original (now at St.-Roch). The painting in the dome is by Pierre Mignard; in the chapel on the right of the choir is a portrait of Anne of Austria borne by an angel; and in the *Chapel of the Sacrament* is the Communion of the Angels, by J.-B. de

Champaigne. The imposing *Cloisters* may be visited, and also, in the former Refectory, a *Museum of Military Hygiene*.

The *Val-de-Grâce* was only one of the many religious houses which, until the Revolution, were established in this district. To the N are the Rue des Ursulines and Rue des Feuillantines (in which the young Victor Hugo spent the years 1808–13), whose names recall vanished convents; almost opposite were the Carmelites (see above); to the S stood Port-Royal (see below), beyond which, in the Blvd Arago, stood a 13C Franciscan nunnery.

To the right on the far side of the Blvd de Port-Royal, a maternity hospital has, since 1814, occupied the buildings of **Port-Royal de Paris**, a branch of the Jansenist abbey of Port-Royal-des-Champs (SW of Versailles; see *Blue Guide France*), destroyed at the instigation of the Jesuits and its site ploughed over in 1709. In the chapel, completed by Le Pautre in 1647, is the tomb of Angélique Arnauld (1591–1661), the reforming abbess.

The extensive buildings of the *Hôpital Cochin* lie to the left of the Rue Faubourg-St.-Jacques. Here, in February 1929, George Orwell was treated for pneumonia; Samuel Beckett was also treated here after being stabbed by a tramp. No. 38 in the street (right), the *Hôtel de Massa* (1784), transferred here from the Champs-Élysées in 1927 and re-erected, has since been occupied by the Société des Gens de Lettres.

We turn up the Rue Cassini, where at No. 2 Alain-Fournier lived in 1910–14, and wrote 'Le Grand Meaulnes' (1913); Balzac lived in 1829–34 at a house on the site of No. 1, where he wrote 'La Peau de Chagrin'.

We pass (left) the entrance of the **OBSERVATOIRE** (Pl. 14;7), founded by Louis XIV in 1667 and completed by Claude Perrault in 1672. It was visited in 1672 by John Locke, in 1680 by Edmund Halley and in 1698 by Dr Martin Lister, all of whom met its director Jean Dominique Cassini (1625–1712), the first of the family of astronomers and cartographers. The famous Danish astronomer Olaf Römer (1644–1710), was also working here from 1672.

The four sides of the building face the cardinal points of the compass, and the latitude of the S side is the recognised latitude of Paris (48°50′11″ N). A line bisecting the building from N to S is the meridian of Paris (2°20′14″ E of Greenwich), which until 1912 was the basis for the calculation of longitude on French maps. The Observatoire is also the headquarters of the *Bureau International de l'Heure*, and a 'speaking' clock (tel. 699 84 00) is installed in its cellars.

Application to attend a guided tour should be made in advance to the Secrétariat at 61 Av. de l'Observatoire.

On the first floor of the main building is a *Museum of Instruments*, and the contents of the Rotunda in the W tower illustrate the history of astronomy. The room on the second floor, on the pavement of which is traced the Paris meridian, contains older instruments. A shaft descending from the roof of the main building into the catacombs has been used for the study of falling bodies. In the E cupola is an equatorial telescope of 38cm aperture.

Turning N from the Observatoire, we shortly cross the Av. Denfert-Rochereau to reach the Carrefour de l'Observatoire.

To the NW is Rude's statue of Marshal Ney (1769–1815), who was shot close by, for ('traitorously') espousing Napoléon's cause on his return from Elba. Among those 'Royalists' who voted for his death were marshals Marmont and Victor. Behind it is the *Closerie des Lilas*, long a literary resort, and frequented by Baudelaire, Verlaine, Gide, Jarry, Apollinaire, et al. To the N is the *Fontaine de l'Observatoire* (1875) by Davioud, Frémiet, and Carpeaux.

The Av. Denfert-Rochereau leads SW to the Pl. Denfert-Rochereau, passing (right) the *Hôpital St.-Vincent-de-Paul*, with a chapel of 1650–55. Chateaubriand lived in 1826–38 in the grounds of the *Infirmerie Marie-Thérèse*, which occupied an adjacent site, and which was directed by his wife.

This focus of traffic (regular buses to Orly airport) was known as the *Pl. d'Enfer* until 1879, when it received its present name in honour of the defender of Belfort during the Franco-Prussian War. The earlier name originated as Via Inferior, the Roman road (now the Blvd St. Michel) leading S to it from the Île de la Cité, parallel to and W of the Via Superior (now the Rue St.-Jacques). In the centre is a reduced copy of Bartholdi's sculpture of the 'Lion of Belfort'.

On the SW side of the Place, in one of the octroi pavilions of the old *Barrière d'Enfer* (by *Ledoux*; 1784), is the main entrance to **Les Catacombes**, a labyrinthine series of underground quarries dating from the time of the Romans and extending from the Jardin des Plantes to the Porte de Versailles and into the suburbs of Montrouge, Montsouris, and Gentilly. In the 1780s they were converted into a charnel-house for bones removed from disused graveyards, and most of the victims of the massacres of the Terror were later transferred here. In 1944 they were a headquarters of the Resistance Movement.

Guided-tours take place Tuesday–Friday between 14.00–16.00, and Saturday–Sunday 9.00–11.00, 14.00–16.00. It is advisable to take a torch. The tour lasts over an hour, through a macabre series of galleries lined with bones and skulls, to a huge ossuary containing the debris of over 6 million skeletons, and tends to be monotonous.

Leading S from the Pl. Denfert-Rochereau, the Av. René-Coty approaches the *Parc de Montsouris*, some 16 hectares in area and laid out in 1875–78. Near its NE corner is a lake (which suddenly dried up on the day of inauguration, and the engineer responsible committed suicide); near the centre of the S side is a reproduction of the *Bey's Palace* at Tunis (erected for the Exhibition of 1867).

Among artists who lived in this quarter was Braque (1882–1963), with a studio in the Rue du Douanier (Rousseau), to the W. Lenin lived at No. 4 Rue Marie-Rose, some minutes walk further NW, in 1909–12.

Facing the S side of the park, flanked by the Blvd Jourdan, is the *Cité Universitaire*, founded in 1922, accommodating c 7000 students in some 37 halls of residence, the individual style of each reflecting the characteristic architecture of their own country. The US foundation dates from 1928; the British hostel from 1937; and the huge Maison Internationale (with a swimming-pool, theatre, etc.) from 1936. Few of these heterogeneous buildings are of any great interest, although those by Le Corbusier (the designer of the Swiss and Brazilian halls) are noteworthy.

Montparnasse. From the Carrefour de l'Observatoire the long Blvd du Montparnasse leads NW across the Blvd Raspail, where to the N stands *Rodin's* statue of Balzac. This junction may be regarded as the centre of a quarter which replaced Montmartre as the principal artistic and bohemian rendezvous, when they no longer found inspiration on the N heights of Paris. Gauguin had a studio at No. 8 Rue de la Grande-Chaumière, leading NE. Then, inexorably, the smaller intimate cafés were replaced by Le Dôme, La Coupole, La Rotonde, etc., and the district was invaded by hangers-on and pseudo-bohemians; the 'boîtes' in the Rue de la Gaité and elsewhere still attract this polyglot crowd.

Nevertheless, the neighbouring streets still retain (fast fading) associations with late-19C and early 20C artists and intellectuals. Trotsky and his fellow-revolutionaries frequented the Rotonde before 1917. Rilke and Modigliani lived in the Rue Campagne-Première, to the SE, as did Whistler, who, with Rodin, had studios at 132 Blvd du Montparnasse (demolished). In earlier decades, Sainte-Beuve, the critic (1804–69), lived at No. 19 Rue N.-D.-des Champs, to the NE, and died at No. 11 Rue du Montparnasse. Romain Rolland lived at No. 162 Blvd du Montparnasse in 1901–14.

Both Henry Miller and Hemingway have described the café life, disreputable and otherwise, of the district in its heyday, which was largely blighted by the mid-1930s. The area is now dominated by the obtrusive **Tour Montparnasse** (1973; 200m high), which has little to recommend it except for the impressive panoramic views (fee) from the 56th floor. An open-air terrace forms its 58th floor.

To the SW and parallel to the Blvd de Montparnasse, is the BLVD EDGAR-QUINET, with the main entrance of the **Cimetière Montparnasse** (Pl. 13;7), an 18-hectare site laid out in 1824. Maupassant, Louÿs, Banville, Baudelaire, J.-K. Huysmans, Leconte de Lisle, and Sainte-Beuve, among writers; César Franck, D'Indy, Saint-Saëns, Chabrier, Jean de Reszké, and Clara Haskil, among composers and musicians; Fantin-Latour, Gérard, Houdon, Rude, Soutine, Zadkine, Bourdelle, Bartholdi, and Brancusi, among artists and sculptors; Pierre-Joseph Proudhon, the social reformer; Arago; and Alfred Dreyfus, are buried here; as are Charles Garnier, the architect; Augustin Thierry, the historian; André Citroën, the car manufacturer; and Pierre Laval, prime minister in the wartime Vichy régime.

From near the SW corner of the cemetery the Rue Raymond-Losserand leads SW. Just S of its junction with the Rue du Château stood, until the turn of the century, the *Château du Maine*, a hunting-lodge of the Duc de Maine, on the road to Sceaux: see Rte 38.

Adjacent to the Tour, and forming part of the glass and concrete complex, is the **Gare Montparnasse** (Pl. 13;7), 18 storeys high, surrounding, on three sides, the station platforms.

At No. 34 in the Blvd de Vaugirard, flanking the station to the NW, is the impressive *Musée de la Poste, a well-displayed collection vividly explaining the history of the postal system from its earliest days, laid out in some 15 rooms, descending in stages from the 5th floor (lift). Sections are devoted to methods of communication and transport; to postmen themselves, illustrated by old costumes and prints, etc; to letter-boxes; to stamps and their printing; and to telecommunication and the mechanisation of the service. The catalogue is well-produced and informative.

Further to the W is the Blvd Pasteur, off which runs the Rue du Docteur-Roux, with (left) the *Institut Pasteur*, founded by Louis Pasteur in 1887–89 and built by private subscription. Pasteur (1822–95) is buried in the crypt; the tomb of Dr Émile Roux (1853–1933), inventor of the treatment of diphtheria by serum-injection, lies in the garden.

At No. 16 Rue Antoine-Bourdelle, N of and parallel to the Blvd de Vaugirard, is a *Museum* devoted to the sculptor *Bourdelle* (1861–1929).

The Métro at Montparnasse-Bienvenue is well-connected with lines returning to the centre.

8   The Faubourg St.-Germain: Eastern Sector
The Institut de France; Hôtel des Monnaies; Palais du Luxembourg; St.-Sulpice; St.-Germain-des-Prés

MÉTROS: Pont-Neuf, Odéon, Luxembourg, St.-Sulpice, St.-Germain-des-Prés, Mabillon.

The district still known as the **Faubourg St.-Germain** stretches S from the Seine opposite the Louvre, from the Institut on the E to the Pont de la Concorde to the W. Until the end of the 16C, much of this area, the property of the *Abbaye St.-Germain-des-Prés*, was open country. In the following century, with the religious revival, several convents were built here, and in 1670, the Hôtel des Invalides was constructed on the outskirts to the W. By 1685 the new Pont Royal provided easy access to the Palais des Tuileries, which became the home of the court during the Regency, and this, together with the creation of the École Militaire, was the main reason for the building of this new aristocratic quarter, which gradually took the place of the Marais. About half the houses were built between 1690 and 1725, a quarter between 1725 and 1750, and most of the rest between 1750 and 1790. In style they are very similar; often the most handsome façade faces the garden, and the gateway or 'Porte-cochère' from the street leads to the 'Cour d'Honneur'.

Today, the main thoroughfares are the Blvd St.-Germain and the Blvd Raspail, which have done much to alter the character of the quarter. The most characteristic streets of the once 'noble faubourg' are now the Rue de Lille, Rue de l'Université, Rue St.-Dominique, and Rue de Grenelle. About a hundred old mansions remain, many of them converted to house embassies or government offices, and the 6th and E half of the 7th arrondissements are still two of the more pleasant districts of Paris in which to linger.

It is convenient to divide the large area into two sections: Rte 8 describing the Luxembourg and St.-Germain-des-Prés (from the Blvd St.-Michel to the Rue des Saints-Pères and Blvd Raspail): Rte 10 describing the rest of the 7th arrondissement.

Facing the Louvre is the PL. DE L'INSTITUT, flanked by the curved wings of the ***INSTITUT DE FRANCE** (Pl. 14;1), surmounted by a dome, which, since its restoration, is one of the more attractive features of this reach of the quays.

The building may be visited on Saturday afternoons by prior arrangement with the Secrétariat, 23 Quai de Conti.

The E wing of the Institut and the adjacent Hôtel des Monnaies (see below) cover the site of the *Hôtel de Nesle* (13C), in which was incorporated the 12C *Tour de Nesle* or *Tour Hamelin*, the river bastion of Philippe Auguste's Wall (which ran SE parallel to the Rue Mazarine). The tower was notorious in legend as the scene of the amours of Marguerite (c 1290–1315) and Jeanne of Burgundy (1292–1325/30), wives of Louis X and Philippe V respectively, who are said to have had their lovers thrown into the river. Later occupants were Isabeau de Bavière, Charles le Téméraire (the Bold), and Henry V of England. The W part, known as the *Petit-Nesle*, and the workshop of Benvenuto Cellini in 1540–45, was demolished in 1663. The E part, or *Grand-Nesle*, rebuilt in 1648 by François Mansart, became the *Hôtel de Conti*, and in 1770, the Mint.

The present building, with its conspicuous cupola, was erected in accordance with the will of Card. Mazarin, who bequeathed 2 million *livres* in silver and 45,000 *livres* a year for the establishment of a college for 60 gentlemen of the four provinces acquired by the Treaties of Münster and the Pyrenees: Flanders, Alsace, Roussillon, and Piedmont (Pinerolo). Designed by Louis Le Vau, it was built in 1662–74, but Christopher Wren suggested that it was set 'ill-favouredly, that he [the architect] might shew his Wit in struggling with an inconvenient Situation'. The official name of the new college was the Collège Mazarin, but its popular name was the Collège des Quatre-Nations. The Institut, founded in 1795, and installed first in the Louvre, acquired the former Collège Mazarin in 1806.

The *Institut de France* comprises five academies: the exclusive *Académie Française*, founded by Richelieu in 1635 and restricted to 40 members (and already satirised by Saint-Évremond in 1643), whose particular task was the editing of the dictionary of the French language; the *Académie des Beaux-Arts* (1816), founded by Mazarin in 1648 as the *Académie Royale de Peinture et de Sculpture*; the *Académie des Inscriptions et Belles-Lettres*, founded by Colbert in 1663; the *Académie des Sciences*, founded by Colbert in 1666; and the *Académie des Sciences Morales et Politiques*, founded in 1795 and reconstituted in 1832. The Institut is also responsible for several collections, among them the Musée Marmottan, and the Musée Condé at Chantilly. An annual general meeting of all five academies is held on 25 October (admission by ticket only).

The Académie Française holds special receptions for newly elected members, tickets of admission to which are much sought after (apply to the general secretary). It was not until 1980 that the first non-male member was elected.

Members are known, ironically, as 'Les Immortels' (cf. Daudet's novel of that title), but among the considerable list of great figures of French literature who were *not* members were Pascal, Descartes, Molière, La Rochefoucauld, Diderot, Rousseau, Beaumarchais, Balzac, Flaubert, Baudelaire, Maupassant, Zola, and Proust.

Passing into the first octagonal courtyard (beyond which are two others, the third being the Kitchen Court of the old Collège Mazarin), the door on the left leads to the Bibliothèque Mazarine, containing c 350,000 vols, 5800 MSS., and 1900 incunabula. Originally the Cardinal's personal library, which, opened to scholars in 1643, became the first public library in France, it was considerably augmented by other collections during the Revolutionary period.

The *Institute Library* is also in this wing, together with a number of rooms decorated with academic statues and busts of distinguished academicians. Among many of little merit, Pigalle's Voltaire is striking.

In the W wing is the *Salle des Séances Solennelles*, in the former chapel. Recent restoration has undone the damage caused by Vaudoyer, and Mazarin's Tomb, by *Coysevox*, has been returned from the Louvre. His niece, Hortense Mancini, Duchesse de Mazarin (died 1699, in London), the famous beauty of the court of Charles II, was also buried here. The room contains some 400 seats (green for members of the Académie Française; red for the others), and is used for receptions and general meetings.

At No. 13 QUAI DE CONTI (the riverside embankment here, as elsewhere in this central reach of the Seine, lined with the bookstalls of the *bouquinistes*) is the *Hôtel Guénégaud* or *de Sillery-Genlis*, by François Mansart (1659), often visited by Napoléon when on leave from the École Militaire. Baron Larrey lived here from 1805 to 1832.

No. 11, the *HÔTEL DES MONNAIES, the *Mint*, is a dignified building by J.-D. Antoine (1771–75). The handsome doorway is ornamented with Louis XVI's monogram and elegant bronze knockers; above is the fleur-de-lys escutcheon with Mercury and Ceres as supporters. From the vestibule, a notable example of 18C architecture, a double staircase on the right ascends to *Musée de la Monnaie* (Monday to Friday, 11.00–17.00), containing an impressive collection of stamping presses, punches, medals, and coins. Medals are for sale in the far wing.

The *Salle Guillaume Dupré*, in the centre of the building, is (apart from the modern ceiling) representative of the best period of the Louis XVI style; showcases display medals from the Renaissance to the present. The *Salle Sage* contains new acquisitions; the *Salle Jean Warin*, portraits of the Walloon medallist Warin (1604–72) and directors of the Mint. The *Salle Denon* is devoted to medals of the Consulate and Empire period and the *Salle Duvivier* displays examples of coins illustrating the evolution of French currency from Merovingian times.

On the right of the second courtyard is the entrance to the *Ateliers* or workshops, where, one may see processes in the production of coins and medals (adm. only Monday and Wednesday from 14.15–15.00; closed during summer vacation). In 1973 the minting of French coins was transferred to a new establishment at *Pessac*, near Bordeaux.

At No. 5, on the corner of the Rue Guénégaud, Col de Marguerittes, of the Resistance, set up his headquarters while conducting operations for the liberation of Paris 19–28 August 1944.

At the end of the adjacent Rue de Nevers (entered below an arch), part of Philippe Auguste's *Wall* is visible.

From the S end of the *Pont Neuf*, the Rue Dauphine leads S, passing (left), at No. 9 Rue Mazet, the site of *chez Magny*, a famous restaurant and literary rendezvous in the 1860s, to the CARREFOUR DE BUCI with its street market. No. 5 Rue Mazet was until 1906 the site of the 'Cheval Blanc' coaching inn, terminus in the 17–18Cs of the diligence to Bourges, Bordeaux, and La Rochelle, etc. The parallel Rue des Grands-Augustins (with the restaurant *Lapérouse* on the corner), contains the *Hôtel d'Hercule*, dating from the 17C (Nos 3–7); No. 21 was the birthplace of the lexicographer Émile Littré (1801–81), and Heine lived at No. 25 in 1841; as had La Bruyère in 1676–91, and Augustin Thierry, the historian, in 1820–30.

At No. 35 QUAI DES GRANDS-AUGUSTINS (where stood the famous convent of that name from 1293 until its demolition in 1797) is another 17C mansion, at the corner of the Rue Séguier, home of the printer François Didot in 1740, and of Laplace during the Directory. This street, lined with old houses, leads S to meet the Rue St.-André-des-Arts, also containing several notable 17–18C buildings (Nos 27, 28, and 52).

From the PL. ST.-ANDRÉ-DES-ARTS, to the E, where at No. 11 Gounod was born in 1818, the Rue Hautefeuille leads S, in which No. 5, the *Hôtel des Abbés de Fécamp*, has a pretty turret. Among its occupiers was Godin de Sainte-Croix, an accomplice of the Marquise de Brinvilliers. Baudelaire (1821–67) was born at No. 15 (demolished).—J.-K. Huysmans (1848–1907) was born at No. 9 Rue Suger, leading W from the Pl. St.-André-des-Arts.

Leading S from the Rue St.-André-des-Arts, the Rue de l'Éperon shortly meets (right) the Rue du Jardinet, in which Saint-Saëns (1835–1921) was born. Further along the alley is the entrance to the *Cour de Rohan* (16–17C), originally part of the palace of the Abp. of Rouen. Turning left on passing through an archway, No. 4 in the ancient *Cour de Commerce-St.-André* is the basement of one of Philippe Auguste's towers. At No. 8, Marat's journal 'L'Ami du Peuple' was printed.

At No. 9, opposite, popular myth has it that Dr Joseph-Ignace Guillotin (1738–1814), a professor of anatomy, perfected his 'philanthropic beheading machine', although in fact he merely proposed to the *Assemblée constituante* that beheading should be the only method of capital punishment, preferably by a machine. A mechanic built one to the specifications of the secretary of the College of Surgeons, a certain Dr Louis, which was put into operation on 25 April 1792, at first being known as the *'Louisette'*.

The Rue de l'Ancienne Comédie (the next street to the W) takes its name from the Comédie Française of 1689–1770, which occupied No. 14, while opposite, the *Café Procope* (after its founder, a Sicilian named Francesco Procopio dei Coltelli), of 17C origin, was a favourite haunt of Voltaire and the Encyclopae-dists, Musset, George Sand, Balzac, Gautier, Gambetta, Verlaine, Huysmans, Wilde, et al.

To the N the Rue Mazarine (in which Smollett stayed—at the Hôtel de Montmorency—in 1763) leads back to the *Institut*, passing the sites (at No. 42) of the *jeu de paume 'de la Bouteille'*, where the Abbé Perrin established the Opéra in 1669–72; occupied by Molière's company in 1673–80, after his death in 1673; and by the Comédie-Française in 1680–89, and (at No. 12), another *jeu de paume*, where the 'Illustre Théâtre' was opened in December 1643 by Molière's company. No. 30, known as the *Hôtel des Pompes*, was until 1760 the headquarters of the *pompiers* or fire brigade of Paris, founded in 1722 by François Dumouriez du Périer, *père*, who died here the following year. He was an actor, and also the father of 32 children (by two marriages, admittedly).

In the mid-19C the BLVD ST.-GERMAIN was cut through this pictures-que area of narrow lanes leading S from the river. Opposite the Rue de l'Ancienne Comédie is the CARREFOUR DE L'ODÉON (Pl. 14;3), beyond the PL. HENRI-MONDOR, both busy crossroads, where the *Benjamin Franklin Library* has replaced the *Café Voltaire* (No. 1), where a banquet was held in honour of Gauguin before he left for Tahiti in 1891. At No. 2 Camille Desmoulins was arrested in 1794; the statue of Danton (1759–94) marks the site of his house, where he too was apprehended.

To the E is a building of the **Faculty of Medicine** (University V) erected by Gondouin in 1769–76 on the site of the *Collège de Bourgogne* and *Collège des Prémontrés*, and since enlarged. The older part, facing the Rue de l'École-de-Médecine, is considered one of the most Classical works of the 18C. The façade facing the Blvd St.-Germain was added in 1878.

In the courtyard is a statue of the anatomist Bichat (1771–1802) by David d'Angers. The *Library* contains c 600,000 vols, and commentaries of the heads of the faculty from 1395 onwards. Also of interest are the *Lecture Hall*, the *Musée d'Histoire de la Médecine*, and the *Salle du Conseil*, hung with four Gobelins tapestries of the Louis XIV period, after Le Brun.

Opposite is the entrance to the former *Refectory* of the *Couvent des Cordeliers*, a 15C Franciscan house, which during the Revolution was a meeting-place of the extremist Club des Cordeliers, the leaders of which were Marat (a doctor by profession, and partly educated at Edinburgh), Camille Desmoulins, and Danton. Marat was stabbed in his bath by Charlotte Corday in 1793 at No. 20 (demolished).

At No. 5, the *Institut des Langues Modernes* occupies the old *Amphithéâtre du Jardin du Luxembourg St.-Côme* (1691–94), with a beautiful portal. This was originally the lecture-hall of the College of

Surgery. A plaque commemorates the birth of the actress Sarah Bernhardt (1844–1923).

Further E (left) at the corner of the S section of the Rue de Hautefeuille (No. 32), Gustave Courbet (1819–77) had his studio in the former chapel of the *Collège des Prémontrés*.

The Rue de l'École-de-Médecine narrows before meeting the BLVD ST.-MICHEL.

From its W end, we may ascend steps before turning left along the Rue Monsieur-le-Prince (de Condé). At No. 10, Auguste Comte (1798–1857), the positivist philosopher, lived from 1841; Saint-Saëns at No. 14 in 1877–89, and Longfellow had lodgings at No. 49 in 1826 (and in a subsequent winter, at No. 5 in the adjacent Rue Racine). At No. 54 (altered) Pascal lived in 1654–62 and wrote his 'Pensées'.—To the left, on meeting the Rue de Vaugirard, is the *Lycée St.-Louis*, built by Bailly on the site of the *Collège d'Harcourt*, the greatest of the University colleges (1280), its entrance facing the Pl. de la Sorbonne. Racine and Boileau studied here.

Adjacent to the S end of the Rue Monsieur-le-Prince is the PL. EDMOND-ROSTAND, with a good view of the *Panthéon* (see Rte 4).—George Sand's last Paris home, in the 1870s, was at No. 5 Rue Gay-Lussac, to the SE.—To the S, on the right of the BLVD ST.-MICHEL, the *École Supérieure des Mines* occupies the *Hôtel de Vendôme*, an 18C building enlarged after 1840, and having its principal façade facing the Luxembourg Gardens. It contains a *Museum of Mineralogy and Geology*. At No. 95 in the Boulevard died César Franck (1890). Leconte de Lisle, leader of the 'Parnassiens', a poetic coterie, lived at No. 64 in 1872–94.

One of many entrances to the *__Jardin du Luxembourg__ (Pl. 14;5) is a few paces S of the Pl. Edmond-Rostand. These extensive gardens (23 hectares), embellished by numerous statues, several of which are notable, form one of the pleasanter and more colourful open spaces in central Paris, and long a favourite with nannies. Laid out in the 17C, they were deplorably mutilated in 1782 and 1867, and little remains of the original garden as known by Marie de Médicis.

Steps descend from the E Terrace to lawns surrounding an octagonal pond with a fountain. Beyond the formal W Terrace is the Jardin Anglais; while to the S, beyond the PL. ANDRÉ-HONNORAT, gardens are continued between the two branches of the Av. de l'Observatoire, which were laid out under the First Empire on the site of a Carthusian monastery demolished at the Revolution.

N of the central octagonal pond, on the right, at the end of an oblong pool, is the *Fontaine Médicis*, attributed to *Salomon de Brosse* (c 1627), moved here in 1861.

In the central niche is Polyphemus about to crush Acis and Galatea; on either side are Pan and Diana, and at the back a bas-relief, the Fontaine de Léda, brought from the Rue du Regard in 1855.

At No. 19 Rue de Médicis, flanking the gardens to the NE, was born André Gide (1869–1951).

The *__PALAIS DU LUXEMBOURG__, once a royal residence, is with its heavily rusticated masonry, more visually attractive externally than internally, although the S façade, facing the gardens, is a 19C copy, by Gisors. The N façade, where the main entrance is surmounted by an eight-sided dome, is original. The two wings, terminating in steep-roofed pavilions, with three orders of columns superimposed, are connected by a single-storeyed gallery.

The Luxembourg was built by Salomon de Brosse in 1615–27 for Marie de

Médicis, widow of Henri IV, who, it is said, wished to have a palace which reminded her of the Pitti Palace in Florence, her birthplace. She also acquired the adjacent mansion of the Duc de Tingry-Luxembourg (the *Petit-Luxembourg*; 1570–1612), hence its name. The building was altered in 1808 and enlarged in 1831–44.

After Louis XIII's death, the palace passed to her second son Gaston, Duc d'Orléans, and the 'Palais Médicis' became known as the 'Palais d'Orléans'. Subsequently, it belonged in succession to Mlle de Montpensier, the Duchesse de Guise (1672), Louis XIV (1694), and the Orléans family. Here from 1724 until she retired to a convent, lived the obstreperous Louise-Élisabeth, the 15-year-old widow of Luis I of Spain. Among prisoners confined here during the Revolution were Marshal de Noailles (executed at the age of 79 with his wife, daughter, and granddaughter); Hébert, Danton, Desmoulins, Fabre d'Églantine, the painter David, and Tom Paine (imprisoned here in 1793 for voting in the Assembly against the king's execution, and who escaped the guillotine only by an accident).

In 1794 the Directory transferred the seat of government from the Tuileries to the Luxembourg, and here Gén. Bonaparte presented them with the Treaty of Campo Formio (1797). In 1800 the 'Palais Directorial' became the 'Palais du Consulat'; under the Empire it was the 'Palais du Sénat', and later, the 'Palais de la Pairie'. Marshal Ney was confined and tried here in 1815. The ministers of Charles X were tried here under Louis-Philippe in 1830, and Louis-Napoléon Bonaparte after landing at Boulogne in 1840. From 1852 to 1940 the Palais was the meeting-place of the Senate, the upper chamber of the French Republic, except in 1871–79, when it was the seat of the Préfecture de la Seine.

In 1940–44 it was occupied by Sperrle, commander-in-chief of the Luftwaffe on the Western Front. In 1946 it was the seat of the Conseil de la République, but in 1958 it reverted to the Senate. Here also was held the ineffectual Peace Conference of 1946.

Admission at 10.00–11.00; 14.30–15.30 on Sunday, when small groups are conducted round parts of the building.

The INTERIOR, drastically remodelled by Chalgrin under Napoléon I, is decorated in the sumptuous but decadent 19C manner, replete with statues and paintings, historical and allegorical, few of which are of any merit. The series of paintings devoted to the Life of Marie de Médicis, by *Rubens*, which once hung in the palace, is now in the Louvre.

By far the most interesting room is the luxuriously gilt *Cabinet Doré*, Marie de Médicis's audience chamber. Other rooms (on the first Floor) opened to the public are the *Salles des Conférences*, the hemicycle of the *Salle de Séances* and the *Library*, overlooking the gardens, which contains some paintings by *Delacroix*, that in the cupola being the Limbo of Dante's Inferno.

The adjoining **Petit-Luxembourg** (now the residence of the President of the Senate) was presented to Richelieu by Marie de Médicis in 1626. It includes the cloisters and chapel of the Filles du Calvaire, for whom the queen built a convent; the chapel is a charming example of the Renaissance style; the cloister forms a winter-garden. To the W is the *Orangery*, once occupied by a museum, some of the former contents of which now embellish the *Musée d'Orsay*.

A few paces to the NE of the Palais stands the ***Théâtre de l'Odéon**, built in the form of a classical temple by Wailly and Peyre in the garden of the *Hôtel de Condé*, which was demolished by Louis XV to this end.

This town house of the family from 1612–1764 stood on the site of Nos 5–9 in the Rue du Condé, parallel to the W. Here was born the Marquis de Sade (1740–1814), his mother being a lady-in-waiting to the Princess.

Inaugurated in 1782, the Théâtre-Français was rebuilt by Chalgrin after a fire in 1799, and re-opened in 1808. Its auditorium is one of the finest in Paris.

From its N entrance, the Rue de l'Odéon, bordered by 18C houses, slopes downhill towards the Carrefour de l'Odéon. At No. 12 once stood the *Librairie Shakespeare*, founded by Sylvia Beach, where in 1922 the first edition of James Joyce's 'Ulysses' was published, in an edition of 1000 numbered copies. At No.

22 in this street lived Lucile Duplessis before her marriage to Desmoulins; No. 26 was the home of Beaumarchais in 1763–76, whose 'Le Barbier de Séville' was produced in 1775.

From the main entrance of the *Palais de Luxembourg*, in the Rue de Vaugirard (the longest street in Paris, stretching from the Blvd St.-Michel to the Porte de Versailles), the wide and stately **Rue de Tournon* leads gently down to the Blvd St.-Germain, N of which it is extended by the Rue de Seine, also containing a number of attractive houses, to the *Institut*.

Balzac lived at No. 2 in the Rue de Tournon in 1827–30; Marie Lenormand, the fortune-teller consulted by Revolutionary celebrities, lived at No. 5 for over fifty years and died there in 1843; Hébert ('Père Duchesne'; 1755–94), the revolutionary journalist, lived here in 1793, and Charles Cros, one of the pioneers of the phonograph, died here in 1888. No. 6, the *Hôtel de Brancas*, was reconstructed during the Regency by Bullet; Alphonse Daudet lived at No. 7, the *Hôtel du Sénat*, when he first came to Paris (1857); Gambetta lived here (on the top storey) in 1858–61. No. 10 (now barracks of the Garde Républicaine) was the *Hôtel de Concini*. Paul Jones, the first admiral of the US navy, died at No. 19 in 1792; the actor Gérard Philipe (1922–59) died at No. 17.

Parallel, to the W, is the Rue Garancière, with the *Hôtel de Sourdéac* (No. 8; 1640).

At No. 20 Rue de Vaugirard stood the *Café Tabourey*, a famous literary rendez-vous; while at No. 48 the composer Massenet (1842–1912) long resided, and died.—Mme de la Fayette (1634–93), author of 'La Princesse de Clèves', died at No. 50, the *Hôtel de la Vergne*; it had been her home since 1655.

The next street, turning right off the Rue de Vaugirard, the Rue Bonaparte (which narrows as it approaches the Seine), contains numerous antique shops and galleries, and is one of the most pleasant and characteristic in the commercial part of the Faubourg. It skirts the PL. ST.-SULPICE (Pl. 13;6), dominated to the E by the church. In the centre is the *Fontaine des Quatre-Évêques*, by Visconti, with statues of four famous preaching bishops: Bossuet, Fénelon, Massillon, and Fléchier.

In 1843–45 Renan was a scholar at the seminary which stood on the S side; opposite, No. 6 is a dignified mansion by Servandoni (1754), the first of a range which never materialised. Many of the neighbouring shops display cloying modern ecclesiastical art and furniture.

ST.-SULPICE, the wealthiest church on the Left Bank, although described by Gibbon as 'one of the noblest structures in Paris', is a somewhat ponderous classical building, imposing mainly for its size. The W front consists of an Ionic colonnade over a Doric. The N tower is 73m high; the S tower is 5m lower.

It was begun in 1646 by Gamard on the site of an older church, and continued on a larger scale by Le Vau in 1655 and Gittard in 1670. After an interval from 1675 to 1719 work was resumed by Oppenordt. The building of the W front was entrusted to Servandoni, who, however, failed to give satisfaction, and was replaced in 1745 by Maclaurin. His successor, Chalgrin, rebuilt the N tower in 1777, since Maclaurin's design had also failed to please, but the S tower was left incomplete.

Camille Desmoulins was married here to Lucile Duplessis in 1790. Under the Convention St.-Sulpice became the 'Temple de la Victoire', and in 1799 a public banquet was given here by Gén. Bonaparte. Saint-Simon, writing earlier, was contemptuous of its clergy, with their 'barbes sales'.

It is noted for its music and organ recitals. Enquire at the church for details.

The stately INTERIOR, a representative example of the 'Jesuit' style, is 110m long, 56m wide, and 33m high.

In the nave are two huge *tridacna gigas* shells serving as holy-water stoups, presented to François I by the Venetian Republic; the marble 'rocks' supporting them were sculpted by *Pigalle*. The late 18C pulpit, by *Wailly*, bears gilded figures of Faith and Hope by *Guesdon*, and Charity by *Dumont*.

The famous *Organ*, one of the largest in existence (6588 pipes), was built in 1781 and remodelled in 1860–62; the case was designed by *Chalgrin*, and is adorned by statues by *Clodion*, and decoration by *Duret*.

In the paving of the S transept is a bronze table connected by a meridian line with a marble obelisk in the N transept; at noon the sun's rays, passing through an aperture in a blind window in the S transept, strike the meridian at different points according to the time of year.

The encircling CHAPELS are decorated with frescoes: in the first (right) are late works by *Delacroix* (1853–63). In the 5th chapel is the tomb, by *Slodtz*, of the curé Languet de Gergy (1674–1750), founder of the *Enfants Malades*, and responsible for the completion of the church. In the *Choir* are works by *Bouchardon*. The *Lady Chapel* was designed by *Servandoni*. In a niche behind the altar is a marble Virgin by *Pigalle*, with angels by *Mouchy*. The wall-paintings are by *Carle Van Loo*; those in the dome, by *Lemoyne*. Remains of the 16C church may be seen in the crypt.

The next cross street to the N is the Rue du Four.——Chardin lived from 1720–44 at No. 1 Rue Princesse, leading S from the Rue du Four, and at No. 13 from 1744–57.

Beyond is the busy intersection of the PL. ST.-GERMAIN-DES-PRÉS (Pl. 13;4). Diagonally opposite, at Nos 170 and 172 respectively, are the *Café des Deux Magots* (grotesque Chinese figures), and the *Café de Flore*; while at No. 151 in the boulevard is the *Brasserie Lipp*. All were once known for the artists and writers who frequented them.

*ST.-GERMAIN-DES-PRÉS, the oldest church in Paris, and also the only one retaining any considerable remains of Romanesque work, dominates the NE of the square. It has been cleaned and restored recently.

The church, a relic of the great Benedictine abbey founded in 558 by Childebert I, who was buried there, as was St. Germanus, Bp of Paris (died 576), was rebuilt at the beginning of the 11C (body of the W tower), in the late 11C (nave), and in the mid-12C (choir), and was consecrated by Pope Alexander III in 1163. It was the chief house of the reformed Congregation de St.-Maur in the 17C, and numbered the scholars Jean Mabillon (1632–1707) and Bernard de Montfaucon (1655–1741) among its distinguished members.

The massive flying buttresses of the choir are among the earliest in France. The W porch dates from 1607, but preserves the jambs of a 12C door and a battered lintel depicting the Last Supper. The transepts were remodelled c 1644. The bell-chamber of the tower was added in the 17C. Flanking the choir are the bases of two towers pulled down in 1822, when the church was drastically restored, after its partial destruction following an explosion and fire in 1794, just prior to which its refectory had been used as a saltpetre store.

The INTERIOR (65m by 21m, and 19m high) would be more imposing if stripped of its 19C decoration; but it is nevertheless interesting architecturally for the combination of Romanesque in the nave with the earliest Gothic in the choir. The vault of the nave and the aisles date from 1644–46. The pillars are flanked by four columns, the sculptured capitals of which in 1848–53 were either re-cut or removed to the Musée de Cluny and replaced by copies, with the exception of one remaining in the NW corner. Both nave and choir are daubed with murals by *Hippolyte Flandrin* (1842–64), among others.

To the right in the S aisle is a marble statue of N.-D. de Consolation, presented to the Abbey of St. Denis by Queen Jeanne d'Évreux in 1340. In the S transept is the tomb, by *Girardon*, of Olivier and Louis de Castellan, killed in the king's service in 1644 and 1669. In the *first ambulatory-chapel* is the tomb of Lord James Douglas (1617–45; son of the first Marquess of Douglas), commander of Louis XIII's Scots regiment, killed near Arras. *2nd chapel*: tombstones of Descartes (1596–1650), removed from Ste.-Geneviève (1819), and of Mabillon (see above). *4th chapel*: fragments of stained glass of 1245–55.

Choir. The small marble columns in the triforium are re-used material from the 6C abbey of St. Vincent; their bases and capitals are of the 12C. The *Lady Chapel* was rebuilt at the beginning of the 19C.

In the *N Aisle* is the tombstone of Nicolas Boileau (1636–1711) removed from the Ste.-Chapelle, and the tomb of William Douglas, 10th Earl of Angus (1554–1611), who died in the service of Henri IV. In the N transept are a statue of St. Francisco Xavier, by *G. Coustou*; and the theatrical tomb, by *G.* and *B. Marsy*, of John Casimir V, King of Poland, who became abbot of St.-Germain in 1669 and died in 1672.

In the garden to the N of the church are fragments of sculptures from the great lady-chapel built in 1212–55 by Pierre de Montreuil within the precincts of the abbey.—In the Rue de l'Abbaye, but further E, are the buildings of the old *Abbot's Palace*, erected c 1586 by Card. de Bourbon, behind which was the *Prison de l'Abbaye* (its site crossed by the present boulevard), where Brissot wrote his memoirs, and Charlotte Corday spent her last days. It was the scene of a beastly massacre of 'suspects' in September 1792.

In 1857, six years before he died at 6 Rue de Furstemberg (or Fürstemberg) Delacroix built a studio in the adjoining PL. DE FÜRSTEMBERG, which with its four Paulownias, is now less a back-water than it once was. This was later shared by Monet and Bazille, and now contains a *Delacroix Museum* (open 9.45–17.15 except Tuesday).

No. 1 Rue Bourbon-le-Château, a few paces E, was Whistler's first home in Paris (1855–56), while the *Pré-aux-Clercs*, which lay to the N (now crossed by the Rue Jacob), was a favourite promenade, and the scene of medieval student brawls.

For streets radiating SW and W of the Pl. St.-Germain-des-Prés, see below.

The Rue Bonaparte continues N, crossing the Rue Jacob. At No. 18 in the former street the Czech government was formed in 1916; No. 14 is the main entrance to the *École des Beaux-Arts* (see below), while the *Hôtel du Marquis de Persan* (Nos 7–9) was the home of Monge in 1803, and the birthplace of Manet (1832–83). The Rev. William Cole, a friend of Walpole, and author of a live 'y description of Paris in 1765, resided in this street, then the Rue des Petits Augustins.

Both the Rue Jacob, and two streets diverging right off the Rue Bonaparte, have interesting associations. Laurence Sterne put up in the **Rue Jacob** on his arrival in Paris in 1762 (at the 'Hôtel de Modène'; as did Philip Thicknesse in 1791), and was later a guest of Mme de Rambouillet at No. 46. Wagner lodged at No. 14 in 1841–42, working on 'The Flying Dutchman'; the social reformer Pierre-Joseph Proudhon later resided at the same address. In 1848 Mérimée lived at No. 18

(rebuilt); No. 32 belonged to du Cerceau, architect of the Pont Neuf; Stendhal stayed at both Nos 28 and 52 in 1808–10. At No. 56 was signed a provisional treaty recognising the independence of the United States (3 September 1783); since 1810 it has been the offices of the printer Didot. In 1765 Horace Walpole lived in the Rue de Colombier, near the E part of the street.

To the N in the parallel Rue Visconti (then the Rue des Marais) Racine (1639–99) lived from 1693 until his death (house demolished); at No. 16 Adrienne Lecouvreur (1692–1730) died in the arms of Marshal Saxe; at No. 17 Balzac had a printing business, liquidated in 1828, and on the 2nd floor is a studio once occupied by Delaroche (1827–34) and Delacroix (1838–43).

In the next street to the right, the Rue des Beaux-Arts, Mérimée and later Corot lived at No. 10; Fantin-Latour lived at No. 8 in 1868. At No. 13 Oscar Wilde, who had styled himself 'Sebastian Melmoth' when on the Continent, died in debt in 1900; his drama 'Salomé' had been produced in Paris in 1896, while he was in Reading Gaol.

The **École des Beaux-Arts** (Pl. 13;4), begun in 1820 by Debret and finished in 1862 by Duban, replaced the convent of the Petits-Augustins, founded in 1608, of which certain relics remain. It was here that Alexandre Lenoir collected together numerous pieces of sculpture, saving them from destruction during the Revolutionary period (cf. St.-Denis). The recently cleaned building, with its main entrance at No. 14 Rue Bonaparte, was further enlarged in 1885 on the acquisition of the *Hôtel de Chimay* (see below). The *Library*, containing c 80,000 volumes and one million engravings and drawings, may be visited by scholars and artists on application to the director.

The main points of interest are the former convent *Chapel* (c 1600), against the S wall of which has been built the central part of the façade of the Château d'Anet, by Philibert Delorme; in the adjoining *Chapel of Marguerite de Valois*, the small domed hexagon has claims to be the first dome built in Paris. Part of a Renaissance façade from the Château de Gaillon (1500–10) in Normandy separates the first courtyard from the second. An arcade from the *Hôtel de Torpane* (c 1570) and the façade from the *Hôtel de Chimay* are also preserved. Both in the courtyards and inside the buildings are many sculptured fragments, antique marbles, etc., while the *Salle de Melpomène* is used for the display of students' work when competing for the Grands Prix de Rome.

Leading SW from the Pl. St.-Germain-des-Prés is the Rue de Rennes, at the far end of which obtrudes the *Tour Montparnasse* (see Rte 7).—A short distance down the street is the Rue Cassette, diverging left, in which Alfred Jarry (1873–1907) died at No. 20. No. 27 was the home of Alfred de Musset's family in 1818–32; Rainer Maria Rilke lived at No. 29 in 1906.

Turning right at the end of this street into the Rue de Vaugirard, we pass domed *St.-Joseph-des-Carmes*, once the chapel of a Carmelite convent, dating from 1613–20, and preserving several 17C canvases. The crypt contains the bones of some 120 priests massacred in the convent garden in September 1792. Prisoners held here and later released included Gén. Hoche, Joséphine de Beauharnais, and Mme Tallien.

Adjacent are the buildings of the *Institut Catholique*, where, in 1890, radio waves were discovered by Édouard Branly (1844–1940).

Some distance S in the next crossroad, the Rue d'Assas, is No. 62, where Strindberg lived in 1895–96, while Auguste Bartholdi (1834–1904), sculptor of the Statue of Liberty (New York), died at No. 82. At 100 bis is the former *Studio* (from 1928–67) of Ossip Zadkine, with a small museum devoted to his work.

Turning right into the Rue d'Assas, and recrossing the Rue de Rennes, we reach the Rue du Cherche-Midi (deriving its name from an 18C sign on No. 19 representing an astronomer tracing a sundial), containing a number of attractive 17–18C houses. For its W section, beyond the *Blvd Raspail*, see p 108.

From the animated CARREFOUR DE LA CROIX-ROUGE (Pl. 13;5) the Rue de Sèvres leads SW. At No. 11 lived J.-K. Huysmans from 1872 to 1898.—Off the N side of the street, the Rue Récamier recalls the *Abbaye aux Bois*, the home of Mme Récamier, where the most frequent visitor to her salon was Chateaubriand, from 1819 to her death, when totally blind, in 1849. Here also, from 1831–38 lived Mary Clarke, who had resided in Paris since c 1816 (see p 107).

For the W section of the Rue de Sèvres and the Rue de Grenelle, which also commences at the *Carrefour de la Croix-Rouge*, see Rte 10. Across this junction is the Rue du Dragon, the possible site of the pottery workshop of Bernard Palissy (1510–89). Hugo lived at No. 30 in 1821, before his marriage to Adèle Foucher.

At No. 71 in the parallel Rue des Saints-Pères, to the W, died Rémy de Gourmont (1858–1915).

At the junction of the Rue des Saints-Pères and the Blvd St.-Germain stood the *Hôtel de Selvois*, where the Duc de Saint-Simon (1675–1755) was born and lived until 1714.—At No. 184 in the Boulevard is the *Hôtel de la Société de Géographie*, founded in 1821.

On the E side of the Rue des Saints-Pères, after crossing the Boulevard, is the *Chapelle St.-Pierre*, rebuilt in 1611, the sole relic of the Hôpital de la Charité, which stood on this site from 1605 to 1937. It is now the church of the Ukrainian Catholic community in Paris (St.-Vladimir-le-Grand). Adjacent are buildings of the *Faculty of Medicine* (1936–53), while opposite, in the 18C *Hôtel de Fleury*, by Antoine, is the *École des Ponts et Chaussées*, a civil engineering school founded in 1747.

Further N, at the corner of the Rue de Lille is the *École des Langues Orientales*, founded by the Convention in 1795. Manet died at No. 5 Rue des Saints-Pères, and the organist Widor (1844–1937) lived at No. 7, the *Hôtel de Falconet* (c 1650). From the *Hôtel Tessé*, on the corner of the Quai Voltaire, the Marquis de Becqueville attempted to glide with wings, Icarus-like, across the Seine in 1742.

In the QUAI MALAQUAIS, leading E to the *Institut*, are some charming 17–18C mansions. Anatole France (1844–1924) was born at No. 19 (the home of George Sand in 1832–36), but until 1853 he lived at No. 15. At No. 17, part of the *Hôtel de Chimay*, built by François Mansart c 1640, and altered in the 18C for the Duchesse de Bouillon (died 1714), the friend of La Fontaine, lived Henrietta Maria (the widow of Charles I) in 1662.

No. 9, at the corner of the Rue Bonaparte, the *Hôtel de Transylvanie*, is a good example of Louis-XIII architecture (1622–28). No. 5 was occupied by Marshal Saxe from 1744 until his death in 1750; and No. 3 was the residence of the naturalist Alexander Humboldt during the Restoration.

9   Musée d'Orsay

MÉTROS: Musée d'Orsay, Solférino.

The Quai d'Orsay is dominated by the huge and ornate bulk of the *MUSÉE D'ORSAY, inaugurated in December 1986 (Pl. 13;1).

The building was originally the Gare d'Orsay, erected in 1898–1900 by Victor Laloux (1850–1937) on the site of the ancient Cours des

Comptes, set ablaze in 1871 during the Commune. Edouard Detaille, the artist, remarked ironically at the time that the railway station looked exactly like a Palais des Beaux-Arts, but 86 years were to elapse before the transformation took place. By 1939 the station had virtually outlived its usefulness because of its comparatively short platforms. During the Second World War it became a depot for parcels destined for prisoners of war, and was later used as a reception centre for those liberated. It then served in part to house a theatre, and became the temporary home of the Hôtel Drouot (the auction house). But the edifice progressively deteriorated, and its demolition was planned—after all, Baltard's pavilions at Les Halles had gone—and there was a project to replace it with a large hotel (the former station hotel had contained 370 rooms). But with the belated revival of interest in the conservation of 19C industrial architecture it was decided to use the structure as a museum rather than attempt to destroy the all-too-solid building.

220m long, and 75m wide, it now contains a vast museum. The coffered vault of its central hall alone—with its 1600 rosettes—which once spanned the platforms (where a snorting engine would still not appear out of place) is 138m in length, 40m wide, and 32m high. For those fascinated by such technical details, the structure contains 12,000 tonnes of metal (compared to the mere 7000 of the Eiffel Tower); 40,000 acoustic resonators; 350 surveillance cameras; 500 radar detectors; and 6500 sensors connected to a central control unit. Some 16,000 square metres are devoted to permanent exhibitions, the space being divided into some 80 separate sections or galleries.

The architects of the new museum were Messieurs Renaud Bardou, Pierre Colboc, and Jean-Paul Philippon of ACT; the architect/designer responsible for the interior was Gae Aulenti. Certain rooms retain their 1900s decoration.

The address of the museum is 62 Rue de Lille, 75007, but the main entrance is at No. 1 Rue Bellechasse, at its W end. **It is closed on Mondays**.

The permanent collections are mainly French works of art dating from 1848 until 1914, although there are certain overlaps, with particular emphasis on the works of artists, sculptors, photographers, and designers born between 1820 and 1870. It is also the venue of numerous temporary exhibitions, occasional concerts and films, and of lectures, etc. Brochures detailing forthcoming events are available. The building also has a restaurant (in the former hotel restaurant), a rooftop café, bookshop, library, and postcard shop (with access from the exterior); postal and exchange facilities are also available.

While a knowledge of the 'Style Pompier' may be useful to appreciate the art of the epoch in its historical perspective, it must be admitted that their very quantity and mediocrity is apt to swamp the more important masterpieces of the period. Numerous canvases from the 'romantic era' to that of the 'Art Nouveau', many extracted from the 'réserves' of museums, where they have long slumbered, now again see the light, and many visitors have wondered to whose advantage. The remarkable collection of **Impressionists**, many of them formerly in the Jeu de Paume (with some remaining in the Orangerie; see Rte 13), have been relegated to a series of rooms on an upper level, which, with certain other important sections, can easily be overlooked by the unwary, and they are not particularly well displayed. The layout is confusing, and the collection very extensive: time and patience are required to cover the ground.

The main permanent collection—approximately 2300 paintings, 250 pastels, 1500 sculptures, 1100 objets d'art, and 13,000 photographs (exhibited in rotation)—is shown on three floors. To view them in approximately chronological order it is suggested that the upper level is visited before descending to the middle level: all three are shown on the ground plan opposite. Separate sections are devoted to individual collections, for instance to the Chauchard, Gachet, Kaganovitch, Mollard, Moreau-Nélaton, and Personnaz collections. Among the more remarkable works are:

GROUND FLOOR, with its entrance below the great *Clock* of the central aisle, where are displayed some of the more important *Sculptures*; among them: *Jean-Baptiste Carpeaux* (1827–75), Ugolin group (1862), the Four quarters of the World bearing the celestial sphere (1867–72), and La Danse (1869; commissioned for the façade of the Opéra.

Vistors are advised, however, to follow the route indicated below, first entering the section to the right of the aisle, marked **(A)** on our plan, displaying *Ingres* (1780–1867), La Source (completed 1856); *Delacroix* (1798–1863), The Lion Hunt, among other characteristic works by the artist; and *Winterhalter* (1806–73), Portrait of Mme Rimsky-Korsakov. Also to be seen here, and in the passage adjacent **(B)** are *Auguste Clésinger* (1814–83), Woman bitten by a snake (marble; 1847; Mme Sabatier being the model), and *Henri Regnault* (1843–71), Gen. Prim on horseback.

The section immediately to the E **(C)** is devoted to the *Decorative Arts* of the period 1850–80. Facing the main aisle is a huge canvas by *Thomas Couture* (1815–79), Roman Decadence (1847). The following section **(D)** contains *Puvis de Chavannes* (1824–98), The poor Fisherman (1881), among other works by the artist, whose Summer is displayed near the museum entrance. New acquisitions by *Puvis de Chavannes* are The Pigeon, and The Balloon, painted during the period of the Siege of Paris (1870–71). Close by are representative paintings by *Gustave Moreau* (1826–98), and early works by *Degas* (1834–1917), including The Bellelli Family (1858/60), Portraits of Hilaire De Gas, the artist's grandfather (painted on a visit to Italy in 1857), and of Thérèse De Gas, The Opéra orchestra, Before the race, and the unfinished Semiramis watching the construction of Babylon.

Crossing the central aisle, enter the section opposite **(E)** to view *Monet* (1840–1926), two sections from Le Déjeuner sur l'herbe (1865/6), Women in a garden, and The Magpie (a snow scene); *Manet* (1832–83), The balcony (with Berthe Morisot in the foreground), Portrait of Zola (1868), Olympia, The fife-player, and Portraits of his parents; *Renoir* (1841–1919), Bazille painting; *Bazille* (1841–70), Portrait of Renoir, The improvised ambulance, The Meeting, and Family reunion.

In section **(F)** are displayed *Millet* (1814–75), The gleaners (1857), The Angelus (1858/9), and several portraits and landscapes; also works by *Théodore Rousseau* (1812–67), *Charles Daubigny* (1817–78), *Corot* (1796–1875), and *Diaz de la Peña* (1807–76); and works by members of the Barbizon School in general. Adjacent is a room devoted to paintings by *Daumier* (1808–79), but also including a remarkable series of 26 painted clay caricature busts of Parliamentarians, modelled from 1831.

In the adjoining passage **(G)** are a number of realistic paintings of the period, among them *Meissonier* (1815–91), Napoléon at the head of his troops. Off this passage opens a section **(H)** largely devoted to *Courbet* (1819–77), including Stags by a stream, Cliffs at Étretat, Burial at Ornans, and The artist's studio (in which Baudelaire is shown on the right, reading). The passage is continued, with several more works by *Monet*, including his Portrait of Mme Gaudibert.

MUSÉE D'ORSAY

Middle Level

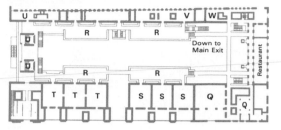

Upper Level

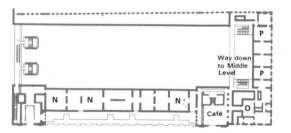

Ground Floor

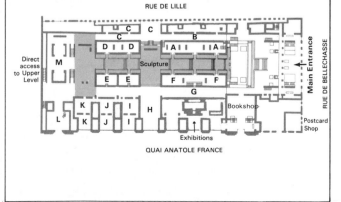

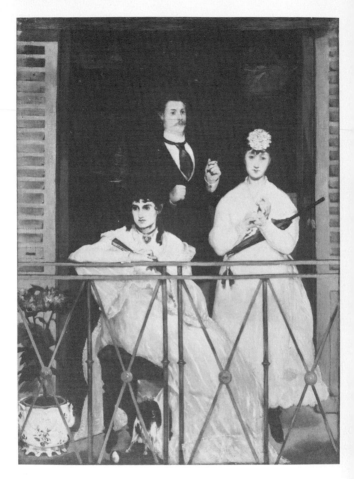

The balcony, by Édouard Manet, *c 1868*

Off this are six rooms **(I,J,K)** displaying *Fantin-Latour* (1836–1904), The studio in the Batignolles (1870), in which Manet is shown painting, while standing (from right to left of the canvas) are Monet, Bazille and—beyond another figure—Zola, and Renoir (with a picture-frame behind him). Close by is *Whistler* (1834–1903), Portrait of his mother, and several characteristic works by *Boudin* (1824–98), *Lépine* (1836–92), and *Jongkind* (1819–91). In section **(J)** are displayed *Manet*, Le déjeuner sur l'herbe (1863), and Blonde with bared breasts; also *Monet*, The poppies, Lilacs, and The railway-bridge at Argenteuil; and *Sisley* (1839–99), The footbridge at Argenteuil. In the adjacent room are the Eduardo Mollard collection of paintings by *Jongkind* (including The Seine at Notre-Dame), *Boudin* (including The beach at Trouville), several remarkable works by *Pissarro* (1830–1903, and *Sisley*, The bridge at Moret-sur-Loing.

Section **(K)** contains representative canvases by *Adolphe Monticelli* (1824–86), among other artists.

Making our exit from this section and turning left, the E end of the museum is reached, where, to the left, is a section **(L)** devoted to *Architectural and Decorative features* of the period 1850–1900, including furniture and other objects produced by members of the British *Arts and Crafts movement* and the *Century Guild*, etc.

Below the main vault of the building is another section **(M)** concerned with *Charles Garnier* (1825–98), and the construction of the Paris *Opéra*, commenced in 1862. This contains a maquette of the entire Opéra quarter at 1:100 as it was in 1914; a model of the Opéra shown as a cross-section; a maquette of the Stage of the Opéra built for the Universal Exhibition of 1900, etc.

A series of escalators ascends to the UPPER LEVEL and a series of rooms devoted to the **Impressionists (N)**, the majority of them moved here from their former home in the Jeu de Paume: and, as has been said, just because Monet painted several views of the Gare St.-Lazare is no reason to assume that he expected any of them to be hung in the upper floor of a former station. They are displayed in roughly chronological order. Among them are *Monet*, Fête in the Rue Montorgueil (1878); several Landscapes by *Pissarro*, including Red Roofs; *Caillebotte* (1848–94), Planing the floor; *Renoir*, Portraits of Monet, of Mme Charpentier, and of Richard Wagner, among others, his Dancing at the Moulin de la Galette, Nude in sunlight, The swing, and The path through long grass; and his sculpted Bust of Mme Renoir. Also in this first section are *Sisley*, Snow at Louveciennes, and Flooding at Port-Marly; and *Berthe Morisot* (1841–95), The cradle.

We pass on to *Degas*, The absinthe drinkers (1876), The Bourse, Women ironing, and several Horse-racing scenes, and of Ballet-dancers, together with examples of his sculptures, including the realistic 14-year-old Dancer wearing her tutu; also *Manet*, The beach at Berck-sur-Mer, and Portraits of Mallarmé, and of Clemenceau. The following section contains *Renoir*, Dance in the country, and Dance in the town, and Girls playing the piano; and *Monet*, Ice thawing on the Seine, The church at Vetheuil, Woman with an umbrella, Blue waterlilies, and the series of five views of The cathedral at Rouen painted in 1892–3. The next section contains part of the Personnaz collection, including *Pissarro*, Winter at Louveciennes; *Guillaumin* (1841–1927), The Place Valhubert; *Mary Cassat* (1844–1926), Woman sewing. This is followed by the Gachet collection, with a number of paintings by *Van Gogh* (1855–90), among them his Portrait of Dr Paul Gachet, Self-portraits, The church at Auvers, The restaurant de la Sirène, L'Arlésienne, His bedroom at Arles, The siesta; and *Cézanne* (1839–1906), The card-players, L'Estaque, Woman with a coffee-pot, and Still lifes; also *Toulouse-Lautrec* (1864–1901), Panels for La Goulue's booth at the Foire du Trône.

In the next two rooms are displayed a number of **Pastels** by *Degas*, including The tub; and *Manet*, Mme Manet on a blue couch.

Adjacent is the *Rooftop Café*, providing a curious view of Paris through the hands of the huge clock, and also from the terrace.

The next series of rooms **(O)** contain several Neo-Impressionist paintings, by *Seurat* (1859–91), including The circus; *Paul Signac* (1863–1935), *Henri Cross* (1856–1910); and *Odilon Redon* (1840–1916), including several pastels by the last.

The Absinthe Drinkers, by Edgar Degas, *1876*

Rooms **(P)** on the W end of the museum, contain *Toulouse-Lautrec*, Jan Avril dancing, La toilette, and Cha-U-Kao (the female clown), among others; *Henri Rousseau* (le Douanier; 1844–1910), Female portrait, and War; *Gauguin* (1845–1905), La belle Angèle, Tahitian women on the beach, Haymaking in Brittany, The white horse, Les Alyscamps, The meal, Arearea, and also several carvings and other souvenirs from Tahiti. Other sections are devoted to the Nabis, including representative examples of the work of *Pierre Bonnard* (1867–1947), among them The croquet party, and Nude; *Paul Sérusier* (1863–1927); *Maurice Denis* (1870–1943); *Félix Vallotton* (1865–1925), The ball; *Edouard Vuillard* (1868–1940), Au lit; and paintings by *Aristide Maillol* (1861–1944).

The last section on this upper level displays the Kaganovitch collection, including *Gauguin*, Breton peasant women, and works by *Monet, Sisley, Renoir, Pissarro, Van Gogh,* et al.

Passing along a passage-way devoted to the *Press*, we reach escalators descending to the MIDDLE LEVEL of the museum and to a section displaying the *Decorative Arts of the Third Republic* **(Q)** and, among paintings, such representative canvases as *William Bouguereau* (1825–1905), The birth of Venus, and *Alphonse de Neuville* (1835–85), The cemetery at St.-Privat. Notable is the decoration of the former *Ballroom* of the station hotel, and the *Restaurant*.

Another passage leads to a landing **(R)** overlooking the Ground Floor, displaying a collection of *Monumental Sculpture* of the period, off which are rooms **(S)** containing a collection of Naturalistic paintings and sculptures, among which are *Bastien-Lépage* (1848–84), Haymaking; *Léon Bonnat* (1833–1922), Portrait of Mme Pasca; *Max Liebermann* (1847–1935), Brewery at Brannenburg; *Valentin Serov* (1864–1955), Mme Lwoff; *Jacques-Émile Blanche* (1861–1942), The Thaulow family; *Giovanni Boldini* (1842–1931), Portrait of Robert de Montesquiou (on whom Proust based his 'Baron Charlus'), together with *Paul Troubetzkoy* (1866–1938), Statuette of Montesquiou seated; also *Boldini*, Mme Max; *Eugène Carrière* (1849–1906), Portrait of Verlaine; and *Burne-Jones* (1833–98), The Wheel of Fortune.

Turning left on regaining the landing we reach an important collection of sculpture by *Rodin* (1840–1917), including a plaster cast of The Gate of Hell, The Baptist, The Bronze Age, and numerous busts, including the marble Head of *Camille Claudel* (1864–1943), whose impressive bronze group entitled L'Age mûr (Maturity) is also in this section.

Adjacent is a further series of rooms **(T)** containing a collection of 'Art Nouveau' material, including jewellery by *René Lalique* (1860–1945); furniture and woodwork by *Hector Guimard* (1867–1942), *Alexandre Charpentier* (1856–1909), *Jean Dampt* (1854–1945), and *F.-R. Carabin* (1862–1932); and glass, ceramics, and enamel work by *Émile Gallé* (1846–1904), and the School of Nancy. More work by *Guimard* may be seen in a room to the left as we cross to the S side of the museum, while other rooms **(U)** contain bentwood furniture by *Michael Thonet* and his brothers (from 1853), and work by *Adolf Loos* (1870–1933), *Charles Rennie Mackintosh* (1868–1928), *Otto Wagner* (1841–1918), and *Josef Hoffmann* (1870–1956); and also examples of the productions of the *Wiener Werkstatte*, including designs by *Koloman Moser* (1868–1918).

The S landing displays more sculpture, among them *Bourdelle* (1861–1929), Hercules drawing his bow, and several works by *Maillol*. Passing a section devoted to temporary exhibitions (often of old photographs; see below), we reach **(V)**, to the left, the last series of rooms containing paintings, largely post 1900, among them further examples of the work of *Bonnard* (Woman with a cat); *Vuillard*, Portrait of Mme de Polignac; *Matisse* (1861–1954), Luxe, calme et volupté; *Gustav Klimt* (1862–1918), Roses under trees; *Edvard Munch* (1863–1944) Summer night at Aasgaarstrand; and lastly, *Henri Rousseau*'s The snake-charmer (previously in the Musée d'Art Moderne of the Centre Beaubourg).

Also reached from the landing is a section **(W)** devoted to the early days of the *Cinema*.

Among collections of early photographs are the work of *Eugène Atget, Édouard Baldus, L.-A. Humbert de Molard, Félix Nadar, Charles Nègre, Pierre Petit, George Charles Beresford, Julia Margaret Cameron, Lewis Carroll, Roger Fenton*, and *George Shaw*.

Also of interest are a collection of drawings from the *Gustave Eiffel* archive.

10   The Faubourg St.-Germain: Western Sector
Palais de la Légion d'Honneur; Palais Bourbon; Musée Rodin

MÉTROS: Solferino, Musée d'Orsay, Chambre des Députés, Invalides, Varenne, Sèvres-Babylone, Rue du Bac (RER)

From the *Louvre*, the *Pont du Carrousel* crosses the Seine to the QUAI VOLTAIRE (Pl. 13;3), which continues the *Quai Malaquais* to the W, (see p 96), and was formerly the *Quai des Théatins*. Voltaire died in 1778 at the house of the Marquis de Villette (No. 27); *St.-Sulpice* refused to accept his corpse, which was rushed by his nephew to the *Abbaye de Sellières*, near Troyes, to save it from a common grave.

Louise de Kéroualle, Charles II's mistress *en titre*, and created Duchess of Portsmouth in 1673, occupied Nos 3–5 in 1695–1701. Ingres died at No. 11 in 1867. At No. 13 was installed the 'Moniteur Universel', an influential newspaper during the Revolution. Here as a tenant in 1829–36, Delacroix was preceded by Horace Vernet and followed by Corot. At No. 19 Baudelaire lived in 1856–58, working on 'Les Fleurs du Mal', while Wagner completed the libretto of 'Die Meistersinger' there in 1861–62; Sibelius, and Oscar Wilde, were later tenants. Alfred de Musset lived at No. 25 in 1841–49; it was later the home of Henri de Montherlant (1896–1972).

To the W extends the QUAI ANATOLE-FRANCE and the QUAI D'OR-SAY (the latter, beyond the Pont de la Concorde, being a focus of 'foreign affairs'). The former is dominated by the new **Musée d'Orsay**; see Rte 9.

Opposite the W end of the museum is the **Palais de la Légion d'Honneur**, flanked by a colonnade with bas-reliefs by Roland on the attic storey. The Corinthian portico in the courtyard is adorned with a frieze of arabesques with the motto 'Honneur et Patrie'. Facing the quay is a rotunda with Corinthian columns and symbolic busts, etc.

Built by Rousseau in 1782–86 for the Prince de Salm-Kyrbourg, at the Revolution it was raffled and won by a former wig-maker's apprentice who had made a fortune. He was later imprisoned for forgery, and the house became the Swedish Embassy in 1797. Mme de Staël, the ambassador's wife, gave her famous receptions here under the Directory, but in 1804 it was bought by the government for the grand chancellory of the Legion of Honour. It was restored in 1878, having been severely damaged by fire during the Commune.

The entrance to the *Musée National de la Légion d'Honneur et des Ordres de Chevalerie*, exhibiting medals, decorations, etc., relating to the history of the Order, together with foreign heraldic trappings, is at No. 2 Rue de Bellechasse, adjoining. This non-hereditary Order, instituted in May 1802, comprises five classes (in ascending order): Chevalier, Officier, Commandeur, Grand-Officier, and Grand-Croix.

At No. 80 Rue de Lille (to the S) is the *Hôtel de Seignelay* by Boffrand, also architect of the adjacent *Hôtel de Beauharnais* (1714), once the home of Queen Hortense, and later the German Embassy (now the ambassador's residence) with a curious neo-Egyptian peristyle. Mérimée lived at No. 52 Rue de Lille for the last 18 years of his life, but his library was burnt out during the Commune a few weeks before his death at Cannes. Mme de Tencin held a literary salon from 1726–40 at her home (from 1715) on the site of No. 75. It was frequented by Montesquieu, Marmontel, Marivaux, Fontenelle, and Helvétius; also Matthew Prior, Bolingbroke and, later, Chesterfield.

A few minutes' walk to the W is the W end of the BLVD ST.-GERMAIN and the **Palais-Bourbon**, seat of the *Assemblée Nationale* (Pl. 12;7), facing the *Pont de la Concorde* (see Rte 13).

In 1722 a mansion was erected on this site for the Dowager Duchess of Bourbon (legitimised daughter of Louis XIV and the Marquise de Montespan), of which only the inner courtyard and main entrance (at 128 Rue de l'Université) have survived. The Prince de Condé, forced to leave his home because of the construction of the *Théâtre de l'Odéon*, bought the palace from Louis XV and enlarged it between 1764 and 1789, incorporating the *Hôtel de Lassay*, in which he lived after the Revolution. The Palais became national property under the name of Maison de la Révolution, the meeting-place of the Council of Five Hundred, and was later occupied by the Archives (1799–1808). Since 1815 it has been used by the *Chambre des Députés*, the French equivalent to the House of Commons, its name being changed to the *Assemblée Nationale* in 1946.

In 1940–44 the *Palais-Bourbon* was the headquarters of the German military administration of the Paris region, and at the time of the Liberation considerable fighting took place in the neighbourhood, causing some damage to the building, and the destruction of over 30,000 volumes in the Library.

Admission. Those wishing to visit the interior, or to attend a session of the Assembly, must first apply in writing to the Questor's Office. The main entrance is in the Pl. du Palais-Bourbon (see below).

The N façade (1804–07), a neo-Hellenistic piece of imperial bombast designed principally to balance the *Madeleine* when seen from the *Pl. de la Concorde*, is entirely decorative, and consists of a portico of twelve Corinthian columns, with statues of statesmen, allegorical bas-reliefs, etc. by Poyet.

The decoration of the interior is of slight artistic merit; certain rooms contain historical paintings by *Horace Vernet* and *Ary Scheffer*, and by *Delacroix* (in the *Salon du Roi* and *Library*); the *Salle des Séances* retains bas-reliefs by *Lemot* (1798).

The *Galerie des Fêtes* (1848) connects the building to the *Hôtel de Lassay* (1724), the official residence of the President of the Assembly.

Further along the QUAI D'ORSAY (with which it is synonymous) stands the *Ministère des Affaires Étrangères* (Foreign Office), built by Lacornée in 1845.

Adjacent, on the ESPLANADE DES INVALIDES is the *Gare des Invalides* and *Aérogare* (or Air Terminus).

For the *Hôtel des Invalides* and *Musée de l'Armée*, see Rte 11.

Turning E along the Rue de l'Université, we shortly reach the PL. DU PALAIS-BOURBON, an elegant ensemble of Louis XVI mansions built to the same pattern after 1776. Maria Edgeworth lived there in 1820.

At No. 108 Rue de l'Université (but with its entrance at No. 121 in the Rue de Lille, parallel to the N) is the *Institut Néerlandais*, with a good collection of Dutch and German paintings (adm. 13.00–19.00, except Mondays). Jacques Turgot (1727–81), the economist, died here; La Fayette lived at No. 123, adjacent, in 1799.

Further E (on the far side of the Blvd St.-Germain), at No. 51 Rue de l'Université, is the *Hôtel de Soyécourt*, of 1707, by Lassurance; No. 24, the *Hôtel de Senneterre*, has a notable façade perhaps by Servandoni in the courtyard (1700). Franklin's first lodging on his arrival in Paris in 1776 was at the Hôtel de Hambourg in this street. Alphonse Daudet (1840–97) died at No. 41; from 1885 he had lived in the neighbouring Rue de Bellechasse. This leads S to regain the BLVD ST.-GERMAIN, flanked to the W, at this point, by the extensive buildings of the *Ministère de la Défense* (by Bouchot; 1867–77), with a clock-tower at the corner of the Rue de Solferino.

Nos 1, 3, and 5 Rue St.-Dominique, running W from the BLVD ST.-GERMAIN, date from c 1710, No. 5 was the home of Gustave Doré

(1832–83) from 1849 until his death. Nos 10–12 (since 1804 part of the *Ministère de la Défense*) occupy the former *Couvent des Filles de St.-Joseph* (1641), established for orphaned girls, and generously supported by Mme de Montespan (1640–1707), who retired here in 1687 after being supplanted in royal favour by Mme de Maintenon (c 1674). Mme du Deffand (1697–1780) in 1755 likewise supported it, and here, until 1764, held her literary salons, being later much neglected, except by a few admirers such as Horace Walpole (1717–97; 4th Earl of Orford), who visited Paris in 1765, '67, '69, '71 and '75.

Nos 14–16, in the same block of buildings, the *Hôtel de Brienne* (1714 and 1730), was once the home of Lucien Bonaparte, and later of Laetitia Bonaparte. No. 28 was the *Hôtel Rochefoucauld-d'Estissac* (1710), while further W, the *Hôtel de Sagan* (No. 57), built by Brongniart in 1784 for the Princess of Monaco, is now the *Polish Embassy*, and was the British Embassy prior to the purchase of the Hôtel de Charost: see Rte 26. It was during this period that David Hume (who had lived in France in 1734–7) was secretary to the embassy (1763–5) and briefly chargé d'affaires. He was an intimate of Mme Geoffrin, D'Alembert, and Turgot.

S of the Rue St.-Dominique rises the uninspired Gothic-revival church of *Ste.-Clotilde*, built in 1846–56 by Gau and Ballu, where César Franck was organist from 1858 until his death in 1890; a commemorative monument, by Lenoir, stands opposite.

The Rue de Grenelle, flanked by a number of Embassies and Ministries, may be conveniently approached by following the Rue de Bellechasse S, in which, at No. 41, the *Conseil de la Résistance* and the *Comité Parisien de la Libération* organised operations for the rising of 19 August 1944.

Turning left at their junction, we pass, at No. 106, the *Temple de Panthemont* (by Constant d'Ivry; 1747–56), once the chapel of a convent where Joséphine de Beauharnais lived for several years. Its main buildings (now Nos 37–39 in the Rue de Bellechasse) housed an aristocratic school for girls, where Jefferson's daughter was a pupil during her father's embassy.

No. 102, the *Hôtel de Maillebois*, built early in the 18C by Deslisle-Mansart, was the home of the Duc de Saint-Simon from 1738, when he was working on his 'Mémoires', until his death in 1755. No. 87 is the *Hôtel de Bauffremont* (1721–36), with a curved façade; No. 85, the *Hotel d'Avaray* (1718; by Leroux), home of Horace Walpole (1678–1757) during his Paris embassy (1727–30), is now the *Netherlands Embassy*. No. 79, the *Hôtel d'Estrées*, the *Soviet Embassy*, was built by Robert de Cotte in 1713.

Retracing our steps towards the W, we pass No. 110, the *Hôtel de Courteilles* (1778; now the *Min. de l'Éducation Nationale*); No. 116, the old *Hôtel de Brissac*, rebuilt for Marshal de Villars by Boffrand and Leroux (1731), and now the *Mairie of the 7th Arrondissement*. No. 101, opposite, the former *Hôtel Rothelin* (or *de Charolais*), built by Lassurance in 1700, is now the *Min. du Développement Industriel et Scientifique*. Nos 138 and 140 were built by Jean Courtonne in 1724 and decorated by Lassurance in 1734 for Mlle de Sens. Marshal Foch (1851–1929) died in the former; the latter is occupied by the *Institut Géographique National*. No. 127, the *Min. du Travail*, was the *Hôtel du Châtelet*, one of the finest examples of the Louis-XV style; it was at one time used as the Archbishop's Palace. The *Hôtel de Chanac*, at No. 142, opposite (by Delamair; 1750), is now the *Swiss Embassy*.

We turn left along the BLVD DES INVALIDES, passing the NE corner of the *Hôtel des Invalides* (see Rte 11), and back into the Rue de Varenne. At No. 77, the **Hôtel Biron* (Pl. 12;4), on the corner, is the ***MUSÉE RODIN** (MÉTRO: *Varenne*), containing an important and impressive collection of sculpture by *Auguste Rodin* (1840–1917), which he left to the State, many being the originals of works executed in marble or bronze, and also a fine selection of drawings.

The mansion, built in 1728–30 by Aubert and Gabriel, was occupied by the Duc de Biron in 1753, after the death there of Louise de Bourbon, widow of the Duc de Maine, and in 1820 by the aristocratic convent of the Sacré-Coeur. The State bought the house in 1901. In 1910 two ground-floor rooms were used as a studio by Rodin, who lived here from 1907 until his death, while Rainer Maria Rilke, at one time his secretary, also had lodgings there (1908–9). Much of the painted and gilt panelling, which had been removed by the Philistine superior of the convent as being mere ostentation, has been recovered and replaced.

Of the many outstanding examples of Rodin's work displayed here, a few only are listed. *Grand Salon*: St. John the Baptist; 'L'Homme qui marche'; the Kiss; the Hand of God; Iris; and two studies of hands.—In a room to the left: 'L'Age d'Airain'; busts of Carrier-Belleuse, Mahler, and Puvis de Chavannes. In rooms to the right of the Grand Salon: the Thinker; Orpheus; Eve; bust of Lady Sackville-West; of Eve Fairfax, the suffragette; Rodin's father.—On the *Staircase*: Three Shades (from the Gate of Hell).

FIRST FLOOR. Case of models for the Gate of Hell; two busts of Victor Hugo; four nude studies of Balzac; Man with a broken nose; the Good Genius; Eternal Spring; Triton and Nereid on a dolphin; Water-fairy; Young Mother. Also shown are dance studies by *Renoir*, and paintings by *Renoir*, *Monet*, and *Van Gogh*, including the latter's Le Père Tanguy.

The *Gardens* are embellished by numerous bronzes and marbles, including: the Thinker; Hugo at Guernsey, formerly in the gardens of the Palais-Royal; Balzac; and the Gate of Hell; also, near the entrance, and seen from the street, the Burghers of Calais.

There is an Annexe to the Museum at *Meudon*, see Rte 33.

No. 72 in the Rue de Varenne is the *Hôtel de Castries* (1700), sacked by the mob in 1790 after the duel between the reactionary Duc de Castries and the radical Comte Charles de Lameth. No. 69, the *Hôtel de Clermont* by Leblond (1708), is now offices of the *Haut Commissariat à l'Énergie atomique*.—At 1 bis in Rue Vaneau (right) André Gide (1869–1951) died.

Just beyond is the **Hôtel de Matignon* (No. 57), built by Courtonne in 1721 and altered in the 19C; having served as the Austro-Hungarian Embassy (1888–1914), since 1935 it has been the residence of the *Présidence du Conseil*. One of the most beautiful mansions in the Faubourg, it has an unusually large garden. Talleyrand lived here in 1808–11.

No. 50, the handsome *Hôtel de Gallifet*, with an Ionic peristyle built by Legrand in 1775–96, is now the *Italian Institute*; their *Embassy* is at No. 47.—See p 108 for the continuation of the route N from the Rue du Bac.

To the S, No. 98 Rue de Bac, with gilt angels above the door, and good iron balconies, was the *Café des Deux-Anges*, the secret rendez-vous of the Chouans (c 1800), and here Cadoudal hatched the conspiracy of 1804. At No. 108 bis died Laplace (1749–1827), the astronomer and mathematician. At No. 110 Whistler (from 1892) was visited by Beardsley and Mallarmé, and scandalised his landlord by letting his child-models run naked in the garden. Nos 118–120, with doors designed by Toro, are the *Hôtel de Clermont-Tonnerre*, where Chateaubriand (1768–1848) lived from 1838 until his death. Here Mary Clarke (1793–1883; Mme Jules Mohl after 1847) had her salon from 1838–76, and was visited by Dean Stanley, Ticknor, Thackeray, Mrs Gaskell, and Florence Nightingale. No. 128 is the *Séminaire des*

Missions Étrangères, founded in 1663, with relics of martyred missionaries. Nos 136–140 are the *Hôtel de la Vallière*, with handsome portals, occupied by the Soeurs de Charité.

To the left is the *Grands Magasins du Bon Marché*, built on the site of an asylum, the Petites Maisons, to the E of which is the SQ. BOUCICAUT (Pl. 13;5; named after the foundress of the *Bon Marché*).

A short distance to the SW, in the Rue de Sèvres, No. 42 is the *Hôpital Laënnec*, formerly a home for incurable women, founded by Card. de la Rochefoucauld c 1635, which retains its original courtyard and chapel. At No. 95 is the *Église des Lazaristes*, with a silver shrine preserving the body of Vincent de Paul (1576–1660), canonised in 1737. Barbey d'Aurevilly (1808–89) lived for thirty years and died at No. 25 in the adjacent Rue ʾousselet.

At No. 31 Rue St.-Placide, the S extension of the Rue du Bac, J.-K. Huysmans (1848–1907) died; David d'Angers and Michelet lived in the same street, while Parmentier resided in the parallel Rue de l'Abbé-Grégoire.

No. 40 in the Rue du Cherche-Midi, near the BLVD RASPAIL, belonged to Rochambeau (1725–1807), who fought for the Americans in the War of Independence, notably at Yorktown. At No. 38, the *Maison des Sciences de l'Homme*, has been built on the site of the *Prison Militaire du Cherche-Midi*, where many French patriots were imprisoned between 1940 and 1944.

The Rue du Bac leads N from the Rue de Varenne, shortly crossing the Rue de Grenelle, where to the right (Nos 57 and 59) is the *****Fontaine des Quatre-Saisons**, designed by Bouchardon in 1739, with sculptures of the City of Paris with the Seine and Marne at her feet, and with bas-reliefs of the Seasons. Alfred de Musset lived at No. 59 from 1824 to 1840.

Half-left across the BLVD ST.-GERMAIN, government offices occupy Nos 244–248, two early-18C houses. No. 246, the *Hôtel de Roquelaure* (1722), by Lassurance and Leroux, has a fine courtyard. Cambacérès, Second Consul in 1799, lived here in 1808.

Guillaume Apollinaire (1880–1918) lived and died at No. 202 BLVD ST.-GERMAIN; off which, to the right, leads the Rue St.-Guillaume, where the 16C *Hôtel de Mesmes* (No. 27), enlarged in 1933, is the *Institut National des Sciences Politiques*; No. 16, the *Hôtel de Créqui*, built in 1660–64, and extended in 1772, was for a time the home of Lamartine, and later of Renan.

Crossing the Boulevard, the Rue du Bac leads N to the Seine, and is named after the ferry operating there before the construction of the Pont Royal.

No. 46 Rue du Bac, the former *Hôtel de Boulogne*, with its courtyard, was built in 1744 by Boffrand for Jacques Bernard, who died after a scandalous bankruptcy in 1753; it was the lodging of Chateaubriand in 1815–18.

To the E is **St.-Thomas-d'Aquin**, begun in 1682 by Pierre Bullet in the Jesuit style, and completed, with the construction of the façade, in 1787. The ceiling-painting in the Lady Chapel is by *Lemoyne*.

11 The Invalides and Musée de L'Armée

MÉTROS: Invalides, Varenne, La Tour-Maubourg,
St.-François-Xavier.

The districts to the W of the Faubourg St.-Germain are overshadowed by the *Dôme* of the *Invalides*, the *Tour Eiffel* to the W, and the *Tour Montparnasse* (cf.) not far to the SE.

From the Right Bank, the best approach is by the *Pont Alexandre-III* (see p 204), which affords an impressive vista of the *Invalides* at the

end of its esplanade. This walk can be conveniently combined with a
return via the Palais de Chaillot.

The ESPLANADE DES INVALIDES 487m by 250m, was laid out in
1704–20 by Robert de Cotte, and planted with trees along the sides. At
its NE corner is the *Aérogare*.

To the W, the QUAI D'ORSAY extends as far as the *Pont de l'Alma*. At No. 63 on the
Quai is the *American Church*, built in a Gothic style in 1927–31; the playwright
Jean Giraudoux (1882–1944) died at No. 89.—For the adjacent public entry to
the *Sewers* of Paris, see p 213.—At No. 7 Rue Edmond-Valentin, a short distance
SW, off the Av. Bosquet, lived James Joyce from 1935 to 1939.

From the PL. DES INVALIDES, S of the Esplanade, the Av. de la
Motte-Picquet leads SW past the front of the *École Militaire* (see Rte
12); the BLVD DES INVALIDES skirts the E side of the *Hôtel des
Invalides*, the formal façade of which contrasts with the domestic
architecture opposite. To the left diverges the Rue de Grenelle and
the Rue de Varenne, and near the corner of the latter is the *Musée
Rodin* (see Rte 10).

The Dôme des Invalides seen from the South

The **HÔTEL DES INVALIDES** (Pl. 12;4; headquarters of the military governor of Paris) was founded by Louis XIV in 1671 as a home for disabled soldiers, the first enduring institution of its kind; at one time it housed between 4000 and 6000 pensioners or *invalides*. At present about 70 wounded live there. The buildings, which form a majestic ensemble, were erected from the designs of *Libéral Bruant* (died 1697), and *J. Hardouin-Mansart* continued the work. Antoine Parmentier (1737–1813) was chemist here, where he carried out researches into the properties of the potato and the processes of baking bread. Sombeuil, governor of the Invalides from 1786, was in 1789 forced by the mob to hand over arms stored there. During the Revolution it was known both as the 'Temple de l'Humanite', and 'Temple de Mars'. It was restored under Napoléon I, who was later buried beneath its Dôme. Part of the building now houses the *Musée de l'Armée*; see below.

Tickets, which may be used on two *consecutive* days, cover both the museums and entry to Napoléon's Tomb (the main entrance to which is in the Pl. Vauban).

Facing the Esplanade are two artillery batteries: the unmounted *Batterie Trophée*, and the *Batterie Triomphale*, whose salvos announcing victory were last heard at the end of the First World War; the latter were removed by the Germans in 1940. Made for Frederick the Great in 1708, these eight pieces were captured by Napoléon at Vienna in 1805.

From the entrance gate we approach the dignified façade, over 200m long. The dormer windows take the form of trophies, each different. Flanking the main entrance are copies of the original statues of Mars and Minerva, by Guillaume Coustou (1735). The equestrian bas-reliefs above the central door, of Louis XIV accompanied by Justice and Prudence, by Pierre Cartellier, replaced (in 1815) an earlier design by Coustou.

Opposite the entrance to the *Cour d'Honneur* (102m by 63m) is the door of the church of St.-Louis, above which are Seurre's original bronze statue of Napoléon, formerly surmounting the *Vendôme Column* (see Rte 17), and an astronomical clock (1781).

On the E side of the courtyard is the main entrance to the *Musée de l'Armée*. At the foot of the staircase to the right of the entrance to the church, is one of the Renault cars (the Marne taxis), which, commandeered by Gén. Gallieni, carried troops to the Front in September 1914.

The *Church of St.-Louis* (the chapel of the *Invalides*) was built by Bruant and Mansart. The imposing interior, decorated with captured regimental colours, has a gallery built at the same level as that of the dormitories of the disabled. In 1837 it resounded to the first performance of Berlioz's 'Grande Messe des Morts', the orchestra being reinforced by a battery of artillery on the esplanade. The *Organ* (1679–87), by Alexandre Thierry, was restored in the 1950s. Concerts still take place here.—Behind the high-altar a sheet of plain glass separates the chapel from the *Dôme des Invalides*.

In vaults below (no adm.) are the graves of numerous French marshals (and generals), among them Jourdan, Bertrand, Grouchy, and Oudinot, and, more recently, Leclerc de Hautecloque, and Juin.

On leaving the chapel, turn left along the Corridor de Nîmes to reach the entrance of the *Dôme*. Visitors approaching from the Pl. Vauban, to the S, will find the ticket-office just W of its main entrance (Pl. 12;4).

The *Dôme des Invalides*, begun by J. Hardouin-Mansart in 1675, and finished in 1706, was added to the church of St.-Louis as a chapel royal. In the niches on either side of the entrance are statues of

Charlemagne and St. Louis by Coysevox and Nicolas Coustou. The ribbed dome is roofed with lead, adorned with gilded trophies, and crowned with a short spire reaching to a height of 107m.

The admirably proportioned interior, 56m square, is in the form of a Greek cross.

The focus of attention is the sumptuous *Tomb of Napoléon, designed by *Visconti*, in which the Emperor was placed in April 1861, forty years after his death at St. Helena. His remains were brought to the Invalides in December 1840 (see *Arc de Triomphe*).

They lay in the Chapel St.-Jérome while this sarcophagus of dark red porphyry (from Finland), resting on a pedestal of green Vosges granite, was being prepared.

The tomb, its dimensions 4m by 2m, and 4·5m high, is surrounded by a gallery with ten bas-reliefs *after Simart* representing the 'benefits' conferred on France by the Emperor, and facing the sarcoph; jus are twelve figures by *Pradier* symbolising his greater victories, between which are six trophies of 54 colours taken at Austerlitz. The statue of Napoléon in his coronation robes is also by *Simart*.

The error of placing the tomb in an inappropriately inferior position as seen from the circular gallery is now generally recognised. An imposing view is gained by descending to the *Crypt*, the inscription on the impost of the entrance to which may be translated: 'I desire that my ashes rest on the banks of the Seine, in the midst of the French people whom I have loved so dearly'.

On re-ascending we may visit the surrounding chapels, passing (in an anti-clockwise direction from the SE) the tombs (some enshrining only hearts) of Joseph Bonaparte (died 1844), Vauban (died 1707), Foch (died 1929; tomb by *Landowski*), Lyautey (died 1934; tomb by *Albert Laprade*); La Tour d'Auvergne (died 1800; 'the first grenadier of the Republic'); and Turenne (died 1675), to reach the Chapel St.-Jérome, standing empty. Relics of the Roi de Rome (1811–32), Bonaparte's only son, who died prematurely of phthisis and was originally buried in Vienna, were brought here by the Germans in 1940 (on the centenary of the burial of his father), and since 1969 have lain in the vaults of the crypt (see above).

The **MUSÉE DE L'ARMÉE** comprises one of the world's most interesting, extensive, and well-displayed collections of arms and armour, weapons, uniforms, military souvenirs, etc., and without an excessive display of chauvinism. The building also houses the *Musée des Plans-Reliefs* (see below), a library, and a small cinema.

From the main entrance (E side of the *Cour d'Honneur*), we may visit first the restored *Salle Turenne* (right), in which colours of French regiments from the First Republic to the present have been re-hung, and the fine frescoes, variously attributed to *J.-B. Martin 'des Batailles'* (1659–1735) or pupils of *Van de Meulen*, are now seen to advantage. The maquette of the Invalides (made prior to 1757) is also of interest.—To the left is the *Salle Vauban*, containing cavalry uniforms and equipment, and similar frescoes.

From the Vestibule, stairs ascend to the SECOND FLOOR. To the right is the entrance to a series of rooms devoted to the military exploits of the Ancienne Monarchie (1618–1792), set out in chronological order. It should be emphasised that most figures are displayed in such a way that the visitor may see them in the round: this applies likewise to the suits of armour to be seen in the W wings. Among the numerous plans, engravings, prints, and portraits, those individual objects which may be pointed out are the cannon-ball that killed Turenne, and the perforated back plate of his cuirass, his marshal's baton, and his portrait attributed to *Le Brun*. Note also the colours of the Irish Clancarty regiment (1642).

Another room contains souvenirs of Gén. La Fayette (1757–1834). We next enter compartments concentrating on the Revolutionary,

Directory, and Consulate periods, with numerous Napoleonic souvenirs, including one of Bonaparte's grey coats; his tent and furniture;
and the stuffed skin of his white horse, 'Vizier', which outlived the
Emperor by eight years. Among portraits of his marshals, that of Ney,
by *Gérard*, is notable. A further series of cabinets devoted to
Napoléon at St. Helena, and the period 1830–52, bring us back to the
stairs.

On the THIRD FLOOR are sections devoted to the Second Empire,
Crimean War, and Franco-German War of 1870, additionally illustrated by early photographs, and paintings by *Alphonse de Neuville*
and *Edouard Detaille*.

On the ATTIC FLOOR are housed the important collections of the
autonomous *MUSÉE DES PLANS-RELIEFS**, recently reorganised
after the roof had been restored, and after the political scandal with
regard to their dispersal had died down, although several of the
models of fortresses near what is now the Belgian border have been
transferred to Lille.

The collection as a whole consists of some 80 models (apart from
those dismounted or in *réserve*), and it is known that another 50
existed, but which have been destroyed. The majority were built to
the scale 1:600, and together with maquettes, maps and plans,
represent the form of fortresses—both in France and near her
frontiers—since the time of Vauban. They are of very considerable
historical, architectural, and topographical interest.

The idea of their construction is attributed to Louvois. Until 1776
they remained secreted in the Louvre, and were only shown to such
important visitors as Peter the Great (1717), who could be trusted.
They were then moved to the Invalides, where—although evacuated
to Chambord during the Second World War—they have for the most
part remained. The models were made during the period 1668–1870,
although many of them have since been restored, and occasionally
somewhat over-restored. The new distribution displays, in some 14
rooms, the following models, apart from sections devoted to military
cartography and descriptive of their construction: *La Kenoque*, no
longer existing, being built over by the Belgian town of Knokke-le-
Zoute; *Fort Quarré*, Antibes; *Constantine*, Tunisia; *Antwerp*; *Metz*;
Berg-op-Zoom; *Landrecies*; *Gravelins*; *Brest*; *Marsal* (Moselle); *Per-
pignan*; *Strasbourg*; *Château-Trompette* (the former citadel at
Bordeaux); and *Briançon*.

On the W side of the *Cour d'Honneur* are the **Collections of Arms
and Armour**, extraordinarily rich in weapons of all periods, many
exhibits being of great artistic interest, and masterpieces of dama-
scening and chasing. To the right, the *Salle François I*, retaining the
original frescoes (restored) of the dining-rooms and a painting of the
Founding of the Invalides by *Pierre Dulin*, contains suits of armour
(including parade armour) and the horse armour of François I, his
sword, and plaques from his tomb. Note the heavy armour of the
Elector Palatine Otto Henry.

A small room near the entrance, containing arms *before the 9C*, may be visited
on request.

To the left of the entrance to this wing is the Salle Henri IV, with
frescoes by *Martin 'des Batailles'*, concentrating on jousting armour.
Note the diminutive 'sample' suits made by the armourer to obtain
orders. Straight ahead of the vestibule are galleries containing the
important **Collection Pauilhac**. Among the numerous medieval and
Renaissance pieces are suits belonging to Louis XIII, Henri III, Henri

IV, and Louis XIV. The extensive *Collection of Firearms*, showing the evolution of such weapons, is outstanding.

Another section is devoted to collections of **'Oriental' arms and armour** from the Balkans, Turkey, Persia, India, and China, etc. Among individual helmets of interest are those of Voivode (Russia; 16C) and of the Ottoman sultan Bajazet II (1447–1512).—On the far side of the adjacent courtyard is a wing containing some thousands of *figurines*.

From these galleries there is a view into adjacent courtyards, in which stand a number of artillery pieces, while the walls of the *Cour d'Angoulême* (N) are embellished by the 'Danube Chain', with which the Turks held their vessels in position during the Siege of Vienna in 1683. Other pieces, usually unmounted, are arranged around the main courtyard.

On the SECOND FLOOR are galleries devoted to the 1914–18 War and France's participation in the 1939–45 War, while 'animated' maps describe graphically the movements of troops during the various campaigns. *Occupied* France, France *Liberated*, and the sad history of deportations are also covered, as are the *Normandy Landings*.

Further rooms on the THIRD FLOOR are devoted to France's Allies during the last war, while in the *Gribeauval Hall* is displayed an extensive collection of scale models of French and foreign artillery of all periods.

12 The École Militaire; The Eiffel Tower

MÉTROS: École Militaire, Cambronne, Bir. Hakeim, Champ-de-Mars, La Motte Picquet-Grenelle.

From the PL. VAUBAN (Pl. 12;4), to the S of the *Hôtel des Invalides*, the Av. de Tourville leads W towards the *École Militaire*, and the Av. de Villars leads SE, shortly meeting the S section of the BLVD DES INVALIDES (by the church of *St.-François-Xavier*; 1875), which continues as far as the Rue de Sèvres, beyond which it is extended by the BLVD DE MONTPARNASSE.

At this latter junction are the buildings of the *Institut National des Jeunes Aveugles (Blind)*, founded in 1793 by Valentin Haüy.—Vincent d'Indy (1851–1931) lived for 70 years and died at No. 7 Av. de Villars.

S of the Rue de Sèvres are the *Hôpital des Enfants-Malades* (founded 1724) and *Hôpital Necker*, once a Benedictine nunnery, founded in 1779 by Louis XVI, directed at one time by Mme Necker, and rebuilt in 1840.

Also radiating from the PL. VAUBAN are the wide tree-lined Av. de Breteuil; and to the SW, the Av. de Ségur, passing (right) the *Min. des Postes et Télécommunications*, and the controversial buildings of the UNESCO headquarters, perhaps best approached by the Av. de Lowendal.

The main **UNESCO Building** (by Breuer, Zehrfuss, and Nervi; 1958), flanking the semicircular Pl. de Fontenoy, consists in fact of three buildings: one for the permanent delegation; a *Conference Building*, with its accordion-pleated concrete roof covered in copper, and containing murals by Picasso and Rufino Tamayo; and the dominating Y-shaped *Secretariat* of seven floors supported by 72 pylons. In the *Piazza* are 'decorative works' by Henry Moore, Alexander Calder, Jean Arp, and Miró, and a Japanese Garden has been designed by

Noguchi. An annexe, to house even more functionaries, lies a short distance due
S. The main building was the object of arson in March 1984.

To the N is the *__École Militaire__ (Pl. 12;3–5), a handsome structure
covering part of the former 'ferme' and 'château' of Grenelle, built by
J.-A. Gabriel, and enlarged in 1856.

The school was founded in 1751 by Louis XV (influenced by Mme de Pompadour)
for the training of noblemen as army officers. It was opened in 1756 and
completed in 1770. Its director in 1775 was Col Drumgold, an Irishman, who Dr
Johnson considered 'a most complete character, for he had first been a professor
of rhetorick, and then became a soldier'. In 1777 its rigid rules for entry were
modified so that it could take in the élite of provincial military academies; thus in
1784 Bonaparte (who was confirmed in the chapel during his training) was
chosen from the Collège de Brienne. It was closed in 1787 and used as a depot
and barracks. It is now occupied by the _École Supérieure de Guerre_, or staff
college.

18C railings separate the _Cour d'Honneur_ from the PL. DE FONTENOY,
which has lost its 18C character. On the entablature of the entrance
façade, the figure representing Victory is in fact Louis XV, a likeness
that escaped destruction during the Revolution.

On written application to the Commandant, 1 Pl. Joffre, a guided tour of the
interior can be arranged. The most impressive room is the _Salon des Maréchaux_,
with its fine _boiseries_. The _Chapel_ is open to the public daily.

A short distance SW is the PL. CAMBRONNE. It was Gén. Cambronne (1770–1842)
who made the famous and defiant expletive—'_Merde!_'—when the Imperial
Guard was summoned to surrender at Waterloo, since known as 'le mot de
Cambronne'. The Rue Frémicourt and its extension, the Av. Émile-Zola, lead due
W to the _Pont Mirabeau_: see below.

Between the _École Militaire_ and the Seine lies the **Champ-de-Mars**,
almost 1km long, laid out in 1765–67 as a parade ground on the old
Plaine de Grenelle, with its market-gardens; it was used as a
racecourse after the Restoration, and converted into a park after 1913.

The ground was the scene of several early aeronautical experiments by the
Montgolfiers, by Charles and Robert, and by Blanchard (1783–84). Numerous
revolutionary festivals were held here, the most famous of which was the Fête de
la Fédération on 14 July 1790, when the king, the Assembly, and the delegates
from the provinces, and the army, took the oath at the Autel de la Patrie to
observe the new Constitution; the 'Champ de Mai', held by Napoléon on his
return from Elba; and several international exhibitions.
Bailly, president of the Constituent Assembly, was brutally executed here in
1793; and Capt. Alfred Dreyfus was publicly degraded here in December 1894.

The **Eiffel Tower** (Pl. 11;7), with its base at the river end of the
Champ-de-Mars, still one of the tallest structures in the world (300m
high, or 320m including the television installation), an inseparable
part of the Paris landscape, continues to dominate this quarter,
although the equally obtrusive _Tour Montparnasse_ threatens to divide
one's attention.

Built in 1889 on the occasion of the important Paris Exhibition, the _Tour Eiffel_ was
originally granted only 20 years of life, but its use in radio-telegraphy in 1904
saved it from demolition. Constructed by the engineer Gustave Eiffel (1832–
1923), the tapering lattice-work tower weighs over 7000 tonnes, and is composed
of 15,000 pieces of metal, fastened by 2,500,000 rivets, while its four feet are
supported by masonry piers sunk 9–14m into the ground.
The first, second, and third platforms, the latter 274m from the ground, are
reached by lift/elevator. On a clear day, particularly about one hour before
sunset, the extensive *views are remarkable.
It may be of interest that among the far-reaching influences of the 1889
Exhibition was the sound of a _gamelan_ orchestra from Jakarta, which here
introduced oriental music to Debussy, Ravel (aged 14), Satie, and Rimsky-
Korsakov, among other composers.

The Eiffel Tower, built in 1889 by Gustave Eiffel

The *Pont d'Iéna* spans the Seine to the *Palais de Chaillot*: see Rte 27.

Further SW is the *Pont de Bir Hakeim* (see p 217), from which the BLVD DE GRENELLE leads SE, on No. 8 of which a plaque records the round-up of some thousands of Parisian Jews in the *Vélodrome* (or cycling-track) here in July 1942 prior to their deportation.

The QUAI DE GRENELLE leads SW, with a view across the *Allée des Cygnes* (an island used as a charnel-house for dead horses in the 18C) to the *Maison de la Radio* (see Rte 27), passing (left) a concrete-jungle area of tower blocks flanking the Seine, joined to the far bank by the *Pont de Grenelle* and *Pont Mirabeau* (1895–97), leading to *Auteuil*.

To the SE, facing the Rue de la Convention, in this not very interesting 15th arrondissement, are the buildings of the *Imprimerie Nationale* (founded 1640), moved here in 1925 from the *Hôtel de Rohan*.

The riverside beyond the latter bridge, until recently the site of a large Citroën factory, is at present being developed.—Beyond the BLVD VICTOR, and the *Pont du Garigliano*, is the BLVD PÉRIPHÉRIQUE (*Quai d'Issy*; with the *Porte de Sèvres* further E), on the far side of which is the *Héliport de Paris*, while adjacent to the E are various buildings of the *Armée de l'Air* and other Service departments, exhibition areas, Palais des Sports, etc.

THE NORTH OR RIGHT BANK: LA RIVE DROITE

13 From the Pl. de la Concorde to the Pl. du Carrousel

MÉTROS: Concorde, Tuileries, Palais-Royal.

The ***PL. DE LA CONCORDE** (Pl. 7;7), occupying a central position by the Seine, and midway between the *Étoile* and the *Île de la Cité*, is still—in spite of the traffic swirling round it—one of the world's most impressive squares. Although its perspectives were evidently a design of the First Empire, the present appearance of the square dates from 1852, when the surrounding ditch was filled in.

The site, then a vacant space to the W of the main built-up area of the city (but within the enceinte of the Fermiers-Généraux raised some 30 years later), was chosen in 1757 to receive a bronze statue of Louis XV commissioned by the 'échevins' (or magistrates, see p 169), and unveiled in 1763. The surrounding square was named after the king. In 1770 panic during a firework display celebrating the marriage of the dauphin Louis and Marie-Antoinette provided its first holocaust (133 dead).

Young was impressed by the Place in 1787: 'a very noble entrance to a great city ... here one can be clean and breathe freely'. In 1792 the statue was replaced by a huge figure of Liberty, designed by Lemot (the object of Mme Roland's famous apostrophe: 'O liberté, que de crimes on commet en ton nom'), and the square was re-named Pl. de la Révolution. In the same year a guillotine was erected here for the execution of the robbers of the crown jewels (cf. below).

Louis XVI was guillotined on 21 January 1793 on the site now occupied by the fountain nearest the river, and between May 1793 and May 1795 the blade claimed among its 1119 victims: Charlotte Corday (17 July 1793), Marie-Antoinette (16 October), the Girondins (31 October), Philippe-Égalité (6 November), Mme Roland (10 November), Hébert (24 March 1794), Danton (5 April), Lavoisier (8 May), Mme Élisabeth (9 May), and Robespierre (28 July). The square first received its present name in 1795 at the end of the Reign of Terror.

On the N side of the square are two handsome mansions designed by Gabriel in 1763–72 (with pediment sculptures by M.-A. Slodtz and G. Coustou the younger) and originally intended as official residences. That to the right, from which the crown jewels were stolen in 1792, is now the *Ministère de la Marine*; that to the left has long been shared between the *Automobile Club* and the *Hôtel Crillon*.

Between these buildings leads the Rue Royale, at the end of which stands the *Madeleine* (see Rte 22), while in the opposite direction the southern perspective is completed by the assertive Classical façade of the *Palais-Bourbon*, see Rte 10.

To the W of the *Pl. de la Concorde*, the *Av. des Champs-Élysées* (see Rte 25) rises gently towards the *Arc de Triomphe*, the vista framed by the **Marly Horses*, two groups by G. Coustou, which were brought from the Château de Marly in 1794 and now form pendants to the winged horses at the W entrances of the *Tuileries*.

In the opposite direction the view extends to the Louvre. On the S side of the Place, the *Pont de la Concorde*, offering magnificent perspectives, was built by Perronet in 1788–90, and widened in 1932. Stone from the Bastille was used in the construction of the upper part; one reason for this is said to be that the Parisians would be able to tread under foot that symbol of royal despotism.

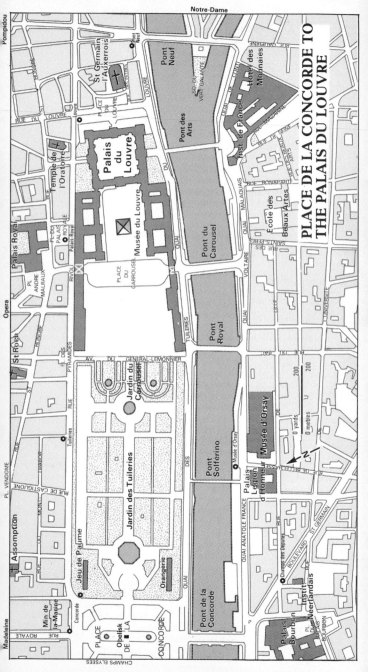

PLACE DE LA CONCORDE TO
THE PALAIS DU LOUVRE

In the centre of the Place rises the **Obelisk of Luxor**, a monolith of pink syenite, almost 23m high and c 230 tonnes in weight. It originally stood before a temple at Thebes in Upper Egypt, and commemorates in its hieroglyphics the deeds of Rameses II (13C BC).

The obelisk was presented to Louis-Philippe in 1831 by Mohammed Ali (the donor of Cleopatra's Needle in London). The pedestal, of Breton granite, bears representations of the apparatus used in its erection in 1836 (see also *Musée de Marine*, Rte 27). The two fountains, by Hittorf, copies of those in the piazza of St. Peter's at Rome, are embellished with figures emblematic of Inland (N) and Marine Navigation.

The eight stone pavilions round the Square, built by Gabriel in the 18C, support statues personifying the great provincial capitals. Strasbourg (as capital of Alsace, lost to France in 1871) was hung with crêpe and wreaths until 1918. Pradier's model for Strasbourg was Juliette Drouet (1806–83), Victor Hugo's mistress.

The public entrance to the *Sewers* of Paris, which used to be near the statue of Lille, has been moved to the S end of the *Pont de l'Alma*: see Rte 27.

The **Jardin des Tuileries**, the tree-lined formal garden of 25·5 hectares, adorned with statues, extends eastwards to the *Pl. du Carrousel*, and is crossed by the Av. du Gén.-Lemonnier, now partly subterranean and providing access to underground parking for the Louvre. The W section was the private garden of the Tuileries, and has been little altered since it was laid out by Le Nôtre in 1664.

The earlier gardens, in the Italian style, had been designed by his grandfather. It became the favourite promenade of the fashionable nobility until superseded by the Palais-Royal just before the Revolution.
  Here, on 1 December 1783, the scientists Charles and Robert made an ascent in a gas-filled balloon, watched by a vast crowd. The first such ascent had been made some 40 days previously: cf. *La Muette*.

The gateway opening from the *Pl. de la Concorde* has pillars crowned by equestrian statues of Fame and Mercury, by Coysevox (brought from Marly in 1719).
  The large octagonal pond is surrounded by statuary of the 17–18C by N. and G. Coustou and Van Cleve; on the steps to the S is 'Hommage à Cézanne' by Maillol; to the N, a copy of Coysevox's bust of Le Nôtre (original in *St.-Roch*).
  Terraces extend along both sides of the gardens. On the S, overlooking the QUAI DES TUILERIES (from which the *Pont Solferino*, demolished in 1963 and replaced by a footbridge, crosses to the *Quai Anatole-France*), is the *Terrasse du Bord-de-l'Eau*. A new road bridge is projected. From beneath this terrace, a passage led from the palace cellars to the *Pl. de la Concorde*, providing Louis-Philippe with an escape route in 1848. At the W end of the terrace is the *Orangerie* (1853), see below.

On the N side, the *Terrasse des Feuillants*, skirting the Rue de Rivoli, is named after a Benedictine monastery which in 1791 was the meeting-place of the 'Club des Feuillants' (moderate republicans, among whom were Lavoisier and André Chénier).
  Below the E side of the terrace are fragments of the *Palais des Tuileries*, *not* in situ. Further E, nearly opposite the Rue de Castiglione, was the site of the *Manège*, the riding-school of the palace, where the National Assembly met from 1789 to 1793, and where Louis XVI was condemned to death.

Here, until its contents were transferred to the Musée d'Orsay, stood the *Musée du Jeu-de-Paume*, so-named because it was accommodated in a real tennis-court built in 1851. It will be the venue of temporary exhibitions of 20C art, after its renovation by Antoine Stinco, and is expected to be reopened by late 1989. On the terrace on its S side is a monument to Charles Perrault (1628–1703), the writer of fairy tales, at whose suggestion the gardens were thrown open to the public by Colbert.

In the **ORANGERIE**, 3 minutes walk to the S across the Tuileries gardens, are displayed *Monet's* series of mural paintings, 'Les Nymphéas' (see also *Musée Marmottan*, Rte 27).

Since 1984 the upper gallery has been the permanent home of the works of art acquired by *Jean Walter* and *Paul Guillaume*, and donated to the State on the condition that they remained a separate collection. It comprises some 144 paintings, not many of which are of the first quality, including 28 examples of the work of *Derain*, 24 by *Renoir*, 22 by *Soutine*, 14 by *Cézanne*, 12 by *Picasso*, 11 by *Matisse*, 10 by *Utrillo*, and 9 by *Henri Rousseau (le Douanier)*, together with representative works by *Sisley, Monet, Modigliani, Marie Laurencin*, and *Van Dongen*. Among the more notable canvases are: *Cézanne*, Portrait of his wife, c 1885; *Renoir*, Gabrielle and Jean, Young girls at the piano, Claude playing, and Dressed as a clown, and Snowscape, and several lush nudes; *Derain*, The artist's niece, and Portrait of Mme Guillaume; *Picasso*, The embrace, and Nude on a red background; *Henri Rousseau*, The wedding, and Père Junier's cart; and *Modigliani*, The young apprentice, and Portrait of Paul Guillaume.

The central avenue of the **Jardin des Tuileries**, of chestnuts and plane trees, leads to the Round Pond. Between the pond and the Av. du Gén.-Lemonnier survive the railings put up by Louis-Philippe to isolate the 'private garden'. *Galignani's* 'New Paris Guide' (1841 ed.) stated that 'Great care is taken in keeping the garden clean; persons in working habits or carrying any parcels, except books, are not allowed to enter it'! Among the flower-beds are groups of sculpture, notably by *G.* and *N. Coustou, Coysevox*, and *Le Pautre*.

The main W wing of the former **Palais des Tuileries** no longer exists, except for the *Pavillons de Flore* and *de Marsan* (to the S and N respectively), both of which have been restored or rebuilt, and which now form the W extremities of the wings of the Louvre; see below. The *Pavillon de Marsan* accommodates the *Musée de la Mode* (see Rte 15).

The Palais des Tuileries was begun in 1564 by Philibert Delorme (c 1515–70) for Catherine de Médicis, who left the *Hôtel des Tournelles* after Henri II's lingering death. The site, beyond the city walls, was known as the 'Sablonnière' and occupied by tile-kilns (*tuileries*). Delorme was succeeded by Jean Bullant and then, in 1595, by Jacques du Cerceau, responsible for the *Pavillon de Flore*. The *Pavillon de Marsan* was built in 1660–65 by Louis Le Vau and his son-in-law François d'Orbay. Both pavilions were rebuilt where necessary and restored in 1875–78 by *Lefuel*.

Louis XVI was confined here after being brought from Versailles (except during his ineffectual attempt to escape in 1791) until the riot of 10 August 1792, when his Swiss Guards were massacred. In 1793–96 it was the headquarters of the Convention. Pope Pius VII was lodged in the *Pavillon de Flore* for four months in 1804–05.

The Tuileries became the permanent residence of Napoléon I, Louis XVIII (who died here), Charles X, Louis-Philippe, and Napoléon III. Eugénie escaped from the palace in September 1870 to the house of Dr Thomas Evans, her American dentist, who cleverly extracted her from Paris. Sir John Burgoyne's yacht awaited the Empress at Deauville. In May 1871 the Communards set fire to the building, which, like the Hôtel de Ville, was completely gutted. Its charred remains stood until 1884, when the main wing was razed, and the site was converted into a garden in 1889. This is embellished by statues in bronze by Aristide Maillol (1861–1944) and Rodin.

The restored and regilt **Arc de Triomphe du Carrousel**, a copy on a reduced scale of the Arch of Septimius Severus at Rome (14·60m high instead of 23m), was begun in 1806 from the designs of Fontaine and Percier to commemorate the victories of Napoléon I in 1805. It then constituted the main entrance to the courtyard of the Tuileries from the Cour du Carrousel.

On the top are figures of Soldiers of the Empire and a bronze chariot-group by Bosio (1828) representing the Restoration of the Bourbons. The original group incorporated (at the suggestion of Baron Denon) the antique horses looted by Napoléon from St. Mark's, Venice, in 1797 and replaced there in 1815 (the sculptor Canova being instrumental in their return). The four sides are decorated with marble bas-reliefs: the Battle of Austerlitz; the Capitulation of Ulm; the Meeting between Napoléon and Alexander at Tilsit; the Entry into Munich; the Entry into Vienna; and the Peace of Pressburg.

The PL. DU CARROUSEL, lying to the E of the Arch, was until the middle of the 19C a small square amidst a labyrinth of narrow and noisome alleys, which for centuries had remained almost encircled by the royal palaces. It derives its name from an equestrian fête given here in 1662 by Louis XIV.

The archways to the N lead to the Rue de Rivoli and beyond to the S end of the Av. de l'Opéra; those on the S give onto the QUAI DES TUILERIES opposite the *Pont du Carrousel*.

To the E lies the *Cour Napoléon*, and the main entrance to the **Musée du Louvre**, below its pyramid (see Rtes 14 and 15); westwards the Place commands a distant view towards the *Arc de Triomphe* and the towers of La Défense beyond.

14 Palais du Louvre

MÉTROS: Tuileries, Palais-Royal, Louvre, Pont-Neuf.

The *****PALAIS DU LOUVRE** (Pl. 13;2), surrounding three sides of a square, and occupying an extensive site between the Rue de Rivoli and the Seine, is one of the most magnificent of the world's palaces, and the most important public building in Paris.

The *Musée du Louvre* is described in Rte 15. For the *Musée des Arts Décoratifs*, see Rte 16.

The name is derived either from an early wolf-hunter's rendez-vous known as 'Lupara' or 'Louverie', or from a 'Louver', a blockhouse. It first appears in history as one of Philippe Auguste's fortresses (1190–1202), part of which may now be seen in the basement; see Rte 15. Charles V made it an official royal residence, and surrounded it with a moat. The W and S sides were rebuilt under François I (1515–47) and extended by Henri II. Catherine de Médicis, Henri II's widow, began the LONG GALLERY, flanking the river, to connect the Louvre with her new palace at the *Tuileries*. The building was further extended during the reigns of Henri IV and Louis XIII, and the quadrangle was completed, on Colbert's orders, during the minority of Louis XIV.

When Christopher Wren visited Paris in 1665, he observed that 'The Louvre for a while was my daily Object; where no less than a thousand Hands are constantly employ'd in the Works; some in laying mighty Foundations; some in raising the Stories, Columns, Entablements, &c. with vast Stones, by great and useful Engines; others in Carving, Inlaying of Marbles, Plaistering, Painting, Gilding, &c.... Mons. Colbert...comes to the Works of the Louvre, every Wednesday, and, if Business hinders not, Thursday'. Wren met Bernini, and remarked 'I would have given my Skin' for his design of the Louvre, 'but the old reserv'd Italian gave me but a few Minutes View'.

But the king soon lost interest in the new buildings, which were left in a state of disrepair and were occupied by squatters. In 1754 Louis XV commissioned Gabriel to renovate and restore the palace. Under Napoléon I the W part of the northern gallery was erected, and under Napoléon III the main wings were completed.

Catherine de Médicis lived in the palace after the death of her husband in 1559. Here she extorted from Charles IX (whose sister Marguerite de Valois had married Henri de Navarre—later Henri IV—five days earlier) the order for the Massacre of St. Bartholomew (24 August 1572). In 1591, during the Wars of the League, the Duc de Mayenne hanged three members of the 'Council of Sixteen' in the *Salle des Gardes* (now the *Salle des Cariatides)*. Henrietta Maria, the widow of Charles I of England, found refuge in the Louvre. In 1658 Corneille's 'Nicomède' was performed in the Salle des Gardes.

In 1793 the *Musée de la République* was opened in the Louvre, which, with a change of name, has remained the national art gallery and museum ever since. The building was attacked during the revolutions of 1830 and 1848, and in 1871 it was set on fire by the Communards, though serious damage was limited to the library: but see *Palais des Tuileries*, above.

Few 19C travellers did *not* visit it. One, according to Crabb Robinson, was Southey, who cared 'for nothing else at Paris but the old book-shops'!

The Louvre consists of two main divisions: the OLD LOUVRE, comprising the buildings surrounding the *Cour du Louvre* (or Cour Carrée); and the NEW LOUVRE, the 19C buildings N and S of the *Cour Napoléon*, together with their extensions to the W. It is proposed to call the whole, once renovated, the THE GRAND LOUVRE. An ambitious project has been under way since February 1983, when M. Mitterrand approved the plan proposed by Ieoh Ming Pei (a Chinese-born American architect). Apart from continuing restoration of the fabric and façades of the Palais du Louvre itself, and the redesigning of the Jardin des Tuileries in due course, it comprises the following transformations. (At the time this edition of the Guide went to press the work taking place in the Cour Napoléon had not been completed, and the description below is therefore provisional).

Firstly, the *Cour Carrée* has been excavated, to expose the foundations of the medieval fortress and the palace of Charles V, now called the 'Crypte Philippe Auguste'; see p 125.

In a central position in the Cour Napoléon, further W, between the Pavillon Denon and the Pavillon Richelieu, rises a *glass* **'Pyramid'** (an idea which might have well be championed by Champollion, but which is, admittedly, less ostentatious than the monument projected there a century ago by Louis-Ernest Lheureux), from its side steps descend into a large well or Entrance Vestibule; see Rte 15. From here passages lead to the basements of the Cour Carrée (and Crypte), to the S Wing of the Louvre, and similarly to the N Wing, into which the museum will eventually expand. It is also expected that direct communication will be provided between the adjacent métro stations and the Louvre. From the W side of the vestibule a passage leads to extensive underground car and coach parks beyond the foundations of the Arc de Triomphe du Carrousel, entered from the now subterranean Av. du Gén. Lemonnier. Below the Pl. du Carrousel and Cour Napoléon will be a complex providing space for the 'reserves' of the Louvre, studios for the restoration of works of art, service areas, and other facilities.

Further information on work in progress, or completed, will be given in the next edition of this Guide. Meanwhile, until the contents of each department of the Louvre have been redistributed—which may take several years—the visitor must expect a certain amount of confusion, nor should one be surprised at the unkempt condition of most of its rooms, awaiting restoration.

On the W side of the restored and cleaned *Cour Carrée*, to the S of the *Pavillon Sully*, is the oldest visible part of the early 16C Palace, by Lescot, with sculptural decorations by Jean Goujon and Paul Ponce. The N half of the W façade, and part of the N façade, were designed by Lemercier in imitation of Lescot; the caryatids on the *Pavillon Sully* are after Sarazin. The remainder of the court was built by Le Vau after 1660.

The top storeys on the N, E, and S sides, out of keeping with Lescot's attic, were added in the 17–18C, to bring them up to the height of the great *Colonnade* of 52 Corinthian columns and pilasters that now forms the exterior E façade. The work of Claude Perrault (1667–70), it was designed without due regard to former dimensions, and to give this E façade its correct proportions, a moat was excavated in 1966–67, and the *terreplein* previously envisaged was added. During these works the base was uncovered of an earlier façade begun by Le Vau (in collaboration with Perrault) and abandoned when Colbert became superintendent of the building.

For *St. Germain-l'Auxerroris*, to the E, see Rte 19.

The *Galerie du Bord de l'Eau*, the long S façade flanking the Seine, was the work of Pierre Chambiges, architect to Catherine de Médicis, and Thibaut Métezeau, as far as the Pavillon de Lesdiguières. Jacques du Cerceau was responsible for the prolongation of this wing, largely rebuilt in 1863–68. The building of the *New Louvre* (N and S of the *Cour Napoléon*) was undertaken by Visconti in 1852 and completed in 1871 by Lefuel. The N side, known as the *Aile Richelieu*, had until recently been occupied by the intrusive *Ministère des Finances*, whose functionaries have now been transferred to a new building at *Bercy*. This long overdue move has enabled the wing to be renovated and adapted to accommodate certain departments of the Musée du Louvre.

Three bridges cross the Seine from the Louvre to the *Quai Voltaire*. To the W is the *Pont Royal*, a five-arched bridge by Père F. Romain and Gabriel (1685–89); the last pillar on either bank has a hydrographic scale indicating the low-water mark (zero; only 24m above sea-level), besides various flood-marks.

The *Pont du Carrousel* (1834, but rebuilt in 1939) retains four seated figures by Petitot and Pradier from the original structure.

The pedestrian *Pont des Arts* was built of cast iron by Cessart and Dillon in 1801–03, deriving its name from the 'Palais des Arts' as the Louvre was then called. It was rebuilt in a similar style to the original in 1983–84, having been dismantled for several years.

15 The Musée du Louvre

MÉTROS: Tuileries, Palais-..oyal, Louvre, and Pont-Neuf.

The exterior of the Palais du Louvre, and its architectural history, is described in Rte 14.

On either side of the open *Passage Richelieu*, at ground level between the Rue de Rivoli and the Cour Napoléon, are two courtyards, which will be covered by glass roofs to protect a collection of large sculptures which will be displayed there.

In the centre of the *Cour Napoléon* stands a glass-covered pyramidal structure, 30m square and 20m high, flanked by three subsidiary pyramids, 5m high. Here is the new principal entrance to the *Musée du Louvre*; see plan, p 128–9,which also shows the position of other entrances.

Admission. The galleries of the Louvre are **closed on Tuesdays**, but are otherwise normally open every day from 9.45 to 17.00 or 18.30 (although entrances will close 30 minutes earlier). Certain rooms may be closed in rotation between 11.30 and 14.00.

Hand cameras are admitted without charge, but a special ticket is required for those with tripods; the use of 'flash' is prohibited.

Cloakrooms, where umbrellas, parcels, capacious bags, etc. must be deposited, are in the entrance foyer, adjacent to which, and elsewhere, are lavatories and other facilities. An Information desk can advise on the times of lectures, guided tours (in English), etc.

Catalogues, photographs, postcards, and books (not necessarily concerned with the collections of the Louvre) are also available here, together with lists of casts (bronze, resin, or plaster), jewellery, and prints which may be purchased: the latter may be seen in the **Chalcographie du Musée du Louvre**, with a range of some 14,000 engravings, many of them from the original plates. Numerous casts (moulages) of objects in the Musées Nationaux, and copies of jewellery, of very fine quality, and priced accordingly, may also be brought.

A catalogue listing some 10,000 colour diapositives of objects in the Musées Nationaux is also produced, and may be obtained at the *Service Commercial de la Réunion des Musées Nationaux*, 10 Rue de l'Abbaye (just N of *St.-Germain-des-Prés*), and at the *Service Photographique des Musées Nationaux*, 89 Av. Victor-Hugo, 16e (MÉTRO: *Victor-Hugo*).

The ***Crypte Philippe Auguste** may be approached by following the subterranean passage leading E from the pyramidal entrance. This passes below the *Pavillon Sully* to enter the moat surrounding the foundations of the two surviving walls forming the N and E sides of the medieval fortress, which stood below the SW corner of the *Cour Carrée*. The area was excavated and the walls strengthened in

1984–87, and the moats provided with a ceiling to sustain this part of the courtyard.

The fort established here at the turn of the 13C by Philippe Auguste, which formed a quadrangle 70m by 77m, was extended by Charles V (1364–80), which is depicted in the miniature of 'October' in the 'Très Riches Heures' of the Duc de Berry. This was razed and the moat round the circular keep was filled in in 1528. The outer moats were filled in by Lemercier in 1624, and Le Vau in ,1660.

The *Tour du Milieu* is first reached, which, like the others, shows considerable batter; and then the *Tour de la Taillerie*, at the NE corner of the castle. Beyond are the basements of the twin towers forming the E entrance of the Louvre, and the support for its drawbridge. At the far end of the moat is an entrance to the *Crypte du Sphinx*, in the basement of the *Pavillon des Arts*, providing access to the *Egyptian collections*. Turning right before reaching this, one may enter the inner courtyard to see the interior moat surrounding the circular foundations of the *Keep*, 15m in diameter and 7m high, and which was formerly 30m in height. A passage to the W leads into a vaulted basement room below the present *Salle des Cariatides*, formerly the *Salle des Gardes*.

It is expected that a selection of the extensive archaeological finds (c 25,000) extracted during the recent excavation of this site and of the *Cour Napoléon* will be displayed in the vicinity.

The collections of the ****MUSÉE DU LOUVRE** are divided into seven sections: these and the pages on which each department is described, are listed below.

A. Paintings (p 127); **B**. Cabinet de Dessins _ (p 138); **C**. Greek and Roman Antiquities (p 138); **D**. Egyptian Antiquities (p 140); **E**. Oriental Antiquities (p 143); **F**. Objets d'Art (p 145); and **G**. Sculpture (p 149).

The approximate position of each department is indicated on the Plan of the Louvre (p 129) by the letters A, B, C, etc., but see *Note* on p 128.

History of the Collections. The nucleus of the royal art collection was formed by François I. At his request Leonardo da Vinci spent the last few years of his life in France, (dying at Amboise in 1519). Henri II and Catherine de Médicis carried on the tradition; Louis XIV made some notable additions to his collection of Old Masters, and Louis XVI acquired some important paintings of the Spanish and Dutch Schools. During the 18C the *Academie de Peinture et de Sculpture* (founded in 1648) had a permanent exhibition in six salons of the Louvre, and also held annual exhibitions of the works of its members there. These, during the years 1759–81, were the subject of Diderot's 'Salons' (written at the suggestion of Baron Grimm), which set a standard for all subsequent art criticism. William Hazlitt spent four months in Paris during the winter of 1802–3 copying paintings in the Louvre.

In 1793 the *Musée de la République* was opened to the public, and during the next few years a large number of the most famous paintings of Europe—spoils of conquest by the victorious Republican and Napoleonic armies—were exhibited here; although after 1815 the French government was obliged to restore some 5000 of them to their former owners. Under Louis XVIII, the Vénus de Milo and over a hundred pictures were acquired.

In 1848 the Museum became the property of the State, and an annual grant was made for the purchase of works of art, and these have been supplemented subsequently by private bequests. During the years 1939–45 the collections were dispersed throughout the country, for the sake of security. There have been a number of changes in layout during post-war decades, and the long-drawn-out process of reorganisation continues: see below.

It is very easy to underestimate the size of the *Musée du Louvre*, and while each Department is described in sequence, this is not in any

*The Grande Galerie du Louvre, painted by Hubert Robert in
1796, showing an artist copying Raphael's Holy Family*

way a suggestion that all the galleries should be seen at one visit.
Most visitors will have their priorities and should plan accordingly.

The picture galleries themselves are enough for one day, for, in the
words of that experienced 19C connoisseur and traveller Richard
Ford, 'picture-seeing is more fatiguing than people think, for one is
standing all the while, and with the body the mind is also at exercise
in judging, and is exhausted by admiration'.

It is perhaps worth mentioning here the more important analogous or
supplementary collections *in Paris*, which will interest the visitor to the
Departments of the Louvre itself: the *Musée d'Orsay*; *Petit-Palais*; the *Cabinet
des Médailles* of the Bibliothéque Nationale; *Musée des Arts Décoratifs*; the
Musées Guimet, Cernuschi, and *d'Ennery* (for Oriental Antiquities); the *Musée
de Cluny*; and the *Musées Carnavalet, Nissim de Camondo*.

Among the more important collections in the immediate *environs of Paris* are
those at *Versailles, St.-Germain-en-Laye* and *Écouen*; and further afield,
Chantilly, and *Fontainebleau*, see Rtes 34, 35, 37, 39, and 40 respectively.

Note. Work is in progress on perhaps the most drastic reorganisation
the Musée du Louvre has yet experienced. Many departments other
than the Greek and Roman Antiquities, and Sculpture, or large
sections of them, are likely to be closed for months at a time and many
objects will be moved from their previous positions.

In view of this general upheaval, it has been decided, reluctantly,
not to attempt to describe the contents of each room, but rather to give
some idea of the range of works which *may* be seen *somewhere* in the
building by listing representative items of outstanding quality or
interest in each Department, and in the section devoted to Paintings,
to sub-divide them into their various Schools. However unsatisfactory
this may be, there appears to be little alternative at present, but it is

hoped that by the time the eighth edition of this Blue Guide is published, the dust might have settled to a certain extent and a more detailed description can again be given. Many of the 19C canvases have been transferred to the *Musée d'Orsay* (see Rte 9) and replaced by others at present out 'on loan' in other museums, by new acquisitions, or by those in 'rèserve'. Meanwhile, the visitor will be directed to those Departments, or parts of them, open to the public.

The plan is to separate the various disparate departments, which at present too often impinge on each other, and in the case of the paintings, to distribute them in chronological order, divided into Schools, which may then be studied without the intrusion of works of other Schools or periods.

Certain rooms, such as the *Chambre à Alcôve*, and *Chambre de Parade* retain restored panelling originally in Henri II's apartments in the Louvre; the vestibule adjacent to the former contains 17C boiseries from the Queen's Pavilion of the Château de Vincennes.

A.   Paintings

The department of Paintings is reached by ascending the *Escalier Daru* (on the landing of which is the *Nike of Samothrace* (see p 139) to the First Floor, and turning through the *Salles Percier et Fontaine*, and *Duchâtel* (both ceilings being painted by *Charles Meynier* in 1819) to enter the *Salon Carré*, in which the wedding feast of Napoléon and Marie-Louise was celebrated in 1810, and also with a richly decorated ceiling. The first of these rooms contains two frescoes by *Botticelli* from the Villa Lemmi, near Florence.

MUSÉE DU LOUVRE

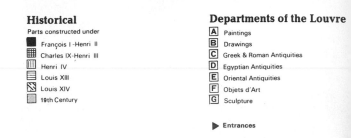

Historical

Parts constructed under

■ François I -Henri II
▦ Charles IX-Henri III
Ⅲ Henri IV
☰ Louis XIII
◩ Louis XIV
▢ 19th Century

Departments of the Louvre

A Paintings
B Drawings
C Greek & Roman Antiquities
D Egyptian Antiquities
E Oriental Antiquities
F Objets d'Art
G Sculpture

▶ Entrances

Historical

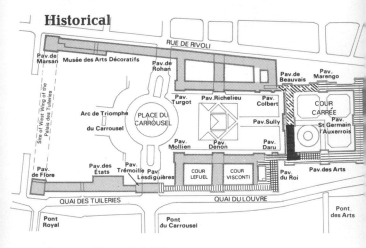

Lower Ground Floor

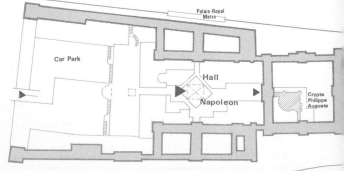

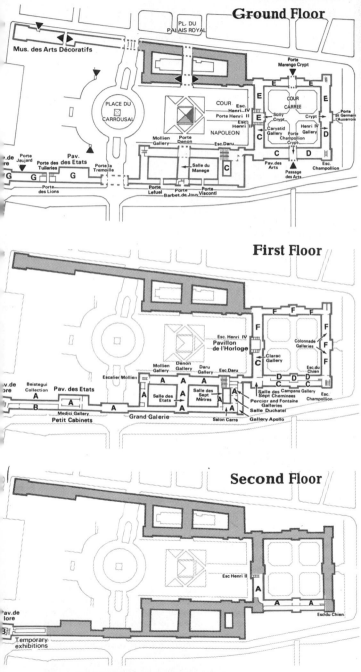

Ground Floor

PL. DU PALAIS ROYAL

Mus. des Arts Décoratifs

PLACE DU CARROUSAL

COUR NAPOLEON

Porte Henri IV
Esc. Henri IV
Porte Henri II
Esc. Henri II

Porte Marengo Crypt

COUR CARRÉE

Porte St Germain l'Auxerrois

Sully Crypt
Crypt
Caryatid Gallery
Henri IV Gallery
Porte Champollion Crypt
Champollion Crypt

Mollien Gallery
Porte Denon
Esc.Daru

Pav. des Etats
Porte Jaujard
Porte des Tuileries
Porte la Tremoille

Salle du Manege

Porte des Lions
Porte Lefuel
Porte Barbet.de.Jouy
Porte Visconti

Pav.des Arts
Passage des Arts
Esc. Champollion

First Floor

Pavillon de l'Horloge
Esc. Henri IV

Colonnade Galleries

Clarac Gallery

Esc.du Chien

Mollien Gallery
Denon Gallery
Daru Gallery
Esc.Daru

Escalier Mollien

Beistegui Collection
Pav. des Etats

Medici Gallery
Petit Cabinets
Grand Galerie

Salle des Etats
Salle des Sept Mètres
Salon Carré

Salle des Sept Cheminees
Campans Gallery
Percier and Fontaine Galleries
Salle Duchatel
Gallery Apollo
Esc. Champollion

Second Floor

Esc Henri II

Esc.du Chien

Pav.de Flore
Temporary exhibitions

French School

14–16Cs: *Girard d'Orléans* ⸦ *Jean Coste*, Portrait of Jean II (le Bon; 1319–64); *Henri de Vulcop*, The raising of Lazarus; *Jean Fouquet* (c 1420–c 1480), Portraits of Charles VII of France, and of Guillaume Juvénal des Ursins; *Jean Hey*, the 'Master of Moulins' (fl. 1480–1500), two panels from a triptych of Pierre II, Duc de Bourbon, and Anne of Beaujeau, and a small portrait of their daughter, Suzanne de Bourbon; *Enguerrand Quarton* (attributed; fl. 1444–66), The Pietà of Villeneuve-lès-Avignon; *School of Avignon*, Three Prophets; *anon.* (Flemish; mid 15C) panel of the Parlement of Paris (note background); *Master of the Annunciation of Aix*, Books in a niche; *Nicolas Froment* (fl. 1461–83), The Matheron Diptych, with portraits of King René of Anjou and his wife Jeanne de Laval; *Josse Lieferinxe* (fl. 1493–1505), Calvary, and Adoration of the Child; *Jean Cousin the Elder* (c 1490–c 1560), Eva Prima Pandora; *Pseudo Félix Chretien*, Portrait of a Man 'à l'antique'; *School of Fontainebleau* (mid 16C), Diana the huntress; *Jean Clouet* (c 1485–c 1540), Portrait of François I; *Toussaint Dubreuil* (c 1561–1602), The toilette; *anon.* Double portrait, possibly by *Daniel Dumonstier* (1574–1646); *anon.* One-eyed flautist (1566); *François Quesnel* (attributed; c 1543–1616), Portrait of Henri III; *School of Fontainebleau* (late 16C), a titillating Portrait of Gabrielle d'Estrées and her sister the Duchesse de Villars; *Corneille de Lyon* (1505–74), Portrait of Pierre Aymeric; Portraits, mostly from the collection of Roger de Gaignières (1642–1715), which included 1096 items, from the workshops of *Corneille de Lyon*, *Pourbus the Younger* (1569/70–1622)—note his portrait of Henri IV—and *François Clouet* (c 1505–72): note the latter's portrait of Elisabeth of Austria, wife of Charles IX, painted in 1571.

17–18Cs: *Valentin de Boulogne* (1591–1634), Tavern scene; *Nicolas Poussin* (1594–1665), Echo and Narcissus, and The poet's inspiration. Among other Arcadian scenes by Poussin are Orpheus and Eurydice, Diogenes throwing his bowl, and the Four Seasons are notable; also a self-portrait; *Philippe de Champaigne* (1602–74), two Portraits of Robert Arnauld d'Andilly, The artist's daughter with Mère Catherine-Agnès Arnauld, and The magistrates of Paris; *Georges de la Tour* (1593–1652), The cardsharper, Adoration of the shepherds, St. Irene weeping over St. Sebastian, Joseph the carpenter, St. Jerome reading, and Mary Magdalen watching a candle; *Louis le Nain* (1593–1648), The guard house, The peasants' meal, and Peasant family, among others; *Lubin Baugin* (1612–63), Still-life; *Sébastien Bourdon* (1616–71), The meeting of Anthony and Cleopatra; *Claude Gellée*, better known as *Claude Lorrain* (1600–82), View of the Campo Vaccino, Rome, Ulysses and Chryseis, and three luminous Port scenes; *Charles le Brun* (1619–90), Chancellor Séguier; *Joseph Parrocel* (1646–1704), Louis XIV's army crossing the Rhine; *François de Troy* (1645–1730), Charles Mouton, the musician; *Hyacinthe Rigaud* (1659–1743), The sculptor Martin Desjardins, Portrait of the artist's mother; *Nicolas de Largilliere* (1656–1746), Self-portrait, with his wife and daughter, Portrait of Président De Laage; *François Desportes* (1661–1743), Self-portrait 'en chasseur'; *Jean-Baptiste-Siméon Chardin* (1699–1779), The skate, and 'Le souffleur'; Boy with a teetotum, and Man with a violin, still-lifes, including Hare and powder-flask, and genre scenes; *Antoine Watteau* (1684–1721), Gilles, the clown; *Jean Honoré Fragonard* (1732–1806), Two figures: Inspiration and Study, Portrait

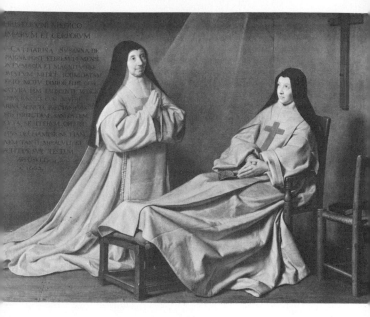

The artist's daughter with Mère Catherine-Agnès Arnauld, by
Philippe de Champaigne

of Marie-Madeleine Guimard; *Jean-Baptiste Oudry* (1686–1755),
Bittern and partridge watched by a white dog; *Louis Tocqué* (1696–
1772), The painter Louis Galloche; *Joseph Silfrein-Duplessis* (1725–
1802), Allegrain, the sculptor; *Pierre Subleyras* (1699-1749), The
Abbé Cesare Benvenuti, Portrait presumed to be of Joseph Baretti;
Joseph-Marie Subleyras, Vien, the artist; *Hubert Robert* (1733–1808),
The Pont du Gard, two imaginary Views of the Louvre, one in ruins,
The Triumphal Arch at Orange, The Maison Carrée and Temple of
Diana (Nîmes); *Élisabeth Vigée-Lebrun* (1755–1842), Portrait of
Hubert Robert; and examples of the work of *François Boucher*
(1703–70), *Nicolas Lancret* (1690–1743), and *Jean-Baptiste Greuze*
(1725–1805), including his Broken pitcher, and Portrait of Claude
Henri Watelet. *Claude-Joseph Vernet* (1714–89), The Ponte Rotto;
Jean-Baptiste Perronneau (1715–83), Mme de Sorquainville;
Jacques-Louis David (1748–1825), M. Sériziat, His wife and son, Mme
Trudaine, The Marquise d'Orvilliers, Alexandre Lenoir, Mme Récam-
ier in a familiar pose, Pope Pius VII, and Coronation of Napoléon I (by
Pope Pius VII in Notre-Dame, 2 December 1804).

19C: *Baron Antoine-Jean Gros* (1771–1835), Portrait of Madeleine
Pasteur, Bonaparte at the bridge of Arcole (1796), Christine Boyer,
first wife of Lucien Bonaparte, Bonaparte visiting the plague-striken
at Jaffa, and at Eylau (with portraits of Berthier, Murat, Soult, and
Davoust); *Baron François Gérard* (1770–1837), Portraits of his wife, of
Comtesse Regnauld de Saint-Jean d'Angély, and of J.-B. Isabey;

The Cardsharper, by Georges de la Tour

Jean-Auguste-Dominique Ingres (1780–1867), Portraits of the Rivière family, and of L.-F. Bertin, senior, of C.-J.-L. Cordier, The Turkish bath, 'La grande odalisque', 'La baigneuse', and the composer Cherubini; *Pierre-Paul Prud'hon* (1758–1823), The Empress Joséphine at Malmaison; *Théodore Géricault* (1791–1824), Officer of the Chasseurs de la Garde, The raft of the 'Medusa', The Vendéen, Equestrian portraits, including horses at Epsom; *Eugène Delacroix* (1789–1863), Self-portrait, Hamlet and Horatio, The orphan at the cemetery, Portrait of Chopin, Liberty leading the people (or 'Les Barricades'), Scenes of the massacre of Chois, Algerian women at home; *Alexandre Decamps* (1803–60), Defeat of the Cimbri; *Gustave Courbet* (1819–77), The wave, Portrait of Pierre-Joseph Proudhon; *Joseph Berger* (1798–1870), Male portrait; *Marie-Guillemine Benoist* (1768–1826), A black woman; *Henri-François Riesener* (1767–1828), Portrait of Maurice Quay; *Martin Drölling* (1752–1817), Kitchen interior; *A.-L.-C. Pagnest* (1790–1819), Portrait of Nanteuil-Lanorville; *Amuray-Duval* (1808–85), Mme de Loynes; *P.-H. Valenciennes* (1750–1819), Views of Rome and the Campagna; *Louis Boilly* (1761–1845), Genre scenes; *A.-E. Michallon* (1796–1822), Landscapes; *Eugène Isabey* (1803–86), The wooden bridge; and *Eugène Fromentin* (1820–76), Hawking in Algeria.

It is possible that one or two of the paintings listed above may have been moved to the *Musée d'Orsay*; see Rte 9.

Flemish and Dutch Schools.

Frans Hals, Portraits of Paulus van Berestyn, and of his third wife, Catherine Both van der Eem; The van Berestyn family, now attributed to *Pierre Soutman*; also by *Hals*, The gipsy girl; *Johannes Cornelisz Verspronck*, Portrait of Anna van Schoonhoven; *Salomon van Ruysdael*, The landing-stage, Still life with a turkey; *Jan van Goyen*, View of Dordrecht. *Rembrandt*: Self-portrait, bareheaded; another wearing a toque and with an architectural background; and a third with a toque and gold chain; a fourth self-portrait is of the artist in his old age (1660) at his easel; Christ at Emmaus, Portrait of Hendrikje Stoffels, Bathsheba bathing, St. Matthew inspired by an angel, The meditating philosopher, and Carcase of an ox.

Albert Cuyp, Cavaliers; *Allart van Everdingen*, Landscape with hunters and fishermen; *Paul Potter*, Horses at a cottage door; *Jacob van Ruysdael*, The bush; *Philips Wouwerman*, Landscape with a cart; *Karel Dujardin*, Italian charlatans; *Jan van der Heyden*, The Town Hall, Amsterdam; *Ferdinand Bol*, The mathematician; *Frans Post*, Tropical landscapes painted in Brazil; *Cornelis van Poelenburgh*, Orpheus charming the beasts, and Ruins of Rome with the Castel Sant'Angelo, etc.; *Willem Claesz Heda*, The dessert; *Willem Cornelisz Duyster*, Robbers; *Pieter Codde*, Dancing-lesson; *Hendrik Pot*, Copy of Daniel Mytens's portrait of Charles I of England; *David Teniers*, The Seven Works of Mercy, 'Les joueurs de Hoquet', Winter scene, Tavern interior; *Frans Francken the Younger*, The Prodigal Son; *Adrien Brouwer*, The inn, Landscape at dusk; *Joos van Craesbeek*, The smoker (? self-portrait); *Denis van Alsloot*, Winter landscape; *Paul Bril*, Landscape with a pond, Fishing; *Gotthard de Wedig*, Still-life; *Roelant Savery*, Polish mercenaries in the forest; *Adriaen Pietersz van de Venne*, Celebrating the truce of 1609; *Jan Brueghel the Younger (Velours)*, The battle of Arbela, Virgin and Child with a garland of flowers, Air and Earth (part of a series of the four Elements: Fire and Water are in the Ambrosiana Museum, Milan), and Landscapes.

Joos van Cleve, Triptych of the Descent from the Cross, St. Francis of Assisi receiving the stigmata, A Dominican offering his heart to the Virgin and Child, and The Last Supper; *Master of the St. Bartholomew Altarpiece*, Descent from the Cross; *Master of the View of St. Gudule*, Pastoral instruction; *Thierry Bouts*, Descent from the Cross, Virgin and Child; *Gérard de Saint-Jean*, Raising of Lazarus; *Jan van Eyck*, Chancellor Nicolas Rolin before the Virgin; *Rogier van der Weyden*, Salvator Mundi, triptych of the Braque family; *Petrus Christus*, Pietà; *Memling*, The Mystic Marriage of St. Catherine, with the donor praying under the protection of St. John the Baptist, Portrait of an old lady, The martyrdom of St. Sebastian, Resurrection of Christ, Ascension, The Virgin of Jacques Floreins; *Gérard David*, Triptych of Mary, Marriage at Cana; *Cornelis van Dalem*, Farmyard in winter; *Brueghel the Elder*, Beggars; *the Brunswick Monogramist*, Sacrifice of Abraham; *Lucas van Leyden*, The card-dealer, Lot and his daughters; *Mabuse*, Diptych of Jean Carondelet (Chancellor of Flanders) and the Virgin; *Quentin Metsys*, Moneylender and his wife, The dead Christ; *van Orley*, Portrait of an old man; *Joachim Patinir* (or *Patenier*), St. Jerome in the desert; *Hieronymus Bosch*, The Ship of Fools; *Lucas van Valckenborgh*, The Tower of Babel; *Brueghel the Elder*, contemporary copy of The blind men; *Antonio Moro* (Anthonis Mor van Dashorst), Card. de Granvella's dwarf, A nobleman in the Cardinal's entourage; *anon*. Portrait of a lady of quality; *Nicolaes*

Berchem, Landscape with animals; *Gérard Dou*, Woman with dropsy; *Gabriel Metsu*, The female toper, Soldier and young girl, and The grass-market at Amsterdam; *Nicolaes Maes*, Bathing scene; *Gerard Ter Borch*, The military gallant, Reading lesson, The concert, Portrait of a man in black; *Pieter de Hooch*, Card-players, 'La Buveuse'; *Jan van der Heyden*, The Herengracht in Amsterdam; *Adriaen Coorte*, Shells; *Vermeer*, The lacemaker; *Adriaen van Ostade*, The schoolmaster; *Michiel Sweerts*, Young man and matchmaker.

The Moneylender and his wife, by Quentin Metsys

Van Dyck, Portraits of the Marchesa Spinola Doria; Francisco de Moncada, Conde de Osuna and Gov.-Gen. of the Spanish Netherlands; the Duke of Richmond; Charles Louis, Elector Palatine, and his brother Prince Rupert, later Duke of Cumberland; Charles I of England; A gentleman with his sword; A lady of quality with her daughter; and A gentleman with his daughter.

Rubens, Kermesse (the village fair), Portraits of his wife Hélène Fourment with two of her children, her sister Suzanne, and Hélène

Fourment descending from her coach, Baron Henri de Vicq—a portrait of the ambassador who obtained for the artist the commission to paint the Medici canvases (see below)—and The Adoration of the Magi; *Jan Fyt*, Still life with game; *Victor Boucquet*, Standard-bearer; *Jordaens*, The king drinks; and *David Teniers the Younger*, Riverside tavern.

Also by *Rubens*, the 21 large allegorical paintings depicting the Life of Marie de Médicis, designed in 1622–25 to decorate the Luxembourg Palace, and executed with the aid of his pupils. The paintings follow a chronological sequence, from Marie's birth in April 1575 to the reconciliation with her son, Louis XIII, in 1619.

Paintings from the *de Croy Bequest* include *Gerrit van Honthorst*, The dentist, and (after Van Honthorst) Portrait of Frédéric-Henri of Nassau; *Samuel van Hoogstraten*, The slippers; *Jan Verspronck*, Young woman from Haarlem; *Joos van Craesbeek*, Spring; *Barent Avercamp* and *Jan van Goyen*, Skating scenes.

German School.

Hans Baldung Grien, A knight, a young woman, and Death; *Master of the Legend of St. Ursula*, Pagan ambassadors at the court of St. Ursula; *anon. painter from Cologne*, Pietà of St.-Germain-des-Prés; *Ludger Tom Ring, the Elder*, Sibyl; also a fine *anon.* (L.C.Z.) Flagellation; *Hans Holbein the Younger*, Portraits of Sir Henry Wyatt, Anne of Cleves, Erasmus (painted for Sir Thomas More), Nicolas Kratzer (Henry VIII's astronomer), and William Warham, Abp of Canterbury; *Dürer*, Self-portrait (1493); *Wolf Huber*, The grieving Christ; *Lucas Cranach the Elder*, Venus in a landscape, A young girl (?Magdalena Luther); *Hans Maler*, Mathäus Schwartz.

Also Studies for the decoration of the Ducal Palace at Urbino, by *Just de Gand (Justus of Ghent)* and *Pedro Berruguete*.

Spanish School.

Jaime Huguet, The Flagellation, and Entombment; *Barnat Martorell*, Four episodes from the life of St. George; *El Greco*, Crucifixion with two donors (signed in Greek characters), St. Louis of France; *Ribera*, St. Paul the hermit; The Entombment, Adoration of the shepherds, and Club-footed boy; *Zurbaran*, St. Bonaventura at the Council of Lyon, The saint's corpse exposed and Sta. Apollina; *Murillo*, Legend of San Diego, known as 'the angels' kitchen' (one of a series of 16 painted for the Franciscan convent at Seville, another of which has been acquired by the Louvre); *Carreño*, Foundation of the Trinitarian Order; *Velázquez*, Mariana of Austria, her daughter the Infanta Margarita, and the Infanta María Teresa; *Francisco Collantes*, The Burning Bush; *Murillo*, Young beggar; *Luis Eugenio Meléndez*, Self-portrait, and Still-life; *Goya*, The unequal wedding, Christ in the Garden of Olives, Woman with a fan, and portraits of Ferdinand Guillemardet, Mariana Waldstein, Marquesa de Santa Cruz, and Evaristo Pérez de Castro.

Portuguese School. *anon*. Man with a glass of wine.

Italian Schools.

14–15C: *Cimabue*, Madonna with angels; *Giotto*, St. Francis receiving the stigmata; an *anon.* 14C Florentine Calvary; *Bernardo Daddi*,

Annunciation; *Bartolo di Maestro Fredi*, Presentation in the Temple; *Barnaba da Modena*, Madonna and Child; *Lorenzo Veneziano*, Madonna enthroned; 12 *anon*. Venetian scenes from the Life of the Virgin; *Simone Martini*, Christ bearing the Cross; *Guido da Siena*, Nativity, and Presentation in the Temple; *Pisanello*, A princess of the House of Este; *Gentile da Fabriano*, Presentation; *Jacopo Bellini*, Madonna and Child with donor; *Benozzo Gozzoli*, The triumph of St. Thomas Aquinas; *Alessio Baldovinetti*, Madonna adoring the Child; *Paolo Uccello*, Battle of San Romano, 1432; *Fra Angelico*, Coronation of the Virgin, and The martyrdom of St. Cosmas and St. Damian; *Sano di Pietro*, Five episodes from the dream of St. Jerome; *The Master of the Observance*, St. Anthony; *Sassetta*, Madonna and Child with angels, St. Anthony of Padua and St. John the Evangelist, and The miraculous deliverance of the poor incarcerated in the prisons of Florence; *School of Fra Filippo Lippi*, Nativity; *Botticelli*, Madonna and Child surrounded by angels, Portrait of a young man, 'The Madonna of the Guidi of Faenza', Madonna and Child with St. John the Baptist; *Mantegna*, St. Sebastian, and Calvary; *Antonello da Messina*, The condottiere; *Catena*, Portrait of Giangiorgio Trissino; *Piero della Francesca*, Portrait of Sigismondo Malatesta; *Bernardo Parentino*, Adoration of the Magi; *School of Fra Angelico*, Herod's banquet; *Pesellino*, St. Francis of Assisi receiving the stigmata, and St. Cosmas and St. Damian nursing the sick; *Signorelli*, Birth of St. John the Baptist; *Bartolomeo di Giovanni*, Marriage of Thetis and Peleus, and Wedding procession; *Ghirlandaio*, The bottlenosed old man and his grandson, The Visitation; *Piero di Cosimo*, Madonna and Dove; *Perugino*, Madonna with saints and angels, and Tondo showing the Madonna and Child with St. Catherine and St. John the Baptist; *Giovanni Bellini*, Crucifixion, Resurrection, and Blessing, Portrait of two men, Male portrait; *Carpaccio*, St. Stephen preaching; *Venetian School*, Reception of a Venetian ambassador in an oriental town; *Cima da Conegliano*, Madonna and Child with St. John the Baptist and the Magdalen; *Jacopo de Barbieri*, Madonna at the fountain; *Marco Palmezzano*, Christ supported by two angels; *Marco Zoppo*, Madonna and Child with angels.

16C. *Veronese's* huge Marriage at Cana; others by Veronese are the so-called 'La belle Nani', a Calvary, and Supper at Emmaus; *Titian*, Lady at her toilet (called 'Alfonso da Ferrara and Laura de' Dianti'), St. Jerome in the desert, Man with a glove, and another Male portrait, Supper at Emmaus, The Entombment, Allegory representing the wife of Alfonso d'Avalos being entrusted to Chastity and Cupid, François I (painted from a medal of the king the artist never saw), Jupiter and Antiope, known as 'the Venus of the Pardo', and Pastoral concert (once attributed to Giorgione); *Tintoretto*, Susanna and the elders, and Self-portrait (1590); *Palma Vecchio*, Adoration of the shepherds; *Giulio Romano*, Portrait of Joanna d'Aragón (the face by *Raphael*); *Andrea del Sarto*, Charity; *Correggio*, The Mystic Marriage of St. Catherine of Alexandria, Jupiter and Antiope; *Lotto*, The woman taken in adultery, Christ bearing the cross; *Raphael*, St. George, and St. Michael, Portrait of Baldassare Castiglione (author of 'The Courtier'), 'La belle Jardinière', Self-portrait with a friend; *Leonardo da Vinci*, Annunciation, Madonna and Child with St. Anne, The Virgin of the Rocks (1482; probably earlier than the similar composition in London), St. John the Baptist (apparently painted from a female model or worked on later by another hand);

School of Leonardo, Bacchus, and the so-called 'La belle ferronnière' (from the chain round her forehead).

A Portrait by *Leonardo da Vinci*, traditionally assumed to be of Monna Lisa Gherardini, third wife of Francesco di Zanobi del Giocondo, hence also 'la Gioconda', or in French, 'La Joconde'.

Leonardo worked intermittently on this portrait between 1503–06. In spite of drastic restoration at different periods, this remains one of the outstanding achievements of the Italian Renaissance. In August 1911 it was stolen from the Salon Carré by a thief disguised as a workman, but was recovered in Florence in December 1913. It has also been claimed that the sitter was Costanza d'Avalos, mistress of Giuliano de' Medici, and that another somewhat similar portrait in a private collection represents Monna Lisa.

17–18Cs. *Caravaggio*, Portrait of Alof de Wignacourt, and The fortune-teller; *Bartolomeo Schedone*, Entombment; *Guido Reni*, St. Sebastian, Ecce Homo; *Domenichino*, Herminia among the shepherds, St. Cecilia; *Pietro da Cortona*, Venus as a huntress appearing to Aeneas; *Carlo Maratta*, Maria-Magdalena Rospigliosi, niece of Pope Clement IX; *Lionello Spada*, Return of the Prodigal Son; *Bernardo Strozzi*, Holy Family; *Salvator Rosa*, Landscape with hunters; *Paolo Porpora*, Still life; *Aniello Falcone*, Battle scene; *Giuseppe Angeli*, The little drummer; *Giuseppe-Maria Crespi*, Woman with a flea; *Guardi*, 8 of 12 scenes depicting festivities organised for the coronation of the Doge Alvise IV Mocenigo, View of the church of SS. Giovanni e Paolo; *Longhi*, The Presentation; *Giovanni Paolo Panini*, Concert in Rome (26 November 1729) to celebrate the birth of the Dauphin Louis to Marie Leczinska and Louis XV, and Preparations for festivities in the Piazza Navona; *Michele Marieschi*, View of S. Maria della Salute, Venice; *Batoni*, Portrait of Charles John Crowle; *Giovanni Battista Lampi*, Count Stanislas Félix Potocki and his sons; *G.-B. Tiepolo*, The Last Supper; *Domenico Tiepolo*, Carnival scene, and The charlatan.

Among the larger 17–18C canvases may be mentioned *Annibale Carracci*, The Virgin appearing to St. Luke and St. Catherine, Hunting, and Fishing; *Caravaggio*, Death of the Virgin; *Louis Bréa*, Pietà; and *Guercino*, The raising of Lazarus.

The undispersed *Beistégui Collection* (donated to the Louvre in 1953) contains an *anon. Franco-Flemish* Virgin and Child; *Master of Moulins*, Portrait of the Dauphin Charles Orlando (1494; son of Charles VIII and Anne of Brittany): among other portraits are *François-Hubert Drouais* (1727–75), Anne-Françoise Doré, his wife; *van Dyck*, A Genoese gentleman (*not* Livio Odescalchi); *Lawrence*, Mrs Cuthbert; *Zuloaga*, Carlos de Beistégui (donor of the Collection); *David*, Gén. Bonaparte, sketched near Rivoli (c 1797), M. Mayer, envoy from the Batavian Republic; *Gérard*, Mme Lecerf, his cousin; *Ingres*, Mme Panckoucke; and *Goya*, The Condesa del Carpio, Marquesa de Solana.

English School.

Ramsay, Lord Elcho; *Gainsborough*, Conversation in the park, Lady Gertrude Alston; *Reynolds*, Master Hare; *Romney*, Sir John Stanley; *Wright of Derby*, The Lake of Nemi; *John Linnell*, Hampstead Heath; *Lawrence*, Charles William Bell, John Julius Angerstein and his wife; *Raeburn*, Capt. Robert Hay of Spott; *Bonington*, The Adriatic; and examples of the work of *John Hamilton Mortimer, Fuseli, Constable*,

Turner (including watercolour View of St. Germain-en-Laye) and *Angelica Kauffmann*.

B.   Cabinet de Dessins

On the SECOND FLOOR of the Pavillon de Flore are displayed a number of masterpieces of *pastel portraiture*, a very small part of the collections of the *Cabinet de Dessins*: also some miniatures.

The **Cabinet de Dessins** itself is not open to the general public, but researchers and connoisseurs (who on their first visit will require a letter of introduction) are courteously allowed to study its superb collections, which include some 1200 miniatures, 30,000 engravings, and 90,000 drawings.

Although drawings had already existed in the Bibliothèque du Roi, it was not until 1671, when Louis XIV acquired the 5542 drawings (in addition to important paintings) collected by *Everard Jabach* (died 1695) that the main nucleus of the Royal Collection was formed. To these were added drawings by Le Brun, Mignard, and Coypel, and by 1730 an inventory included some 8593 works, to which were added some 1300 drawings collected by the great connoisseur *Pierre-Jean Mariette*. By 1792 some 11,000 drawings were listed, and in following decades the figure almost doubled (including the Saint Maurice collection, the collection of the Dukes of Modena, and of Filippo Baldinucci, etc.).

The Codex Vallardi (including a number of drawings by Pisanello) was acquired in 1856, and Jacopo Bellini's sketchbook in 1884, and the collection was further enriched by a number of important donations in succeeding years. Among more recent collections thus acquired by the Cabinet des Dessins have been those of Gustave Caillebotte, Isaac de Camondo, Étienne Moreau-Nélaton, Walter Gay, D. David-Weill, Carle Dreyfus, and Baroness Gourgaud.

Approximately one hundred pastel portraits are exhibited in rotation, among them: *Leonardo da Vinci*, Isabella d'Este, Duchess of Mantua; *Charles Le Brun* (1619–90), Three portraits of Louis XIV; several by *Robert Nanteuil* (c 1623–78); *Joseph Vivien* (1657–1734), the sculptor François Girardon, and the architect Robert de Cotte, among others; *Rosalba Carriera* (1675–1757; who did much to popularise the technique in France), Young girl with a monkey (the model may have been the daughter of the financier John Law); *Maurice-Quentin Delatour* (1704–88), ·Hermann-Maurice, Comte de Saxe, Philibert Orry, Jacques Dimont, and The Marquise de Pompadour; *Jean-Baptiste Perronneau*, Abraham van Robais, The engraver Laurent Cars; *Chardin*, His second wife, Self-portraits, with spectacles, with a green eye-shade, and at his easel.

Other portraits by *Gustav Lundberg, Adélaïde Labille Guiard* (1749–1803), *Joseph Boze*, and *John Russell* (1745–1806) may be displayed, together with a representative selection of 19C pastels; later examples may be seen in the *Musée d'Orsay*; see Rte 9.

C.   Greek and Roman Antiquities

The larger objects are now displayed in a series of rooms on the GROUND FLOOR, extending E from the *Galerie Denon-Daru*; around the *Cour du Sphinx*, and at the SW corner of the *Cour Carrée*. The first section is devoted to 7–6C BC sculpture, including the so-called *Dame d'Auxerre* (c 630 BC), of Cretan origin; the *Hera of Samos* (c 570–550

BC), one of the oldest and best authenticated works of island sculpture, inscribed *Cheramues*; the *'Rampin Head'* (6C BC), with a plaster cast of the equestrian figure (in the Acropolis museum at Athens); bas-reliefs from the architrave of the Temple of Assos (near Troy, in Asia Minor) representing Hercules battling against the Triton, a banquet, a procession of animals and centaurs, etc.

R2 The *'Apollo of Piombino'*, a 5C bronze figure, with copper encrustations—lips and nipples—which was retrieved from the sea near Piombino, and perhaps a replica of a work by *Kanachos*; the upper part of the stele *'Exaltation of the Flower'*, from Pharsalus; the torso of *Apollo* (Miletus; 5C BC).—**R4–5** Fragments of the E frieze of the Parthenon at Athens (5C BC)—the greater part of the frieze, which represents the Panathenaic procession, is in the British Museum; the *'Laborde Head'*, from the pediments of the Parthenon.—**R9** The so-called *'Kaufmann Head'*, after Praxiteles; the *Venus 'de Milo'*, found in five fragments by a peasant in 1820 on the island of Melos in the Greek archipelago and now regarded as a 2C BC copy after a 4C BC original.—**R10** The late Hellensitic *'Borghese Warrior'*, signed on the tree-trunk by *Agasias* (c 100 BC), found at Anzio in the 17C.—**R13** *Apollo Sauroktonos* (about to kill a lizard), after Praxiteles; the *Aphrodite of Cnidos*; the *'Venus of Arles'*.—**R14 Salle des Cariatides**, the oldest surviving room in the palace, was built by *Pierre Lescot* for Henri II, who commissioned *Jean Goujon* to execute the caryatids supporting the gallery at the far end. Other decoration and the chimney-piece at the near end, are by *Percier* and *Fontaine* (c 1806). Mary Stuart married François II in this room in 1558, and here Louis XIV washed the feet of 13 poor men on Maunday Thursdays. It contains *Hermes fastening his sandal* and *Artemis, the huntress*, known as the 'Diana of Versailles', acquired from Rome by François I.

R15 Etruscan antiquities, including five terracotta plaques from Cerveteri (c 530 BC); the imposing terracotta *Sarcophagus* (also discovered at Cerveteri, by Campana, in 1850), on which, as if on a funeral couch, recline the lifelike figures of a man and his wife represented as if still alive and conversing. The woman wears a cap (tutulus) and a small gorget; the man, bare-footed, is draped. Further examples of Etruscan antiquities, including cinerary urns, bronze figurines, mirrors, jewellery, and ceramics, are found in the adjacent **RR16–17**.

RR18–26 Roman portraits and reliefs, and busts—among which those of *Agrippa*, and *Livia* (in black basalt) are outstanding—frescoes, mosaics, cameos, sarcophagi, etc.

R27 (the **Cour du Sphinx**, with a façade by *Le Vau*), on the floor of which is a huge mosaic of *The Seasons* (c AD 325) from a villa near Antioch. On the walls, a frieze from the temple of Artemis at Magnesia on the Maeander, depicting a battle between Greeks and Amazons (2C BC); the *God of the Tiber*, a colossal group found in the 16C.

On the landing of the monumental *Escalier Daru*, stands the **Nike of Samothrace**, or *'Winged Victory'*. This imposing statue of Parian marble, the centrepiece of a fountain, was found in the Sanctuary of the Great Gods, on the island of Samothrace, in 1863. Further excavations in 1950 led to the discovery of the mutilated right hand (in a case to the right), and established the probable date of the statue as c 200 BC. The breast and left wing are of plaster.

FIRST FLOOR Passing through an upper rotunda, we see to the right the impressive wrought-iron gates of c 1650, brought from the Château de Maisons (see p 266), which close the *Galerie d'Apollon*.

The gallery, built during the reign of Henri IV, was burnt in 1661 and rebuilt by *Le Brun*. It is admirably decorated; the central ceiling painting, by *Delacroix*, depicts Apollo's Victory over the Python.

The first room entered contains the *'Treasure of Boscoreale'* a collection of superbly decorated silver objects discovered in 1895 in a fine state of preservation on the site of a villa overwhelmed by the eruption of Vesuvius in AD 79; two silver masks from the Gallo-Roman *'Treasure of N.-D. d'Allençon'*, and the silver *'Treasure of Graincourt lès-Havrincourt'*.

Among exhibits of the pre-Hellenic civilisations: pithoi from Knossos (Crete; 1700–1600 BC), and from Thera and Rhodes (14C BC); marble idols from the Cyclades (2500–2000 BC); terracotta and bronze figurines and painted ceramics (Minoan) from Crete (14–12C BC), and funerary objects.

Other impressive collections of Greek and Roman bronzes, jewellery, arms, utensils, etc., are arranged in chronological and geographical groups, outstanding among which are: ARCHAIC GREEK ART—a *Minotaur*; statuette of *Athene*; a Warrior; a Javelin-thrower; and *Silenus* dancing (all 6C BC).—*Pan* and his syrinx.—mirrors, including one in its box decorated with scenes in relief.—CLASSICAL GREEK statuettes (5C BC); Group of *Lycurgus and the Maenads*; a Stag; *Hercules fighting*; and *Zeus*.—Athlete's head (Greek; 5C BC), found at Benevento, Italy.—HELLENISTIC ART—*Aphrodite fastening her sandal*; an Hermaphrodite figure; and 'Napoléon's cist' (a cylindrical box in which jewels and toilet accessories were kept).—ROMAN GAUL. Statuettes and busts: note eyes; Bull; and Boar; and a Cock found at Lyon.—A Winged helmet encircled by a gold crown; Gladiator's armour; and a collection of jewellery and goldsmiths' work from all the periods and regions covered by other exhibits.

Among the superlative collection of **Antique Pottery** from the 10C BC to the 4C BC, are examples of the Geometric style; Boeotian figurines, etc.; Attic vases found in the Dipylon cemetery (c 800 BC); pottery from the Greek islands; and vessels in the 'orientalised' style; pottery from Corinth; Tyrrhenian amphorae, kraters, and other vessels; and black-figure Attic ceramics; oenochoai and vases in the Attic style, including both black and red figures; coloured terracottas; Attic red-figure pottery (c 500 BC), including a large krater depicting the combat of Hercules and Antaeus, a kylix on which are Eros and Memnon, and an amphora showing Croesus on a pyre; terracotta figurines, and statuettes from Tanagra; figurines of the Hellenistic period; and antique glassware.

D. Egyptian Antiquities

This department may be entered direct from the *Porte Champollion*, on the S side of the *Cour Carré*, named after the great Egyptologist and first curator, Jean-François Champollion (1790–1832), who had in 1826 acquired the collection of the British Consul-general Henry Salt (1780–1827), to which others were added in subsequent decades.

The *Crypt du Sphinx* is first entered, passing the stele of Antef, first herald in the service of King Thothmes III (1504–1450 BC), and other steles of the 12th Dynasty; the crypt itself contains a stele dedicated by Queen Hatshepsout to her father Thothmes (1530–20 BC); a colossal sphinx in pink granite, from Tanis (Lower Egypt; Old Kingdom).

Among remarkable objects in the collection are a colossal statue of Seti II (19th Dynasty) in red sandstone; the limestone cult chamber of the 'mastaba' or tomb of Akhouthotep, an Egyptian dignitary (c 2500 BC; 5th Dynasty), found at Sakkara: inscribed in the architrave above the door are the occupant's name and titles. Within, the walls are covered with vivid scenes in bas-relief of contemporary life in the Old Kingdom, as well as depicting the funeral of the deceased, some of them among the finest extant examples of the art. The offerings of food and drink were placed on the adjacent table of pink granite.

Among smaller objects from the Egyptian collection, are, from the PREHISTORIC AND THINITE PERIODS (4000–2800 BC): schist palettes, for grinding and mixing paints, one decorated with a bull—symbolising the king—pinning an enemy to the ground, and another depicting both imaginary and real animals (giraffes, etc.); a knife from Gebel-el-Arak (c 3400 BC), and small ivory nudes, known as 'concubines of the dead'.

THINITE EPOCH (c 3100–2700 BC). Stele of King Zet, known as the Serpent King, his name being represented here as a serpent; the falcon above symbolises Horus, the god of kingship: it was found near the king's tomb at Abydos (c 3000 BC).

OLD KINGDOM (c 2700–2200 BC). Stele of Nefertiabet (4th Dynasty), in painted stone: she is seated before a table of offerings, dressed in a leopard's skin; three fine columns of pink granite with palm-leaf capitals, one being marked with the name of King Uni (5th Dynasty); the other two, which were taken by Rameses II, are of the same period. Sarcophagus in the 'palace façade' style, found at Abu Roash (5th Dynasty): note the charming low relief in limestone of a girl smelling a flower; finds from the pyramid of Didoufri, son of Cheops, including a red quartzite head of King Didoufri. Small limestone figure of a scribe seated cross-legged, known as the 'Scribe accroupi', remarkable for its lifelike appearance, with eyes of white quartz, and rock crystal. Limestone group of the official Raherka, and his wife Merseankh (5th Dynasty); alabaster and hard-stone vessels dating from pre-dynastic times to the 6th Dynasty (c 3400–2300 BC).

MIDDLE KINGDOM (2200–1750 BC). Limestone lintel of Sesostris III (1887–1850 BC): the king is shown making an offering of bread to the hawkheaded god Montou; sandstone statue of the scribe Mentuhotep; statuette of Sesostris III in green schist, and part of the head of the same king in grey granite; statues in black granite of Sesostris III in his youth, and as an old man. Silver and lapis lazuli treasure discovered in four bronze caskets, marked Amenemhat II (1938–1904 BC), in the foundations of the temple of Tod; a portico with papyrus-like columns (13th Dynasty).

ARCHITECTURAL and colossal stone pieces, including Black granite statue of the god Amon protecting King Tutankhamen (18th Dynasty); the head (the right half eroded by sand and wind) and feet of a huge pink granite statue of Amenophis III (18th Dynasty), with a list of the peoples he subdued inscribed on the base; the sarcophagus of Rameses III (20th Dynasty), the lid of which is in the Fitzwilliam Museum at Cambridge; painted bas-relief of Seti I and the goddess Hathor, from the tomb of the former (19th Dynasty); a red granite fragment from the base of the Obelisk of Luxor (see Rte 13), with four cynocephali (dog-faced baboons) adoring the rising sun, and cartouches of Rameses II; also several statues of Sekhmet, the lion-headed goddess; Hathor capital of pink granite, from Bubastis, where Sekhmet was especially worshipped; limestone statue of a dog; a statue of a Nubian woman from Korosko; and mummy-shaped sarcophagi, including that of Tenthapi.

The **Crypt** contains a number of imposing funerary monuments of the late period, among them a wooden statue of Osiris; also smaller funerary objects and statues—many zoomorphic—of the Ptolemaic and Roman periods. On the ceiling, the large circular sandstone zodiac is from the temple of Hathor at Dendera.

Coptic Antiquities: painted cloths used as shrouds, showing masks of the deceased, outstanding among which is the Fayoum portrait, and the mummy of a woman showing the form of its wrapping, and how the mask was mounted; plaster mask of a child; and colourful Coptic woven fabrics; fragments of mural-paintings from one of the first monasteries, and a collection of bronze statuettes, crosses, lamps, candlesticks, etc.; reconstructed part of the nave of the monastery of Bawit (5–9C AD): note the Coptic icon, painted on wood, of Christ protecting Apa Mena, superior of the monastery.

On the staircase leading up to the first floor are displayed objects discovered by François-Auguste-Ferdinand Mariette (1821–81) in 1850–53 at the Serapeum at Memphis, including the limestone sphinxes which bordered its approach. (Mariette provided the librettist of Verdi's 'Aida' with the plot.) The serapeum itself was the underground burial-chamber of the sacred bulls, and canopic jars held the entrails of two Apis bulls (18th Dynasty). Note also a limestone statue of the god Bes from the temple of Nectanebo, and a limestone statue of the bull of Apis, of the 30th Dynasty (378–341 BC).

FIRST FLOOR. Note the sphinx from Medamoud, and a huge bust of Amenophis IV (who adopted the name Akhnaton), from Karnak.

R 'A': MIDDLE KINGDOM (continued): models of granaries; funerary furniture from the tomb of Chancellor Nakhti, and wooden statue of the same, one of the largest wooden funerary effigies known of this period; statue of stucco and painted wood known as the 'Porteuse d'Auge', a young girl, clothed in a tunic of netted pearls, carrying on her head a trough containing a joint of an ox, an essential of the funerary offering; statuette of a concubine (nude), her thumbs having been intentionally cut off; five wooden figures of girls carrying offerings; the inner case of the coffin of Chancellor Nakhti (note the two mystical eyes painted on the outside); models of funerary boats for transporting the dead down the Nile; examples of blue-glaze ware, including several hippopotami.

R 'B': BEGINNING OF THE 18TH DYNASTY (c 1555–1365 BC): Prince Ahmosis, a seated statue of painted limestone; a wooden one of the priestess Toui (1200 BC); life-size statues of Seny Nefer and his wife Hatchepsout; two statuettes of the scribe Nebmertuf writing to the dictation of the cynocephalic god Thot.

R 'C': NEW KINGDOM: household objects; furniture; musical instruments; games; the toilet, etc.

R 'D': AMARNA PERIOD: limestone bust of Akhnaton, and statuette of the young king with his wife Nefertiti, also a bas-relief of the royal couple; painted limestone head of a princess of El-Amarna; quartzite female torso; objects from the time of Tutankhamun, and Horemheb, and reliefs from the tomb of the latter; a royal head in blue glass paste; and fragments of reliefs of this period.

R 'E': RAMESSIDE PERIOD: (1320–1086 BC): green enamelled schist statuette of the priestess Nacha. Note the wooden statues, among them that of Piay; statue of the scribe Sethi, kneeling, and holding a naos containing a figure of Osiris (19th Dynasty). Note, in the showcase containing jewellery, the gold shell of the Middle Kingdom; a bracelet of sphinxes of King Ahmosis (New Kingdom); a collar with gold pendant fishes; General Djchouty's gold and silver bowl; jewels from the tomb of Prince Khaemouaset, son of Ramses II; the triad of Osorkon II, in gold and lapis lazuli, with the divinities Osiris, Isis, and their son Horus; necklace of Pinedjem I, of gold and lapis lazuli; and Roman jewellery from Egypt.

R 'F': THIRD INTERMEDIATE PERIOD (1085–663 BC): large bronze statues: note that of Horus, the falcon-god, making a libation; bronze sistrum; bronze tablet-cover, decorated in silver, gold, and electrum; bronze figures of kings and priests; a damascened bronze statue of queen Keramana, wife of Takelot II (847–823 BC); bronze statuette of King Taharqa on a silver-plated wooden stand, kneeling before the falcon-god Hemen, of gold-plated schist. A showcase displays 'Sha-wabty' figures, placed in tombs to serve the dead; sarcophagi and other funerary objects of the 21st Dynasty.

R 'G': SAÏTE PERIOD (663–525 BC), and the last native dynasties (525–333 BC): Portrait reliefs; bronzes representing Bastet, the cat-faced goddess of Bubastis; images of Bes, god of recreation, and other deities in the form of animals; protective steles, amulets, and other objects associated with magic and superstitious beliefs, and a black basalt 'healing statue' representing Horus on the crocodiles, covered with magical signs.

R 'H': PTOLEMAIC AND ROMAN PERIOD (332 BC–AD 337): Ptolemaic and Roman sculpture; highly decorated 'Mit-Rehineh' faïence objects; a section devoted to mummification; portrait masks, which covered the deceased; and papyrus 'Book of the Dead', etc.

E.   Oriental Antiquities

This department is concerned with objects from the *Middle East*, apart from Egypt: antiquities from the *Far East* may be seen in the *Musée Guimet* (p 215).

The *Crypte Sully* at present contains antiquities from Palestine, including an ossuary in the form of a house, from Azor (4th millennium), and one of the jars in which were preserved the 'Dead Sea Scrolls' (2C BC and 1C AD), found by Bedouin in 1947; jewellery, glass, and metal objects; the Moabite Stone, or stele of Mesha, king of Moab (842 BC), discovered in 1868 in a remote village E of the Dead Sea.

The 34-line inscription, recording victories over the Israelites in the reigns of Omri, Ahab, and Ahaziah, is one of the most important, if not the earliest, examples of the alphabetic writing which has come down to us from the Phoenicians through Greek and Latin.

SUMERIAN ANTIQUITIES: objects from Lagash (Mesopotamia), and Semitic reliefs and sculptures of the Akkadian Dynasty (2340–2190 BC) from Susa; bas-reliefs of a 'plumed figure' from Girsu (Sumer; 3rd millenium) and of Ur-Nanshe, prince of Lagash, carrying a basket of bricks on his head, with his sons; bronze bull's head, etc.; stele of the

Vultures, commemorating the victory of Eannadu, king of Lagash, over a rival city, Umma; silver vase of Entemena, with a frieze of incised animals and the Lagash 'crest', a lion-headed eagle; stele of the victorious Naram-Sin, king of Akkad.

NEO-SUMERIAN ANTIQUITIES of c 2150 BC: eleven diorite statues of Gudea, ruler of Lagash; a large clay cylinder recording, in cuneiform, Gudea's achievements as a builder; 'turbaned' head (Gudea); goblet belonging to Gudea, decorated with serpents and winged dragons with scorpion tails; alabaster statuette of Ur-Ningirsu, son of Gudea; woman with a scarf, from Girsu; the dog of Sumu-ilu; terracotta figurines (one strangling a bird); late cuneiform documents (3–2C BC); seals and cylinders.

MARI AND LARSA: objects from the temple of the goddess Ishtar (c 2500 BC) at Mari, including an alabaster statue of the intendant of Mari, Ebih-II, and head of Ishtar; mosaic panel showing a scene of war; two murals from the 2nd millennium palace, depicting Ishtar investing King Zimrilim with regal powers, and a·sacrificial scene; two bronzes, one of Hammurabi on bended knee, his face and hands covered in gold leaf: the other of a group of three rampant ibex, with horns interlaced, from Larsa; ceremonial vase from Larsa, with Ishtar and figures of animals; relief of a goddess smelling a flower; statuette of Idi Ilum, prince of Mari; a bronze lion from the temple of Dagon.

BABYLON: alabaster statuettes, including reclining female figures, some with jewelled eyes and navels; bronze horned dragon (6C BC), symbol of Marduk, terracottas (c 2000–1700 BC); and the *Codex of Hammurabi*, a block of black basalt, covered with the closely written text of 282 laws embracing practically every aspect of Babylonian life of c 1800 BC at the top of which the god Shamash dictates the law to the king; 'Kudurrus' or boundary-stones, with inscriptions; statues of the princes of Ashnunnak, a rival state, captured by Shutruk-Nakhunté, an Elamite prince, who erased the original inscriptions and substituted his own (c 1100 BC).

SUSA: pottery and the first attempts at metallurgy from Susa (Mesopotamia; 4th millennium), northern Iran (3–2nd millennia), Tepe Giyan and Tepe Sialk; silverware and jewellery (12–5C BC): note the ornamental vase-handle in the form of a winged ibex (6C BC); brick reliefs from Achemenian times, of lions, winged bulls, and griffins.
    Susa (3–2nd millennia): vase 'à la cachette', with treasure hidden inside it; headless bronze statue of Queen Napir Asu, and ritual scene celebrating the sunrise, known as the Sit Shamshi; vessels in bitumen and terracotta; votive offerings, and toys; monumental capital in grey marble from the palace of Darius I at Susa (521–486 BC); lion in enamelled terracotta (700 BC); reliefs in enamelled brick of a winged bull and a lion, and two warriors; two rhytons (silver and bronze); bronze fibula; alabaster vase; and a bronze cup decorated with an ostrich hunt, etc.; *Charter of Darius*, reporting how he had the raw materials required for building his palace brought from distant lands; friezes of enamelled brick with royal archers in relief; also lions, griffins, and winged sphinxes, from the palace of Darius; sculpted head in stone; bronze lamp with a monkey on the lid, etc.; Luristan bronzes; four large earthenware pots from Susa (3–2C BC); funerary lions; cast of a mural niche from the palace of Shapur (3–4C AD), and Parthian and Sassanid antiquities (3–9C AD).

The *Crypte Marengo* contains lead Phoenician sarcophagi, and the black sarcophagus of Eshmunazar, king of Sidon (5C BC), which although Egyptian in style, has an inscription in Phoenician (cursing the eventual violator of the tomb); also statues from the sanctuary of the god Mithra.

Busts and funerary reliefs from tombs found at Palmyra in Syria, and three divinities in military attire (2–3C AD); PHOENICIAN sculptures, and collections of objects from their great cities of Baalbek (Heliopolis), Sidon, Tyre, Byblos, and Rase-Shamra (Ugarit); bust of the pharaoh Osorkon (924–895 BC); the 'Lady of Byblos' stele (5–4C BC), and an unusual three-sided stele in relief; woman's head in marble (3C BC); statuettes of Jupiter of Heliopolis, flanked by bulls (3–2C); votive hand, and other examples of the same cult; head of a sphinx (Roman; Baalbek); terracotta figurines; gold plaquettes; Syrian glass, etc.; a headless Aphrodite from Dura-Europos; wall-painting of a wild-ass hunt (194 BC); gilded bronze figurines of the god Reshef, from Byblos; sphinx dedicated by princess Itar, daughter of pharaoh Amenemhat II, found at Qatna.

Antiquities from excavations at Ugarit; Cypriot, Mycenaean, and Canaanite pottery; ivory pyxis depicting a goddess of fertility in Minoan style; gold cup with hunting scene; bronze and gold figurines of the god Ba'al; alphabetic tables describing Canaanite epics.

Reliefs from the great ASSYRIAN palaces of Nimrud, Khorsabad, and Nineveh (9–7C BC); carved ivories from Arslan-Tash; a bronze lion, and winged bulls from Khorsabad (7C BC), each with an extra leg, for the sake of symmetry: note the reliefs of Kings Assurnasirpal, Tiglathpileser III, and Sargon with his ministers; reliefs from the palace of Assurbanipal at Nineveh; two bulls from the temple of Arslan-Tash (8C BC).

CYPRUS: 'Vase of Amathus', a huge monolithic cistern (5C BC); statues of the 'King of Cyprus' (5C BC); sculptured heads in the Greek style; a bronze charioteer with silver inlay; gold jewellery and repoussé work from Enkomi; Bronze Age ceramics; Mycenaean kraters, terracotta and painted stone figurines, etc.

The HITTITE, CAPPADOCIAN and ISLAMIC antiquities are not at present on display.

F.   Objets d'Art

The collections of this department may—for the time being—be conveniently divided into the art of the Gold and Silversmith, some examples of which may be displayed in other sections; Medieval and Renaissance Objets d'Art; and French Furniture and Objets d'Art or de Vertu, mostly 16–early 19C.

The display of MEDIEVAL AND RENAISSANCE GOLDSMITHS' WORK may also contain some furniture and furnishings, including a Florentine mosaic table from the Château de Richelieu, a coloured marble table-top dating from the reign of Louis XIV, and one of 13 Savonnerie carpets (1667; usually rolled).

A number of items were originally part of the collection of the French royal house, including semi-precious vessels of lapis lazuli, jade, amethyst, amber, red and green jasper, agate, sardonyx, and basalt, etc. Individual objects include: the crowns of Louis IX (c 1255) and of Louis XV (1722; after his coronation the gems were replaced by coloured stones, according to custom); crown of Napoléon I (after Charlemagne's), never placed on his head; the Crown Jewels retained when the rest were sold in 1887, including the Regent diamond (137 carats), discovered in India, and bought by the Regent in 1717; the 'Côte de Bretagne' ruby, once owned by Marguerite de Foix, Anne of Brittany, Claude de France, and François I, and later cut into the shape of a dragon as a decoration of the Order of the Golden Fleece; the 'Hortensia' diamond, acquired in 1691; reliquary brooch of the Empress Eugénie (1855); and plaque of the Order of St.-Esprit.

Ecclesiastical ornaments from the Abbey of St.-Denis, presented by Abbot Suger; antique porphyry vase mounted in silver gilt as an eagle; rock-crystal vase given by Eleanor of Aquitaine to Louis VII, who gave it to Suger; rock-crystal vase with decorations illustrating Noah in his vineyard, and other vessels; antique sardonyx ewer, mounted c 1150; crystal ewer of the 10C (Islamic); serpentine paten inlaid with gold dolphins (5–6C) set in an 8–9C border; lapis lazuli plaque with figures of Christ and the Virgin (Byzantine; 11–12C); two Byzantine reliquary plaques from the Ste.-Chapelle and the so-called 'Ring of St. Louis' (14–15C) from St.-Denis; silver-gilt statuette of the Virgin (14C), presented in 1339 to St.-Denis by Jeanne d'Évreux; gold sceptre of Charles V; gold coronation spurs, set with garnets and fleurs-de-lys (12C; restored); coronation sword 'of Charlemagne' (? 11C); enamelled gold shield and morion of Charles IX; sword of Charles X; candlestick and rock-crystal mirror presented to Marie de Médicis on her marriage to Henri IV (1600); sword and dagger of the Grand Master of the Knights of Malta (Augsburg; 16C), given to Napoléon in 1797; reliquaries and plate from the chapel of the St.-Esprit, founded by Henri III in 1578.

MEDIEVAL AND RENAISSANCE OBJETS D'ART: four ceremonial mantles of the Order of St.-Esprit; tapestry of the Battle of Jarnac, from the workshop of *Claude de Lapierre*; a chest belonging to Marie de Médicis, with her monogram; a richly decorated late 17C altarpiece; a Mortlake tapestry (1630–35), and 17C wall-hangings in silver thread; the shrine of St. Potentin, in copper gilt, from Steinfeld, near Trèves (13C); other tapestries include an Adoration of the Magi (15C Flemish); St. Luke painting the Virgin (Brussels; 16C), the Virgin in Glory (Flanders; 1485); three hangings illustrating the life of St. Anatole de Salins (Bruges; early 16C); an embroidered cross from a chasuble (Bohemia; early 15C); two porphyry columns from the 4C basilica of St. Peter at Rome.

A beautiful and extensive collection of **ivories**, including the Harbaville triptych (Byzantine; 10C); triptych of the Nativity (Byzantine; 11C); caskets with scenes from the Life of Christ (Metz; 10C), and with mythological scenes (Byzantine; 10C); plaques, including Christ and St. Peter (5–6C), Miracle of the Loaves (Ottoman; 10C), and the Rout of Silenus (Alexandria; 3C); two 6C pyxes; Virgin (English?; 11C); liturgical comb depicting Samson and the lion (Metz; 10–11C); 12C chessmen; a huge ivory altarpiece by the *Embriachi* (c 1400), presented to the abbey of Poissy by Jean, Duc de Berri; 13–14C ivories from Paris workshops, some with distinctive decoration (c 1320–40); and of Spanish and Italian origin.

Among **enamels**: the reliquary of the arm of Charlemagne (Mosan; c 1170) from Aix-la-Chapelle; cross-reliquary given to the abbey of St.-Vincent at Laon (1174–1205); champlevé work from Cologne and the Moselle (12–13C); chalice and paten (Spanish; c 1200); Limoges and other enamels of the 12–13C, including a small shrine, a

Crucifixion, and a Eucharistic dove; the casket of St. Louis, a wooden box with enamel and metal decoration (Limoges; late 13C); enamelled ciborium, signed 'G. Alpais of Limoges' (mid 13C); Limoges enamels with repoussé and champlevé work; and Spanish and Italian enamels, notably a Spanish 14C communion cup.

Reliquaries, including that of the arm of St. Louis of Toulouse (Italian; 1337), of St. Martin (14C), and of Jaucourt (Byzantine 11–12C work with French 14C supporters); a ring containing a portrait of Jean sans Peur, and a ring of the Black Prince; a bronze equestrian statue of Charlemagne (9C); 12–15C metalwork and 'dinanderie'; and fragments of 13C stained-glass from Reims.

Renaissance **bronzes** of the Florentine and Paduan Schools (15–16C), including a Flagellation attributed to *Donatello*, Gnome with a snail (Paduan; 15C), and eight bronze reliefs from the tomb of Marcantonio della Torre, in San Fermo, Verona, by *Andrea Riccio* (1470–1532), and examples by *Bellano*; a collection of French and Italian **medals** by *Pisanello, Matteo de'Pasti, Germain Pilon*, and *G. Dupré*; 16C engraved Italian crystals, including work by *Valerio Belli*; twelve small busts of Caesars (16C); the 'Spinario', a Renaissance cast of the antique original (c 1541); 16C Florentine table, with a bronze fountain (Spanish).

Later Italian and Limoges enamels (15–16C), including superb examples from the workshops of *Poillevé, Jean* and *Pierre Pénicaud, Jacques* and *Pierre Nouailher, Jean* and *Suzanne de Court, Pierre Courteys, J. Pierre*, and *Martial Reymond, Jacques I* and *Jacques II Laudin*, and *Jean* and *Léonard Limousin*, including a Portrait of the Constable Anne de Montmorency by the latter (1556); also a medallion with a self-portrait by *Jean Fouquet*.

An impressive collection of Hispano-Moresque, French, and Italian **ceramics** of the 15–17C, with fine examples of the art of *Bernard Palissy* (c 1510–89), and from the St.-Porchaire workshop. Notable are three intarsia panels attributed to *Fra Vicenzo da Verona* (c 1500), and four ceramic medallions attributed to *Girolamo della Robbia*, from the Château of St.-Germain-en-Laye (16C). Also a series of twelve tapestries of the months, 'Les Chasses de Maximilien', *after Van Orley* (Brussels; c 1530).

FRENCH FURNITURE AND OBJETS D'ART: among tapestries, etc., the Martyrdom of St.-Mammès, by *Jean Cousin the Elder*, and another of an Elephant Hunt (mid 16C); pre-Gobelins tapestries *after Simon Vouet*, including Moses in the bulrushes; a Gobelins tapestry of the Life of Scipio, from designs by *Giulio Romano* (1689); Gobelins tapestry of Sheepshearing (1735); Gobelins tapestries, and bed-hangings from the Chambre Rose, woven for the Condé family at the workshop of *Neilson*, c 1775; Gobelins tapestries representing the story of Don Quixote, *after Tessier* and *Coypel* (c 1785); and 'Chinese' hangings *after Blain .de Fontenay* and *Vernansal* (Beauvais; early 18C); also a screen woven in the Savonnerie after a design by *Desportes*.

Notable examples of furniture include a walnut coffer from the Château of Azay-le-Rideau, in the Italian manner; an inlaid desk belonging to Marie de Médicis; the 'nécessaire' of Marie Leczinska (1729); examples of the ornate style of *André-Charles Boulle* (1642–1732), and other furniture of the period, including a pair of ebony cupboards once owned by William Beckford; French Regency furniture, by *Charles Cressent* (1685–1768); a bureau by *Mignon* and *Dubois*; four armchairs by *Nicolas Heurtaut* (c 1755–75); works by the ébéniste *Jean-François Oeben* (c 1720–63); roll-top desk 'of the King of Sardinia' (c 1770), by *Mathieu-Guillaume Cramer* (died 1794); a flat-topped bureau by *Hauré* and *G. Beneman* (1787) made for Louis XVI's library at Fontainebleau; roll-topped secrétaire in mottled mahogany (1784) by *Jean-Henri Riesener* (1734–1806); a large commode by *Beneman*, from Compiègne; armchairs by *J.-B. Sené* (1748–1803); lacquered corner-pieces and commodes by *Martin Carlin* (c 1730–85), in the Chinese taste; Marie-Antoinette's travelling-case, made in Paris c 1787; chairs by *Rode*, and *Georges Jacob* (1739–1814).

The latter, who usually signed his work 'G. Jacob', had two sons, and their furniture was often marked 'Jacob Frères' until 1804, after which François-Honoré-Georges Jacob—'Jacob Desmalter'—worked on his own for another decade. The latter's son—Alphonse Jacob—signing his work 'Jacob', flourished in the 1840s.

Napoléon's throne from St.-Cloud, by *Jacob Desmalter*, and a cradle for his son, by the same ébéniste and *Pierre-Philippe Thomire* (1751–1843) after a design by Proudhon (1811); the 'Grand Écrin' jewellery-case by *Jacob Desmalter* and *Thomire* after a design by *Percier* (1809); a commode decorated with Wedgwood plaques (1790); and a nécessaire by *M.-G. Biennais* (1764–1843) and *Lorillon*, offered by Napoléon to Tsar Alexander I in 1808; a bed belonging to Louis XVIII at the Tuileries, by *Jacob Desmalter*.

Also preserved are panels of Chinese papers of the late 18C, and gilt and white panelling from the Hôtel de Luynes. Sections are devoted to the display of a magnificent collection of **silverware** (16–18C), including work by *Thomas Germain* (1674–1745); a silver-gilt tea-service by *Biennais* ordered by Napoléon for his marriage with Marie-Louise, and a Sèvres porcelain coffee-service decorated with views of Egypt, made for the wedding, and which the Emperor took with him to St. Helena. Also notable are bronzes from the workshops of *Jean de Bologne* (*Giambologna*) and *Pietro Tacca*; and a superb collection of snuffboxes and watches of the 17–18C, with examples dating from 1746–59, by *Moynat, Noël Hardivilliers* (1752–79), *J.-J. Barrière* (1765–76), the *Drais* family (1769–82), and *P.-J. Menière* (1773–82), as well as representative works from other countries, notably Switzerland, together with more silverware, jewellery, clocks, 15–16C ivories, a Delft tulipière (17C), etc.

Individual Donations are displayed in separate rooms, among them that of ADOLPHE DE ROTHSCHILD, containing a 15C Flemish tapestry of the Miracle of the Loaves; a bas-relief of the Madonna and Child by *Agostino di Duccio*, and a remarkable late 13C polyptych-reliquary from the abbey of Floreffe, Flanders.

The COLLECTION CAMONDO contains four armchairs by *S. Brizard* (c 1775), a chaise-longue by *Delanois* (c 1765); a bed, signed *G. Jacob*, covered with Genoa velvet; six chairs by *Tilliard* (c 1755); a marble clock, 'the Three Graces', attributed to *Falconet* (c 1770), and a collection of Meissen porcelain, etc.

The COLLECTION SCHLICHTING: a roll-top desk (c 1780) attributed to *David Roentgen* (1743–1807), once the property of the Tsarina Catherine II; a child's armchair (? the Dauphin's) by *Gay* (1780); and a portrait of Louis-Élisabeth de Maillé by *Drouais*.

The COLLECTION THIERS preserves a number of Italian Renaissance bronzes, ivory carvings, etc., collected by the statesman, together with examples of Sèvres and Vincennes porcelain (18C), among others.

G. Sculpture

The collections of Medieval, Renaissance, and 17–19C Sculpture are at present displayed in the Pavillon de Flore, entered by the *Porte de la Trémoille* and *Porte Jaujard.*

MEDIEVAL PERIOD. 11–12C: Two capitals from Moutiers-St.-Jean, one depicting the vintage, rare at this period; a marble Merovingian capital recarved in the 11C of Daniel in the Lions' den, from the former abbey of Ste.-Geneviève, Paris; a relief of St. Michael and the Dragon, from Nevers; a Descent from the Cross (painted wood), probably Burgundian (early 12C); a carved wooden seated Virgin and Child (from the Forez; 12C); Doorway from the priory of Estagel (Gard) and a remarkable head of St. Peter (1170–89), with eyes lined with lead, from Autun.

Early French 'Gothic' Sculpture: fragments of a frieze from N.-D-en-Vaux (Châlons-sur-Marne); column-statues of Solomon and the Queen of Sheba from N.-D. de Corbeil (c 1180–90); two historiated spiral columns from the abbey of Coulombs (mid-12C).

13–14C: the Virgin 'de la Celle' (Île de France; 14C); tomb statues of Charles IV (le Bel) and Jeanne d'Évreux, from the abbey of Maubuisson (1372), by *Jean de Liège*; statues of Charles V, and Jeanne de Bourbon, from the Palais du Louvre; two *pleureurs* from the tomb of Jean, duc de Berry (died 1416) by *Étienne Bobillet* and *Paul Mosselman.*

15–early 16C: tomb of Philippe Pot, Grand Seneschal of Burgundy (died 1493), formerly in the abbey of Cîteaux; marble high relief of St. George and the Dragon, by *Michel Colombe* (c 1508); marble tomb (1515–24) of Renée d'Orléans-Longueville, from the Célestins church, Paris; tomb of Louis de Poncher and his wife, from St.-Germain-l'Auxerrois.

FRENCH 'RENAISSANCE': The Three Graces, *Germain Pilon* (c 1535–90); a funeral monument for the heart of Henri II; Diana leaning on a stag, an early garden figure, from the Château of Anet; tomb-statue of Adm. Philippe Chabot in armour, attributed to *Pierre Bontemps* (1505–68); Deposition and the Evangelists (reliefs, c 1545), *Jean Goujon*; effigies of the Constable Anne de Montmorency and his wife, *Barthélemy Prieur* (c 1540–1611); and tomb of Valentine Balbiani, by *Pilon.*

ITALIAN SCULPTURE. A collection of enamelled earthenware from the Florentine *workshop of Della Robbia*; Madonna and Child surrounded by angels (marble bas-relief), by *Agostino di Duccio*; Dietisalvi Neroni (marble), by *Mino da Fiesole* (1418–81); Madonna and Child, by *Donatello* (1386–1468); Bust of a Woman, in painted and gilded wood, and St. John the Baptist as a youth, attributed to the *workshop of Desiderio da Settignano*; Mercury, by *Giambologna* (1529–1608); Monumental portal of the Palazzo Straga at Cremona, attributed to

Pietro da Rho; the Nymph of Fontainebleau, a bronze bas-relief by *Benvenuto Cellini* (1500–72); the Two Slaves, by *Michelangelo Buonarotti* (1475–1564), intended for the tomb of Pope Julius II, but given to Henri II in 1550 by Robert Strozzi; and a bronze bust of Michelangelo by one of his pupils.

GERMAN SCULPTURE. Virgin of the Annunciation, kneeling, by *Tilman Riemenschneider* (1468–1531), of painted and gilded marble; a naked Magdalen, 'the beautiful German girl', by *Gregor Erhardt* (1470–1541), of painted wood.

FRENCH 17–19C SCULPTURE. Representative works by *Antoine Coysevox* (1640–1720), *Sébastien Slodtz* (1655–1726), *Nicolas* and *Guillaume Coustou* (1658–1733, and 1677–1746 respectively), *J.-L.* and *J.-B. Lemoyne* (1665–1755, and 1704–78), *René Fremin* (1672–1744), *Edme Bouchardon*(1698–1762), *Christophe-Gabriel Allegrain* (1710–95), *J.-B. Pigalle* (1714–85), and *Étienne-Maurice Falconet* (1716–91).

Pierre Julien (1731–1804), sculptures of Poussin, and La Fontaine; *Jean-Jacques Caffieri* (1725–92), Corneille; *Augustin Pajou* (1730–1809), Pascal, Mme du Barry, and Mme Vigée-Lebrun; a bronze bust of Lemoyne, his master, and a bust of Pajou by his pupil *Roland* (1746–1816). Among works by *Jean-Antoine Houdon* (1741–1828), a bronze Diana (1790), and busts of his contemporaries, including Voltaire, the singer Sophie Arnould, Rousseau, Houdon's smiling wife (original plaster), Diderot, Washington, Franklin, the Brongniart children, and Mme Adelaïde.

Among other notable sculptures are *F.-N. Delaistre* (1746–1832), Cupid and Psyche; *Claude Ramey* (1754–1838), Sappho; *Claude Michallon* (1751–99), Alexandre Lenoir; *Antonio Canova* (1757–1822), Psyche revived by the kiss of Cupid, and Cupid and Psyche standing; *Charles-Louis Corbet* (1758–1808), La Tour d'Auvergne; *Jacques-Edme Dumont* (1761–1844), Gén. Marceau; *Joseph Chinard* (1756–1813), bust of a young woman; *James Pradier* (1790–1852), Niobe wounded; *François Rude* (1784–1855), Mercury, and Louis David, showing the deformation of his mouth; Works by *Antoine-Louis Barye* (1795–1875), and other early 19C French sculptors of varying merit. See also *Musée d'Orsay*, Rte 9.

16 Musée des Arts Décoratifs; Musée des Arts de la Mode

MÉTROS: Tuileries, Palais-Royal.

The autonomous **MUSÉE DES ARTS DÉCORATIFS, with its main entrance at No. 107 Rue de Rivoli, is housed in the *Aile de Marsan*, the NW wing of the *Palais du Louvre* (Pl. 8;7).

It contains an outstanding collection of French *decorative and ornamental art* from medieval times to the present, and is one of the most rewarding museums to visit in Paris. As with the Musée du Louvre, it has been in the throes of a thorough reorganisation of its extensive collections, which the quality of the objects it contains deserves. Some sections may still be closed, and the provisional description given below is only a rough indication of the future rearrangement and display, and lists only a number of representative objects in order to give some idea of their value and range.

Its history is bound up with the 'Union Centrale des Beaux-Arts appliqués à l'Industrie' and the 'Société du Musée des Arts Décoratifs' (founded in 1864 and 1877 respectively), which in 1882 merged to become the *Union Centrale des Arts Décoratifs*. In 1901 work commenced on the rehabilitation of the interior of the Pavillon de Marsan, then ceiling-high with archives and dossiers from the Cours des Comptes, and the Musée des Arts Décoratifs was inaugurated in May 1905. Today, its inventory lists some 80,000 items.

It is affiliated with the *Musée des Arts de la Mode* (see below), the *Musée Nissim de Camondo*, 63 Rue de Monceau, 8e, and the *Musée de la Publicité* (posters), 18 Rue de Paradis, 10e: see Rtes 26 and 23 respectively.

It also accommodates the *Centre National d'Information et de Documentation sur les Métiers d'Art*, and an important specialised *Library* (over 100,000 volumes, and 1500 periodicals) with a Photographic Service.

A new and enterprising departure is the department selling replicas of choice objects from the collections themselves, or of contemporary design, their reproduction being undertaken in collaboration with Tiffany, and in co-operation with French manufacturers and craftsmen of quality. For the most part they will be porcelain or faïence objects, silver, glass, and jewellery.

Temporary exhibitions, usually in the fields of design and decoration, are held here throughout the year.

Among sections which may be visited by appointment are the *Cabinet des Dessins* (containing some 15,000 drawings), and the *Departments of Textiles*, and of *Wallpapers* (among the latter are the series depicting Views of Naples, and the 'Inca' series of wallpapers manufactured by Dufour, Leroy, Zuber, and others, in the 1820s).

The six main floors of the wing are arranged as follows: GROUND FLOOR: entrance hall, information desk, shop, bookshop, etc.; FIRST FLOOR: Late 19C, 20C and Contemporary collections. Notable is the *Salle 1900*, with art nouveau woodwork by *Georges Hoentschell* (1855–1915), and furniture by *Hector Guimard*.

The SECOND FLOOR is devoted to collections of the Gothic and Renaissance periods, with 13–16C tapestries—among them the 'Woodcutters' (Tournai; 15C)—among other hangings, and furniture; also representative examples of German woodcarving; medieval metal work and Renaissance bronzes; a richly carved retable (Brussels; early 16C); an *anon.* Portrait of a young girl (Bruges; c 1550), and a Portrait of Madeleine de France, Queen of Scotland, by the '*Maître de Marie Tudor*'.

Another section illustrates the arts of Spain, including Catalan paintings by *Jaume* and *Pere Serra*, and the Retable of the Baptist (c 1415–20) by *Luis Borrassa*; also stalls from Rueda (Valladolid; early 16C); and stamped leather panels or *guadameciles*.

The THIRD and FOURTH FLOORS are mainly devoted to collections from the time of Louis XIII to the Second Empire period (17–early 19C), among which will be found examples of panelling of c 1707 from No. 7 Pl. Vendôme, and oak-panelling of c 1735; a ceiling of c 1710 by *Claude Audran* (1658–1734) from the Hôtel Bertier de Flesselles, Rue de Sévigné, and another of c 1715 from the Hôtel de la Comtesse de Verrie in the Rue du Cherche-Midi; also decorative panels by *N. Coypel*, and by *Hubert Robert*; painted panels in the Etruscan style (c 1780), and a number of carved wood brackets, panels, picture-frames, mirrors, etc.

The furniture includes a collection of 17–18C chairs arranged to show their evolution in style; a fine marquetry cabinet of c 1670; a marquetry armoire attributed to *Boulle* of c 1680, and another by *Charles Cressent* (c 1725); and examples in the Chinese taste, together with other Chinoiserie objects. Also chairs by members of the *Jacob family*; a boat-shaped bed by *F. Baudry* (1827).

Among the paintings are a Portrait of the Chancellor d'Anguesseau by *Robert Tournières*; a pastel of Molière; Venetian scenes by *Michele Marieschi*; and Monastic scenes by *Alessandro Magnasco*; Garden scenes by *Pillement*; Flower studies (1614–15) by *G. Pini*; watercolours by *Lavreince, J.-B. Huet, Debucourt*, and *Mallet*; an early work (c 1806) by *Ingres*, The Casino de Raphael at Rome; and Houdon's Studio, and the Gohin family, both by *Louis Boilly*. Note also a series of wax-portrait moulds, some by *G.-B. Nini* (c 1717–80), and a collection of portrait-miniatures.

The Gohin family, by Louis Boilly; *Musée de Arts Décoratifs*

Among the extensive ceramic collections are examples from St.-Cloud, Moustiers, Strasbourg, Rouen (some exhibiting strong Chinese influence—Oriental works of art at that time entering France at Dieppe), Sceaux, Sinceny, Marseille; faïences 'en trompe-l'oeil', and 'fine blanches'; ware from Vincennes, Sèvres, Mennecy, and Chantilly; biscuit figures, and a curious terracotta of a girl playing with her pet dog, by *Clodion* (1738–1814); an important collection of Chinese cloisonné; and Delft, and Meissen porcelain, etc.

Complementary collections, which may be shown with other displays of their period, or 'thematically' and separately, are such diverse objects—usually of very fine quality—as door furniture; bronze appliqués, and ornaments (and also a 'coiffeuse' used by Joséphine at the Tuileries); silverware; mathematical instruments; pewter; clocks and watches; ivory boxes; snuff grinders; rings; cutlery; 'nécessaires'; embroidered purses; shuttles; walking-sticks; paperweights; pipes; plaster plaques; statuettes; glass ornaments; decorative embossed leather cases; toys; and book-bindings.

The third floor also contains space for temporary exhibitions, and the *Jean Dubuffet Donation*; the fourth floor will display furniture and furnishings in the Louis-Philippe taste, and in the style of the Second Empire (Napoléon III). The *Islamic Collection* is now to be seen in the Museum of the Institut du Monde Arabe; see Rte 6. *Charles Le Brun*'s projects for tapestries of The Months, and certain other sections, are not at present on display.

The *Salle Grasset*, and *Salon Barriol*, have recently been inaugurated, containing collections of art nouveau, and 18C furniture, respectively.

Anonymous portrait of mother and child, c 1860;
Musée des Arts de la Mode

The adjacent **Musée des Arts de la Mode**, with its entrance at 106 Rue de Rivoli, was inaugurated in 1985 in the *Pavillon de Marsan*, the NW extremity of the *Palais du Louvre*; see Rte 14 for its History. It had its origins in the *Union Française des Arts du Costume*, established in 1901, since when its collections of costumes and accessories has been very considerably increased, partly due to donations. A proportion has been acquired with the participation of several famous fashion houses—among the more notable names being *Balenciaga, Chanel, Dior, Fath, Givenchy, Lanvin, Patou, Ricci, Rochas, Saint-Laurent, Schiaparelli, Ungaro,* and *Worth*. (Charles Frederick Worth (1825–95), who had been apprenticed to Messrs Swan & Edgar in London, was employed as a ladies tailor in Paris from 1858, and worked independently from 1870.) The growth of the industry was spectacular during the latter half of the 19C; the Bottin directory of 1850 listed some 158 couturiers in Paris. By 1872 this had risen to 684, and in 1895 to 1636 (six of whom employed 400–600 workers each), not including small independent dressmakers.

Its *réserves* at present contain over 9000 costumes and over 32,000 accessories of all types (including a rare collection of umbrellas, Second Empire hats, costume jewellery, fans, shoes, handbags, gloves, and what not) apart from collections of materials, prints, tapestries, laces, embroideries, braids, patterns and pattern-books, etc. And these holdings are being increased continually. The specialised *Library* contains an extensive collection of books on European costume, fashion magazines, photographs, prints, designs, and catalogues, slides, etc., and the building also contains a laboratory for the restoration of fabrics.

It is the venue of important temporary exhibitions of costumes on the 7–9th floors, while there is a permanent exhibition on the 5th level.

17   North of the Rue de Rivoli
Pl. Vendôme; Palais-Royal;
Banque de France

MÉTROS: Concorde, Tuileries, Pyramides, Palais-Royal.

The **Rue de Rivoli**, constructed in 1811–56, and named in honour of Bonaparte's victory over the Austrians in 1797, runs E from the *Pl. de la Concorde* (Pl. 7;7; see Rte 13). It skirts the *Tuileries Gardens* and the *Louvre*, and in its W half, is flanked by uniform ranges of buildings above arcades. No. 107 is the entrance of the *Musée des Arts Décoratifs* and adjacent, at No. 109, that of the *Musée de la Mode*; see Rte 16.

Oscar and Constance Wilde stayed at the Hôtel Wagram, which was at No. 208 Rue de Rivoli, on their honeymoon in 1884. No. 220 was the home of Léo Delibes.

No. 224 is *Galignani*'s Bookshop, established here since 1855.

The first English bookshop and circulating library had been opened c 1800 at No. 18 Rue Vivienne by Anne Parsons, who had married M. Galignani when he worked in London some five years earlier. In 1815 they were publishing 'Galignani's Messenger' a newspaper for the English community, a Guide to Paris with English and German descriptions on opposite pages for the use of the occupying troops, and—until 1852—reprints of English books. The house in Rue Vivienne soon became a club and reading-room for English residents. In 1852 Thackeray, when visiting Paris, contributed to the 'Messenger'.

At the W end, at the corner of the Rue St.-Florentin, stands the 18C *Hôtel de la Vrillière*, or *de Talleyrand*, built to designs by Chalgrin, where Talleyrand (1754–1838) died, and where the Princesse de Lieven held her salon in 1846–57. The design of the *American Embassy* (see Rte 25) was inspired by this building, and completes the symmetry of the N side of the PL. DE LA CONCORDE. At No. 228 Rue de Rivoli, the *Hôtel Meurice*, Gen. Von Choltitz, commander of the German forces in Paris, allowed himself to be captured (25 August 1944), having refused orders to destroy the capital's principal buildings. No. 374 was the home of Mme Geoffrin (1699–1777) from 1750, where she entertained many of the artists, writers, and intellectuals of the day, among them Marivaux, Helvétius, Saint-Lambert, Diderot, d'Alembert, Falconet, Boucher and Delatour.

On the left is the Rue Cambon, where at No. 5 (previously No. 3) Stendhal lived from 1810–14, and where Hubert Robert died in 1808 (at No. 21), the birthplace likewise of Eugène Sue (1804–75). In the Rue du Mont-Thabor, which it crosses, at No. 6 died Alfred du Musset (1810–57); Washington Irving lodged at No. 4 in 1821. The Rue Cambon continues N to the Rue St.-Honoré, leading E, parallel to the Rue de Rivoli.

At its junction with the Rue Cambon stands the church of the *Assumption*, built in 1670 as the chapel of the convent of the Haudriettes and now used by the Polish community. Funeral services for La Fayette and Stendhal were held here. At No. 398 (opposite) stood the house where Robespierre lodged with the cabinet-maker Duplay from July 1791 until his arrest three years later.

Turning E, we shortly cross the Rue de Castiglione, where in the *Hôtel Lotti* (No. 7) George Orwell was employed as a *plongeur*, as described in 'Down and out in London and Paris' (1933). The street leads N into the octagonal **PLACE VENDÔME* (Pl. 7;8),—in fact a rectangle of 213m by 124m with canted corners—a superb example of the Louis XIV style, surrounded by houses with uniform façades, designed by Hardouin-Mansart. Many of the buildings here were erected after Mansart's death, but the façades of all conformed to the original design. Originally called *Pl. des Conquêtes*, it owes its present name to a mansion built here in 1603 by César, Duc de Vendôme, son of Henri IV and Gabrielle d'Estrées.

A number are now luxury hotels (the *Bristol* at No. 3; the *Ritz* at No. 15), or shops. Nos 5, 22, and 28 were built for John Law (who also lived at No. 23 as controller-general of finance); Chopin died at No. 12 (1849); Nos 11–13 are the *Ministère de la Justice* (since 1815); No. 16 was let to Dr Mesmer, the famous quack, in 1778; the composer Piccini lived at No. 17 in 1787.

The centre of the Place is dominated by the **Vendôme Column*, constructed by Denon, Gondouin, and Lepère in 1806–10 in the style of Trajan's Column in Rome. It replaced an equestrian statue of Louis XIV by Girardon, which stood there previously.

Encircling the column (43·50m high) is a spiral band of bronze bas-reliefs, designed by Bergeret and made of the metal of some 250 Russian and Austrian cannon, in which the principal feats of arms in the campaigns of 1805–07 are glorified. The statue of Napoléon surmounting it is a copy (1863) of the original by Chaudet torn down by the royalists in 1814 and replaced at the Restoration by a fleur-de-lys. In 1833 Louis-Philippe put up a statue of Napoléon, which is now at the Invalides. The present statue narrowly escaped destruction in 1871, when a group of Communards led by Gustave Courbet, the artist, brought the whole column—which was felled like a tree—crashing to the ground. Courbet preferred exile in Switzerland rather than ruin himself by paying—as he was ordered—for its re-erection (in 1873–74).

The once fashionable Rue de la Paix (now lined with travel agencies and airline offices) leads N to the *Pl. de l'Opéra* (see Rte 22), crossing the Rue Danielle-Casanova (named after a Resistance heroine; previously Rue des Petits-Champs), with 17–18C houses, where at No. 22 Stendhal (1783–1842) died of apoplexy.

We may return to the Rue St.-Honoré via the Rue du Marché-St.-Honoré, passing the site of a Dominican convent where the Jacobin Club met in 1789–94.

To the E, steps ascend to Baroque **ST.-ROCH** (Pl.7;8), begun by Jacques Lemercier in 1653. Work was abandoned in 1660, but a donation by John Law on his conversion to Rome in 1719 enabled the nave to be completed; Robert de Cotte was responsible for the façade (1735). The church was consecrated in 1740.

The unkempt INTERIOR (126m long) contains monuments of interest. To the left of the entrance is a medallion of Corneille (1606–84), who died in the neighbouring Rue d'Argenteuil (plaque on No. 6), and is buried in the church. In the 1st bay (right) are a bust of François de Créquy (died 1687) by *Coysevox*, and the tomb of the Comte d'Harcourt (died 1666) by *Renard*. 2nd bay: statue of Card. Dubois (died 1723) by *G. Coustou*, and a monument to the astronomer Maupertuis (1698–1759; the first Frenchman to be made a member of the Royal Society, London), by *Huez*. In the Lady Chapel, by *Hardouin-Mansart*, is a marble group of the Nativity by *François* and *Michel Anguier*, from Val-de-Grâce.

W AISLE. On the last pillar of the ambulatory (right) is a bust of Le Nôtre (died 1707) by *Coysevox*. The 3rd chapel (beyond the transept) contains a mourning figure, by *J.-B. Lemoyne the Elder*, of Catherine, Comtesse de Feuquières (c 1700) incorporated in a monument, the central feature of which is the bust of her father, Pierre Mignard (1610–95), by *Girardon*. Diderot, Holbach (1723–89, whose hospitable home from 1759 was No. 8 in the Rue des Moulins, a few minutes walk to the N), Mme Geoffrin, Le Nôtre, Cherubini, and the Abbé de l'Épée (see p 82) are also buried in St.-Roch.—The Organ-case dates from 1755.

The adjoining Rue St.-Roch, where Vauban (1633–1707) died, rejoins the Rue de Rivoli just W of the PL. DES PYRAMIDES, with a bronze-gilt statue of Joan of Arc, by *Frémiet*.

Continuing E along the Rue St.-Honoré, the scene both here and in neighbouring streets of Bonaparte's suppression of the royalist rising of 5 October 1795 (some marks of his 'whiff of grape-shot' may be detected on the front of St.-Roch), we shortly enter the PL. ANDRÉ MALRAUX (Pl. 8;7), with a view NW towards the *Opéra*. The two fountains are by Davioud. To the S the short Rue de Rohan reaches the Rue de Rivoli opposite the arch leading to the *Pl. du Carrousel*.

On the E of the Place stands the **THÉÂTRE FRANÇAIS**, built in 1786–90 by Victor Louis, but largely remodelled after a fire in 1900, and recently restored again.

As an institution the *Théâtre-Français* (or *Comédie-Française*) dates from the amalgamation in 1680 of the Hôtel de Bourgogne actors with Molière's old company, which had already absorbed the Théâtre du Marais. In 1812 Napoléon signed a decree (at Moscow) reorganising the Comédie-Française, which is still a private company although controlled by a director nominated by the government and enjoying a state subsidy.

The vestibule contains, among other statues of actors, Talma, by *David d'Angers*; the staircase and foyer display busts of eminent dramatists including Dumas fils by *Carpeaux*, and Mirabeau by *Rodin*, a statue of George Sand by *Clésinger* (her son-in-law), and a *Seated statue of Voltaire by *Houdon*. The chair in which Molière was sitting when acting in 'Le Malade Imaginaire' and taken fatally ill, is also preserved. The Library may be consulted.

An inscription at the corner of the Rue de Valois (on the E side of the *Palais-Royal*) marks the site of the 'Salle de Spectacle du Palais-Cardinal', occupied by Molière's company from 1661 to 1673, and by the 'Académie Royale de Musique' from 1673 until a fire in 1763.

Galeries du Palais Royal, 1809, by Louis Boilly *(detail; Photographie Girandon)*

Abutting the *Théâtre Français*, the *PALAIS-ROYAL** and its surroundings constitute one of the most attractive and interesting areas of Paris. (It is hoped, however, that the black and white truncated columns by Daniel Buren misguidedly placed there under the aegis of M. Lang, will be removed.) The name Palais-Royal is now applied not only to the original palace, but also to the extensive range of buildings and galleries surrounding the gardens to the N. This pedestrian thoroughfare, entered from neighbouring streets by several passages, is now a delightful backwater and haunt of the philatelist. It played an important role in the Revolutionary period, and among the profligate society of the late 18th and early 19C, was the scene of unbridled licence and revelry, packed with '*tripots*' or gaming-houses, cafés, restaurants, and numerous haunts of lesser repute. Thicknesse, on his last visit to Paris, in 1789, refers to it as in itself 'a great City: it consists of seven theatres, forty public gaming-tables, two thousand *filles de joye*, and every kind of luxury, dirt, and magnificence, imaginable'.

The Palais-Royal proper was originally known as the 'Palais-Cardinal', having been built by Jacques Lemercier in 1634–39 for

Richelieu, who, as chief minister, wished to be near the Louvre. He died there in 1642. (It contained a *salle de spectacle*, later used for operas.) Bequeathed to Louis XIII, it was first called 'Palais-Royal' during the residence of Anne of Austria (died 1666), then regent, and her sons Louis XIV and Philippe d'Orléans. Richelieu's apartments were then occupied by Card. Mazarin. During the Fronde they all had to escape to St.-Germain-en-Laye; Louis XIV therefore disliked the palace and it was Philippe and his wife Henriette d'Angleterre who returned to live there, although the king housed the Royal Academy of painting and sculpture in the W wing, and also his mistress Louise de la Vallière. This was the period of Mansart's alterations.

In 1692 the palace was given by Louis to his brother and his heirs. It acquired an equivocal reputation from the dissolute 'petits soupers' given by the Regent, Philippe, duc d'Orléans (1715–23). Changes were made for his son, Louis, by Constant d'Ivry and Jean-Silvain Cartaud. In 1763 a fire destroyed the E wing and the theatre. The houses and galleries around the gardens were built in 1781–86 as a speculation by Philippe-Égalité, the Regent's great-grandson, under pressure of debt, and let out as shops and cafés, etc. He also built the *Théâtre-Français*; and the *Théâtre du Palais-Royal*, in the NW corner, dates from the same period.

The cafés became a rendez-vous for malcontents, since the police were excluded from entry, and on 13 July 1789 Camille Desmoulins delivered in the gardens the fiery harangue which precipitated the fall of the Bastille the following day.

The name Palais-Royal was changed to the 'Palais-Égalité', and it was used as government offices. In 1814 it was returned to the Orléans family, and reverted to its earlier name; and Louis-Philippe lived there until 1832. In 1848 it was plundered by the revolutionaries, and occupied for a time by the 'Rights of Man' club. During the Second Empire it was the residence of Jérôme Bonaparte; Taine, Flaubert, Sainte-Beuve, and the brothers Goncourt were often entertained there. The palace was rebuilt by Chabrol in 1872–76 after damage during the Commune. It is now occupied by the *Conseil d'État* and the *Ministère des Affaires Culturelles*.

The **Hôtel de Rambouillet**, built on part of the site of the Palais-Royal, and the town house of Catherine de Vivonne, Marquise de Rambouillet (1588?–1665; known in her refining circle as 'Arthénice'), was, during c 1618–50, a famous intellectual centre, Vincent Voiture, Saint-Évremond, Malherbe, Godeau, La Rochefoucauld, the Scudérys, Bossuet, and the Duchesse de Longueville being among its habitués.

The buildings in the *Cour de l'Horloge*, facing the PL. DU PALAIS-ROYAL, were erected by Constant d'Ivry (1763–70), with sculptures by Pajou (left wing) and Franceschi (right; 1875). The façade on the N side, overlooking the *Cour d'Honneur*, was begun by d'Ivry, continued by Louis, and completed by Fontaine, who also restored the E and W wings. The so-called 'Galerie des Proues', on the E side of the court, is the only relic of Lemercier's 17C building. To the N, the *Cour d'Honneur* is separated from the gardens by the *Galerie d'Orléans*, a double Doric colonnade by Fontaine (1829–31), which was restored and cleared of its shops in 1935.

The *Gardens of the *Palais-Royal* are surrounded on three sides by arcades and buildings (by Louis; 1781–86), still occupied by shops and dwellings, altogether a charming and harmonious ensemble. Among residents in recent times were Jean Cocteau, and Jean Marais, while Colette (1873–1954) lived from 1938 until her death at No. 9 Rue de

Beaujolais, beyond the *Galerie Beaujolais* to the N. On the W side is the *Galerie de Montpensier*, and opposite is the *Galerie de Valois*, where at No. 113 Le Peletier de Saint-Fargeau was assassinated in 1793. Nos 79–82 Galerie de Beaujolais, the *Grand Vefour*, was the fashionable rendez-vous of writers in the Second Empire. Earlier, in the same house, Mlle de Montansier entertained the leaders of the Revolution in 1789. No. 17 Galerie de Montpensier was in 1785 a museum of waxworks, founded by Curtius, the uncle of Mme Tussaud. Here (Nos 83–86) Fragonard died in 1806. The *Café du Caveau* (Nos 89–92) was the rendez-vous of the partisans of Gluck and his rival Piccini; other habitués were Méhul and Boïeldieu.

Immediately E of the *Palais-Royal* is the Rue de Valois, with (Nos 1–3) the *Pavillon du Palais-Royal* (1766, by d'Ivry and Moreau); at Nos 6–8, once the *Hôtel Melusine*, took place the first meetings of the French Academy in 1638–43, and the ox sculptured above the door recalls its period as the restaurant 'Boeuf à la Mode' from 1792 to 1936.

In the parallel street to the E, the Rue Croix-des-Petits-Champs, is the entrance to the **BANQUE DE FRANCE** (Pl. 8;7), founded in 1800 and accommodated here in 1811.

The buildings incorporate the former *Hôtel de la Vrillière*, built by Mansart in 1635–38 and restored by Robert de Cotte in 1719. Later known as the *Hôtel de Toulouse* from its occupancy by the Comte de Toulouse, son of Louis XIV and Mme de Montespan, it became the residence of the Princess de Lamballe, murdered in the prison of *La Force* in 1792.

The profusely decorated *Galerie Dorée*, within the Bank, may be visited by those providing suitable bona fides.

The *Hôtel Portalis* (by Ledais; 1750) stands at the corner of the Rue de la Vrillière and the Rue Croix-des-Petits-Champs, No. 13 in which is the site of a house occupied by Malherbe from 1606–27. Vincent de Paul lived in the street in 1613–16, and Bossuet in 1699–1702, at No. 52. Another resident was Mme de Pompadour (1721–64), from 1725 to 1745, before her introduction to Versailles; she was born (as Jeanne Antoinette Poisson) in the Rue de Cléry, a short distance to the NE. Richelieu is believed to have been born (in 1585) in a house on the corner of the Rue du Bouloi, just to the E. Corneille lived in this street from 1665–81; La Rochefoucauld also resided here in his youth.

No. 33 in the Rue Radziwill, on the N side of the *Banque de France*, has an unusual double staircase; while Mansart's projecting angle here, supported by a brackct, is a masterpiece of stonework.

To the NE of the Bank lies the circular *Pl. des Victoires, laid out by Jules Hardouin-Mansart in 1685; the surrounding houses were designed by Pradot. The equestrian statue of Louis XIV by Bosio (1822) replaces the original, destroyed in 1792; the bas-reliefs on the pedestal depict the Passage of the Rhine, and Louis XIV distributing decorations.

The Rue Hérold, to the SE, is named after the composer Louis-Joseph-Ferdinand Hérold (1791–1833), born at No. 10.

Immediately NW is the PL. DES PETITS-PÈRES, with a surprisingly provincial appearance, off which the Rue du Mail leads NE, where Colbert lived (at No. 5, richly decorated), and Mme Recamier reclined (No. 12), while Liszt was a frequent visitor at No. 13 between 1823 and 1878. The composer Gasparo Spontini (1774–1851) also lived in this street in 1803.

On the N side of the Place stands **N.-D.-des-Victoires**, or the church of the *Petits-Pères*, dedicated in 1629 by Louis XIII to commemorate the capture of La Rochelle from the Huguenots in the previous year. Replacing a chapel, it was not actually begun until 1666, and only finished in 1740. Every interior wall is plastered with ex-voto tablets. In the 2nd chapel on the left is the tomb of the composer Jean-Baptiste Lully (1633–87) by *Pierre Cotton*, with a bust by *Gaspard Collignon*; in the choir are elaborately carved stalls, and seven paintings by *Charle Van Loo*.

The adjoining street leads N to the **Bourse des Valeurs** or *Stock Exchange*, built by Brongniart and Labarre in 1808–27, and resembling the Temple of Vespasian in Rome. The N and S wings were added in 1903.

The Rue Feydeau, to the N, built on Louis-XIII fortifications, and the Rue des Colonnes, to the W, retain some interesting houses in an old district through which the Rue du Quatre-Septembre was driven in 1864, before being renamed on the proclamation of the Third Republic.

The Rue Vivienne leads S from the Bourse along the E side (right) of the *Bibliothèque Nationale* (see below), and retains several 17–18C houses; Simón Bolívar lived at No. 2 bis in 1804.

Of more interest is the parallel Rue de Richelieu, to the W, laid out by the cardinal, running S to the Pl. André Malraux. Rossini and Meyerbeer lived in its N half; Grétry resided at No. 52, further S, in 1780. No. 101, with decorative masks in the courtyard, was the home of the Abbé Barthélemy (1716–95), the antiquary, author of the 'Voyage du jeune Anacharsis', and curator of the royal collection of medals, then housed in the *Hôtel de Nevers* (see below). Anthelme Brillat-Savarin (1755–1826), author of the 'Physiologie du goût', died at No. 66; Ninon de Lenclos (1620–1705) had lived there in 1653–59.

On the left, at the corner of the Rue Colbert, stands part of the *Hôtel de Nevers*, built by Mazarin in 1649 to house his library (see below). As the home of the Marquise de Lambert (1647–1733) it was a famous literary salon from 1710, where Montesquieu and Marivaux met.

Further on is a fountain of 1708, and beyond (right) in the SQ. LOUVOIS (Pl. 8;5–6), the *Fontaine Louvois*, by the younger Visconti (1844).

The *Square* was laid out in 1839 on the site of a theatre (the *Salle Louvois*) built in 1794, which housed the Opéra until 1820. On 13 February 1820 the Abp of Paris was called here to administer the last sacraments to the Duc de Berry (assassinated here—by Louis Pierre Louvel—while on his way to watch the dancing of his mistress, Virginie Oreiller), consenting to do so on such unholy ground on condition that the theatre was afterwards pulled down (see Rue le Peletier).—Donizetti lived at No. 5 Rue de Louvois in 1840.
Bossuet (1627–1704) died at No. 46 Rue Ste.-Anne, the street to the W.

For the **Bibliothèque Nationale**, on the E side of the square, see Rte 18.

Immediately S of the *Bibliothèque Nationale* is the Rue des Petits-Champs; No. 45 was the residence of Lully, built with financial help from Molière until 1683; the garret of No. 57 was the home of Rousseau and Thérèse Levasseur c 1754; Mme Récamier (1777–1849) died (of cholera) at No. 8.

Chamfort (1741–94), the author of posthumously published 'Maximes', attempted suicide in 1793 at No. 10 Rue Chabanais, immediately to the W. No. 12 in this street had an equivocal reputation in the late 19C. Holbach entertained Diderot, Marmontel, Grimm,

Helvétius, and Saint-Lambert here during the years 1759–89 at No. 6 Rue des Moulins, further W. Its interior was also the setting of Toulouse-Lautrec's painting 'Au Salon' (1894).

Continuing S, at the corner of the Rue Molière (where at No. 37 lived Voltaire and Mme du Châtelet) is the *Fontaine Molière*, by Visconti (1844; the dramatist is by Seurre, and the figures of Comedy by Pradier).

Molière (1622–73) died in a house on 'he site of No. 40 Rue de Richelieu. Denis Diderot (1713–84) died at No. 39; and Pierre Mignard (1610–95) at No. 23. No. 21, formerly the *Hôtel Dodun*, by Bullet (1715), preserves some of its 18C grandeur; the composer Maria Gasparo Sacchini (1730–86) died at No. 14.

The street ends at the PL. ANDRÉ-MALRAUX (previously the Pl. du Théâtre-Français); see p 156.

18 Bibliothèque Nationale; Cabinet des Médailles et Antiques

MÉTROS: Bourse; Pyramides, 4 Septembre.

On the E side of the Sq. Louvois (with its entrance at No. 58 Rue de Richelieu) rises the W façade of the **BIBLIOTHÈQUE NATIONALE**.

Admission. Most departments of the *Bibliothèque Nationale* are open daily from 9.00 or 10.00–18.00, except public holidays. Foreigners wishing to use the Library should apply to the reception desk with some form of identity, two passport-type photographs and a letter of recommendation (in the case of students, from their director of studies). Information regarding the completion of requisition forms, photocopying services, etc., is freely available. Catalogues may be bought at No. 71 Rue de Richelieu, opposite. Frequent temporary exhibitions are also held in the library.

The Library is divided into the following departments: *Maps and Plans*; *Prints*; *Printed Books*, *Manuscripts*; *Oriental Manuscripts*; *Music* (at No. 2 Rue de Louvois); *Periodicals*; and *Medals* (see below). The *Bibliothèque de l'Arsenal*, a subsidiary collection, is at No. 1 Rue de Sully (see Rte 19).

The *Bibliothèque Nationale* ranks with the British Library as one of the two largest libraries in W Europe. The extensive buildings were erected at various times on the site of the 17C *Hôtel Mazarin*, and include the *Hôtel Tubeuf*, whose brick and stone façade, set back in the Rue des Petits-Champs, was built by Le Muet in 1635.

Formerly known as the *Bibliothèque Royale* and the *Bibliothèque Impériale*, it originated in the private collections of the French kings. Largely dispersed at the end of the Hundred Years War, the Library was refounded by Louis XII, and moved to Blois. During the next two centuries it was at Fontainebleau, and then Paris, before finding its present home in the Rue de Richelieu in 1721. Guillaume Budé (c 1468–1540) had earlier been appointed the first Royal Librarian. It was enriched by purchase or by gift of many famous private libraries and smaller collections (including that of Colbert), and at the Revolution its range was further increased with the confiscation of books from numerous convents and châteaux. In 1793 it was enacted that a copy of every book, newspaper, etc. printed in France should be deposited by the publishers in the Bibliothèque Nationale.

The main entrance vestibule is on the right of the *Cour d'Honneur*. The *Reading Room* (seen through glass doors opposite), roofed by nine faïence domes, seats 360 readers who have access to over 10,000 works of reference. The *Galerie Mansart* to the right at the foot of the

stairs, was formerly Mazarin's sculpture gallery; note his arms above
the door, and the carved foliage and paintings by *Grimaldi*. It is now
used for exhibitions. The *Cabinet des Estampes*, beyond, contains
over 5 million prints. The Department of Music contains over 300,000
works including collections of musical scores, books on music, and
MSS. (among them Mozart's 'Don Giovanni') previously in the Library
of the *Conservatoire de Musique* (see Rte 29).

The *MUSÉE DU CABINET DES MÉDAILLES ET ANTIQUES,
beyond the iron gates on the first floor landing reached by stairs to the
left of the main entrance, and entirely reformed in 1981, is of
considerable interest to the connoisseur and should not be overlooked. The collection, founded in the 16C, but containing objects
known to be in royal hands some time prior to that date, preserves c
250,000 coins and medals, in addition to antiquities of outstanding
quality, only a small proportion of which are on display.

To the right of the entrance is a Parian marble torso of Aphrodite
(Hellenistic period), while in a series of showcases on this and on the
mezzanine floor are selected examples of French and foreign coins
and medals, engraved cameos, jewels, etc. Notable is the 'Grand
Camée', from the Ste.-Chapelle, representing the Apotheosis of
Germanicus, with Tiberius and Livia—the largest antique cameo
known; the aquamarine intaglio of Julia, daughter of Titus, one of the
best glyptic portraits extant; an engraved Chaldaean stone (1100 BC),
found near Baghdad; the agate nef from St.-Denis; the Dish of
Chosroes II, king of Persia (c 600 AD); the sardonyx Cup of Ptolemy;
the 'Patère de Rennes' (a Roman gold dish found in 1774); a
Merovingian chalice and oblong paten (6C), from Gourdon, in the
Charollais; a bust of Constantine the Great, once the head of the
cantor's wand at the Ste.-Chapelle; and a series of ivory chessmen
(11–12C), which were once reputed to have belonged to Charlemagne (died 814).

Other cases contain Renaissance medals and bronzes; Egyptian
terracottas, and painted limestone statuettes; Roman bronze statuettes; ancient arms and armour, and domestic utensils; Greek and
Etruscan vases, etc., including a red-figured amphora, signed Ama-
sis; cyclix of Arcesilaus, king of Cyrene; vase of Berenice (239–227
BC), from Bengazi, and other ceramics; gold objects from the tomb of
Childeric I, at Tournai; ivory consular diptychs, and Byzantine
diptychs; gold bullae of Charles II of Anjou, king of Naples (1285–
1309), of Baldwin I, Emperor of Constantinople in 1204–06, and of
Edmund, Earl of Lancaster, titular king of Sicily, 1255–63; gold coins
found at Chécy (Loiret); a Celtic bracelet (Aurillac; 5–6C); a silver
hoard from the temple of Mercurius Canetonensis (Berthouville,
Eure), including silver figurines and vessels of the 2C BC and others of
the best Greek period.

Also displayed is the so-called Throne of Dagobert, on which the
kings of France were crowned: a Roman curule chair of bronze, with
arms and back added in the 12C by Suger.

The restored Salon Louis XV, decorated by *Van Loo* and *Natoire*, with dessus de
portes by *Boucher*, retains its original coin cabinets.

On the floor above, is (right) the **Manuscript Room** (with more than
130,000 MSS., of which some 10,000 are illuminated); and left, the
Galerie Mazarine, by *Mansart* (1645), with a ceiling by *Romanelli*.
Beyond is the *Department of Maps and Plans*.

19 From the Pl. du Palais-Royal to the Pl. de la Bastille
St.-Germain l'Auxerrois; the Bourse du Commerce; St.-Eustache; the Forum des Halles; St.-Merri; Hôtel de Ville; St.-Gervais-St.-Protais; St.-Paul-St.-Louis; Hôtel de Sully

MÉTROS: Palais-Royal, Louvre, Les Halles, Étienne-Marcel, Châtelet, Rambuteau, St.-Paul, Sully-Morland, Bastille, and Châtelet-les Halles (RER).

Proceeding E from the Pl. du Palais-Royal, with the façade of the *Palais-Royal* on our left (see Rte 17), we follow the Rue St.-Honoré, skirting the N side of the **Louvre des Antiquaires**.

The building, of 1852, formerly the department store of the *Grands Magasins du Louvre*, was acquired in 1975 by the British Post Office Staff Superannuation Fund as an investment, and gutted. Since 1978 it has tastefully accommodated, on three floors, some 250 professional antique-dealers' stalls, open to the public daily from 11.00–19.00, except Monday (also closed on Sunday from mid July–mid September). They can also organise transport, settle customs formalities, and provide certificates of authenticity, etc. Lectures and exhibitions are frequently held there.

A short distance to the E is (right) the **Temple de l'Oratoire**, designed by Clément Métezeau the younger and Jacques Lemercier, and built in 1621–30 for Card. Bérulle as the mother church in France for his Congregation of the Oratory. In 1811, Napoléon assigned it to the Calvinists. The portal was added in 1845.

Against the apse is a monument to Adm. Coligny (1519–72), the chief victim of the massacre of St. Bartholomew, who was wounded in a house now replaced by No. 144 Rue de Rivoli, and murdered in the Louvre, where the king had given him sanctuary. Here stood the *Hôtel de Ponthieu*, where the actress and singer Sophie Arnould (1764–1804) was born.
Further E in the Rue-St.-Honoré, in which are several well-preserved 17C houses, Molière was born on the site of No. 96 in 1622; opposite is the *Fontaine du Trahoir* (rebuilt by Soufflot in 1778, replacing an earlier fountain by Goujon), with its stalactites and shells. The chemist Lavoisier (1743–94) owned No. 47; and Riesener (1734–1806), the cabinet-maker, died at No. 2.
Gallows stood at the point where the street is intersected by the Rue de l'Arbre-Sec, and nearby Card. de Retz was attacked during the Fronde (1648). Gabrielle d'Estrées (1573–99) died at the *Hôtel de Sourdis* (No. 21 Rue de l'Arbre-Sec) a few days before she was to have married Henri IV.

A short distance E of the *Oratoire* the Rue-St.-Honoré is intersected by the Rue du Louvre. By turning right here, and—crossing the Rue de Rivoli, with a view of the E façade of the *Palais du Louvre*—the PL. DU LOUVRE is reached, which claims to be the area where Caesar's legions encamped in 52 BC. Opposite stands the *Mairie of the 1st Arrondissement* (1859), which, according to Viollet-le-Duc, seems to have been intended as a caricature of the adjoining church, to which the conspicuous N tower was added in the following year.
*ST.-GERMAIN-L'AUXERROIS (Pl. 14;1), a Gothic church of the 13–16C, was itself drastically restored in the 18–19C. The most striking exterior feature is the porch, by Jean Gaussel (1435–39), with a rose window, and above it, a balustrade which encircles the

building. The transeptal doorways (15C) and Renaissance doorway (1570), N of the choir, are noteworthy. Nothing remains of the cloister.

In 885, the Norman invaders turned the church, dedicated to the 5C St. Germanus, Bp of Auxerre, into a fortress. A second church was built on the site in the 11C, which, in the following century, being the parish church of the adjacent palace, was found to be too small, and was replaced by the present building in the 13C. The ringing of its bells for matins on 24 August 1572 was the signal for the slaughter of Huguenots to commence, known as the Massacre of St. Bartholomew.

Molière was married and his first son baptised here, and Danton was also married here. During the Revolution, having first served as a granary and then as a printing-works, it became the 'Temple of Gratitude'. It was sacked by a mob in 1831 during a mass celebrated on the anniversary of the death of the Duc de Berry (see p 000), and poorly restored after 1838.

Among those buried in St.-Germain are the poet Jodelle, and Malherbe; the architects Lemercier, de Cotte, Gabriel, and Le Vau; the artists Coypel, Boucher, and Chardin; the sculptors Coysevox, N. and G. Coustou; and the engraver Israël Silvestre.

The INTERIOR (78 by 39m) is double-aisled. The 'restoration' of 1745, mingling the classicism of the 18C with 14–15C architecture, mangled the choir-arches, converted the piers into fluted columns, and heightened their capitals. Fragments of the destroyed rood-screen are preserved in the Louvre. The pulpit and royal pew are fine examples of late 17C woodwork by *François Mercier* (designed by *Le Brun).* Behind the latter is a sculptured triptych with painted wings (16C; Flemish), and in the aisle-chapel opposite is another altarpiece (1519; from Antwerp) in carved wood. The wrought-iron choir-railings date from 1767. On the left at the choir entrance is a wooden statue of St. Germanus; on the right a stone figure of St. Vincent (both 15C).

The outer S aisle is occupied by the *Chapelle de la Vierge* (late 13C), containing a 14C Virgin of the Champagne School, a 15C St. Mary of Egypt, a 13C St. Germanus (of the Paris School), and a 13C wooden Crucifixion. The transepts alone have preserved their 15–16C stained-glass. Above a small door in the *Ambulatory* (S side) is a late-15C polychrome Virgin. The first inner bay is the base of the 12C belfry. In the 4th chapel are marble statues of Étienne d'Aligre and his son, both Chancellors of France (died 1635; 1677); 6th chapel, a relic of a Pietà by *Jean Soulas* (1505); and in the 7th chapel, effigies from the tomb of the Rostaing family (1582 and 1645).

Immediately to the S is the Rue des Prêtres; No. 17 was the site of the *Café Momus* from 1841 to 1861.

At No. 11 Rue du Louvre, leading N from the Rue-St.-Honoré to the small PL. DES DEUX-ÉCUS, are slight remains of Philippe Auguste's fortifications. Off the Rue Jean-Jacques Rousseau (leading SW from here) is the once fashionable *Véro-Dodat arcade* (1822), named in fact after two characters—M. Véro and M. Dodat—and beyond, the Rue du Pélican, which long lived up to its original name of 'Poilcon'.

To the E of the Pl. des Deux-Écus stands the **Bourse du Commerce** (Pl. 8;8), formerly the *Corn Exchange,* a circular mid 18C building, which Arthur Young considered 'by far the finest thing' he had seen in Paris—'so well planned and so admirably executed'. It was remodelled in 1888.

A fluted Doric column abutting its SE side is the only relic of the *Hôtel de la Reine* (later *Hôtel de Soissons,* in the garden of which stock-jobbing took place from 1720), built for Catherine de Médicis in 1572 on the site of the earlier *Hôtel d'Orléans* which had belonged to Blanche of Castile (died 1252). The column may have been used as an astrologer's tower.

This building, recently cleaned, is now the only remaining relic in Paris of the *Halles Centrales*, which by mid 1969 had been moved to extensive modern markets at *Rungis* (c 11km S of Paris and a short distance N of *Orly* airport). Markets had stood here since the early 12C, but the huge pavilions constructed by Victor Baltard (1805–74) in the 1850s immediately to the E were needlessly torn down and demolished by 1974 (with the exception of No. 8, which was re-erected at *Nogent-sur-Marne*).

What Zola called 'Le ventre de Paris' is no more, although the excavated site some distance further E was for a decade known as the *'trou'* or hole; and more recently it has been gratuitously endowed with the epithet *'cul'* de Paris. For the area immediately to the N, see below.

Work on the radical redevelopment of the whole area of **Les Halles** has only recently been completed, and has been much criticised, not only for the overall design, which had been subject to numerous changes and compromises, too involved to detail here. A number of architects took part in the project, among the foremost being Ricardo Bofill, who later left the scene.

The technical problems posed and resolved were prodigious. These included the siting of the important underground railway-station at the intersection of the N–S and E–W lines of the RER system at the bottom of the 'trou'; the provision of road tunnels, and underground parking facilities; air-conditioning plants, skilfully disguised behind the façades of houses; and the erection of new blocks of buildings, which to some extent harmonise with the old.

Certainly *St.-Eustache* (see below) comes into its own (as does the *Bourse du Commerce*), while the restored *Fontaine des Innocents* (see below) is also now seen to advantage. Large areas have been designated a pedestrian precinct—indeed the Pl. Ste.-Opportune has already been styled Ste.-Importune—both in streets to the E and W of the transverse BLVD SÉBASTOPOL, and there has been a notable revival of *trade* in the district, which has, with the improvements in communication, become a hub of activity of all kinds, some of it distasteful.

The much-vaunted **Forum des Halles**, its ribbed and glazed courtyard forming the sunken lid to the 'trou', and embellished by curious pink marble statuary entitled 'Pyègemalion' (sic), by Julio Silva, has been the object of considerable critical comment since it was inaugurated in September 1979. Most of the building is on three subterranean floors, and although partially lit from the central square, and supplied with numerous escalators and lifts, the feeling experienced by many visitors is of claustrophobia combined with agoraphobia. There is little in it which is imaginative. Certain walls, ceilings, and pillars in passages are decorated with examples of pop art; the various levels contain eight cinemas, and some 200 shops.

To the N and E of the Forum are terraces on which mirrored mushroom-shaped pavilions have sprung up. *Gardens* have been laid out further W, and near St.-Eustache, together with an open-air auditorium with a covered swimming-pool below; aquariums and dolphin-pools; conservatories and hanging-gardens, etc., all of which must be seen to be believed.

From the W side of the *Bourse du Commerce* the Rue du Louvre continues N, on the right of which is the **Hôtel des Postes** (1880–84), the main *Post Office* of Paris: opposite, in the elegant *Hôtel d'Ollone* (built in 1639 and altered in 1730), the *Caisse d'Épargne* (or Savings Bank) is installed.

From the 13th to the 18C the *University of Paris* was responsible for the postal service for private citizens, while from 1461 the royal mail was carried by relays of post riders. In 1719 the University lost its privilege and all mail was controlled by the royal service. In 1757 the postal headquarters was in the *Hôtel d'Hervart*.

On the E façade of the *Hôtel des Postes*, facing the N extension of the Rue Jean-Jacques Rousseau (where Rousseau lived at No. 52 in 1776), is an inscription marking the site of the Hôtel which had been occupied by La Fontaine (1621–95) at the time of his death. Nos 64 and 68 in the street are worth noting.

Richard Twiss visited Rousseau in 1776, to ask him to copy out some music for him, and remarked that Rousseau—who at that time was thus supporting himself (refusing to draw his British pension)—had apparently only two books with him: 'Robinson Crusoe', and Tasso's 'Gerusalemme Liberata'.

From just N of the *Bourse du Commerce*, the Rue Coquillière (with a remarkable shop selling kitchen utensils) leads E.

*ST.-EUSTACHE (Pl. 8;8), just beyond, in detail and decoration a Renaissance building, but in plan and in its general lay-out of medieval design, dominates the area.

Begun in 1532, perhaps by Pierre Lemercier, it was consecrated in 1637. The main W doorway was rebuilt in 1754–88 in a completely inharmonious classical style. Both transepts have handsome round-headed doorways (c 1638–40). The N transept is approached by a passage from the Rue Montmartre. The open-work bell-tower ('Plomb de St.-Eustache') above the crossing, has lost its spire. Above the Lady Chapel in the apse is a small tower built in 1640 and restored in 1875.

The church was the scene of the riotous Festival of Reason in 1793, and in 1795 it became the 'Temple of Agriculture'. Molière was baptised here in 1622, and Antoinette Poisson (Mme de Pompadour) in 1721; Lully was married here in 1662. In 1791 the body of Mirabeau lay in state here before its removal to the Panthéon. Among those buried here are Colbert (1619–83), Adm. de Tourville (died 1701), and Rameau (1683–1764). *St.-Eustache* has always been noted for its music. It was here that Berlioz conducted the first performance of his 'Te Deum' (1855), and Liszt his 'Messe Solenelle' (1866). It is the venue of frequent organ recitals.

The INTERIOR is unusual in its striking combination of classical forms with a Gothic plan. The double aisles and chapels of the nave are continued round the choir. The square piers are flanked by three storeys of columns in Renaissance variants of the classical orders. The chapels are decorated with paintings from the time of Louis XIII, but restored. The 11 lofty windows of the apse were executed by *Soulignac* (1631), possibly from cartoons of *Philippe de Champaigne*. The churchwardens' pew by *Pierre Le Pautre* dates from c 1720. The stalls come from the convent of Picpus.

S Aisle. The 2nd chapel commemorates Rameau; by the transept doorway is a 15C statue of St. John the Evangelist; the 2nd choir chapel has a Pietà attributed to *Luca Giordano*. In the Lady Chapel, on the altar, is a Virgin by *Pigalle*; the murals are by *Thomas Couture*.

N Aisle. In the 1st choir chapel as we return is the tomb of Colbert, designed by *Le Brun*, with statues of Colbert and Fidelity by *Coysevox*, and of Abundance by *Tuby*. Above the W door is the Martyrdom of St.-Eustache, by *Simon Vouet*.

The Rue de Turbigo leads NE from *St.-Eustache* towards the *Pl. de la République*, soon reaching the Rue Étienne-Marcel, in which, to the left (at No. 20), rises the *Tour de Jean-sans-Peur*, a graceful defensive tower of c 1400 once incorporated in the *Hôtel de Bourgogne*. Part of this mansion (see No. 29) was used from 1548 until the turn of the 18C as a theatre, where Corneille's 'Le Cid', and Racine's 'Andromaque' and 'Phèdre' were performed.

The next street to the E is the old Rue St.-Denis.

At No. 135, in its N section, an inscription indicates the former position of the *Porte St.-Denis* or *Porte aux Peintres*, a gateway in the *Walls* of Philippe Auguste. At the corner of the Rue Tiquetonne (then the Rue du Petit-Lion), stood the old shop bearing the sign of the 'Cat and Racket', celebrated in Balzac's story 'La Maison du Chat qui Pelote'. On No. 142 is the *Fontaine de la Reine* (1730).

Walking S down the street, where at No. 133 are some statues from the medieval *Hospital of St.-Jacques* (on this site), we reach (left) **St.-Leu-St.-Gilles**, built in 1235, and first rebuilt after 1319. The nave is of this date; the aisles were added in the 16C; the choir, still partly Gothic, in 1611 (and reconstructed in 1858–61 to make way for the adjacent boulevard). The façade and windows were remodelled in 1727, and a crypt excavated in 1780. The church contains three Nottingham alabaster reliefs (in the sacristy entrance) and a sculptured group of St. Anne and the Virgin, perhaps from Écouen, by *Jean Bullant* (2nd S chapel). The organ gallery is by *Nicolas Raimbert* (1659).

Marivaux (1688–1763) was born on the site of No. 106 Rue Rambuteau, two streets further S.

Continuing S in the Rue St.-Denis, we reach the small SQ. DES INNOCENTS, on the site of the medieval *Cimetière des Innocents*, the main burial ground of Paris until 1785, when the remains, probably including those of La Fontaine, were transferred to the *Catacombs* (see Rte 7). According to Pantagruel, 'the grave-digging rogues of *St. Innocent* used in frostie nights to warme their bums with dead mens bones'. Traces of the arches of the cemetery galleries are still to be seen on Nos 11 and 13 in the Rue des Innocents.

The charming Renaissance *Fontaine des Innocents** (1548; recently restored) was originally erected in the neighbouring Rue St.-Denis by Pierre Lescot, with bas-reliefs by Jean Goujon (now in the Louvre). It was remodelled and set up here by Payet c 1788, the S side (for it had earlier abutted a building) being decorated by Pajou.

To the S is the Rue de la Ferronnerie, where, in front of No. 11, Henri IV was assassinated by Ravaillac in 1610.

No. 33 Rue St.-Denis has an 18C sign, 'Au Mortier d'Argent'. The playwright and librettist Eugène Scribe (1791–1861) was born at No. 32.

Across the ugly BLVD DE SÉBASTOPOL (left) is the narrow Rue Quincampoix (parallel to the E), one of the oldest streets in Paris (and still, apparently, partly devoted to the oldest profession), although most of the houses date from the 17–18C. At No. 43 John Law (1671–1729, in Venice), the celebrated Scottish financier, established in 1716 his Mississippi bank which, after frenzied speculation, obstructed by jealous rivals, ended in a bankruptcy (1720) even more catastrophic than the 'South Sea Bubble'. No. 54 (demolished) was the Cabaret de l'Épee de Bois, where the *Royal Academy of the Dance* had its origins in 1658. After the creation of Law's bank the wealthy 'Mississipiens' made it their club, when it was frequented by Louis Racine and Marivaux. Nos 10, 12, and 14 (further S) have rococo façades: No. 36 is also worth noting.

To the E opens the PL. EDMOND-MICHELET (or *Sq. de la Reynie*), diagonally across which we obtain a view of the *Centre Beaubourg* on

approaching the *Piazza Beaubourg*, flanked to the W by the Rue
St.-Martin.

At No. 168 in this street (then No. 96) was born Gérard de Nerval (1808–55). At
the junction of the Rue Bernard-de-Clairvaux, leading E into this recently
re-developed *Quartier de l'Horloge*, and the Rue Brantôme, is an imaginative
modern *Clock*, with automata, by Jacques Monestier (1979). For the **Centre
Beaubourg** or **Pompidou**, see Rte 20.

Immediately S of the *Centre*, is the PL. IGOR-STRAVINSKY, flanked by
relics of the Rue Brisemiche, in which Pascal's family once lived.

Here rises **ST.-MERRI**, built in the Flamboyant style (1515–52) on
the site of at least two older churches, which covered the grave of St.
Médéric of Autun (died c 700). In 1796–1801 it was called the 'Temple
of Commerce' (much of which in this area, from the 14C at least, was
of the carnal kind). The W front is notable for its rich decoration, but
the statues are mostly poor replacements of 1842. The NW turret
contains the oldest bell in Paris (1331); the SW tower lost its top storey
in a fire. The nave has a double aisle on the right; a single, on the left.
The pulpit was designed by *Michel-Ange Slodtz* (1753), who also
altered the choir. The organ dates from 1567; Saint-Saëns was
organist here. The remaining stained-glass windows, contemporary
with the church, are good.

In the *right aisle*, the 1st outer chapel preserves remains of the 13C
church; further on is a large chapel by *Boffrand* (1743–44), with
decorations by *Paul-Ambroise Slodtz*. In the *left aisle*, the 1st chapel
contains a 15C tabernacle; the 3rd a Pietà attributed to *Nicolas
Legendre* (c 1670); the 4th, a painting by *Coypel* (1661). From the 5th,
a staircase descends to the crypt (1515), which has grotesque corbels,
and the tombstone of Guillaume le Sueur (died 1530). In the *N
Transept* is St. Merri delivering prisoners, by *Simon Vouet*. Among
other paintings are a late-16C work of the Fontainebleau School (S of
the *Lady Chapel*) of St. Geneviève guarding her flocks, with Paris in
the background.

The quarter round *St.-Merri*, with its narrow and picturesque alleys, retains
several characteristic old houses, which have survived the rage for demolition
during the Halles-Beaubourg redevelopment scheme.

Traditionally Boccaccio (1313–75), whose mother was French, was born near the
junction of the adjacent Rue des Lombards and the Rue St.-Martin (in which note
the 17C bas-relief of the Annunciation on No. 89). No. 14 in the Rue des
Lombards (now a restaurant) preserves in its basement the vaulted chapel of the
former women's prison of St.-Merri. This ancient street is continued to the E by
the Rue de la Verrerie, in which both Boucher and Bossuet were born (on the
sites of Nos 60 and 83 respectively).

We regain the Rue de Rivoli just S of St.-Merri. This E section of the
street was laid out under Napoléon III to allow a rapid access for
troops to the *Hôtel de Ville* in case of emergency.

In the centre of the SQ. ST.-JACQUES rises the only relic of the church
of *St. Jacques-la-Boucherie* (demolished 1797), the Flamboyant
Gothic **Tour St.-Jacques**, dating from 1508–22, and now serving as a
meteorological station. It was used as a shot-tower after 1836, until
'restored' in 1858 by Ballu.

Among its 19C statues is one of Pascal, who in 1642 verified here (or on the tower
of St.-Jacques-du-Haut-Pas) the barometric experiments he had set up on the
Puy de Dôme.

Adjoining, to the SW, is the PL. DU CHÂTELET (Pl. 14;2), bounded by
the Seine, here crossed by the *Pont au Change*: see Rte 1.

The square is named after the vanished *Grand Châtelet*, a fortress gateway leading to the Cité, once the headquarters of the Provost of Paris and the Guild of Notaries. It was begun in 1130, and demolished between 1802–10. Both François Villon and Clément Marot—in 1448 and 1526 respectively—were confined here. There is a plan of the fort on the front of the *Chambres des Notaires* on the N side of the square.

On the E side is the *Théâtre de la Ville*, restored after a fashion and reopened in 1980, only to be severely damaged by fire in 1982. To the W is the *Théâtre du Châtelet* (1862), in which the Communards were court-martialled in 1871. Jacques-Louis David (1748–1825), the artist, was born in a house which stood on the S side of this site. In the centre of the square is the *Fontaine du Châtelet* (or de la Victoire, or du Palmier) dating from 1808 and 1858. An inscription indicates the position of the 'Parloir aux Bourgeois', the seat of the municipality of Paris from the 13C until 1357 (see below).

From the N side of the Square, the Avenue Victoria (named in honour of Queen Victoria's visit to Paris in 1855) leads E to the **Pl. de l'Hôtel-de-Ville** (Pl. 14;2), known until the Revolution of 1830 as the PL. DE GRÈVE, for here, since the 11C, ships had moored on the strand, or *grève*.

This square was the usual site for public executions: among the more famous of which (many incredibly barbarous) were those of the Comte de St.-Pol (1475), Constable of France, on the orders of Louis XI; Briquemont and Cavagnes, the Huguenot leaders (1572; among many other Protestants); the Comte de Montgomery (1574), captured at the siege of Domfront and formerly captain in the Scottish Guard; François Ravaillac, the assassin of Henri IV (1610); Eléonore Galigaï (the favourite of Marie de Médicis), executed for sorcery in 1617; the Marquise de Brinvilliers (1676), poisoner; the highwayman Cartouche (1721); and Damiens (1757), for attempting to murder Louis XV. In 1789, Foullon (controller-general of finance) and his son-in-law Bertier were hanged here by the Revolutionary mob. In 1795 Fouquier-Tinville suffered the same fate as his countless victims. Louvel, who assassinated the Duc de Berry, was executed here in 1820.

It was often a rendez-vous for unemployed or dissatisfied workers, who were said to 'faire grève', which came to mean 'to go on strike'.

The **HÔTEL DE VILLE**, on the E side of the Square, stands on the site of its historic predecessor, begun c 1532, and burnt down by the Communards in 1871. This caricature replica, in the style of the French Renaissance, was erected (on a larger scale) in 1874–84 from the plans of Ballu and Deperthes.

Its over-decorated façades are embellished with statues of eminent Frenchmen: its interior is also lavishly adorned in the official taste in architecture of the period, with sculpture, elaborate carvings, mural paintings, etc., including *Puvis de Chavannes'* The Seasons.

At No. 29 Rue de Rivoli, on the N side of the building, is the Municipal Tourist Office.

In 1264 Louis IX created the first municipal authority in Paris by allowing the merchants to elect magistrates ('échevins'), led by the 'prévôt des marchands', who was also head of the 'Hanse des marchands de l'eau'. This merchant guild, which had the monopoly of the traffic on the Seine, Marne, Oise, and Yonne, took as their emblem a ship, a device which still graces the arms of the city. Their first meeting-place was known simply as the 'Parlouer aux Bourgeois'; later they met at the *Grand-Châtelet* itself; and finally, in 1357, the Provost Étienne Marcel bought the 'Maison aux Piliers' or 'Maison du Dauphin', a mansion in the *Pl. de Grève*, for their assemblies. In 1532 plans for an imposing new building were adopted, but work was stopped at the second floor, and the new designs approved by Henri II in 1549 were not completed until 1628.

In 1789, the 300 electors nominated by the districts of Paris met there. On 17 July, Louis XVI received the tricolour cockade from the hands of Jean Sylvain Bailly, the Mayor. On 10 August 1792, the 172 commissaries elected by Paris gave the signal for a general insurrection. In 1794 Robespierre took refuge here, but was arrested on 27 July and, his jaw smashed by a bullet, dragged to the Conciergerie. In 1805 it became the seat of the Préfet de la Seine and his council, and was the scene of numerous official celebrations (on Napoléon's marriage to Marie-Louise, etc.).

The Swiss Guards put up a stout defence of the building during the stormy days of 1830. In 1848 it became the seat of Louis Blanc's provisional government, and witnessed the arrest of the revolutionary agitators Armand Barbès and Louis-Auguste Blanqui. Verlaine was employed here in the mid-1860s. The Third Republic was proclaimed here in 1870 (4 September), and in the following March, the Commune. On 24 May 1871 the building was evacuated before being set ablaze by its defenders.

In 1944 the *Hôtel de Ville* was a focus of opposition to the occupying forces by the Resistance movement, who by 19 August had established themselves in the building, repelling German counter-attacks until relieved by the arrival of Gen. Leclerc's division five days later.

From the NE corner of the *Hôtel de Ville*, we may cross the Rue de Rivoli to the **Temple des Billettes**, at No. 22 Rue des Archives, which is conveniently approached from here. It was built in 1756 for the Carmelites, but since 1812 has been used as a Lutheran church. Abutting it to the N, the *cloister*, the only medieval example in Paris, is a relic of an older convent (1427).

The Rue de Rivoli, and its E extension, the Rue St.-Antoine, split the ancient **Marais** district into two unequal sections; the smaller, to the S, is described below; for the area to the N, see Rte 21.

To the E of the *Hôtel de Ville*, between two of its annexes, lies the PL. ST.-GERVAIS, with its elm tree, a reminder of the famous elm of St.-Gervais, beneath which justice used to be administered; the proverbial expression for waiting for Doomsday is, ironically, 'Attendre sous l'orme' (the elm). This was one of the first inhabited areas on the Right Bank, and the Rue François-Miron follows the course of a Roman road which led from Lutetia to Senlis.

To the E it is dominated by *ST.-GERVAIS-ST.-PROTAIS (Pl. 15;1–3), which, founded in the 6C, dates in its present form from the rebuildings of 1494–1578 (choir and transepts) and 1600–57 (nave, chapels, and tower).

The original plans are attributed to Martin Chambiges, whose work was continued by his son Pierre. The lower stages of the tower are an early 15C survival. The façade (1616–21), by Clément Métezeau and (probably) Salomon de Brosse, is thought to be the earliest example in France of the superimposition of the three classic orders—Doric, Ionic, and Corinthian. In 1795 the church was converted into a 'Temple of Youth'. Bossuet preached here; Mme de Sévigné was married here (1644); and Philippe de Champaigne (1602–74), Scarron (1610–60), and Crébillon the Elder (1674–1762) are buried here.

François Couperin (1668–1733) and seven members of his family served as organists here from 1653 to 1830, and their organ, restored, survives. Couperin 'le Grand' was born in a house on the site of No. 4 Rue François-Miron.

The INTERIOR, impressive for its loftiness and unity of style, is remarkably rich in works of art. The high windows of both nave and choir contain much stained-glass of c 1610–20 by *Robert Pinaigrier* and *Nicolas Chaumet*. The nave was completed in Flamboyant Gothic at a time when Renaissance influence was strongest.

S Aisle. The 2nd chapel has an altar commemorating some 50 victims of the bombardment of Good Friday, 1918, when a German shell struck the church. In the 3rd, seven low 17C painted panels of the Life of Christ; 5th and 6th, stained-glass of 1531. In the 8th chapel, the tomb of Michel Le Tellier (died 1685), by *Mazeline* and *Hurtrelle*; the bearded heads supporting the Chancellor's sarcophagus are from the tomb of Jacques de Souvré (died 1670), by *François Anguier*, the rest of which are in the Louvre. The *Lady Chapel*, an overdecorated example of Flamboyant Gothic (1517), has fine contemporary glass.

The Sacristy, in the N choir aisle, retains a good iron grille of 1741. In the N transept is a restored mid 16C Flemish painting of the Passion. From the next chapel we may enter the well-restored *Chapelle Dorée* (1628); in the adjacent chapel are a 13C high relief of the Dormition of the Virgin (below the altar), and a portrait by *Pajou* (1782) of Mme Palerme de Savy.

In the *Choir*, the stalls are of the 17C (W end) and mid-16C, the latter with curious misericords. Against the N entry-pillar is a 14C Virgin, known as N.-D. de Bonne-Délivrance; and on either side of the altar, wooden statues of the patron saints, by *Michel Bourdin* (1625). The 18C bronze-gilt candelabra are by *Soufflot*.

The S façade of the church can now be seen since the area has been the subject of clearance and restoration. Note the façades of some houses in the Rue des Barres, behind the building.

The stepped Rue François-Miron, leading NE from *St.-Gervais*, is one of the more imposing streets in the district. Nos 2–14, built c 1735, are adorned with wrought-iron work displaying the famous elm (see above); Nos 30, 36, and 42 all have good features.

No. 26 in the Rue Geoffroy-l'Asnier (right) is the *Hôtel de Chalons-Luxembourg* (1608), with a magnificent doorway (1659) and an attractive Louis XIII pavilion in the courtyard. No. 22 also retains a handsome 17C façade. No. 17 is a *Jewish Study Centre*, with a memorial.

Further E in the Rue François-Miron (off which diverges the Rue de Jouy; see below) is the mutilated *Hôtel de Beavais* (No. 68; by Le Pautre), with an interior courtyard, ornate circular vestibule, and carved staircase. From its balcony Anne of Austria and Card. Mazarin watched the entry of Louis XIV and Marie-Thérèse into Paris in 1660.

It had been built in 1655 for Pierre Beauvais, on the proceeds gained from having ignored the fact that his 40-year-old wife Catherine-Henriette Bellier, a 'lady-in-waiting' to the queen-mother (and known as 'Cateau-la-Borgnesse', for she had only one eye), had taught the 14-year-old king certain essential facts of life.

Christina of Sweden was a later tenant, and here in 1763 Mozart (aged 7) was the guest of the Bavarian ambassador.

The balcony of the *Hôtel du Président Hénault* (No. 82) should be noted.

To the right in the Rue de Jouy, No. 7, the *Hôtel d'Aumont*, by Le Vau (1648) and François Mansart (1656), retains some of its original decoration, including work by Le Brun.

Beyond, the Rue du Figuier diverges right to the **Hôtel de Sens** (Pl. 15;3), built c 1474–1519 for the archbishops of Sens, at a time when the bishopric of Paris was suffragan to the metropolitan see of Sens (before 1623); it is older than the *Hôtel de Cluny* (cf.), the only other important example of 15C domestic architecture in Paris. Unfortunately it has suffered a long period of neglect, and has been poorly restored. It now houses the *Bibliothèque Forney*, a reference library devoted to the fine arts.

Marguerite de Valois (1553–1615), whose memoirs may well have assisted Brantôme in the composition of his 'Dames illustres', passed peccant years here with her younger lovers, one of whom, in 1605, she had executed for the jealous murder of another on her very doorstep.

To the W are the modern buildings of the *Cité Internationale des Arts*, providing accommodation and facilities for foreign art students.

To the E, the QUAI DES CÉLESTINS, commanding attractive views of the *Île St.-Louis*, passes (left, at No. 32) the site of the *Tour Barbeau*, completing, on the river bank, the N perimeter of Philippe Auguste's defensive *Wall*, a section of which may be seen from the adjacent Rue des Jardins-St.-Paul.

Here also stood the tennis-court of the Croix-Noire, where Molière performed in 1645 until his arrest for debt. Rabelais (1494?–1553) died in the Rue des Jardins-St.-Paul, and was buried in the vanished church of *St.-Paul-des-Champs* (see below), as were the Mansarts (1666, and 1708), and the 'Man in the Iron Mask', who had died in the Bastille (1703).

The neighbouring Rue St.-Paul had acquired its name before 1350; at No. 32, part of the church belfry survives.—See below for the eastern end of the Quai des Célestins. Turning at the N end of this street, and then left brings us to the Rue St.-Antoine, an ancient thoroughfare retaining several elegant façades.

A few paces to the W is **St.-Paul-St.-Louis** (Pl. 15;3), or the *Grands-Jésuites*, built for that Society by Louis XIII in 1627–41 to replace a chapel of 1582. St.-Paul was added to the original name in 1796 to commemorate the demolished *St.-Paul-des-Champs*.

Designed by François Derrand, its florid style, founded on 16C Italian churches, is the earliest example of the Jesuit school of architecture in France. Richelieu said the first mass here. The handsome Baroque portal is by Martellange. The interior is over-decorated but imposing, and contains, in the left transept, a Christ in the Garden by *Delacroix*; and in the right, Louis XIII offering a model of the church to St. Louis, by *Simon Vouet*. Bp Huet (died 1721), the original editor of the Delphin classics, is buried here, and so is Louis Bourdaloue, who made most of his famous orations here: 'he preached like an angel', commented Mme de Sévigné.

Gérard de Nerval, who was educated at the adjacent *Lycée Charlemagne*, occupying a 17C Jesuit house, was found hanged in the old Rue de la Vieille Lanterne, near the *Sq. St.-Jacques* (see above) in 1855.

Turning E along the Rue-St.-Antoine, we shortly reach (left; No. 62) the **Hôtel de Sully ◇* (or de Béthune-Sully), now occupied by offices of the *Caisse Nationales des Monuments Historiques*, who can give information about guided tours to the sites and monuments of Paris; they also publish a review devoted to the restoration of architecturally important buildings: 'Monuments Historiques', and have a bookstall. Their publications are also available at Porte F of the *Grand Palais*, facing the Cours-la-Reine.

The mansion, by Jean du Cerceau (1624–30), was acquired by Sully, the minister of Henri IV, in 1634. The courtyard, a particularly fine example of the Louis-XIII style, the entrance pavilions, and the interior, retaining 17C ceilings and panelling, have been the subject of extensive restoration. The *Hôtel de la Mouffle* had previously stood on this site, from 1407.

The extensive *Photographic Archives* of the Caisse Nationale, invaluable to the student of French art and architecture, are at 4 Rue de Turenne, adjacent to the W.

From just E of the Hôtel de Sully, the short Rue de Birague approaches the S entrance of the *Pl. des Vosges* (see Rte 21); Nos 12 and 14 have elegant features.

Opposite, from the S side of the Rue St.-Antoine, leads the Rue Beautreillis. Beneath the carriage-entrance of No. 22, the *Grand Hôtel de Charny* (where Baudelaire lodged in 1858–59), are some woodcarvings in the purest Louis XIII style. No. 16, the *Petit Hôtel de Charny*, was the birthplace of the dramatist Victorien Sardou (1831–1908).—To the right in the Rue Charles V, is the imposing *Hôtel d'Aubray* (No. 12; 1620), residence of the notorious Marquise de Brinvilliers (1630–76), the poisoner. No. 10, the *Hôtel de Maillé*, retains its Louis XIII façade, and No. 15, opposite, dates from 1642.

No. 10 Rue Beautreillis was the *Hôtel des Princes de Monaco*, built c 1650, but altered in the 18th and 19Cs; No. 7, with a wooden staircase and wrought-iron balcony, is one of the finest bourgeois houses of its period in Paris (late 16C).

On reaching the Rue des Lions, with a number of 17–18C mansions, including No. 10 (the passage in the modern façade leads to a courtyard of 1642) and No. 11, in which Mme de Sévigné lived in 1645–50, turn left and then right to regain the Quai des Célestins.

At No. 4 QUAI DES CÉLESTINS is the stately *Hôtel de Fieubet*, with an interesting courtyard, built by *Jules Hardouin-Mansart* (1676–81) for Gaspard de Fieubet, chancellor to Anne of Austria; unfortunately it was badly disfigured in 1857, and now accommodates the *École Massillon*. The *Hôtel de Nicolai*, No. 4, is also of the late 17C.

At No. 1 Rue de Sully, on the far side of the BLVD HENRI-IV, in the Quartier de l'Arsenal (named after the arsenal established here by Henri IV), stands the **Bibliothèque de l'Arsenal** (Pl. 15;4).

The library, opened to the public in 1797, was founded in 1757 by Antoine-René d'Argenson, Marquis de Paulmy (1722–87), and sold by him to the Comte d'Artois in 1785. It is partly installed in the former residence of the Grand Master of Artillery, built in 1594 for Sully. The façade in the parallel BLVD MORLAND (facing the starkly functional *Préfecture de Paris)* is by Boffrand (c 1723).

The library possesses some 15,000 MSS, one million printed volumes, and 120,000 engravings. It is known particularly for its incomparable series of illuminated MSS, and its almost complete collection of French dramatic works. The Gordon Craig collection was acquired in 1957. Among its archives are the papers of the Bastille; documents relative to the 'Man in the Iron Mask', and the 'Affair of the Diamond Necklace'; letters of Henri IV to the Marquise de Verneuil, etc.; also Louis IX's Book of Hours, and Charles V's Bible, among others. Nodier, Hérédia, Mérimée, and Anatole France were librarians here.

Noteworthy are the *Salon de Musique*, by *Boffrand*, with superb Louis-XV woodwork, and the *Apartment of the Duchesse de La Meilleraie*, with a ceiling by *Simon Vouet*.

Turning NE (right) past the *Caserne des Célestins* (barracks of the Gendarmerie Mobile, built on part of the site of the famous Celestine monastery founded in 1362, but suppressed in 1779), we shortly diverge left off the BLVD HENRI-IV, to regain the Rue St.-Antoine (via the Rue Castex). On the corner is the circular *Temple de Ste.-Marie*, originally the chapel of the convent of the Visitation, and now a Protestant church. It was built by François Mansart in 1632–34.

The unscrupulous Surintendant des Finances, Nicolas Fouquet (1615–80) and Henri de Sévigné (Mme de Sévigné's husband, killed in a duel in 1651) were buried here. Vincent de Paul was almoner of the convent for 28 years.

A few paces to the W, at No. 21, is the *Hôtel de Mayenne* (or *d'Ormesson*), retaining a turret and charming staircase. Now the *École des Francs-Bourgeois*, it was built by Jean du Cerceau in 1613–17. It is flanked by the Rue du Petit-Musc, a corruption of the name it went by in the 14C, which was either 'La pute y Muse' or 'La Pute qui muse'.

Turning E we pass (right) the Rue de Lesdiguières, where at No. 9 was Balzac's first Paris lodging, in a garret at three *sous* a day. A tablet on No. 5 Rue St.-Antoine marks the position of the court of the *Bastille* (see below), by which the Revolutionary mob gained access to the fortress. Near the junction of this street and the PL. DE LA BASTILLE was the site of the great barricade of 1848, and also the last stronghold of the Communards in 1871. See also p 177.

20 The Centre Beaubourg or Centre Pompidou

MÉTROS: Rambuteau, Hôtel de Ville, Châtelet.

The **CENTRE BEAUBOURG** is officially called the **Centre National d'Art et de Culture Georges-Pompidou**, named after the well-meaning Président, who in 1969 conceived the idea of a form of cultural centre. It is also known by the initials CNAC, or merely as the **Centre Pompidou** (Pl. 14;2;16).

The building—selected from 681 projects received—designed by the Anglo-Italian team, Richard Rogers and Renzo Piano, in association with G. Franchini, and the Ove Arup group, was inaugurated early in 1977, and already looks the worse for wear, which is not surprising. The superstructure is 166m long from N to S, 60m wide, and 42m in height. Its superficial area is 103,300m², with a floor area on eight open-plan levels comprising 60,000m², of which 19,000m² is available for exhibitions, semi-permanent and temporary. The glazed surface is 11,000m²; the *'ossature métallique'* weighs 15,000 tonnes, 3000 more than that of the *Musée d'Orsay*.

On its W side the animated 'Piazza Beaubourg' slopes down from the Rue St.-Martin to the main entrance on the ground floor of the Centre. Here a variety of 'manifestations' and exhibitions—both impromptu and organised—take place (beware of pick-pockets).

To the N is a reconstruction of a studio, once at No. 11 Impasse Ronsin, which belonged to *Constantin Brancusi* (1876–1904).

Stairs and escalators (left) rise to a mezzanine floor on a level with the Rue Beaubourg to the E. Turning left again we reach an 'external' escalator traversing a glazed intestine-like tube, which writhes up to connect a series of platforms, each providing access to the upper five floors. On the first three are sections of the *Library* (Bibliothéque Publique d'Information; BPI), containing over 350,000 volumes (less quantities 'missing' shortly after its opening); 250,000 transparencies; 12,000 records; reference material; films; video-cassettes; etc.

These levels are also partly occupied by the *Centre de Création Industrielle* (CCI), and the sonorous-sounding *Institut de Recherche et de Coordination Acoustique/Musique* (IRCA/M; director Pierre Boulez), happily muffled in sound-proof bunkers (below ground between the Centre and St.-Merri). (The institute may be moved to the projected *Cité de Musique* at *La Villette*; see Rte 29.)

On the THIRD LEVEL is the entrance to the *MUSÉE NATIONAL D'ART MODERNE; see below. It extends to the floor above, reached by an interior escalator. On the top floor, devoted to temporary exhibitions (and occasional 'animations') is a *Cinémathèque*;, a restaurant, and a terrace (in addition to others on a lower level) providing some unusual views over Paris.

If the success of a museum or monument is to be gauged by the number of people whose curiosity has provoked them to enter it, then the *Centre Georges-Pompidou* has been a spectacular success, even if only a comparatively small proportion visit the permanent exhibition of modern art. Some have asserted that it is 'a remarkable achievement': others have been less kind. There have been varied reactions to the ungainly and incongruous physical appearance of what has been well-described as a 'culture factory' in the midst of the staid *Marais*, with its dignified 17–18C architecture.

For visitors with an interest in modern art, who will want at least to visit the collections on the third and fourth floors, what is perhaps more disturbing is to contemplate the likely *condition* of the paintings within a very few years unless

The housing of the external escalator of the Centre Pompidou

something is done soon to protect them from the dust and general contamination stirred up—in spite of air-conditioning—by the many thousands who press past them daily.

Neither the canvases nor the dividing screens are adequately labelled and there is no recommended route for the visitor, but by following a vaguely clockwise direction after turning half-right on entering the museum one can *see* everything.

The position of canvases may be changed without notice.

On the first landing are *Bonnard*, 'en barque'; *Picasso*, Recumbent nude (1901), Seated nude (1905), and Tête de femme rouge (1906); and examples of the art of *Vlaminck, Matisse, Derain, Marquet*, and *Dufy*.

R1 *Matisse; Robert Delaunay*, Portrait of Henri Carlier; *Manguin*, Portrait of Ravel.—**R2** *Albert Marquet*, Bassin du Havre; Portrait of

Marquet, by *Camoin; Utrillo*, L'Impasse Cottin, Jardin de Montmagny.—**R3** *Kupka*.—**R4** *Vlaminck; Dufy; Roger de la Fresnaye*, La Ferté-sous-Jouarre, The cuirassier.

R5 *Picasso*.—**R6** *Picabia*, Young girl (1912).—**R7** Sculpture by *Gaudier-Brzeska*. Returning through R5 are, opposite, examples from the Cubist period of *Picasso, Braque, Chagall*, and *Léger*, backing onto which is *Braque*, Girl playing mandolin.

A later section is devoted to *Robert Delaunay*, including his La Ville de Paris, Eiffel Tower, Towers of Laon, Self-portrait, and La verseuse; *Sonia Delaunay*, Prismes électriques, Marché au Minho (together with others in **R13**).—**R14** *Kandinsky*.—**R15** *Kupka; Dufy*, Three bathers. The following section contains *Chagall*, Double-portrait with a glass of wine; *Robert Delaunay*, Le manège de cochons, works by *Gris*, and sculpture by *Lipchitz*.

Below the 'Escalier mécanique' is *Marie Laurencin*, Apollinaire and his friends.

At the top of this escalator is *Lipchitz*, Head of Gertrude Stein (1920), and *Matisse*, Plaques of female bottoms, turning discreetly from which we may enter **R16** containing *Picasso*, La Liseuse (1920), and **R17** devoted to *Braque*.—**R18** *Jacques Villon; Gargallo*, Statue of the Prophet.—To the W are displayed *Picasso*, Minotaure (1927), Confidences (1934), and Nature morte à la tête antique.

Continuing in an anti-clockwise direction, we pass works by *Schwitters*; and *George Grosz*, Remember uncle August, the unhappy inventor.—**R20** *Klee*, and *Ernst*.—**R23** *Kandinsky*; Sculpture by *Antoine Pevsner*.—**R24** *Matisse*, L'Odalesque à la culotte rouge, and La blouse roumaine. Nearby are rooms devoted to *Peyronnet*, and *Dubuffet*.

Continuing N, we pass *Chagall*, The acrobat, and **R25** *Derain*, Nude against green curtain; *Marquet*, Seated nude; *Bonnard*, The toilette, and Landscapes.—**R26** *Suzanne Valadon*. The blue room; *Soutine*, The groom, and Portrait of Miestchaninoff; *Kisling*, Woman with Polish shawl; *Modigliani*, Portrait of Dédié; *Felix Vallatton*, Romanian woman in a red dress.

Outside **R26**, *Chagall*, Guerre (1943), and *Rouault*, The wounded clown; and close by, works by *Miró*. Another section (right) is devoted to *Dalí; Man Ray*; and *Magritte*, Le modèle rouge.—**R29** *Andrè Masson*. The next section displays *Matisse*, Le Ciel; *Picasso*, Portrait of Mme Paul Éluard, and in **R30** *Picasso*, Portrait of Dora Maar, Two women on a beach.—**R31** Sculpture by *Julio González*.

Near the adjacent terrace are works by *Balthus*, and in adjoining rooms, examples of sculpture by *Giacometti* and *Kemeny*; and Three people in a room, by *Bacon*.

The collection is continued in the N part of the building devoted to aspects of modern art with which the Editor has little sympathy and would prefer not to commit his opinions to print. But to quote from a recent brochure, sections are concerned with 'abstraction lyrique', 'nouveau réalisme', 'abstraction géométrique', 'art cinétique', 'Pop art', 'Hyperréalisme et la nouvelle figuration', etc.

21 The Marais

MÉTROS: Bastille, St.-Paul, Hôtel-de-Ville, Rambuteau, Temple, Arts-et-Métiers, Réaumur-Sébastopol.

The **Marais*, one of the most interesting districts of old Paris, is bounded by the *Grands Boulevards* on the N and E, by the Blvd de

Sébastopol to the W, and by the Seine to the S. It includes the greater part of the 3rd and 4th arrondissements. In spite of past neglect, demolition, and some rebuilding, it remains substantially as developed in the 17C, and contains numerous buildings of outstanding architectural interest, affording a fascinating and unique reminder of the elegance of this period.

The S sector of the *Marais* and the *Centre Beaubourg* are described in Rtes 19 and 20.

So called from the marshy land ('marais', marsh or morass), the *Marais* only became habitable with the arrival of the Knights Templar and other religious houses, who settled here in the 13C, and converted the marshes into arable land. Royal patronage began with Charles V, who, anxious to forget the associations of the *Palais de la Cité* with the rebellion of Étienne Marcel in 1358, built the *Hôtel St.-Paul* here. In the 16C, the *Hôtel de Lamoignon* and *Hôtel Carnavalet* were built, but the seal of royal approval came with the building of the PL. ROYALE (1605; later known as the *Pl. des Vosges*, see below).

Courtiers built themselves houses as near to the Pl. Royale as possible, and the Marais remained the most fashionable residential area of Paris until the creation of the Faubourg St.-Germain in the early 18C. The Revolution ended its long reign of splendour. The nobles had to flee; the State confiscated their property and sold it to the craftsmen, mechanics and merchants who flooded into the area, who appeared to take a brutish pleasure in disfiguring as much as possible. Much of the Marais continues to be a commercial district, even if its architectural merits are more appreciated as the value of its properties has increased.

Immediately E of the *Marais* lies the **Pl. de la Bastille** (Pl. 15;4), laid out in 1803.

The ground plan of the famous fortress prison is marked by a line of paving-stones in the Place, beneath which some cellars are said to survive.

Its keep (a model of which may be seen in the *Musée Carnavalet*) stood on the W side, across the end of the Rue St.-Antoine, and the main drawbridge was slightly N of the junction with the *Blvd Henri-IV*. The *July Column* (see below) stands approximately in the centre of what was the E bastion. The *Canal St.-Martin* now runs beneath the Place, appearing to the S in the *Gare d'eau de l'Arsenal*, which flows into the Seine.

The **Bastille** (more correctly the *Bastille St.-Antoine*) originated as a bastion-tower defending the E entrance to Paris. It was developed under Charles V into a fortress with eight massive towers, immensely thick walls, and a wide moat. Nevertheless, in October 1559 Edward Grimston, who had been taken prisoner at the fall of Calais, contrived to escape from confinement here. By the reign of Louis XIII, the Bastille had become almost exclusively a state prison for political offenders, among whom were the mysterious 'Man in the Iron Mask' (1698–1703), and Voltaire (twice). The arbitrary arrest by '*lettre de cachet*' of persons obnoxious to the Court, and their protracted imprisonment without trial, made the Bastille a popular synonym for oppression. Bassompierre was imprisoned in 1629 for twelve years by Richelieu, 'not that he had done wrong, but for fear he might be led into mischief'. Bernard Palissy was incarcerated here in 1588, at the age of 78; and among other notable temporary residents were Cagliostro, Marmontel, the Duchesse du Maine, and Mme de Tencin. In 1657 John Harwood, one of the first Quakers to visit France, was briefly incarcerated here. A certain 'Dr Du Moulin of Aberdeen', with whom John Ray, Sir Philip Skippon, and Martin Lister had travelled to Paris in 1666, was held there for ten months, arrested on suspicion of being an English agent among the Huguenots of

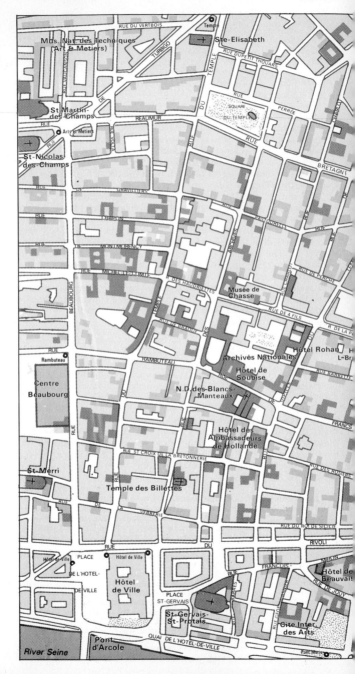

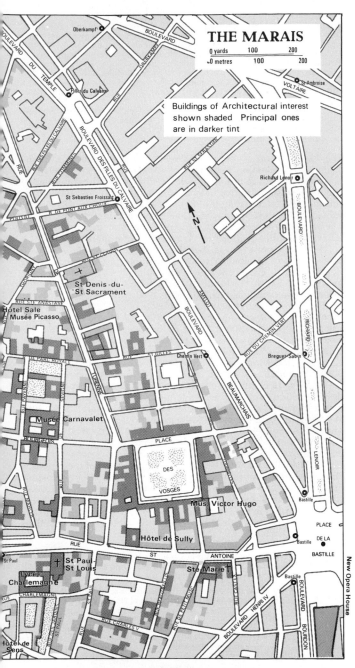

THE MARAIS

0 yards	100	200
0 metres	100	200

Buildings of Architectural interest shown shaded Principal ones are in darker tint

Oberkampf

BOULEVARD

BOULEVARD DU TEMPLE

Filles du Calvaire

St-Ambroise

VOLTAIRE

RUE

BOULEVARD DES FILLES DU CALVAIRE

St Sebastien Froissart

Richard Lenoir

BOULEVARD

POITOU

R DE PON AUX CHOUX

RUE S. SEBASTIEN

St-Denis-du-St Sacrament

RICHARD

BEAUMARCHAIS

AMELOT

RUE DU CHEMIN VERT

RUE ST ANASTASE

Hôtel Salé
Musée Picasso

DE PARC ROYALE

RUE ST GILLES

Chemin Vert

Breguet-Sabin

TURENNE

LENOIR

Musée Carnavalet

BOURGEOIS

PLACE

DES

VOSGES

Bastille

Mus. Victor Hugo

PLACE

DE LA

BASTILLE

Hôtel de Sully

Bastille

RUE

ST

ANTOINE

New Opera House

St Paul

St Paul-St Louis

Ste Marie

Bastille

BOULEVARD

Lycée Charlemagne

CHARLEMAGNE

RUE CHARLES V

BOULEVARD HENRI IV

BOURDON

Hôtel de Sens

Languedoc. Vanbrugh enjoyed Louis XIV's hospitality (for obscure reasons) for most of 1692; and Col. John Parker, in 1702, for offending Maria of Modena. Linguet's 'Memoires' (1783, published in London) describe his own experiences when incarcerated there in 1780–82. Another inmate was the notorious Marquis de Sade, who here wrote 'Justine' and other lubricious works. Mirabeau the Younger was also imprisoned here, another victim of the practice of arrest by 'lettre de cachet', albeit at his father's instigation. (Malsherbes reported to Walpole that the mistress of a former administrator, 'Madame Sabatin, had a bureau of printed *lettres de cachet* with blanks, which she sold for twenty-five louis apiece'.)

On 14 July 1789, the Revolutionary mob, aided by a few troops, attacked and overwhelmed its defenders, and murdered the governor, the Marquis de Launay, and freed a handful of prisoners. In the same year the building was razed. Its key, presented by La Fayette to Washington, is now at Mount Vernon.

The **July Column** (*Colonne de Juillet*) is not connected with the storming of the Bastille, but was erected by Louis-Philippe in 1840–41 to commemorate the 504 victims of the three days' street-fighting of July 1830, who are buried in vaults beneath the circular base of the column. The victims of the Revolution of February 1848 were subsequently interred there, and their names added to the inscription. The bronze-faced column, 51·50m high, is surmounted by a bronze-gilt figure of Liberty; its ascent is provisionally suspended.

The new **Opéra de la Bastille**, designed by *Carlos Ott*, a Uraguayan-born Canadian (chosen from 744 projects: that of the Centre Pompidou was one of a mere 680!) is being raised on a site immediately SE of the Pl. de la Bastille, and the building itself is planned to be completed by the end of 1989.

Nos 2–20 in the BLVD BEAUMARCHAIS, leading N from the *Pl. de la Bastille*, are built on the site of a luxurious mansion and garden belonging to the dramatist Caron de Beaumarchais (1732–99). The Hôtel de Mansart-Sagonne (see below) is well seen from Nos 21–23 in the boulevard, which with its continuation, the BLVD DES FILLES-DU-CALVAIRE (recalling the site of a former convent; 1633–1790) and BLVD DU TEMPLE (see p 197), leads to the *Pl. de la République*.

The Rue de la Bastille leads NW from the *Pl. de la Bastille* to the Rue des Tournelles, No. 28 in which is the *Hôtel de Mansart-Sagonne*, built for himself in 1674–85 by Jules Hardouin-Mansart (1646–1708), and decorated by Le Brun and Mignard. No. 50 has a splendid façade. The cultured courtesan Ninon de Lenclos (1620–1705) lived here from 1644, and died at No. 56.—Before reaching these two houses, the Rue du Pas-de-la-Mule leads left to the *Pl. des Vosges*.

The *****PLACE DES VOSGES** (Pl. 15;2–4), the heart of the *Marais*, a large quadrangle surrounded by 39 houses in red brick with stone facings, was built on a uniform plan with arcaded ground floors (1606–11), and is one of the most attractive squares in Paris. Trees were not planted in the central gardens until 1783, and although they provide welcome shade, they spoil the effect of harmonious symmetry.

The main approach to the *Pl. des Vosges*, from the Rue St.-Antoine, is by the Rue de Birague (see p 172), passing through the *Pavillon du Roi* (see below). The whole square is at present being restored.

It occupies the site of the royal *Palais des Tournelles*, the residence of the Duke of Bedford, regent of France in 1422, after the death of Henry V; in 1559 this was the scene of the fatal tournament when Henri II was accidentally killed by Montgomery, and it was in consequence abandoned by his widow, Catherine de Médicis. The square in its present form was laid out for Henri IV, probably by Baptiste du Cerceau, as the PLACE ROYALE and opened in 1605; the king's pavilion was above the gateway in the centre of the S side, while the queen's was the corresponding building on the N (No. 28). In the earlier part of the reign of

Louis XIV this was one of the most fashionable addresses in Paris, and the centre of the 'Nouvelles Précieuses' satirised by Molière. It only acquired its present name in 1799, the department of the Vosges having been the first to discharge its liabilities for the Revolutionary Wars.

At the corners of the square are fountains (1816), and in the centre a poor equestrian statue of Louis XIII (1825) set up to replace one destroyed in 1792. Mme de Sévigné (1626–96) was born in the *Hôtel de Coulanges* (No. 1 bis; built 1606), next to the *Pavillon du Roi*; No. 3 is the *Hôtel d'Estrades*.

No. 6, in which Victor Hugo (1802–85) lived in 1832–48 (2nd floor), is now the **Musée Victor-Hugo** (admission daily 10.00–17.40, except Monday), perhaps of more interest for his numerous pen and wash *Drawings (c 350) displayed there than for the family souvenirs.

Note the bust of Hugo by *Rodin*; portrait of Juliette Drouet by *Bastien-Lepage*; The Première of Hernani, by *Besnard*; portrait of Adèle Foucher, the poet's wife, by *Louis Boulanger*; Hugo on his death-bed, by *Bonnat*; and works by *Célestin Nanteuil* and *Delacroix*. Note also the furniture and woodwork, designed or carved by Hugo.

No. 7, the *Petit-Hôtel de Sully*, was built by Jean Androuet du Cerceau. Both Gautier (in 1831–4) and Daudet lived at No. 8, the *Hôtel de Fourcy* (1605). No. 9, the *Hôtel de Chaulnes*, was from 1856 the residence of Rachel, the tragedienne (died 1858). No. 11 was occupied by Marion Delorme, the courtesan, in 1639–48. No. 21 was the mansion of Card. de Richelieu (1615), in front of which, on the day after his edict against duelling, took place the duel between François de Montmorency and Des Chapelles against Bussy and Beuvron (1627). No. 12 occupies part of the *Hôtel Dangeau*, the home of Philippe, Marquis de Dangeau (1638–1720), the memorialist.

From the NW corner of the *Pl. des Vosges* we cross the Rue de Turenne (where to the left, in the court of No. 23, is the *Hôtel de Villacerf*, of c 1660, with a fountain), and enter the Rue des Francs-Bourgeois, taking its name from the citizens who, being vassals to a feudal lord, were exempt from municipal taxes. For the N part of the Rue de Turenne, see p 188.

The *MUSÉE CARNAVALET*, or *Musée Historique de la Ville de Paris* (Pl. 15;1; MÉTRO: *St.-Paul*), at the corner of the Rue des Francs-Bourgeois and the Rue de Sévigné, is a highly important collection illustrating the history of Paris from the 16C to the middle of the 19C.

The museum is housed in the *Hôtel Carnavalet, an imposing mansion begun in 1544 for Jacques de Ligneris, President of the Parlement, and adorned with sculptures by Jean Goujon. It was altered in 1660 by Mansart, who built the present façade, but retained the 16C gateway with its Goujon sculptures (on the keystone, a winged figure of Abundance standing on a globe which was later carved into a carnival mask, in punning allusion to Carnavalet). Further alterations and enlargements were made earlier this century.

The project to extend the museum into the adjacent *Hôtel Le Pelletier de St.-Fargeau* (see below) is now under way.

The name Carnavalet was derived from the Breton family of Kernevenoy, the second owners of the building. Mme de Sévigné lived here from 1677 until her death in 1696; her apartments, which were shared by her daughter, Mme de Grignan, and her uncle, the Abbé de Coulanges, were in the SE corner of the first floor. The building was acquired by the municipality in 1866, and the museum was inaugurated in 1880.

The bronze statue of Louis XIV in the centre of the courtyard is by Coysevox. Of the sculptures in the courtyard, the best are those by

MUSEE CARNAVALET

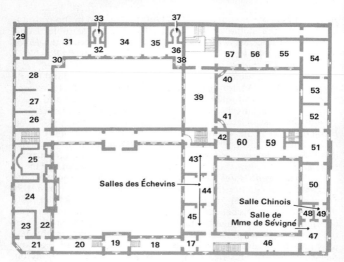

First Floor

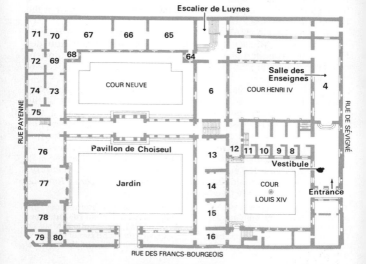

Ground Floor

Jean Goujon on the entrance arch and above the door on the left. The reliefs of The Seasons, on the side opposite the entrance, were probably done under his direction. On the right, the relief above the door is a 19C copy of the one opposite; those on the first storey are by Van Obstal (1660).

Some rooms are being rearranged, but the following itinerary will take the visitor round the building in an approximate chronological progression, with one or two slight breaks in continuity. **RR7–11** (once stables), to the left of the entrance vestibule, are reserved for temporary exhibitions.

The *Salle des Enseignes* (**R4**), with a wrought-iron grille, contain material relative to trades and guilds, including a collection of shop and tavern signs of the 15–19C. In the central cases are weights and measures, models of glassworks and locksmiths' works, merchants' tokens etc.—In **R5**, continuing the display, is the front of an apothecary's shop of the First Empire.

R6 (left) conserves some magnificent gilt panelling from the *Hôtel d'Uzès*, Rue Montmartre, from designs by *Ledoux*, while the adjoining room, also by *Ledoux* (1752), was saved from the 'café Militaire' in the Rue St.-Honoré. Behind is a large 19C maquette of the *Palais-Royal*.

RR12–16 contain engravings of Paris from the 16th to early 17C.

FIRST FLOOR. **RR17–25** illustrate the topography of Paris from the 17C to the beginning of the 18C. Note also the *anon.* 16C Flemish painting of the Prodigal Son in the company of courtesans, and a portrait of Mary Stuart in a white mourning veil (1561) in **R19**, and the views of Paris by *Pierre-Denis Martin* in **RR20, 22**, and **24** (the Inauguration of the church of Les Invalides). **R23** contains the richly painted and gilded *boiseries* (c 1656) from the *Hôtel Colbert de Villacerf* at 23 Rue de Turenne; **R24** is the 'grand cabinet doré', by *Le Vau*, from 14 Pl. des Vosges; the ceiling painting is by *Le Brun*, as is that in **R25**, of 1651, with decorations from the same mansion.

Boiseries from the Hôtel Colbert de Villacerf

Returning through these rooms, enter **R46**, devoted to Mme de Sévigné, with a pastel portrait by *Nanteuil*, and of her daughter Mme de Grignan, by *Mignard*, and other souvenirs.—**R47** contains paintings of St.-Germain, and Vincennes, by *Van de Meulen*.—**RR45–43**, the *Salles Des Echevins*, displays portraits of aldermen by *Largillierre, de Troy*, and *Duplessis*, and the Allegory of the Peace of Aix-la-Chapelle (1749) by *Dumont le Romain*. In **R45** is a monumental chimneypiece of the Louis-XIII period.

R39 is the first of a series of rooms (**RR39–42, 60, 59, 58, 51–53**) accommodating the important collection of furniture donated by Henriette Bouvier in 1965.—To the right of **R51**, **R50** contains an early painting by *Chardin* of a game of billiards. **R49**, adjoining, displays examples of 18C furniture, in the Chinese taste.

RR54–57, well-panelled, concentrate on furniture of the period of Louis XV. **R56** is devoted to the theatre; **R57** to Rousseau and Voltaire, with a portrait of the latter, aged 24, *after Largillierre*.—Across the landing of the Escalier des Luynes (a reconstruction of a stairway from the *Hôtel de Luynes*, decorated with wall-paintings of the family, by *Brunetti*, of 1748, is **R36**, with a portrait of Benjamin Franklin, by *Duplessis*, and **R37**, with the rotunda from the ground floor of the *Hôtel de Fersen*. The following suite of rooms is devoted to furniture of the Louis-XV–XVI from the Bouvier collection; **R31**, painted by *Boucher* and *Fragonard* (1750–65), is from the house of the engraver Gilles Demarteau in the Rue de la Pelleterie.

R26 contains views by *A.-J. Noël*, and *J.-B. Lallemand*, among others.—The adjoining stairs lead to the *Library*, with an extensive reference section devoted to the history of Paris.—The gallery opposite (**RR61–63**), displays topographical views of 18C Paris by *Nicolas* and *J.-B. Raguenet*, among others. Turn left through **R39**, descend the *Escalier de Luynes*, and cross **RR64–68**, with archaeological collections, to reach the wing (**RR69–75**) devoted to the period from the Revolution to the present. Sections cover the Pillage of the Invalides, containing a portrait by *Vestier* of Dr John Moore (1729–1802), the author of descriptions of Paris during this disturbed time; a model of the Bastille cut from one of its stones under the direction of *Palloy*, the demolition contractor; a painting of the Storming of the Bastille, by *Henry Singleton*, and of its Destruction, by *Hubert Robert*; 'Lettres de Cachet' signed by Louis XV; busts, documents, and portraits (Marat, Danton, Robespierre, et al.) of the period; and souvenirs of Louis XVI and his family during their imprisonment in the Temple. Other sections are devoted to Napoleon and his family, with personal souvenirs. Note the portraits of Napoleon by *Lefèvre*; of Mme Récamier, by *Gérard*; and of Talleyrand in 1809, by *Prud'hon*.

Aspects of Paris (literary, theatrical, etc.) are also covered.—From the hall beyond **R75** cross the central colonnade of the *Pavillion de Choiseul* to regain the entrance vestibule.

No. 29 Rue de Sévigné was formerly the *Hôtel Le Pelletier de Saint-Fargeau* (by Bullet; 1687). No. 48, opposite, the *Hôtel de Jonquières*, retains the relief (1810) from an old fountain; No. 52, built by Pierre Delisle-Mansart for himself, has been much altered.

In the Rue Payenne, immediately W of the *Hôtel Carnavalet*, No. 11, the *Hôtel de Polastron-Polignac*, now houses the *Swedish Cultural Centre* and *Musée Tessim*, containing paintings by Alexander Roslin (1718–93), among others. No. 13, the *Hôtel de Lude*, is another good example of an early 18C mansion. There is a small lapidary collection in the SQ. GEORGES-CAIN opposite.

S of the *Hôtel Carnavalet*, on the corner of the Rue Pavée, No. 24 is the **Hôtel Lamoignon**, built in 1584 for Diane de France, the legitimised daughter of Henri II, but named after Lamoignon, President of the Parlement of Paris (1658), a later occupant, and enlarged in the 17C. Daudet set up house here on his marriage in 1867.

It now houses the *Bibliothèque Historique de la Ville de Paris*, containing over 400,000 vols and 100,000 MSS. relating to the history of the city, and to the Revolution.—Adjacent are traces of the notorious prison of *La Force* (demolished 1850), where some 170 victims of the Revolution were massacred in September 1792.

On the S side of the Rue des Francs-Bourgeois, No. 31 is the *Hôtel d'Albret*, built c 1640 by François Mansart, with an 18C street façade. At the end of the courtyard of No. 33 is a fragment of the *Walls* of Philippe Auguste. The *Hôtel de Guillaume Barbès* (No. 35) was built in the second half of the 17C.

In 1642 Ninon de Lenclos lived at No. 16 in the Rue Elzévir (leading off the N side of the Rue des Francs-Bourgeois); No. 8, the *Hôtel Denon*, with a good façade, will be the future home of the *Musée Cognacq-Jay*; see p 193.

No. 26, the *Hôtel de Sandreville* (late 16–18C); and No. 30, the *Hôtel d'Alméras*, a red-brick mansion of the Henri IV period, are noteworthy. The Allée des Arbalétriers (No. 38) was one of the entrances to the *Hôtel Barbette* (see p 187), and led to the field alongside the walls, once a practice ground for crossbowmen.

On the corner of the transverse Rue Vieille-du-Temple (right; No. 54) survives the pretty turret (c 1510; restored) of the *Hôtel Hérouët*.

A short distance S is the **Hôtel des Ambassadeurs de Hollande** (No. 47), built by Cottard in 1657–60. On this site was the house of the Maréchal de Rieux, in front of which, returning from Isabeau de Bavière's residence (see below), the Duc d'Orléans was assassinated in 1407 by the hired bravos of Jean sans Peur (Duke of Burgundy).

The building was never in fact the property of the Dutch ambassadors, but in 1720–27 belonged to the chaplain of their Embassy, and its chapel was used several times for Protestant ceremonies. Mlle Necker (later Mme de Staël) was baptised there in 1766, and Franklin's daughter was married there. Beaumarchais also lived here, where he wrote his 'Mariage de Figaro' (accepted in 1781 by the Comédie-Française, but owing to the royal veto, not publically produced until 1784); in 1788 he turned the house into a provident institution for poor nursing mothers.

Nos 36, 24, and 15 (the *Hôtel de Vibraye*) further S, are of some interest.

For the N half of this street, see below.

On the left is **N.-D. des Blancs-Manteaux** (deriving its name from the white habits of an order of mendicant monks established here in 1285 by Louis IX); the 18C door came from St.-Barthélemy in the Île de la Cité, demolished in 1863. The church contains a rococo pulpit in the Flemish style (1749) and a good organ (restored).

At No. 55 Rue des Francs-Bourgeois are the offices of the *Crédit Municipal*, formerly the Mont-de-Piété (a government pawnbroking establishment), founded by Louis XVI in 1777.

Among other striking houses in the Rue des Francs-Bourgeois are Nos 54, the *Hôtel de Camus*; 56, the *Hôtel de Fontenoy* (early 18C); 58, which belonged to Louis Le Tonnelier, Baron de Breteuil, minister of Louis XVI; and 58 bis, the *Hôtel d'Assy* (early 17C).

Beyond is the imposing portal of the *****HÔTEL DE SOUBISE** (No. 60; Pl. 15;1), the greater part of which was built by Delamair in 1706–12 on the site of the mansion of the Duc de Guise. The *Archives Nationales* have been housed here since 1808, ensuring the survival of the interior decoration (1712–45) by *Natoire, Boucher, Van Loo, Restout, Lemoyne*, et al. The splendid *Cour d'Honneur*, with its colonnade, has copies of The Four Seasons by Robert Le Lorrain on the façade.

The earlier entrance, the turreted Gothic gateway of 1380 (at No. 58 Rue des Archives), was part of the *Hôtel de Clisson*, built in 1372–75 by the Constable Olivier de Clisson, a supporter of Charles V against the English. Bolingbroke (later Henry IV) gave a farewell banquet there in 1399 before setting out for England. During the English occupation of Paris (1420–35) Thomas, Duke of Clarence (died 1421) and later the Duke of Bedford, lived here. With its purchase in 1553 by Anna d'Este, wife of François de Lorraine, Duc de Guise, it became the *Hôtel de Guise* remaining in the family until 1696, when Anne de Soubise bought it. Another occupant during this period was Henri II de Lorraine, who killed the last of the Colignys in a duel in the *Pl. des Vosges* in 1643: his grandfather had instigated the murder of Adm. Coligny in the massacre of St. Bartholomew. Here he entertained lavishly, and gave hospitality to Corneille.

The *Chapel* bears traces of the *Chapelle de Clisson* of 1375 transformed in 1533 for the Guise by *Primaticcio*. The *Oval Room* is a masterpiece of the style of transition from Louis XIV to Louis XV. Here and elsewhere are exhibited some outstanding documents arranged to show the development of French institutions etc.

Among the earliest is a will of 627; others concern Clovis and Charlemagne. Among letters from foreign potentates and statesmen are some from the Emperor Charles V, Christina of Sweden, Tamerlane, Franklin, and Washington; among treaties displayed are those of Brétigny, Westphalia, and the Pyrenees; the Edict of Nantes (with the signature of Henri IV) and its Revocation; the Oath of the Jeu de Paume; Marie-Antoinette's last letter, and Louis XVI's will; also his diary with 'rien' written against the date 14 July 1789, etc. The Orléans archives were donated to the Archives Nationales in 1969.

From the Rue des Archives, skirting the W side of the Hôtel de Soubise, leads the Rue de Braque, in which Nos 4–6, the *Hôtel Le Lièvre de la Grange*, is a fine late-17C mansion; No. 7 belonged to Vergennes, foreign minister to Louis XVI and supporter of American Independence.

At the corner of the Rue des Archives and the Rue des Haudriettes, further N, is a fountain, with a naiad sculpted by Mignot (1765).

Diagonally opposite is the *Hôtel de Guénégaud* (No. 60 Rue des Archives) by François Mansart (c 1650), containing a **Musée de la Chasse**, and an exclusive Hunting Club (with an annexe at Chambord).

The first room displays a portrait, in falconer's costume, of Philip the Handsome (Felipe I of Castile; the father of the Emperor Charles V), and 'La Chasse de Diane' by *Brueghel le Velours* and *Van Balen*. Stairs ascend to rooms containing hunting weapons, powder flasks, daggers, crossbows, etc., and to the second floor. Here are collections of stuffed big game, swords, porcelain decorated with hunting scenes, and paintings by *François Desportes* (1661–1743), *Chardin, Oudry, Carle Vernet*, and others.

No. 62, adjacent, the *Hôtel de Montgelas* (1709), is noteworthy.

No. 22 Rue des Quatre-Fils, leading SE, was the home of the Marquise du Deffand (1697–1780). Her salon was frequented by Voltaire, Montesquieu, d'Alembert, Condorcet, Turgot, and Hénault.

She later became blind, and Mlle de Lespinasse, her companion in 1756–64, set up a separate salon; see p 106.

No. 20, retaining a fine doorway, was the residence, after 1800, of the Comte de Sèze (1748–1828), Louis XVI's lawyer.

In the Rue Charlot, leading NE from the Rue des Quatre-Fils, is *St.-Jean-St.-François*, built as a Capuchin chapel on the site of a *jeu de paume*, and completed in 1715. No. 7, opposite, the *Hôtel de Brévannes*, is partly 17C.

Further along the Rue des Quatre-Fils we regain the Rue Vieille-du-Temple, in which, at No. 87, a few paces to the right, stands the **Hôtel de Rohan**, known also as the *Hôtel de Strasbourg*, begun in 1704 by Delamair.

It was successively inhabited by four cardinals of the Rohan family, all of whom were bishops of Strasbourg. From 1808 to 1925 the mansion was occupied by the *Imprimerie Nationale* (cf.), after which it was thoroughly restored to house certain departments of the *Archives Nationales* not accommodated in the neighbouring *Hôtel de Soubise* (see above). In the second courtyard is a fine relief of the Horses of Apollo by Robert Le Lorrain; the *'Cabinet des Singes'* contains paintings by *Christophe Huet* (1745–50). It was here that the Card. Edouard de Rohan was arrested during the 'Affaire du Collier' (1783–84; see p 257).

Slightly to the S, No. 17 in the Rue Barbette (recalling the name of the *Hôtel Barbette*, the favourite residence from 1403, of Isabeau de Bavière, which stood on this site) retains a badly damaged door, with two medallions.

From the intersection of the Rues Vieille-du-Temple (in which No. 90 was the site of the *Jeu de Paume des Marais*, used as a theatre from 1634–73) and des Quatre-Fils are made towards the NE section of the Marais via the *Hôtel Salé* (see below). Its garden façade is approached by turning right off the former street along the Rue des Coutures-St.-Gervais, lined with a number of 17C houses.— Alternatively, one may follow the Rue de la Perle SE to the tastefully redeveloped PL. DE THORIGNY, passing (right; No. 1) the restored *Hôtel Libéral-Bruant*, built in 1685 for his personal use by the architect of Les Invalides. The pedimented façade, decorated with four busts in niches, is notable. The building now houses the *Musée de la Serrure* (or *Musée Bricard*, after Eugène Bricard, the 19C collector of this splendid decorative door-furniture, including locks, keys, handles, and plaques of all periods).

A few paces to the SE bring one to the Rue du Parc-Royal, in which Gautier lived from 1822–31 at No. 4, built c 1620. No. 10, the restored *Hôtel de Vigny*, of the same date, is now the offices of the *Centre National de documentation du patrimoine—Inventaire Général* (admission 12.00–17.00 Monday to Friday). The Rue Payenne (cf.) leads back towards the *Hôtel Carnavalet*.

By turning NE up the Rue de Thorigny, we reach at No. 5 (left) the *Hôtel Salé* (Pl. 15;1) an impressive mansion also known as the *Hôtel Aubert de Fontenay*, after the financier for whom it was built in 1656–60 by Jean Boullier de Bourges. It was once called the *Hôtel de Juigné*, but became known as the *Hôtel Salé* on account of the huge profits its owner had made out of the salt tax. The decoration of the staircase is superb. The whole fabric has undergone a thorough and well-deserved restoration since being put to commercial use in the 19C, and now houses a museum devoted to the work of *Pablo Ruiz Picasso* (1881–1973).

The *MUSÉE PICASSO* comprises an extensive collection of works of art by that prolific artist, acquired by the State in lieu of death duties, together with a number of canvases by other artists once owned by Picasso. It includes among works by Picasso, some 230 paintings, 140 sculptures, 45 ceramics, almost 1500 drawings and over 1650 prints (displayed in rotation), apart from several 'constructions', etc. They are displayed in approx. chronological order, and are representative of most of his 'periods', although weak in youthful works.

Notable among the comparatively few works of outstanding importance are his Self-portrait (with a blue background; 1901); Self-
portrait unshaven; The two brothers; Les demoiselles d'Avignon
(1907); Sculpted female head (Fernande); Still-life with a cane chair
(1912); Portrait of Olga Khoklova seated (1917); Bathers (Biarritz,
1918); Jug and apples; Women running along a beach (1922); Paul 'en
arlequin' and 'en pierrot'; Female bust (1932); Corrida (1933); Portrait
of Marie-Thérèse Walter (1937); Portraits of Dora Maar (1937); Maya
and her doll (1938); Cat with a bird (1938); Massacre in Korea (1951);
The picnic (after Manet; 1960); The young artist (1972); sculpted
Nanny-goats; and among drawings, The frugal meal (1904), Young
girl wearing a hat (c 1920), and Minotaur (1936).

Also *Balthus*, The children; *Cézanne*, The Château Noir; *Corot*,
Little Jeannette; *Miró*, Self-portrait; *Modigliani*, Seated girl; *Henri
Rousseau*, Self-portrait with lamp, The artist's wife, and The sover-
eigns; *Renoir*, Seated bather; and works by *Braque*, *Matisse*, and
René-Hilaire de Gas (1770–1858; grandfather of Edgar Degas).

It is likely that Marion Delorme died in a house on the site of No. 2 in
1650. Nos 6, 8, and 10 were built together as the *Hôtel de Percey*; No.
8 belonged to Mme de Sévigné in 1669–72.

The Rue Ste.-Anastase leads right off the Rue de Thorigny into the
Rue de Turenne, where (right) Nos 52–54 form the 17C *Hôtel de
Montrésor*. No. 56 was once the home of Scarron (1610–60; who died
there) and his wife Françoise d'Aubigné (1635–1719; grand-daughter
of the poet Agrippa d'Aubigné), later Mme de Maintenon. Crebillon
the Elder died here in 1762; and Le Sage was a later occupier. No. 60
is the *Hôtel du Grand-Veneur*, with a boar's head on the façade, while
No. 66 retains traces of the *Hôtel de Turenne*, built for the great
marshal's father. On the site of the chapel of the convent later
installed here, the church of **St.-Denis-du-St.-Sacrement** was built in
1835 in the Grecian style, by Godde. No. 80, a short distance N,
belonged to the Marquis de Launay, the last governor of the Bastille.

The nearby Rue Debelleyme, leading NW, crosses the Rue Vieille-
du-Temple, at the junction of which (No. 110) is the *Hôtel d'Espinay*
(which belonged to a favourite of Henri III), with a remarkable
staircase. Nos 106–100 (to the left) all preserve features of the early
17C.—Just to the N, the Rue de Poitou leads back across the Rue de
Saintonge, retaining some attractive façades, to the Rue Charlot (in
which No. 28, a short distance to the right, is the *Hôtel de Béramcourt*;
1690). Straight across is the Rue Pastourelle, off which (right), in the
Rue de Beauce, Mlle de Scudéry (1607–1701) lived from 1670, and
died.

To the left in the Rue des Archives (the next main street), at No. 70,
died Lamennais (1782–1854), the subversive religious writer. No. 78,
to the right, was built by Bullet (c 1660), with a beautiful staircase by
Le Muet, and was the residence of Marshal Tallard (1712). Further N
at No. 90 are traces of the *Hôpital des Enfants-Rouges*, founded by
François I and his sister Marguerite in 1534, so-called because the
children wore a red uniform.

Just beyond is the SQ. DU TEMPLE (Pl. 9;7), the centre of the densely
populated **Quartier du Temple**, laid out in 1857 on the site of the
late-12C stronghold of the Knights Templar, and the headquarters of
their order in Europe until 1313, when it was occupied by the Order of
St. John.

The area owned by the Templars lay for the most part between this point and the
Pl. de la République, to the NE (see p 197). Before the Revolution it was occupied

by wealthy noble families, artisans who did not belong to the corporations and therefore were free from many restrictions, and debtors who were protected here from legal action.

The palace of the Grand Prior of the Knights of St. John was reputed for luxurious living, but with the Revolution the Tour du Temple, of 1265, was transformed into a prison, and in August 1792 Louis XVI and the royal family were incarcerated here. On 21 January 1793, the king was taken from here to the guillotine; Marie Antoinette was transferred to the *Conciergerie* on 2 August; and on 9 May 1794, Mme Elisabeth was carried off to execution. The Duc de Normandie ('Louis XVII'; born 1785, but never reigned) is believed to have died here on 9 June 1795. The sole survivor, Mme Royale (Marie Thérèse de France; 1778–1851, in Vienna), was released on 19 December of the same year. Adm. Sir Sidney Smith, captured off La Havre, escaped from here in 1798 after two years' imprisonment. The tower was demolished by Napoleon I, and its last vestiges were razed under Napoleon III.

A short distance to the N (195 Rue du Temple) is **Ste.-Élisabeth**, founded in 1630 by Marie de Médicis. The façade is a copy of the original design of the façade Sta. Maria Novellà in Florence. The main feature is the *boiseries*, including, in the ambulatory, 16C carvings of scriptural scenes from the abbey of *St.-Vaast* at Arras.

The Rue Réaumur leads W from the Sq. du Temple, passing (left) the Rue Volta, in which No. 3, of c 1300, is possibly the oldest surviving house in Paris. The Rue Réaumur crosses the Rue de Turbigo to meet the Rue St.-Martin (the original Roman road to the N from Lutetia) between the former priory of *St.-Martin-des-Champs* (right) and (left) *St.-Nicolas-des-Champs*.

The **MUSÉE NATIONAL DES TECHNIQUES**, or *Conservatoire National des Arts et Métiers*, with its entrance at No. 292 Rue St.-Martin (Pl. 9;7), occupies the site of the ancient priory of *St.-Martin-des-Champs*. The exterior of the *Church* is best seen from the Rue Réaumur, to the S.

During the Revolution, these were taken over by the Société des Jeunes Français, an educational institution, and later were used as a small-arms factory. In 1798 they were assigned to the Conservatoire des Arts et Métiers, which had been founded by a decree of the Convention in 1794, and here were assembled the collections of Vaucanson and other scientists. Its administrator was Joseph-Michel Montgolfier (1740–1810), who with his brother Jacques-Étienne (1745–99; a paper-manufacturer) were the inventors of the air-balloon (1783).

Two important buildings remain of the earlier priory, founded in 1060 by Henri I and presented to the Abbey of Cluny by Philippe I in 1079, which until the early 14C stood outside the city walls.

To the right of the entrance courtyard (its gateway is of 1850) is the *Refectory, a 13C masterpiece, built by Pierre de Montreuil (architect of the *Ste.-Chapelle*). This remarkable hall (42·80 by 11·70m), its vaulting sustained by a central row of columns (recalling those of the *Église des Jacobins* at Toulouse), now accommodates the Library. Note the 13C reader's pulpit at the E end. The external side of the S doorway is a good example of decorated Gothic, and the sole relic of the original cloisters. Further S one may see the restored 13C portal of the church (not entered from here; see below). The turret is a comparatively recent addition.

On the GROUND FLOOR are models of locomotives and rolling-stock; rooms on the left, and in the wing beyond, display an extensive collection of astronomical and surveying instruments; clocks (by Berthoud, Lepaute, Bréguet, Janvier, and other famous 18C horologists); and a collection of elaborate automata, including Marie-Antoinette's 'Joueuse de Tympanon'.

On the FIRST FLOOR are rooms (left) displaying examples of machinery employed in the processes of printing; apparatus used by Daguerre, Niepce,

The former refectory of St.-Martin-des-Champs

Lumière, et al, in the pioneering days of photography and cinematography; and historical equipment illustrating the development of recording, television, radio-astronomy, etc.

To the right on the first floor, are rooms devoted to domestic lighting and heating; models of machines, including the 'Machine de Marly' (see end of Rte 35).

From the far end of this wing, steps descend to the former Abbey Church of **St.-Martin-des-Champs**, now sheltering a curious congregation of cars and planes. Although 'restored' in 1854–80, the fabric of the choir, with its apse chapels, is perhaps the earliest Gothic vault in Paris (1130–40), while the aisleless nave dates from the 13C.

Among the prototypes of the motor-car are Cugnot's steam-carriage of 1770, and one by Serpollet (1888); petrol-driven vehicles include a Panhard (1896), Peugeots of 1893 and 1909, a Berliet phaeton (1898), a De Dion-Bouton (1899), and a Renault of 1900. Among the aeroplanes are those of Ader (1897), Esnault-Pelterie (1906), the plane in which Blériot made the first flight across the Channel (1909), a Bréguet of 1911, etc.

Most other sections of the museum, including that devoted to agriculture, are at present closed or are being reformed.

At the NW corner of the building is the *Fontaine du Vertbois* (1712), which, with the adjoining tower, has been restored.

Adjacent is **St.-Nicolas-des-Champs**, with a square tower, built in 1420 but enlarged in 1541–87, when the choir was rebuilt and the outer nave aisles added. At the Revolution, it served as the 'Temple of Hymen'. The original W doors have survived, and the fine S portal (c 1576), after Philibert Delorme, also retains its contemporary doors.

There is good woodwork in the nave vestibule. Paintings include a Baptism of Christ by *Gaudenzio Ferrari*, and Madonna and Saints by *Amico Aspertini* (both c 1500). The ambulatory chapels have 17C wall-paintings; also (1st S chapel), Our Lady of Victories (c 1610–20) and (6th chapel) a 14C Italian altarpiece. The Apostles at the tomb of the Virgin, with the Assumption (on the 17C high altar), is by *Simon Vouet*.

Guillaume Budé (or Budaeus; 1468–1540), Théophile de Viau (1590–1626), Gassendi (1592–1655), the astronomer, and Mlle de Scudéry (1607–1701), are buried here.

We return to the Rue du Temple by turning E along the Rue des Gravilliers (just S of *St.-Nicolas-des-Champs*). Balzac lived at No. 122 Rue du Temple in 1814–19; at No. 13 Rue Chapon (the first turning right, going S), with an interesting court, was the house of the archbishops of Reims. No. 115 Rue du Temple marks the probable site of a residence of Jean Bart (1650–1702), a privateer created Admiral of the Fleet by Louis XIV. Nos 101–103, the *Hôtel de Montmorency*, the residence of Fouquet in 1652, has its entrance at No. 5 Rue de Montmorency. No. 51 in this street, the *Maison du Grand-Pignon*, restored in 1900, was built in 1407 by Nicolas Flamel.

The Rue Michel-Le-Comte, parallel to the S, retains a number of early 17C houses, including the *Hôtel Le Tellier* (No. 16), with a fine courtyard; No. 21, the home of Verniquet, architect to Louis XVI; and No. 28, the *Hôtel d'Hallwyll*, transformed by Ledoux in 1787, and the birthplace of Mme de Staël (1766–1817).

Nos 67–87, on the W side of the Rue du Temple, provide a charming ensemble of 17C houses, of which Nos 71, 73, and 75 form the *Hôtel de St.-Aignan*, built by Le Muet in 1640–50; the courtyards and gate are particularly elegant. No. 79, dating from c 1620, but altered after 1751, is the *Hôtel de Montmor*, also with a good gateway and an attractive pediment in the courtyard.

No. 62 was the site of a house in which Anne de Montmorency, Constable of France, died in 1567; No. 41, the *Auberge de l'Aigle d'Or* (17C), is the last remaining example in Paris of a coaching inn of the period. The square turret on No. 24 dates from 1610; and an inscription on No. 17 indicates the site of the house of Du Guesclin (1372–80).

We regain the Rue de Rivoli at the *Hôtel de Ville* (see Rte 19).

22 The Grands Boulevards: from La Madeleine to the Pl. de la République La Madeleine; Opéra

MÉTROS: Concorde, Madeleine, Opéra, Richelieu-Drouot, Rue Montmartre, Bonne-Nouvelle, Strasbourg-St.-Denis, République.

The Grands Boulevards, a succession of wide thoroughfares extending in a curve from the Pl. de la Concorde to the Bastille, were laid out in 1670–85 on the site of the inner ramparts, demolished in previous decades. These had comprised the E part of the 'enceinte de Charles V', erected after 1370, and the new fortifications to the W built by Louis XIII in 1633–37.

Young visited them in 1787 after attending a theatre, and remarked: 'Coffee-houses...music, noise and *filles* without end; everything but scavengers and lamps. The mud is a foot deep; and there are parts of the boulevards without a single light'. They have since changed in some respects.

Although the Western Boulevards are no longer the centre of fashion they once were, they are still busy shopping and commercial areas.

The Rue Royale forms a convenient approach to the Boulevards from the PL. DE LA CONCORDE. As far as the Rue St.-Honoré it is lined with uniform 18C houses, with shops below, including that of *Lalique*. René Lalique (1860–1945), also a goldsmith and jeweller, caused a sensation when he displayed his designs in glass at the International Exhibition of 1900. No. 3, *Maxim's*, was a haunt of 'high society' in the 1890s; the *Café Weber*, celebrated earlier in the century as a literary forum, stood at No. 21. Mme de Staël lived briefly on her last visit to Paris (1816–17) at No. 6; No. 8 was the home of the architect Gabriel.

The street is dominated by *Ste.-Marie-Madeleine*, or simply **LA MADELEINE** (Pl. 7;6); built in the style of a Roman temple, and surrounded by a majestic Corinthian colonnade.

Two earlier churches had been demolished unfinished in 1777 and 1789, before P. Vignon commenced work in 1806 on the orders of Napoléon, who, before he had thought of the *Arc de Triomphe*, intended it as a 'Temple of Glory' for the 'Grande Armée'. It was finished by Huvé in 1842. In the pediment is a relief of the Last Judgement (restored), by Lemaire; the bronze doors are adorned with bas-reliefs from the Decalogue by Triqueti (1838). Some 300 insurgents were massacred here by M. Thiers's troops during the last days of the Commune.

The INTERIOR consists of a domed cella, meretriciously decorated and inadequately lit. In chapels on either side of the entrance are the Marriage of the Virgin, by *Pradier*, and the Baptism of Christ, by *Rude*; the affected group of the Ascension of the Magdalen, on the high-altar, is by *Marochetti*.

The statue of St. Luke at the back of the building was decapitated in May 1918 by a shell from 'Bertha', the German long-range gun.

On the E side of the PL. DE LA MADELEINE, is a small flower market. At No. 2 stood the *Café Durand*, which played a dominant role in the 1848 Revolution, and where Zola wrote 'J'Accuse', an open letter denouncing the army, and in defence of Dreyfus, published in 'L'Aurore', 13 January 1898.

Pamela Fitzgerald, wife of Edward Fitzgerald (died 1798), the Irish patriot, died in the Rue Richepance, SE of La Madeleine, in 1831.

Marcel Proust spent much of his youth at No. 9 in the BLVD MALESHERBES, leading NW from the *Madeleine*, its S section dominated by *St.-Augustin*, an early example of the use of iron in church-construction (1860–71), by Baltard, architect of the former *Halles*.

The BLVD DE LA MADELEINE, the westernmost of the Grands Boulevards, leads NE. Marie Duplessis (1824–47), the prototype of 'La Dame aux Camélias', died at No. 15 (formerly 11).—The *Crédit*

Foncier occupies an 18C mansion in the neighbouring Rue des Capucines, leading SE towards the *Pl. Vendôme* (see Rte 17). The boulevard is continued by the BLVD DES CAPUCINES, crossing the *Pl. de l'Opéra* (see below). Offenbach (1819–80), who had lived in Paris since 1833, died at No. 8 Blvd des Capucines.

Opposite the *Théâtre des Capucines*, the Rue Édouard-VII leads N to a small Place containing an equestrian statue of Edward VII (by Landowski), who as Prince of Wales and King was a frequent visitor to Paris, and a promoter of the 'Entente Cordiale'.

At No. 14 in the boulevard a tablet records the first exhibition of a cinema film (in the 'Salon Indien' of the *Grand Café*) given by the brothers Louis and Auguste Lumière (28 December 1895). The first demonstration of X-rays, a discovery of Dr Roentgen, took place in the same room a few days later.

The *MUSÉE COGNACQ-JAY, a small elegant collection of French 18C furniture and works of art, occupied three floors at No. 25 Blvd des Capucines but is now temporarily closed. It was originated by Ernest Cognacq, founder of the 'Magasins de la Samaritaine', advised by Camille Gronkowski, then conservateur of the Musée du Petit Palais, and was inaugurated in 1929. The collection will be transferred to the *Hôtel Denon*, 8 Rue Elzévir (near the Musée Carnavalet) within the next year or two.

One room on the third floor preserves panelling from the Château of Eu, in Normandy; and among furniture, much of it marquetry, is a good desk; also a Louis XVI bed 'à la polonaise'; and a set of chairs covered with Beauvais tapestry. Among objets d'art, three colourful 'Kien-Lung' porcelain birds are notable; also terracotta busts by *Jean-Baptiste Lemoyne* of the Maréchal de Saxe, and the Maréchal de Lowendal. Likewise a collection of Meissen porcelain and French terracotta figures, including *Clodion*, Project for the tomb of Mme Dubarry's dog; and another collection of enamelled and jewelled boxes.

Outstanding among the portraits are: *Boucher*, Mme Baudouin, his daughter; *Francis Cotes*, Charles Colmore; *Drouais*, Alexandrine Lenormant d'Étioles (daughter of Mme de Pompadour); *Daniel Gardner*, Lady Auckland and her daughter, and Albinia Hobart; *Baron Gérard*, Mme Bauquin du Boulay and her niece; *Marguerite Gérard*, Claude-Nicolas Ledoux, the architect; *Hugh Douglas Hamilton*, Lady Carhampton (?); *Adélaïde Labille Guiard*, Comtesse de Maussion; *Largillierre*, The Duchess of Beaufort (?); *Maurice Quentin Delatour*, Mme La Présidente de Rieux, Self-portrait, Man in a blue waistcoat, and The Marquis de Bérenger; *Lawrence*, Princess Clémentine de Metternich, and a copy of The Calmady children; *Lépicié*, La Coiffe blanche; *Nattier*, Madame Henriètte, Marie Leczinska; *Perronneau*, Charles Lenormant du Coudrey; *Reynolds*, Lord Northington (once in an oval frame); attributed to *Romney*, Female portrait; *John Russell*, Miss Power; *Mme Vigée-Lebrun*, The Vicomtesse de Mirabeau playing a guitar, and A Dancer; and an *anon.* Portrait of the Marquise de Sassenage.

Other works include *Boucher*, La belle cuisinière, and attributed to him, The Music Lesson; *Canaletto*, two Venetian scenes; *Chardin*, Still life with a copper cauldron; *Morland*, The first steps; *Rembrandt*, Balaam's ass, an early work (1626); *Ruisdael*, The old oak; *Giovanni-Battista Tiepolo*, Cleopatra's banquet; *Watteau*, Assembly in the park; a number of *galante* scenes by *Baudouin, Boilly, Jollain,*

Lavreince, and *Mallet*, and representative works by *Boucher*, *Fragonard*, *Greuze*, *Guardi*, and *Hubert Robert*.

At No. 35 in the Blvd des Capucines, once the studio of Nadar (Félix Tournachon; 1820–1910), the portrait-photographer (and aeronaut), took place the exhibition of paintings (1874) by Renoir, Manet, Pissarro, and Monet, which included the latter's 'Impression—Soleil levant', which gave the group its name. See *Musée Marmottan*.

The PL. DE L'OPÉRA (Pl. 7;6), a busy focus of traffic, is dominated to the N by the opera-house, while to the NW is the *Café de la Paix*, once a fashionable meeting-place for visitors to Paris.

The grandiose **OPÉRA*, an appropriate monument to the most extravagant and brilliant period of the Second Empire, was built in 1861–75 from the designs of Charles Garnier (1825–98), the successful entrant of 171 competitors. Although covering a huge area, it contains only 2158 seats, few in comparison with some other large theatres.

The first opera-house in Paris was established in 1669 by Perrin, Cambert, and the Marquis de Sourdéac on the Left Bank, between the Rue de Seine and the Rue Mazarine, and the first director was Lully (from 1674), under whom it acquired its secondary title of *Académie Royale de Musique*.

The façade, flanked by a flight of steps, is lavishly decorated with coloured marbles and sculpture. On either side of the arcade opening into the vestibule are allegorical groups, including (right) The Dance, by Carpeaux (a copy of the original, which now graces the interior of the *Musée d'Orsay*). Above are medallions of composers; and bronze-gilt statues of other composers and librettists are seen between the monolithic columns of the loggia. Behind the low dome of the auditorium is a triangular pediment crowned by a statue of Apollo of the Golden Lyre.

The E pavilion in the Rue Halévy is the subscribers' entrance; to the W, in the Rue Auber, is the 'Pavillon d'Honneur', and the entrance to the *Museum* and *Library*, containing a complete collection of the scores of all operas and ballets performed here since its foundation, and over 100,000 drawings of costumes, and scenery, and photographs of artistes, etc.

This latter entrance, originally known as the 'Pavillon de l'Empereur', was designed so that his coach could be driven up to the level of the dress circle—a precaution welcomed since Orsini's attempt on the life of Napoléon III on his way to the old Opera-house in 1858, and a device which won Garnier the competition, so it was rumoured: see Rue le Peletier, below.

The *Hall d'Acceuil* contains a shop selling objects on themes associated with the Ballets Russes, among others (open 10.00–17.00 and on the evenings of performances). The second vestibule contains the box-office (open 11.00–18.30), beyond which is the *Grand Staircase*, with its white marble steps 10m wide, and with a balustrade of onyx and rosso and verde antico. On the first floor, where the staircase divides, is the entrance to the stalls and the amphitheatre, flanked by caryatids, and on each floor are arcades of monolithic marble columns. The *Avant-Foyer* leads to the *Grand Foyer*; glass doors communicate with the Loggia overlooking the *Pl. de l'Opéra*, and by the middle door is a bust of Garnier by *Carpeaux*.

The *Auditorium*, resplendent in red plush and gilt, and with five tiers of boxes, is—except during performances—not normally on view, but visitors may apply to join a guided tour. The dome, resting on eight pillars of scagliola, was redecorated in 1964, many would say inappropriately, by *Chagall*. The huge stage is 60m high, 52m wide, and 37m deep, behind which is the *Foyer de la Dance* (the scene of many paintings by Degas; see p 101), with a mirror measuring 7 by 10m.

The AV. DE L'OPÉRA leads SE to the *Pl. André-Malraux* (see Rte 17), its southern reaches now more oriental than occidental in character! It is crossed by the Rue Louis-le-Grand, in which (at No. 3) Mme de Montespan and the painter Hyacinthe Rigaud (1659–1743; who died at No. 1), had houses. Napoléon and Joséphine Beauharnais were married in 1796 at No. 3 Rue d'Antin (the next cross-street), which was then the Mairie of the 2nd arrondissement. The *Fontaine Gaillon* (1828), just to the E in the Rue St.-Augustin, is by Visconti and Jacquot.

Immediately behind the *Opéra*, facing the PL. DIAGHILEV, are the department stores of *Galeries Lafayette* (1898) and, to the W, *Du Printemps* (1889; but remodelled after a fire in 1921, and since), with huge and remarkable central halls.

Just E of the former is the Rue de la Chaussée-d'Antin, leading N to *La Trinité* (see p 199). In its S section, at No. 2, Rossini lived from 1857–68. No. 5 (rebuilt) was the home of Baron Grimm, frequented by Mme d'Épinay, and which sheltered Mozart in 1778 after the death of his mother: it was the residence of Chopin in 1833–36. No. 7 (also demolished) was the home of the Neckers, who entertained Gibbon here; in 1798 it was bought by Jules Récamier, the banker, whose wife here presided over the most distinguished salon of the Directory, frequented also by Lord and Lady Holland, and many other English *en passage*.

The BLVD DES ITALIENS (the continuation NE of the *Blvd des Capucines*), whose many cafés have been largely replaced by cinemas and commercial buildings, derived its name from the *Théâtre des Italiens* (1783), where Donizetti's 'Don Pasquale' was first performed in 1843. Grétry lived at No. 7 from 1795 to 1813.

In 1784–85, Jefferson had lodgings in the Impasse Taitbout (now Rue du Helder), leading left. No. 5 Rue Taitbout, further E, was the house of Sir Richard Wallace, where Lord Hertford accumulated the works of art now in the Wallace Collection, London (see also p 223). Wagner lived at No. 25 in 1840–41.

At the corner of the next street, the Rue Laffitte (named after Jacques Laffitte, 1767–1844, the financier; see Maisons-Laffitte, Rte 35), stood the house of Mme Tallien (1773–1835), daughter of the Spanish financier Cabarrus, and wife of the revolutionary, and later Princesse de Chimay. Part of the building (No. 20) became the *Café Hardy*, rival of the *Café Riche* at No. 16 ('Il faut être bien riche pour dîner chez Hardy, et bien hardi pour dîner chez Riche').

At the far end of Rue Laffitte is seen *N.-D.-de-Lorette* (Rte 23), with *Sacré-Cœur* in the background. No. 17 was the residence of Queen Hortense of Holland, and here Napoléon III was born in 1808. From No. 27, then Laffitte's residence, was issued the manifesto of Thiers proposing the coronation of Louis-Philippe. At Nos 39 and 41 stood Ambroise Vollard's art gallery, where many paintings by Gauguin and Cézanne were first displayed. Vollard was also responsible for the first exhibitions in Paris of works by Picasso and Matisse (in 1901 and 1904, respectively).

It was in the parallel Rue Le Peletier (to the E) that the 'Carbonaro' Orsini flung a bomb at the carriage conveying Napoléon III to the opera, killing or injuring 156 people, but leaving the emperor unharmed (1858). No. 3 was the *Café du Divan*, frequented by Balzac, Gautier, de Nerval, and Baudelaire. On the site of No. 6 stood the *Salle Le Peletier*, an opera-house from 1821 until 1873, when it was burned out. Here the works of Meyerbeer, and Wagner's 'Tannhäuser', among many others, were first performed.

In the Rue de Marivaux (opposite) stands a building until recently the *Opéra-Comique*, but now housing an experimental *Opéra-Studio*.

The Opéra-Comique originated in a company which produced pieces during local fairs, and in 1715 purchased from the Opéra the right of playing vaudevilles interspersed with ariettas. Discord between the two theatres continued until in 1757 Charles Favart (1710–92) finally established the rights of the Opéra-Comique, which moved to the 'Salle Favart' on this somewhat confined site in 1783, since rebuilt.

At the junction of the boulevard with that of the BLVD MONTMAR-TRE and BLVD HAUSSMANN (only extended to this point in 1927), the Rue Drouot leads N past (No. 6) the *Mairie of the 9th arrondissement* in a mansion of 1746–48, and No. 9 (left), the *Hôtel des Ventes de Paris*, or **Nouveau Drouot**, the main auction-rooms of Paris, where important sales are held from February to June, and which since 1801 has occupied the same place in Parisian life as Christie's or Sotheby's in London. It has been rebuilt recently in an ugly 'modern' style.

To the S, the Rue de Richelieu leads to the *Bibliothèque Nationale* (see Rte 18). Thomas Paine wrote 'The Age of Reason' at No. 95 in this street (1793).

The short BLVD MONTMARTRE, in spite of its name, is some distance from Montmartre. At No. 10 (left) is the *Musée Grévin*, a waxwork collection equivalent to Mme Tussaud's.—On the right is the Rue Vivienne, leading to the *Bourse*; the *Passage des Panoramas* (named after an entertainment displaying views of cities, introduced to Paris by the American Robert Fulton, who had also tested his first steamboat on the Seine in 1803); and the *Théâtre des Variétés*, scene of several of Offenbach's successes.

The Rue Montmartre, already so named in 1200, leads SE towards *St.-Eustache* (Rte 19).—Émile Zola (1840–1902) was born at No. 10 Rue St.-Joseph, a short distance S; the family moved to Aix-en-Provence in 1842.

The Rue du Faubourg-Montmartre, diverging NW towards the 'suburb' of Montmartre, recalls the time when the boulevard formed the city boundary. Lautréamont (1846–70) died at No. 7, where he had written 'Les Chants de Maldoror'.—The Rue Geoffroy-Marie, a turning off to the right (commemorating a saddler and his wife who in 1260 presented to the *Hôtel-Dieu* a little farm which sold for over 3 million francs in 1840), leads to the titillating cabaret known as the *Folies Bergère* (originally the *Café Sommier élastique*, founded in 1869 to produce vaudevilles), situated in a mainly Jewish enclave, and a centre of the diamond trade.

Continuing E along the BLVD POISSONNIÈRE (in which No. 27 was Chopin's first Paris home, in 1831–32), we pass (right) the Rue du Sentier, where, opposite the end of the Rue du Croissant, Mozart and his mother lodged in 1778. In the same year she was buried in the vanished *Cimitière St.-Joseph* nearby, also the original burial-place of Molière.

Necker lived in 1766–89 at the junction of the adjacent Rue de Mulhouse and the Rue de Cléry (in a house replaced by No. 29) and here every Friday Mme Necker (Suzanne Churchod; 1739–94) held her salon, frequented by Voltaire, Diderot, d'Alembert, Marmontel, Buffon, et al.

To the N, at No. 2 Rue du Conservatoire (beyond the Rue Rougemont), is the *Conservatoire National d'Art Dramatique*, a small theatre of 1802, reputed for its excellent acoustics.

The boulevard is now crossed by the Rue Poissonnière (right) and its N extension, the Rue du Faubourg-Poissonnière, both named after the fishmongers who used to pass by on their way to the *Halles*. Corot (1796–1875) died at No. 56 Rue du Faubourg-Poissonnière. Beyond this junction, the line of boulevards is continued by the BLVD DE BONNE-NOUVELLE, on the N side of which is the façade (1887) of the *Théâtre du Gymnase*, where Rachel made her début in 1837.

At the far end of the next street running N rises the church of *St.-Vincent-de-Paul* (see Rte 23).
   To the S, steps lead up to *N.-D. de Bonne-Nouvelle*, rebuilt in 1824. André Chénier (1762–94) lived in 1793 at 97 Rue de Cléry, close by; the same street was Corneille's home in 1665–81.

The short BLVD ST.-DENIS (Pl. 9;5) lies between the *Porte St.-Denis* and the *Porte St.-Martin*, beyond which the *Blvd St.-Martin* continues as far as the *Pl. de la République*. The **Porte St.-Denis**, a triumphal arch 23m high, designed by Blondel, was erected in 1672 to commemorate the victories of Louis XIV in Germany and Holland.

The bas-reliefs were designed by Girardon and executed by the brothers Anguier. It faces the Rue St.-Denis, or 'Voie Royale', once the processional route of entry into Paris, and last so used on the occasion of Queen Victoria's visit in 1855.

On the far side of the BLVD DE SÉBASTOPOL, which with its N extension, the BLVD DE STRASBOURG, stretches from the *Pl. du Châtelet* to the *Gare de l'Est*, we pass the **Porte St.-Martin**, another triumphal arch in honour of Louis XIV, c 18m high, built in 1674 by Bullet, and decorated with bas-reliefs of contemporary campaigns, by Desjardins and Marsy (S side), and Le Hongre and the elder Legros (N).

At No. 6 in the *Blvd St.-Denis* stood the 'Cinéma St.-Denis', opened in 1896 by the brothers Lumière, which claimed to be the first cinema.

The Rue St.-Martin (the original Roman road leading N from Lutetia) leads S to the *Conservatoire National des Arts et Métiers*, and *St.-Nicolas-des-Champs* (see Rte 21), off which the Rue N.-D. de Nazareth diverges left. The façades of Nos 41–49 are of interest; Rudolf Diesel (1858–1913), the inventor of the engine which bears his name, was born at No. 38.

We pass two famous theatres in the BLVD ST.-MARTIN, just E of the Arch, the *Théâtre de la Renaissance* and *Théâtre de la Porte-St.-Martin*, both rebuilt after being burnt down during the Commune.

The 'Renaissance' was managed by Sarah Bernhardt in 1893–99. The 'Porte-St.-Martin', in its original form a foundation of Marie-Antoinette (who had it built in 75 days in 1781 to house the opera), is remembered as being the theatre of Frédérick Lemaître (1800–76). Here Coquelin aîné (who created the name-part in Rostand's 'Cyrano de Bergerac') was seized by a fatal illness during a rehearsal of 'Chantecler' in 1909..
   Paul de Kock (1794–1871), the novelist, died at No. 8 in the boulevard.

The **Pl. de la République** (Pl. 9;8), on the site of the Porte du Temple, and the junction of seven important thoroughfares, was laid out in 1856–65 by Haussmann for strategic reasons, but it has maintained a political role as the scene of radical demonstrations. The pedestal of the *Monument de la République* (1883; 25m high), has bronze bas-reliefs by Dalou.
   At the corner of the Rue Léon-Jouhaux (previously Rue de la Douane) leading NE from the Place, was Daguerre's workshop (1822–35). Gounod's 'Faust' was first performed in 1859 in the *Théâtre Lyrique*, one of many (including 'Des Funambules', 1816–62) which stood on a section of the BLVD DU TEMPLE demolished by Haussmann, known earlier in the 19C from the melodramas enacted

here as the 'Boulevard du Crime', and immortalised by Marcel Carné
in the film 'Les Enfants du Paradis' (1945).

Beyond the *Pl. de la République* the boulevards are of slight interest, and change
their character. The BLVD DU TEMPLE, with its continuations, leads SE to the *Pl.
de la Bastille* (see Rte 21). Flaubert lived at No. 42 in this boulevard in 1856–69;
and a little to the N is the site of the house from which Fieschi discharged his
'infernal machine' at Louis-Philippe in 1835, killing Marshal Mortier and several
others, but not the king.—Just to the W, at No. 5 in the parallel street named after
him, died Béranger (1780–1857).

23   Gare de l'Est to Gare St.-Lazare (Faubourg St.-Martin and Faubourg St.-Denis)

MÉTROS: République, Gare de l'Est, Gare du Nord, Poissonnière,
N.-D.-de-Lorette, Trinité, St.-Lazare, St.-Augustin, Madeleine.

The BLVD DE MAGENTA leads NW from the *Pl. de la République* to
meet the outer boulevards beyond the *Gare du Nord*.

Just E of its intersection with the BLVD DE STRASBOURG is **St.-
Laurent**, one of the oldest foundations in Paris. Gregory of Tours
mentions that a church existed here near the Roman road as early as
583.

The present building, begun before 1429 but retaining an older N tower, was
continued in the 16–17C, the nave having been vaulted and the choir
remodelled in 1655–59, with a high-altar by *Antoine Le Pautre*. The *Lady Chapel*
dates from 1712. The 17C façade was demolished in 1862–65, when the
Flamboyant W front was built and the spire erected. The roof has elegantly
carved pendentives. Mme du Barry (Jeanne Bécu; 1746–93) was married here in
1764.

The courtyard of the **Gare de l'Est** (Pl. 9;3; the terminus of the line to
Strasbourg, etc.) just to the N, occupies the site of the medieval St.
Lawrence fair.

To the W of the boulevard at this point stood the *Prison de St.-Lazare* (since 1935
partly demolished and rebuilt as a hospital), from 1632 the headquarters of the
Lazarists or Priests of the Mission, founded in 1625 by Vincent de Paul
(1576–1660). Among its inmates were André Chénier and Hubert Robert.

The boulevard next crosses the Rue La Fayette before passing (right)
the **Gare du Nord**, by Hittorf (1863), the terminus of the line from
Calais, Boulogne, etc. (Pl. 9;3), and also of a rapid shuttle service to the
Charles de Gaulle airport.

There is little of interest in the thickly populated cosmopolitan Quartier de la
Chapelle to the N. Adjacent to an ugly modern basilica stands *St.-Denis-de-la-
Chapelle* (13C, but much restored), where Joan of Arc received communion in
November 1429 before besieging the walls of Paris.

Turning SW along the Rue La Fayette, we pass (right) **St.-Vincent-de-
Paul** (1824–44), by Lepère and Hittorff, with two square towers
dominating a pedimented portico of twelve Ionic columns, and
approached by a monumental flight of steps.

At No. 58 Rue d'Hauteville, leading S, is the *Hôtel de Bourrienne*
(1787), finely decorated in First Empire style by Napoléon's secretary.

This street is crossed by the Rue de Paradis, where at No. 30 bis is the shop of the glass-maker Baccarat, replacing one existing since 1764, with a *Museum* adjoining.

At No. 18 in this street is the colourful entrance of the **Musée de la Publicité** (posters), opened in 1978 as a department of the Union Centrale des Arts Decoratifs, containing the Pochet, Buquet, and Roger Braun collections, among others. Its computerised catalogue is of assistance in searching for subjects, etc. among over 70,000 examples.

No. 9 Rue de Montholon (leading E from the SQ. DE MONTHOLON) was the residence of Liszt in 1831.

We shortly diverge due W along the Rue de Châteaudun, to pass (right) **N.-D.-de-Lorette**, another drearily magnificent basilican church, built in 1823–36 by Hippolyte Lebas, with a portico of four Corinthian columns.

Bizet (1838–75), born at No. 26 Rue de la Tour-d'Auvergne (leading off the Rue des Martyrs, ascending behind the church), was christened here.—The Rue des Martyrs, the ancient approach to Montmartre, was already well known for its 'cabarets' in the 18C; Géricault (1791–1824) died at No. 49, later occupied by Béranger.

The Rue N.-D.-de-Lorette ascends NW from the church through a quarter whose name was synonymous with the *demi-mondaine* or *femmes entretenues* of the mid-19C who congregated here, and to whom newly-built dwellings in the neighbourhood were let off cheaply until the plaster dried! These 'Lorettes', a favourite subject of the caricaturist Gavarni (1801–66), are represented on his monument in the small PL. ST.-GEORGES, which the street crosses. Delacroix lived from 1844 to 1857 at No. 58 (then 54) in the Rue N.-D.-de-Lorette; Gauguin was born at No. 56 in 1848.

No. 27 in the PL. ST.-GEORGES is the *Hôtel Thiers*, the residence of President Thiers (1797–1877) from 1833.

Burned down by the Communards and reconstructed at public expense, it now contains the *Bibliothèque Thiers* (80,000 vols on the history of France since the Revolution; and the Napoleonic collection of Frédéric Masson, of 30,000 vols; drawings by *David*; and a bust of Joséphine by *Houdon*, etc.). Contact the Librarian, Institut de France, 23 Quai de Conti for permission to visit.

At No. 28, opposite, Thérèse Lachman, later Marquise de Païva, held her salons in 1851–66, at which the brothers Goncourt, Gautier, Sainte-Beuve, Taine, and Wagner, were frequent visitors. Mallarmé (1842–98) was born in the nearby Rue Laferrière (No. 12).

The Rue St.-Georges runs downhill, and crosses the Rue de Châteaudun. The Goncourt brothers lived at No. 43 from 1849 to 1868. Auber (1782–1871) lived for thirty years and died at No. 22; Henry Murger (1822–61), author of 'Scènes de la Vie de Bohème', was born the son of a concierge at No. 19.

In the Rue Taitbout (parallel to the W) lodged Rossini (at No. 28), when musical director of the *Théâtre des Italiens* (1824–25); and Mirabeau (1749–91) died at No. 42.

In 1842–47 Chopin and George Sand lived at Nos 5 and 9 respectively in the SQ. D'ORLÉANS, off the E side of the N end of this street.—At No. 14 Rue de la Rochefoucauld, to the W at this level, is the *Musée Gustave Moreau* (admission 10.00–12.45, 14.00–17.15 except Tuesday), containing an extensive collection of paintings and drawings left by Moreau (1826–98) to the State.

To the W stands **La Trinité**, a conspicuously ugly church built in 1863–67 by Ballu in a hybrid style, with a tower 63m high. It was erected on the site of the disreputable Cabaret de la Grande Pinte, later Les Porcherons. It was here that Berlioz's funeral service took place (11 March 1869).

From a point NE of the church, the Rue Pigalle and Rue Blanche ascend NE and N towards Montmartre. To the W of the church the Rue Clichy (in which, at No. 21, Hugo lived in 1880) ascends N to the *Pl. de Clichy*. No. 16 is the *Casino de Paris*, a famous music-hall.—To the S, the Rue de Mogador leads to the *Opéra*.

The Rue St.-Lazare leads W from the SQ. DE LA TRINITÉ. Mme Vigée-Lebrun died at No. 29 in 1842. Just E of the **Gare St.-Lazare** (Pl. 7;4), the Rue d'Amsterdam leads N, in which lived Manet (at No. 77; in 1879–83) and Alexandre Dumas, père (No. 97; from 1854).

The station itself is a terminus of the western region of the SNCF. The *Hôtel Terminus* was the home of Georges Feydeau, who, intending to stay a week while his family moved house, remained a decade (1909–19).

To the W of the station, the Rue de Rome leads NW, in which No. 89 was the home of Mallarmé from 1885, and here his friends—among them George Moore—would congregate on Tuesday evenings.

At No. 14 Rue de Madrid, diverging W off this street, stood, since 1911, the **Conservatoire National Supérieur de Musique**, which together with its fine collection of musical instruments, is in the process of moving to the Cité de la Musique at La Villette; see Rte 29.

Jules Renard (1864–1910), author of 'Poil de Carotte', died at No. 44 Rue du Rocher, to the W, where he had lived since 1888.

The Rue du Havre leads S from the *Gare St.-Lazare*, where No. 8, the *Lycée Condorcet*, founded in 1804, occupies the former buildings (with a Doric cloister court) of a Capuchin convent; on the site of its chapel (in the parallel street to the E) is *St.-Louis d'Antin*, by Brongniart (1782). Proust was one of the school's many eminent pupils.

The street is continued S of the *Blvd Haussmann* by the Rue Tronchet (in which Chopin lived, at No. 5, in 1839–42) to the *Madeleine* (see Rte 22).

The BLVD HAUSSMANN, one of the main streets in the area, commemorates Eugène-Georges, Baron Haussmann (1809–91) who, as Préfet de la Seine, initiated extensive urban development in central Paris. Work began here in 1857 as part of a scheme to construct an unbroken thoroughfare from the *Blvd Montmartre* to the *Arc de Triomphe*, and was only completed in 1926.

A short distance to the W, on the S side of the *Blvd Haussmann*, is the SQ. LOUIS XVI (Pl. 7;5), formerly the *Cimetière de la Madeleine*, where rest the bodies of the victims of the panic of 1770 in the *Pl. de la Concorde* (see Rte 13), together with the Swiss guards massacred on 10 August 1792, and all those guillotined between 26 August 1792 and 24 March 1794 (among them Charlotte Corday and Philippe-Égalité).

The **Chapelle Expiatoire** ◊ (admission 10.00–17.00 or 18.00), erected in 1815–26 from the plans of Percier and Fontaine, stands in the SW corner of the Square. The chapel, in the style of a classical funeral temenos, was built by order of Louis XVIII and dedicated to the memory of Louis XVI and Marie-Antoinette, whose remains, first interred in the graveyard on this site, were removed to St.-Denis in 1815; see Rte 36.

Inside are two marble groups: Louis XVI and his confessor Abbé Henry Essex Edgeworth (1745–1807), by *Bosio* (below which is inscribed the king's will, dated 25 December 1792) and Marie-Antoinette supported by Religion, by *Cortot*, the latter figure bearing the features of Mme Élisabeth. (Below is inscribed a letter said to have been written by the queen to her sister-in-law from the Conciergerie on 16 October 1793.) The bas-relief by *Gérard* above the doorway represents the removal of the remains to St.-Denis.

24 Montmartre

Best approached from the MÉTRO stations of Clichy, Lamarck-Caulaincourt, or Anvers.

The PL. DE CLICHY (Pl. 7;2) was the site of the 'Barrière de Clichy', which on 30 March 1814 was defended against the approaching Russian troops by pupils from the École Polytechnique and the Garde Nationale under Moncey, an action commemorated by a bronze group by Doublemard (1869).

To the E lies the wide BLVD DE CLICHY, forming, with its continuation, the BLVD DE ROCHECHOUART, the S boundary of Montmartre proper.

The first turning right off the Blvd de Clichy is the Rue de Douai: at No. 30, the house of Turgenev and Mme Viardot, the singer, Dickens met George Sand in 1856 and found her 'just the kind of woman in appearance whom you might suppose to be the Queen's monthly nurse'. The street shortly crosses the PL. ADOLPHE-MAX, in which Vuillard had a studio. Zola (1840–1902) died at No. 21 bis Rue de Bruxelles, crossing this square. Berlioz (1803–69) died at No. 4 Rue de Calais, leading SE; and Arnold Bennett lived in an apartment in this same building from late 1903 to late 1906, when writing 'The Old Wives' Tale' (1908).

Montmartre on 15 July 1789

The *Blvds de Clichy* and *de Rochechouart* are now the focus of the seedy night life of an increasingly sordid area, where colourful crowds congregate in the cafés and around the so-called 'cabarets artistiques' of the PL. BLANCHE, on the N side of which stood the *Moulin Rouge*, built 1889, where one of the star performers was Joseph Pujol, (1857–1945, 'Le Pétomane'), and PL. PIGALLE.

A century has passed since *Montmartre* was made more accessible by the construction of new streets ascending through the N slums, and poor artists, migrating there because it was both picturesque and cheap, made it for about 30 years an artistic centre. Among those who vividly depicted this bohemian era was Toulouse-Lautrec (1864–1901), whose studio was at No. 5 Av. Frochot, near the *Pl. Pigalle.*—No. 16 in the adjacent Rue Frochot was the home of Mme Sabatier (1822–89; 'La Présidente', the mistress of Richard Wallace after 1866), often the rendez-vous of Alfred de Musset, Flaubert, Sainte-Beuve, Clésinger, Feydeau, Gautier, and Baudelaire.

About 1881 the famous 'Le Chat Noir' (No. 84 Blvd de Rochechouart; closed in 1897) was opened, advertising the attractions of the district and inviting a tide of pseudo-bohemians, tourists, and less desirable hangers-on, before which the serious artists retired, and have now all but vanished. There remain, however, a few old-fashioned streets and backwaters, made familiar in the paintings of Utrillo, among others, and an hour or two may be pleasantly spent wandering around the 'Butte' (see below), preferably during daylight.

Seurat and Signac had adjoining studios at No. 128 bis BLVD DE CLICHY in 1886; Seurat (1859–91) died at No. 39 Rue André-Antoine (leading N from the Pl. Pigalle). Picasso lived at No. 130 in 1909; and Degas died at No. 6 in 1917.

The short Av. Rachel, the first turning on the left off the *Blvd. de Clichy* going E, leads to the main entrance of the **Cimetière de Montmartre**, on the W slope of the Butte (Pl. 7;2), partly spanned by a viaduct.

Although less important than that of *Père-Lachaise*, it contains the graves of many famous 18–20C writers, including Gautier, de Vigny, the Goncourt brothers, Alexandre Dumas (fils), Stendhal, Heine, Murger, Zola, Feydeau, Maxime du Camp, Renan, and Giraudoux; among composers, Berlioz, Delibes, Offenbach, Halévy, Adam, and Ambroise Thomas; also Adolphe Sax; among artists, Fragonard, Greuze, Delaroche, Carle Vernet, Horace Vernet, Diaz de la Peña, and Degas; the actors Frédéric Lemaître and Louis Jouvet; the dancers Vestris, Taglioni, and Nijinsky; Mme Récamier, Pauline Viardot, and Marie Duplessis ('La Dame aux Camélias'); Waldeck Rousseau, Marshal Lannes (heart only), Hittorff, Fourier, Ampère, Dr Charcot, and Miles Byrne, the United Irishman.

From the *Pl. de Clichy*, the Rue Caulaincourt is carried over the cemetery by a viaduct, which is the most convenient approach to Montmartre by car.—Continuing along the BLVD DE CLICHY, we pass (left) the once-famous *Moulin Rouge* (now a cinema; see above), facing the PL. BLANCHE and turn left up the steep Rue Lepic (at No. 54 lived van Gogh in 1886) towards the rebuilt *Moulin de la Galette*. Turning E along the Rue Norvins, we shortly reach the central PL. DU TERTRE (Pl. 8;1–2), with the former Mairie (No. 3), now much commercialised, and surrounded by cafés, etc.

To the E of the *Pl. du Tertre* stands the old church of **ST. PIERRE-DE-MONTMARTRE**, the successor of an earlier building erected to commemorate the martyrdom of St. Denis, a relic of a Benedictine nunnery founded in 1134 by Adélaïde de Savoie (died 1154). It was consecrated in the presence of her son Louis VII by Pope Eugenius III in 1147. In 1794 it served as the 'Temple of Reason'.

The façade dates from the time of Louis XIV. Inside, against the W wall, are two ancient columns with 7C capitals; two other capitals, one at the apse entrance and another in the N aisle, are of the same date. The nave has 15C vaulting; the aisle vaulting was added in a restoration of 1900–05. The apse has also been almost entirely rebuilt, but the choir retains perhaps the earliest example of an ogee arch in Paris (1147). The foundress's tomb lies behind the altar.

In the *Jardin du Calvaire*, S of the church, are Stations of the Cross executed for Richelieu; foundations of a Roman temple have been discovered to the N of the building, while in the derelict graveyard is the tomb of the navigator Bougainville (1729–1811); also buried here are the ¬culptor Pigalle (1714–85) and members of the Fitz-James family.

The Rue Azais, to the S, leads past a water-tower to the terrace below the *Basilique du Sacré-Cœur*, with extensive views S over the entire city with its changing skyline. Commanding Paris in this way, the history of the Butte Montmartre is one long series of sieges and battles.

The **Butte Montmartre** rises 130m above sea-level and 104m above the level of the Seine, and is traditionally the highest point in Paris; cf. *Belleville*. The name has been variously derived from Mons Mercurii, Mons Martis, and Mons Martyrum; the two first presuppose the existence of a Roman temple on the hill; the last the probability that St. Denis and his companions, SS. Rusticus and Eleutherius, were beheaded at the foot of the hill, St. Denis afterwards walking to the site of the Basilica of St.-Denis (see Rte 36), 'with his head in his hands'. The *Chapelle du Martyre* (in the convent at 9 Rue Yvonne-le-Tac, just E of the Métro Abbesses) occupies the probable position of a chapel erected on the site of the martyrdom. It was in its crypt that Ignatius de Loyola and his six companions, including Francisco Xavier, took the first Jesuit vows, in 1534, thus founding the Society of Jesus. The Butte was occupied by Henri of Navarre in 1589, and here in 1814 took place the final struggle between the French and the Allies.

On 18 March 1871, at No. 6 Rue des Roses—then called des Rosiers—to the NE of the *Butte*, Generals Clément Thomas and Claude Martin Lecomte were captured and murdered by insurgents when attempting to seize cannon entrusted to the National Guards. Their deaths to a certain extent precipitated government action against the Communards.

In 1873 the National Assembly decreed the building of a basilica here as an expiatory offering after the Franco-Prussian War of 1870–71. The result, the **SACRÉ-CŒUR**, only too visible from almost every part of Paris, is a conspicuous oriental-looking white stone edifice in a neo-Romanesque-Byzantine style derived from *St.-Front* at Périgueux. Its ugliness does not seem to deter a constant press of visitors.

Work was begun in 1876 from the plans of *Abadie* (who had restored *St.-Front*), and although used for services in 1891, it was not consecrated as a basilica until 1919. 100m long, and 75m across the ambulatory, it is surmounted by a dome 83m high, and abutted by a square bell-tower. The undaunted tourist may survey its meretriciously decorated interior, and, for a fee, visit both the crypt and dome (for the panoramic view).

Flights of steps descend the steep slope of the Butte to the SQ. WILLETTE (there is a funicular railway on its W side), and the Rue de Steinkerque leads downhill to the Pl. d'Anvers and Blvd. de Rochechouart.

Not much remains of 'Old Montmartre', with its cottages and little gardens, although in the Rue des Saules, leading N from the Rue Norvins, one may see the last surviving vineyard of Paris. No. 4 in this street is 'Au Lapin Agile', made famous by its artistic clientele. Harriet Smithson (Mme Berlioz; 1800–54, who had married the composer in 1833), Honegger (1892–1955), and Utrillo (1883–1956) are buried in the nearby *Cimetière St.-Vincent*.

At No. 42 Rue des Saules is the *Musée d'Art Juif*.

At No. 17 in the Rue St.-Vincent, to the right beyond the vineyard, steps climb to the *Musée de Vieux-Montmartre*, installed in a 17C house once belonging to Roze de Rosimond, a member of Molière's 'Illustre Théâtre'. It contains, apart from ephemera and material of very local interest, a small collection of Clignancourt (or Montmartre) porcelain, made in 1767–99 in a pottery at the junction of the Rues du Mont-Cenis and Marcadet. This house was occupied by Renoir in 1875, and later by Utrillo, and Dufy, among others.

At the corner of the Rue St.-Vincent, at No. 24 Rue du Mont-Cenis (house rebuilt) lived Berlioz and Harriet Smithson in 1834–37.
    Not far S of the Rue Norvins, the PL. ÉMILE-GOUDEAU was a favourite 'artistic' residence c 1910, where (at No. 13, the 'Bateau-Lavoir'; rebuilt since a fire in 1970) lived Modigliani, Picasso, and Max Jacob, and where a banquet was given in honour of 'Douanier' Rousseau.

25   From the Pl. de la Concorde to the Arc de Triomphe: the Av. des Champs-Élysées; Petit Palais; Arc de Triomphe

MÉTROS: Concorde, Champs-Élysées-Clemenceau, Franklin D. Roosevelt, George-V, Charles de Gaulle-Étoile.

To the W of the *Pl. de la Concorde* (see Rte 13) extend the *Champs-Élysées*, through which the wide *Av. des Champs-Élysées* gently ascends to the *Arc de Triomphe*. The lower-lying area, drained and planted in 1670 according to *Le Nôtre's* designs, was replanned in 1770 by the Marquis de Marigny (brother of Mme de Pompadour), who prolonged the avenue to the Pont de Neuilly in 1774. Cossacks encamped there in 1814, as did English troops in the following year. It was a fashionable promenade under the Second Empire, but time has treated it harshly, and although still crowded, few of its attractions are of an aesthetic nature, however imposing may be the vistas.

The **Champs-Élysées** consist of two parts; the first, forming a park, extends to the ROND-POINT DES CHAMPS-ÉLYSÉES; the increasingly commercialised avenue, flanked by the offices of airline companies, car showrooms, cinemas, banks, and expensive cafés, continues NW towards the commanding bulk of the *Arc de Triomphe*, a striking silhouette against the setting sun.
    Skirting the N side of the *Champs-Élysées* is the Av. Gabriel, with the *American Embassy* (1931–33) at the corner of the Rue Boissy-d'Anglas, built on the site of a mansion of 1769 belonging to Laurent Grimod de la Reynière, a noted gourmand, and later to his more famous son, Alexandre-Balthazar (1758–1838), author of the 'Almanach des Gourmands', etc.
    Further on (right) are the gardens of the British Embassy, and then those of the *Palais de l'Élysée* (see Rte 26).
    From the PL. CLEMENCEAU the Av. de Marigny leads N, off which (left) is the *Théâtre Marigny*, and an open-air stamp market (Thursday and Sunday). To the S the Av. Winston Churchill, with a fine view of *Les Invalides* (see Rte 11), leads between the *Petit-Palais* (left) and *Grand Palais*, both built for the Exhibition of 1900, to the wide *Pont Alexandre-III* (1896–1900) a single steel arch 107·50m in length.
    The **PETIT PALAIS**, or *Musée des Beaux-Arts de la Ville de Paris* (Pl. 7;7), in itself a building of no great merit (by Girault), contains various ***Collections of paintings**, etc., donated to the city by private collectors, which are often unjustifiably ignored by the visitor. Unfortunately the quality of display leaves something to be desired. It

is also the site of temporary exhibitions. It was here that, in 1905, Alain-Fournier briefly met Yvonne de Galais.

MÉTRO: *Champs-Élysées-Clemenceau*. The entrance, with a domed vestibule, is on its W side, in the Av. Winston-Churchill.

The collections may be roughly divided into four sections. First the 19–early 20C **French** paintings, including representative canvases by *Édouard Vuillard* and *Pierre Bonnard*, and *Gustave Courbet*'s portraits of M. Corbinaud, of his Father, of Pierre-Joseph Proudhon and his children, and Self-portrait with his dog. Among other important works may be mentioned: *Fragonard*, Portrait of Lalande, the astornomer; *Cézanne*, Portrait of Ambroise Vollard, and wallpanels of the Seasons (signed 'Ingres' in derision); *Gauguin*, Old man with a stick; *Toulouse-Lautrec*, the Nice mail-coach, Portrait of André Rivoire; *Renoir*, Portrait of A. Vollard, Woman with a rose; *Mary Cassatt*, Head of a girl (pastel), Portraits of Lydia Cassatt and of 'M.D.'; Landscapes by *Sisley* and *Pissarro*; *Monet*, Sunset at Lavacourt; *Manet*, Portrait of M. Duret; *Marie Bashkirtseff*, Self-portrait; *Berthe Morisot*, A young girl, In the park; *Baudry*, Mme Singer; *Sargent*, Mme Allouard-Jouan; *Bonnat*, Mme Ehrler; and *Jongkind*, View of Notre-Dame from the Quai de la Tournelle.

Paintings of the **Dutch** school include: *Willem van de Velde*, Marine views; *Hobbema*, Mills, Forest scene; *van Goyen*, Landscapes; *Willem de Heusch*, Landscape; *Ter Borch*, The fiancée; *Adriaen van Ostade*, The gazette, Woman with a letter, The analyst; *Pot*, Portrait of a man; *Metsu*, The toilet, Woman playing the virginal; *Rembrandt*, Self-portrait in oriental costume; *Neefs*, Church interior; *Palamedes*, Palace interior, 'Réunion galante'; *Isaak van Ostade*, Farmyard; *Teniers the Younger*, Tavern scenes; *Jan Steen*, Idiot begging alms; *Willem Claesz. Heda*, Still life; *Wouwerman*, Gypsies, The cavaliers' halt; *Jordaens*, Diana's repose; *Brakenburgh*, Tavern interior; *Adriaen van de Velde*, Landscape; *van der Meulen*, Cavalry combat; *Both*, Landscape; *Berghem*, The watering-place; *Hackert* and *van de Velde*, Ash-trees; *Jouvet*, Portrait of Corneille.

The **Edward Tuck Collection**: Chinese porcelain of the K'ang-Hsi period (1662–1722; famille noire); Battersea enamels; Meissen figures; 18C Beauvais tapestries, *after Boucher* and *Huet*; *Greuze*, Portrait of Benjamin Franklin; terracotta bust of Franklin by *Houdon*; and a representative collection of Louis XV furniture.

The **Dutuit Collection**: among the paintings, *Cranach*, The burgomaster's daughter; *Brueghel (de Velours)*, Wedding; and *Cima de Conegliano*, Madonna and Child. Also an impressive collection of Grolier bindings, among others; Gubbio and Urbino majolica; Limoges enamels; ivories; German and Burgundian wood carvings; Gallo-Roman bronzes; Egyptian statuettes; and an extensive collection of Greek ceramics, etc.

The **Grand Palais**, facing the *Petit*, with a classical façade, surmounted by a lofty portico, accommodates various exhibition-halls. Its W half contains a *Planetarium* and the *Palais de la Découverte*, devoted to the popularisation of scientific knowledge (admission 10.00–20.00, except Tuesday).

Publications of the *Caisse Nationale des Monuments Historiques* are available from Porte F, facing the Cours-la-Reine; those of the *Inventaire général des Monuments et des Richesses artistiques de la France*, from Porte D.

Six avenues radiate from the ROND-POINT DES CHAMPS-ÉLYSÉES, with its six fountains. At No. 3 Av. Matignon, leading NE, died Heinrich Heine (1799–1856); to the SW extends the wide Av. Montaigne.

On the right at the beginning of the built-up area of the Av. des Champs-Élysées are the offices of the newspaper *Le Figaro*.

Two streets beyond, at No. 107 Rue La Boétie, are showrooms of the *Institut Géographique Nationale*, where a large range of French maps may be bought: see p 29.—At the corner of the Rue de Berri, parallel to the W, a plaque marks the site of a mansion in which Thomas Jefferson lived in 1785–89 as American minister.

No. 25 in the avenue, since 1904 the *Travellers' Club*, was built in 1855–66 by Pierre Maugin in an ostentatious Renaissance style for the Marquise de Païva. Here she continued to hold the artistic and political salon which advanced her career of adventuress and spy (see also p 199). Dickens lived at No. 49 in 1855–56.—Byron stayed in the street named after him, N of and parallel to this section of the avenue.

At No. 127 (left) beyond the upper end of the Av. George-V, is the **Office de Tourisme de Paris**: see p 43.

Twelve avenues radiate starwise from the PL. CHARLES-DE-GAULLE (formerly **Pl. de l'Étoile**, and still commonly known as such: Pl. 6;5). The uniform façades facing it between each avenue were designed by Hittorff in 1854–57.

In the centre stands the grandiose ***ARC DE TRIOMPHE ◇**, the largest triumphal arch in the world (almost 50m high, and 45m wide). It is under restoration.

Designed by Chalgrin, and begun in 1806, it was not completed until 1836. The main façades of the arch are adorned with colossal groups in high relief. Facing the *Champs-Élysées* are (right) the Departure of the Army in 1792 (otherwise known as 'La Marseillaise') by Rude, and (left) the Triumph of Napoléon in 1810, by Cortot; facing the Av. de la Grande-Armée are (right) the Resistance of the French in 1814, and (left) the Peace of 1815, both by Étex.

The four spandrels of the main archway contain figures of Fame by Pradier, and those of the smaller archways have sculptures by Vallois (S side) and Bra. Above the groups are panels in relief of incidents in the campaigns of 1792–1805. On the row of shields in the attic storey are inscribed the names of 172 (victorious) battles of the Republic and the Empire, including some claimed to be French victories, but in fact not so! Below the side arches are the names of some hundreds of generals who took part in these campaigns, those who fell in action being underlined. A discreet silence is maintained with regard to the other hundreds of thousands of Frenchmen who fought for the Emperor, both in his victories and defeats, and who also died.

Beneath the arch is the *Tomb of the Unknown Soldier*, symbolic of the dead of both World Wars. Its flame has burnt constantly since 11 November 1923. At its foot is a bronze plaque representing the 'Shaef' shoulder-flash, and dated 25 August 1944, the day of the liberation of Paris after the German occupation. On the summit is a platform commanding panoramic views of Paris: admission 10.00–17.00 or 18.00 daily; fee.

Since 1840, when the route was followed by a cortège bearing Napoléon's ashes, watched, despite the intense cold, by 100,000 people, the Champs-Élysées has been used for state processions on a number of occasions, funereal, triumphal, and in celebration of liberation, etc.

Richard and Minna Wagner lived in the Rue Newton, a short distance to the S, in 1859–60.

To the W, in the Rue Rude, is the *Irish Embassy*. In The Av. de la Grande Armée lived Maud Gonne (Mme Gonne MacBride) in the 1890s, who founded the French society of Friends of Irish Freedom.

26 From the Rue du Faubourg-St. Honoré to the Parc Monceau
The British Embassy; Musée Jacquemart-André; Musée Nissim de Camondo; Musée Cernuschi

MÉTROS: Concorde, Madeleine, St.-Philippe-du-Roule, Pl.-des-Ternes, Villiers, Monceau, Charles de Gaulle-Étoile.

The RUE DU FAUBOURG-ST.-HONORÉ, the NW continuation of the Rue St.-Honoré, extends from the Rue Royale (leading from the *Pl. de la Concorde* to the *Pl. de la Madeleine*, see Rte 22) to the *Pl. des Ternes* (NE of the *Arc de Triomphe*), following the course of the medieval road from Paris to the village of *Roule*.

It became fashionable at the end of Louis XIV's reign, and in the 18C its splendid mansions made it a rival to the Faubourg St.-Germain as an aristocratic quarter. Its pretensions are now sustained by a succession of luxurious and expensive boutiques, jewellers, and fashion houses.

At No. 8 Rue d'Anjou, leading N, died La Fayette (1757–1834); Benjamin Constant (1767–1830) died at No. 29.

On the left is the exclusive *Cercle Interallié* (No. 33; of 1714), the Russian Embassy during the Second Empire; and adjacent (No. 35), the *Hôtel de Charost*, since 1825 the **British Embassy** (Pl. 7;5), formerly at the *Hôtel Sagan*.

The 4th Duc de Charost commissioned Antoine Mazin to build the mansion in 1722. In 1785 it was let to the Comte de La Marck, during whose tenancy much of its interior decoration was completed, and the 'jardin à l'anglaise' laid out. It was bought in 1803 by Pauline Bonaparte (later Princess Borghese), much of whose furniture remains, and was sold by her to the Duke of Wellington in 1814 for £32,000, the figure including numerous clocks, chandeliers, candelabras, and chimney-pieces, etc.

Sydney Smith preached an eloquent sermon in the dining-room (then serving as a chapel), and here were married Berlioz and Harriet Smithson (with Liszt as their best man) in 1833; and Thackeray to Isabella Shawe in 1836. Sir Edward Blount, attaché here in 1829, later promoted French railways, constructing lines from Paris to Rouen and from Amiens to Boulogne, in 1843 and 1845 respectively, thus making his contribution to the improvement in communications between the two countries. Bertram Russell was briefly attaché in 1894. Somerset Maugham (1874–1965), whose father was solicitor to the Embassy, was born at the residence, at No. 39 in the street. (A new law in 1870 proposed that anyone born on French soil was liable to conscription. His family lived at No. 25 Av. d'Antin—now F.D. Roosevelt—until 1884.)

A few diplomatic representatives have distinguished themselves—like Duff Cooper (who held the post of Ambassador immediately after the last war), ably assisted by his indulgent wife—by throwing lavish parties, which some older men and women might prefer to forget, but protocol is perhaps now less lax; the scene more sober. Among ambassadors of consequence during the last 160 years were Granville, Cowley, Lyons, Lytton, Bertie, Derby, and Tyrrell.

In 1572, until shortly after the massacre of the Eve of St. Bartholomew, Sir Philip Sidney spent some months at a former embassy as guest of the Ambassador, Sir Francis Walsingham (who in 1583 was to be his father-in-law). In 1619–24 Lord Herbert of Cherbury (who had visited Paris in 1608, during the embassy of Sir George Carew) was Ambassador; his 'De Veritate' was published there in 1624. Thomas Carew, the poet, accompanied Herbert to Paris in 1619.

Thomas Hobbes spent the years 1640–52 in Paris, having also lived there in 1634. Many Englishmen were forced or chose to seek exile there during the period of the Civil War and after, including Charles II himself (from October 1651 to June 1654), and Sir Kenelm Digby. Sir John Suckling died in Paris in 1642 and was buried in the old Protestant Cemetery, which was near St.-Germain-des-Prés. Edmund Waller spent some time here during 1644–51, and—according to Aubrey—confirmed that William Cavendish, Duke of Newcastle (in Paris in 1645–48) was 'a great Patron to Dr Gassendi, and M. Descartes, as well as Mr Hobbes, and that he hath dined with them all three at the Marquis's Table at Paris'. Abraham Cowley, who was employed on several diplomatic missions, lived in Paris intermittently after 1645, in which year he met Richard Crashaw there, at that time in straitened circumstances. William D'Avenant was occasionally in Paris during this period, where he wrote the first part of 'Gondibert'. Richard Cromwell lived in Paris under the name of John Clarke from 1660–c 1680. Matthew Prior was in Paris in 1711–14. The 2nd Earl of Stair, minister and later Ambassador there (1715–20), was responsible for the expulsion of James Edward, the 'Old Pretender' from Paris. In 1721–24 Sir Luke Schaub was Ambassador.

The old *Embassy Church* (St. Michael's), in the Rue d'Aguesseau, opposite, demolished in 1971, has been replaced by a functional modern basement hall.

No. 41 is the *Hôtel Pontalba*, built by Visconti and restored by E. de Rothschild; No. 45 was the residence of Thiers at the end of his term as President, in 1873.

The **Palais de l'Élysée** (no admission), stands at the corner of the Av. de Marigny. This heavily guarded mansion (since greatly altered and enlarged) was built by Molet as the *Hôtel d'Évreux* in 1718.

It was occupied by Mme de Pompadour, Murat, Napoléon I (who signed his second abdication here in 1815), Wellington, and Napoléon III, who lived here as Président from 1848 until he moved, as Emperor, to the Tuileries in 1852. It then reverted to its use as a residence for visiting heads of state (including Queen Victoria in 1855, and Elizabeth II in 1957). Since 1873 it has been the official residence of the President of the Republic. Here, in 1899, Felix Faure (President from 1895–99) died in the arms of Mme Steinheil.

To the right, the Rue des Saussaies (in which No. 11 was the Gestapo headquarters in Paris during 1940–44) leads to the PL. DES SAUSSAIES and the *Hôtel du Maréchal Suchet* (No. 16 Rue de la Ville-l'Évêque), built by Boullée c 1750. Alexis de Tocqueville (1805–59), author of 'Democracy in America', was born at No. 12 in the same street.

Passing (right) the *Ministère de l'Intérieur* (Home Office), built in 1769—in which the poet Marquis de Saint-Lambert (1716–1803) died—flanking the PL. BEAUVAU, continue along the Rue du Faubourg-St.-Honoré.—Beyond the Av. Matignon is the Rue de Penthièvre (right), in which No. 26 may occupy the site of Benjamin Franklin's city office. Meyerbeer (1791–1864) died in the Rue Jean-Mermoz, to the left.

Further on, to the right, stands **St.-Philippe-du-Roule**, built in 1769–84 by Chalgrin on the site of the parish church of Roule and later enlarged.

At No. 45 Rue La Boétie (to the right) is the *Salle Gaveau*, one of the more important concert-halls in Paris.

The Rue du Faubourg-St.-Honoré soon meets the wide Av. de Friedland, which leads W to the *Arc de Triomphe* (see Rte 25).

Alfred de Vigny (1797–1863) died at No. 6 Rue d'Artois, parallel to and S of the Rue du Faubourg-St.-Honoré here.

At No. 208 in the Rue du Faubourg-St.-Honoré, beyond the Av. Friedland, are the buildings of the old *Hôpital Beaujon* (1784); opposite, at No. 11 Rue Berryer, is the former *Hôtel Salomon de Rothschild*, where Président Doumer was assassinated by a Russian emigré in 1932. At No. 12 Rue Balzac (then No. 22 Rue Fortuné, demolished), leading SW, is the site of the house where Honoré Balzac (1799–1850) died.

Just beyond the intersection with the Av. Hoche is the *Salle Pleyel* (1927), the largest concert hall in Paris, radically revamped in 1981.—Mme de Caillavet held her salon, frequented by Anatole France, Maupassant, and Proust, at No. 12 Av. Hoche.

In the Rue Daru, parallel to the N, is the neo-Byzantine Russian Orthodox church of *St.-Alexandre-Nevsky* (1859–61).

Gustave Flaubert (1821–80) lived from 1875 until his death at No. 240 Rue du Faubourg-St.-Honoré; from 1869 to 1875 he had lived at No. 4 Rue Murillo, just S of the Parc Monceau.

From behind St.-Philippe-du-Roule (see above) the Rue de Courcelles crosses the *Blvd Haussmann*. At No. 38 in the Rue de Courcelles (then No. 48) Dickens lodged in 1846; Proust lived at No. 45 in 1901–05, containing his cork-lined 'sound-proof' room, before moving to No. 102 Blvd Haussmann where he remained until 1919. Saint-Saëns lived at No. 83 bis. Henri Barbusse (1873–1935) died at No. 105.

The *MUSÉE JACQUEMART-ANDRÉ (Pl. 6;4), at No. 158 BLVD HAUSSMANN (MÉTRO: *St.-Philippe-du-Roule*), contains collections of French art of the 18C (on the Ground Floor), and Renaissance and Italian art on the First Floor. It is at present (1989) closed.

The house was built c 1870 by Édouard André (died 1894), who in 1881 married the painter Nélie Jacquemart, who survived her husband until 1912, bequeathing their collection to the Institut de France.

From the entrance hall, we turn left into **R2**, with four Gobelins tapestries, and a Savonnerie carpet (1663), and displaying *Nattier*, Portrait of the Marquis d'Antin; *Prud'hon*, Cadet de Gassicourt; and busts of Caumartin by *Houdon*, the architect Gabriel by *Coysevox*, the artist Nicholas Vleugels by *Slodtz*, and the Marquis de Marigny by *Lemoyne*.—**R3**, with Beauvais tapestries of Russian games after *Le Prince*.—**R4** *Rubens*, Hercules strangling the lion, and (from his studio) Portrait of a Flemish couple; *van Dyck*, Count Henry of Peña; *Rembrandt*, Amalia von Solms, Pilgrims at Emmaus, Dr Arnold Tholinx; *Hals*, Portrait of a man; *Philippe de Champaigne*, Male portrait; *Ruysdael*, Landscape; *Jan de Bray*, Portrait; *School of Bruges*, Virgin and Child illuminating a book; and in a case, the *Boucicaut Book of Hours, which belonged to Diane de Poitiers.

R5 *Canaletto*, St. Mark's Square and The Rialto, Venice; *Chardin*, Still life; and drawings by *Lancret, Pater, Watteau*, and *Boucher*.—**R6** *Tocqué*, Male portrait; *Vigée-Lebrun*, Countess Skravonska; *Greuze*, Girl in confusion; *Perronneau*, Woman in a bonnet, Portrait of the artist Gillequin, and *Chinard*, A woman's head; in a case, book-bindings. We return to **R7**, with *Mantegna*, Madonna and Child between two saints, and Mocking of Christ; *Quintin Metsys*, Posthumous portrait of an old man; *Luini*, Virgin with SS. Margaret and Augustine; a bronze plaque of the Martyrdom of St. Sebastian, by *Donatello*; a horse in gilt bronze, attributed to *Leonardo da Vinci*; ivories, and an enamelled plaque by *Jean Pénicaud I*.

From the Winter Garden (**R8**) turn left into **R9**, dominated by *Uccello*, *St. George killing the dragon; *di Conti*, Head of a man; *Pontormo*, An old woman; book-bindings.—On the *Staircase*, frescoes by *G.-B. Tiepolo*, including Henri III welcomed by Federigo Contarini to the Villa de Mira. **R10** is devoted to the arts of the Italian

Renaissance. On its walls a number of 15C marble doorways have been re-erected, one with a sculpted frame attributed to *Benedetto da Rovezzano*. Among terracottas from the della Robbia workshops, a Madonna and Child by *Luca della Robbia*; the Legend of St. Emilian, a marble bas-relief in the form of a triptych (*Venetian School*); *Donatello*, two bronze winged torch-bearers, and bust of Lodovico Gonzaga, Marquis of Mantua; and *Ricciarelli*, posthumous Bust of Michelangelo (bronze).

R11, with Brussels tapestries, *after van Orley*; *Botticini*, The dead Christ with the Virgin, saints, and others; Portrait of a young man (*Venetian School*), and marquetry choir-stalls, c 1505 (N Italian). **R12**, adjoining, retains 25 ceiling panels in grisaille attributed to *Girolamo Mocetto* (15C).

On the Ground Floor, **R13** contains a Bust of Richelieu by *Warin*, and a fine collection of Sèvres, Meissen, Vincennes, and Vienna porcelain, and Chinese porcelain and stoneware.

A short distance E, the Rue de Téhéran leads N across the Av. de Messine to meet the Rue de Monceau.

At No. 8 Rue de Monceau Théodore Herzl, proselyte of Zionism, lived in 1891–95; No. 28 belonged to Prince Murat; and No. 32 was the birthplace of Oscar I of Sweden (1799–1859), son of Bernadotte and Désirée Clary.

The *****MUSÉE NISSIM DE CAMONDO**, at 63 Rue de Monceau (Pl. 7;3; MÉTRO: *Villiers*|), an annexe to the *Musée des Arts Décoratifs* is housed in a tastefully furnished mansion, containing a large number of Savonnerie and Aubusson carpets. It was bequeathed by Count Moise de Camondo (died 1935) as a memorial to his son Nissim, killed in 1917 (his daughter and grandchildren died at Auschwitz). A high proportion of the individual pieces of furniture are of outstanding quality. The museum has been restored recently, and the gardens, kitchens, orangerie, and stables, will be shortly.

Salon Huet, the Musée Nissim de Camondo

From the entrance hall, with a red marble fountain (1765) from the Château de St.-Prix, Montmorency, and a writing-desk by *Riesener*, stairs lead up past two lacquered Louis XV corner cupboards in the Chinese style, and a pair of Regency armchairs upholstered in Savonnerie tapestry.

FIRST FLOOR. *Grand Bureau*: white marble chimneypiece of c 1775, inlaid with bronze; a pair of low cabinets by *Leleu*; cylinder-top desk and secretaire by *Saunier*, the latter from the château de Tanly; desk-armchair of 1778; a white marble-topped table by *Martin Carlin* from the château de Bellevue; pair of low chairs by *Séné*; eight chairs by *Nicolas-Quinibert Foliot* covered in Aubusson tapestry (scenes from La Fontaine); Aubusson tapestries with six fables from La Fontaine after *Oudry*, and a Beauvais screen with the fable of the Cock on the Dunghill; bronze bust of Mme Le Comte by *Guillaume Coustou*; *Vigée-Lebrun*, Bacchante.

Grand Salon: White and gold panelling of c 1775–80 from No. 11 Rue Royale; marquetry cabinet and tables by *Jean-Henri Riesener*; round table and bureau de dame (with Sèvres porcelain plaques) by *Carlin*; a pair of low tables by *Adam Weisweiler*; oval table by *David Roentgen*, and one by *Lacroix (Roger Vandercruse)*; suite of furniture (which belonged to Sir Richard Wallace), including two sofas and an armchair by *Georges Jacob*; four chairs by *Henri Jacob*; a six-leaved Savonnerie screen; 'L'Été' (Hubert Robert's daughter), a marble bust by *Houdon*: *Vigée-Lebrun*, Mme Le Coulteux du Molay; 'La Pêcheuse', a Beauvais tapestry *after Boucher*; and among Savonnerie carpets, one ('L'Air') woven for the Grande Galerie of the Louvre (1678) and one made in 1660.

Salon Huet: Seven panels and three dessus de portes of 'Scènes pastorales' painted by *Jean-Baptiste Huet*, dated 1776; cylinder-top desk by *Oeben*; pairs of small cabinets by *Garnier* and *Carlin*, the latter once belonging to Adm. de Penthièvre; sofa, two bergères, and eight chairs by *Séné*; table with chased bronze given by Louis XVI to Vergennes; silver-gilt candlesticks by *François-Thomas Germain* (1762) embossed with the arms of Mme de Pompadour.—*Salle à Manger*: console and a pair of ebony and chased bronze tables by *Weisweiler*; pair of small cabinets by *Leleu*; silver, including two tureens by *Auguste* and *Roettiers* (the latter's work was ordered by Catherine II of Russia for Orloff).—*Cabinet des Porcelaines* (with a view of the *Parc Monceau*), with services of Sèvres, Chantilly, and Meissen porcelain; silver-gilt service by *Dehanne* and *Cardeilhac*, etc.—*Galerie*: sofa and chairs by *Pierre Gillier*; Aubusson tapestries after *Boucher* ('La Danse Chinoise', etc.).

Petit Bureau: furniture by *Topino*, *Riesener*, and *Lacroix*, among others; snuffboxes, clocks, Chinese porcelain (Kien-Loung; 1736–95); terracotta medallions by *J. B. Nini*; marble bust of Mme Le Comte by *Coustou*; four views of Venice by *Guardi*; portrait of Necker by *Duplessis*; *Oudry*, eight sketches for Gobelins tapestries of 'Les Chasses de Louis XV'; three paintings by *Hubert Robert*.—On the *Stairs* leading to the second floor, two Aubusson tapestries in the Chinese style, *after Boucher*.

SECOND FLOOR. *Galerie*: sofa and chairs by *Nogaret*; a series of engravings after *Chardin*; 18C Chinese porcelain. Turning right into the *Salon Bleu*: pair of tables attributed to *Riesener*; bookcase attributed to *Carlin*; red morocco casket embossed with the arms of Marie-Antoinette; views of Paris by *Bouhot* (1813), *Canella* (1830),

Demachy (1774) and *Raguenet* (1754); a family portrait by *Gautier-Dagoty* (1740–86); watercolour of the Quai Malaquais by *Thomas Shotter Boys*; Chinese porcelain of the period 1662–1795.

Bibliothèque (oak-panelled): secretaire by *Leleu*; two bronze and Sèvres biscuit candelabras by *Blondeau* after Boucher; two paintings by *Hubert Robert*; Aubusson tapestry screen (1775).—*Chambre à Coucher*: furniture by *Cramer*, *Topino* and *Jacob Frères*; six-leaved screen by *Falconet* (1743). Among paintings: *Danloux*, Rosalie Duthé; *Lavreince*, The singing lesson; *Lancret*, Les Rémois; *Houdon*, Sabine Houdon (?), a plaster bust; *Drouais*, Alexandre de Beauharnais as a child; Savonnerie carpet (1760) for the chapel at Versailles.—*Deuxième Chambre*: secretaire attributed to *Riesener*; screen by *Canabas*; 'Scènes de chasse' by *de Dreux*, *Shayer*, *Fontaine*, *Horace Vernet*, et al.

At No. 7 Av. Vélasquez, a parallel street to the N (MÉTROS: *Villiers* or *Monceau*), is the **MUSÉE CERNUSCHI**, bequeathed to the city in 1895 by the collector (of Maltese origin) and, in many ways a pendant to the more comprehensive collections of Oriental art in the *Musée Guimet* (see Rte 27).

Of particular interest are the funerary figurines of the T'ang and Wei dynasties, neolithic terracottas, and bronze vases, etc., of the Chang dynasty (14–11C BC), while outstanding are the paintings on silk of horses and grooms of the T'ang period (8C). Note also the collections of clasps, mirrors, jade amulets, etc. On the FIRST FLOOR is an extensive collection of bronze objects from Louristan and Iran (8–7C BC), a bronze basin of 5–3C BC, and porcelain of various periods.

The neighbouring *PARC MONCEAU (Pl. 6;4; 88 hectares) derives its name from a vanished village, and is a remnant of a private park laid out by *Carmontel* in 1778 for Philippe-Égalité d'Orléans, Duc de Chartres, and father of Louis-Philippe. Its gardener was Thomas Blaikie (1750–1838), a Scotsman. It was then known as the 'Folie de Chartres', and certain 'picturesque' details remain.

Near the NE corner is the *Naumachie*, with a Corinthian colonnade which may have come from either the Château du Raincy or from the projected mausoleum at St.-Denis for Henri II and Catherine de Médicis. To the E of the lake is a Renaissance arcade from the *old Hôtel de Ville*; to the W is the *Rotonde de Chartres*, a toll-house (by Ledoux) of the 18C city wall erected by the Farmers-General. Used as a keeper's lodge, the building was disfigured in 1861 by fluting its columns and adding a dome.

There are a number of imposing mansions in the streets to the N, including those in the Rue de Prony, leading NW. Off this street the Rue Fortuny (where at No. 2 Edmond Rostand lived in 1891–97, and wrote 'Cyrano de Bergerac') turns NE to the re-named PL. DU GÉN. CATROUX (but still Métro *Malesherbes*). Slightly to the N is the *Salle Cortot*, a concert-hall (78, Rue Cardinet).

Further NE, in the **Batignolles**, some quaint areas still survive the pressures of modernisation, and deserve exploration. The Quartier gave its name to a school of Impressionist painters under the leadership of Manet (see the painting by *Fantin-Latour* in the *Musée d'Orsay*).

In the **Cimetière des Batignolles** (best approached by the Av. de Clichy, and some distance NW of the Cimetière de Montmartre) lie Verlaine, André Breton, and Léon Bakst. (Chaliapine has been transferred to Russia.)

The Av. de Villiers leads NW from the Pl. Malesherbes, in which No. 43 is the *Musée Henner*, devoted to the work of Jean-Jacques Henner (1829–1905).— Some distance further W, near the *Porte de Champerret*, stands *Ste.-Odile* (1938–46), with a flattened dome and rocket-like tower.

27 Chaillot, Passy, and Auteuil
Musée d'Art Moderne; Musée Guimet; Palais de Chaillot; Musée de la Marine; Musée Marmottan

MÉTROS: Concorde, Alma-Marceau, Iéna, Trocadéro, Passy, Muette, Porte-d'Auteuil.

From the *Pl. de la Concorde* (see Rte 13), the COURS LA REINE with its extension, the COURS ALBERT-1ER (in which No. 40 preserves glass doors by *Lalique*, whose home it was), leads W to the *Pl. de l'Alma*. It was laid out in 1616, and followed the old road to the villages of Chaillot, St.-Cloud, and Versailles, and the Roman canal which brought water from Chaillot.

The sculptures embellishing the so-called 'Maison de François-Ier', which stood from 1826 to 1957 in the Cours-la-Reine, have been returned to Moret-sur-Loing.

The parallel PORT DE LA CONFÉRENCE, flanking the Seine, takes its name from the *Porte de la Conférence* (demolished in 1730), through which the Spanish ambassadors entered Paris in 1660 to discuss with Mazarin the projected marriage between Louis XIV and María Teresa.

The *Pont des Invalides*, beyond the *Pont Alexandre-III* (see p 108), of 1827–29, was rebuilt in 1879–80 and enlarged in 1956.—The *Pont de l'Alma* (1970) retains the figure of a Zouave from its predecessor, which was long used as a gauge in estimating the height of the Seine in flood.

Immediately E of the S end of the Pont de l'Alma is the public entrance to the **Sewers** (*Égouts*) of Paris, a formidable system laid out by the engineer *Eugène Belgrand* (1810–78). Part of it may be visited between 14.00–17.00 on Monday and Wednesday, and the last Saturday in each month: closed when raining. The tour is not so hazardous as that experienced by Jean Valjean in 'Les Misérables'. The total combined length of the sewers of Paris which may be entered has been estimated at 2100km.

Several handsome streets radiate N from the PL. DE L'ALMA (Pl. 11;6), many of the mansions being the showrooms of *haut-couturiers*, who have replaced the once ubiquitous Parisian *midinette* in the folklore of fashion.—At No. 13 Av. Montaigne, leading NE, is the *Théâtre des Champs-Élysées*, by *A.* and *G. Perret* (1911–13), with bas-reliefs by *Bourdelle*.—On the W side of the Av. George-V, leading N, is the American church of the *Holy Trinity* (1885–88), built in a Gothic style by *G.S. Street*.

The Av. de New York, with its continuations, skirts the N bank of the Seine for some distance before bearing W to the *Porte de St.-Cloud*. Parallel to the long narrow *Allée des Cygnes* (or 'Isle of Swans') lying in mid-stream S of the *Pont de Bir-Hakeim*, is (right) the cylindrical **Maison de la Radio** (or de l'ORTF), designed in 1960 by *Henri Bernard*, impressive in size even if its tower is out of proportion to the rest of the building, the only one of note in the area (Pl. 10;8). A *Museum* devoted to radio as a means of communication has been installed here (116 Av. due Président-Kennedy, 16e), but it may only be seen on written application one month in advance of the intended visit!

On the S extremity of the *Allée des Cygnes*, crossed here by the *Pont de Grenelle* (rebuilt 1875), and facing downstream, is a reduced bronze replica of *Bartholdi's* statue of Liberty, presented to France by the United States, where the original stands at the entrance to New York harbour.

The Av. du Président-Wilson leads W from the PL. DE L'ALMA, from which the Av. Marceau immediately diverges right uphill towards the *Arc de Triomphe*, passing (left) *St.-Pierre-de-Chaillot* (1937), built in a bogus Byzantine/Romanesque style by *Émile Bois*, and replacing the parish church of 1750, in which Proust's funeral service took place in November 1922.

To the right in the Av. du Président-Wilson is the main façade, behind gardens, of the *Hôtel Galliéra* (1888), built to house the collections of the Duchesse de Galliéra (died 1889), who subsequently changed her mind and bequeathed the majority of them to the city of Genoa. At present it accommodates the **Musée de la Mode et du Costume** (of the Ville de Paris), with its entrance at No. 10 Av. Pierre-1er de Serbie. Parts of the extensive collections, enriched by numerous donations, are usually shown in rotation in a series of temporary exhibitions covering specific themes or periods.

Normally there is a display of dresses, designs, costume and fashion-plates, and photographs, and an astonishing variety of accessories: belts, buttons, and ribbons; scarves, feathers, and gloves; handbags and hats; fans, and parasols; stays, and stockings; and numerous other forms of clothing, from costume jewellery to shoes, apart from dolls, wigs, etc.

On the S side of the avenue stands the **Palais d'Art Moderne**, constructed for the Exhibition of 1937 (by *Aubert, Dondel, Viard*, and *Dastugue*) on the site of a military bakery, itself replacing the old *Savonnerie* (see p 80). The wall of the terrace is decorated with bas-reliefs by *Janniot*; and here, with other statues by *Bourdelle*, is 'La France', in memory of French patriots who fell in the Second World War.

It consists of two wings, that to the E housing the **Musée d'Art Moderne de la Ville de Paris**, often showing temporary exhibitions. The permanent collection is arranged on two floors, but contains few canvases of great interest. Near the entrance are two series of engravings: *Picasso's* Vollard Suite, and *Derain's* suite 'Le Satyricon'. Notable is *Modigliani*, Woman with a fan; also on view are representative works by *Jules Pascin, André Lhote, Chaim Soutine, Othon Friez, Marie Blanchard, Marcel Gromaire*, and *Jean Lurçat*. Among other works on the floor below are: *Francis Gruber*, Nude in a red waistcoat (sic); *Buffet*, three Nudes, and Self-portrait; *Foujita*, The bistro; and *Pierre Soulages*, Composition.

The W wing, now styled the **Palais de Tokyo**, was, until the translation of its contents to the *Centre Beaubourg*, and the *Musée d'Orsay*, known as the *Musée National d'Art Moderne*.

In the Autumn of 1989, after its reconstruction and restoration, the building will be inaugurated in its entirety as the **Centre National de la Photographie**. This will comprise a *Cinémathèque*, already functioning; a *Bibliothèque* and *Médiathèque*; the *Mission Photographique du Patrimoine*; the *Service Photographique de la Délégation aux Arts Plastiques*; and the *Fondation Européenne des Métiers de l'Image et du Son* (FEMIS).

To the W is the PL. D'IÉNA (Pl. 11;5), from which seven streets diverge. No. 2 Av. d'Iéna is the residence of the US ambassador. To the N of the Place stands the *Musée Guimet* (see below).

At No. 24 Rue Boissière, to the NW, the poet Henri de Régnier (1864–1936) died; at No. 44 Rue Hamelin, leading N, died Marcel Proust (1871–1922).

In the Rue Paul-Valéry (the continuation NW of the Rue Hamelin), No. 40 was from 1902 the home of Paul Valéry (1871-1945) and had been from 1883 the studio of his aunt by marriage, Berthe Morisot (died 1895), and a favourite literary and artistic rendez-vous.

The *MUSÉE GUIMET, installed at No. 6 Pl. d'Iéna (MÉTROS: *Iéna* and *Trocadéro*), was founded at Lyon in 1879 by Émile Guimet, presented by him to the State, and transferred to Paris in 1888. In 1945 it officially became the *Département des Arts Asiatiques des Musées Nationaux*, the original collection having been considerably augmented, and now including those of the Asiatic department of the *Louvre*, illustrating the arts of India and the Far East. The building also houses a *Library* and photographic section.

GROUND FLOOR. From the vestibule we pass into **R'N'**, which together with **RR'L'**, **'O'**, and **'H'**, are devoted to Khmer sculpture from *Cambodia*, including a statue of Hari-Hara (pre-Angkorian style; late 6C), uniting in one person the two gods Siva and Vishnu; lintel of 7–12C; sculpture of 9–10C; Vishnu in the Kulen style; Brahma in the Koh Ker style; pediment from the temple of Banteai Srei (967); seated Buddha in the style of Angkor Wat (early 12C); carvings of a lion, an elephant, and of the magic serpent, Naga (12C). Also sculptures in the Bayon style (12–13C); each meditative statue wears the enigmatic 'Angkorian smile'; portrait of King Jayavarman VII; frieze of dancing *apsaras*.

R'M': *Champa Art of Assam* (central Vietnam). Note the head of Buddha (9C) and a dancer with two young elephants (10C).

R'K' (left): *Java*: Heads of Buddha (8–9C); lintel decorated in the Prambanan style (9C); bronzes (7–9C), and statuettes of Avalokitesvara and Kubera, gods of riches—note the seven treasure-pots at his feet; leather marionettes for a shadow-theatre, and a painted fabric calendar from Bali.

(Centre): *Siam* (Thailand): stuccoes from P'ra Pathom (c 8C); Buddhas of the Schools of Sukhodava and U-Thong (14–15C); head of Buddha (16C); on the walls, painted and worked leather hangings.— *Laos*: Buddha with a begging-bowl.—*Burma*: lacquered wooden Buddha, and illuminated MSS.

Tibetan Art (continued in **R'J'**): Statue in gilded bronze of Dakini; and statuettes decorated with coloured stones; religious objects, jewellery, silverwork, etc. On the walls, paintings illustrating the life of Buddha, gods and saints.—**R'I'**: *Nepal*: Buddhist paintings and statues of wood and gilded bronze.

FIRST FLOOR. **RR'K'** and **'J'**: *Indian Art*. Funerary furniture and stone sculpture from near Pondicherry; clay sarcophagus, pottery, and jewellery. Mathurâ and Amarâvatî sculpture (2–4C); serpent-king (sandstone); marble bas-reliefs; Buddhas. Among objects of the 'classical' period (4–8C), a Buddha in the Gupta style; steles of *Pâla Art* (8–12C); S Indian stone sculpture; bronzes of Siva; *gouaches and watercolours of the Mogul, Rajput, and Pahâri period (16–18C), including one of Louis XIV when young.

RR'M' and **'P'**: *Pakistan, and Afghanistan*, including examples of Græco-Buddhist Gandara sculpture (1–5C); decorative bas-relief (schist); figurines from the Buddhist monastery of Hadda, including a Genie carrying a floral offering, and a demon in a fur; fragments of frescoes from the monastery of Kakrak (c 5C); and the Treasure of Begram (1–2C): Græco-Roman and Syrian objects, Indian ivories, and

Chinese lacquer-work discovered together by the French archaeological mission to Afghanistan in 1937 and 1939–40.

RR'N', 'F', 'G', and **'H'**: the *Arts of China*. Carved bone objects of the Chang Dynasty (16–11C BC), and important collections of archaic bronze implements, ritual vases, and arms, etc., from Ngan-Tang, capital city of the dynasty; ritual vase in the shape of an elephant; a 'p'an' bowl of the Chou Dynasty (11–5C BC); the Treasure of Li-Yu, a remarkable find from the 'Fighting Kingdoms' Dynasty (5–3C BC), notably a jade, turquoise, and gold-ornamented sword.—Jades: the earlier ones in the form of symbols (Pi, the sky; Tsong, the earth; Kwei, the mountain, etc.), and bronzes. Tombstone (Han Dynasty; 206 BC–AD 220); Buddha from Yun-Kang (5C); heads of Bodhisattva and Kasyapa, from Long-men (early 6C); Ananda and Kasyapa, disciples of Buddha (Suei Dynasty; 561–618), marble with traces of polychrome; Dvarapàla, guardian of the temple, and funerary statuettes of the T'ang Dynasty (618–906); gilded bronzes of the Wei, Suei, and T'ang dynasties (5–10C), including a small stele representing Sakyamuni and Pradhutaratna, dated 518; lacquer-work; polychrome bowls of the Han Dynasty and Sung Dynasty (960–1279); black lacquer cabinet decorated in gold (17C).

SECOND FLOOR. **R'K'**: the *Arts of Japan*. Jômon and Yayoi pottery (2000–1000 BC and 1C BC–3C AD respectively); figurines (Haniwa) of the era of the Great Tombs (5–6C); wooden Buddhas (8–9C); carved masks of the Nara Dynasty (8C); portraits of bonzes (14–15C); pottery for the Tea Ceremony ('Cha-no-yu'); Imari Kakiemon, and Satsuma porcelain; sword-furniture (kozukas); screens, one illustrating the arrival of the Portuguese in Japan (16C).

R'K: *Korea*: Gilded bronze crown, and silverware, from the kingdom of Silla (5–6C); and ceramics.

RR'D', 'L', 'P', and **'I'** contain an important collection of *Chinese* porcelain, formed principally from the Calmann Collection—'three colour' ware (T'ang Dynasty), celadon, black and white wares (Sung Dynasty)—and from the Grandidier Collection: Ming (1368–1643) and Ch'ing (1644–1912) dynasties.

R'M': *Central Asia*. Buddhist paintings from Touen-houang; votive banners, one representing Kasyapa in old age, dated 729.

Among recent acquisitions are the Torso of a finely sculpted sandstone Buddha (India; mid 5C), and of a Female divinity (Khmer sculpture, from Cambodia; early 9C).

The Annexe, at No. 19 Av. d'Iéna, is devoted to Oriental *Religious* Art.

To the SW is the *Palais du Conseil Économique et Social*, by *Auguste Perret* (1937–38), originally designed for a Musée des Travaux Publics. The N wing was added in 1960–62, to house the *Western European Union*. No. 34 in the Av. du Président-Wilson was the home of Laure Haymann, the model for Proust's Odette de Crécy.

The Av. du Président-Wilson ends at the PL. DU TROCADÉRO (Pl. 10;6), semi-circular in shape, from which six thoroughfares fan out. In the centre stands an equestrian statue of Maréchal Foch (1851–1929). It is flanked to the SE by the *Palais de Chaillot* (see below). The Place is situated on the 'Colline du Trocadéro' (named after a fort near Cádiz occupied by the French in 1823).

Catherine de Médicis built a country house on this hill; later embellished by Anne of Austria, it was sold to Maréchal de Bassompierre, and in 1651 Henrietta Maria bought it from his heirs and established the *Convent of the Visitation* here. This was destroyed during the Revolution, and Napoléon planned to use the site for a palace for his son which would be more magnificent than the Kremlin, but the disasters of 1812 intervened.

To the W, steps ascend to the small **Cimetière de Passy**, where Debussy, Gabriel Fauré, Manet, Berthe Morisot, Marie Bashkirtseff, and Las Cases are buried.

The **PALAIS DE CHAILLOT** (MÉTRO: *Trocadéro*), on the SE side of the *Pl. du Trocadéro*, was erected for the Paris Exhibition of 1937, and replaced the earlier Palais du Trocadéro designed for the 1878 Exhibition. The new building (by *Carlu, Boileau*, and *Azéma*) encases in its two curved wings the two wings of the original structure. Between them is a square, its terrace affording a striking perspective towards the *Eiffel Tower* and across the *Champ-de-Mars* to the *École Militaire* and the *Unesco* buildings beyond: see Rte 12.

Below the square, adorned with gilded bronze statues, is an *Aquarium*, and the *Théâtre de Chaillot*, seating over 2000, the home of the Théâtre National Populaire (decorated by *Bonnard, Dufy*, and *Vuillard*, among others). Here took place the third General Assembly of the United Nations (1948).

To the right and left of the Colline du Trocadéro, gardens flank fountains which include a battery of 20 jets shooting almost horizontally towards the Seine, crossed here by the *Pont d'Iéna* (1806–13, and since twice widened).—The next bridge downstream is the *Pont de Bir-Hakeim* (formerly the *Pont de Passy*, 1903–06), a double bridge; the upper part being used by the Métro. It is named after a French exploit in N Africa in 1942.

The *Palais de Chaillot* at present accommodates four museums: in the E wing, the *Musée des Monuments Français* and *Musée du Cinéma*; in the W wing, the *Musée de la Marine* and the *Musée de l'Homme*.

The **Musée des Monuments Français** was founded by Viollet-le-Duc in 1879 as the *Musée de Sculpture Comparée*, and although it only contains *copies* of masterpieces of French sculpture, mural paintings, and stained-glass, they are faithfully copied, and the collections are exhibited with ingenuity and taste.

It provides both an interesting introduction to the range of early French sculpture and architecture, displaying examples from all over France, and valuable reproductions of early wall-paintings, many of which have since deteriorated. The items shown are well lit and well labelled. The *Sculpture* is arranged in a series of rooms to the left of the entrance.

The *Wall-paintings* occupy rooms to the right, and on the three floors above, outstanding among which are:

FIRST FLOOR: mural and ceiling paintings from St.-Gilles (Montoire); Berzé-la-Ville (near Cluny); St.-Martin at Vicq (near Nohant); St. Michael, from Le Puy cathedral; St.-Aignan-sur-Cher; St.-Chef (Isère); Rocamadour; and St.-Savin-sur-Gartemp.

SECOND FLOOR: Asnières-sur-Vègre; St.-Julien at Le Petit-Quevilly (near Rouen), St. Jean at Vic-le-Comte (Puy-de-Dôme); dome of Cahors cathedral; Frétigny (Eure-et-Loire), Étigny (Yonne); La Clayette (Saône-et-Loire); Chapelle du Chalard, St.-Geniès (Dordogne); the Tour Ferrande, Pernes (Vaucluse); Chartreuse at Villeneuve-lès-Avignon; crypt of Auxerre cathedral; walls of the château of Ravel (Puy-de-Dôme); Les Brignes (Alpes-Maritime); and Transfiguration from Le Puy cathedral.

THIRD FLOOR: Kernascléden (Morbihan); Abondance (Haute-Savoie); La Chaise-Dieu; château de Dissay (Vienne); château du Pimpéan (near Angers); Ennezat (near Riom); château de Rochechouart (Haute-Vienne); and Albi cathedral.

The devotee of the art of the film will find much of interest in the **Musée du Cinéma** located in the basement of this wing, established by the late Henri Langlois (1914–77). Over 3000 items are displayed in 60 sections, vividly presenting diverse aspects of the history of the film during its earlier decades. At present it may only be visited by a guided group at 10.00, 11.00, 14.00, 15.00, and 16.00, except Tuesday.

On the GROUND FLOOR of the W wing of the *Palais de Chaillot* is the *MUSÉE DE LA MARINE*, with a remarkable collection of material illustrating French naval history, including an outstanding series of ship models, and paintings of maritime subjects, among which are Vernet's *Ports of France*.

The main gallery, right of the entrance, is dominated by the richly carved poop of the 'Reale' (1690–1715), some of the sculpture of which is attributed to *Puget*. Note the paintings (Nos 61 and 62) of the Embarkation of Henry VIII for the Field of Cloth of Gold, by *Bouterwerke* (a copy of the original by *Vincent Volpi*) and a View of Amsterdam by *Bakhuysen* (1664). Four *anon.* views of Malta (Nos 138–9) and two views of Port Mahon (Nos 147 and 416, the latter by *Joseph Chiesa*) are also of interest, and a number of marine paintings by *Jean-François Hue* (1751–1823).

In the centre of the gallery are displayed 13 (of the 15 completed of the original 24 commissioned) views of the *'Ports of France'* painted between 1754–65 by *Claude-Joseph Vernet* (1714–1789), depicting Dieppe, Antibes, tunny-fishing near Bandol, Rochefort, La Rochelle, Cette, two views of Toulon, two of Bordeaux, two of Bayonne, and Marseille.

We pass the Emperor's Barge (1811) before entering a section devoted to early steamships. **R15**, at the far end of the wing, contains recent models and paintings, and a section concentrating on the Fleet Air Arm, etc.

Along a parallel gallery are further sections displaying marine instruments, diving and underwater exploration equipment, a model of a nuclear submarine, models of the careening of a ship, and of the raising and transportation of the obelisk of Luxor (now in the *Pl. de la Concorde*: see Rte 13), of ship construction, etc. Among individual items are a sectional view of the transatlantic liner 'Normandie', and Dr Bombard's raft.

The **Musée de l'Homme**, housed on the First and Second Floors of this wing, was formed by the amalgamation of the *Galerie d'Anthropologie* and the *Musée d'Ethnographie du Trocadéro*. A comprehensive library, photographic library, cinema, and various technical services are also accommodated in the building.

In comparison with some more recently installed museums (such as the *Musée National des Arts et Traditions Populaires*; see Rte 28), its quality of display leaves something to be desired, but the items exhibited are more or less self-explanatory.

The sections devoted to Anthropology, Paleoanthropology and Prehistory, Africa, the Near East, and Europe, are found on the FIRST FLOOR. On the SECOND are rooms displaying exhibits from the Arctic, Asia, Indonesia and Oceania, and America.

The Rue Franklin (No. 8 in which was Clemenceau's residence from 1883 to 1929) leads SW from the *Pl. du Trocadéro*, and is continued by the Rue Raynouard.—From their junction, the PL. DE COSTA RICA, the Rue de Passy, high street of the old village of **Passy**, runs W to the *Jardin du Ranelagh* (see below).

Steps descend to the left in the Rue Raynouard to the *Sq. Charles Dickens*, in which the vaulted medieval cellars of a *Musée du Vin* may be visited.

No. 47 Rue Raynouard is **Balzac's House** (admission daily except Monday 10.00–17.40), containing souvenirs of the novelist, who lived here in 1841–47, where he wrote 'La Cousine Bette' and 'La Cousin Pons' among other novels.

It is worthwhile entering the unexpected ivy-covered Rue Berton, behind the house, one of the more charming lanes remaining in Passy.

Earlier inhabitants of the Rue Raynouard include the architect Robert de Cotte, the Abbé Prévost, and Benjamin Franklin (in 1777–85), who erected on his house (the *Hôtel de Valentinois*, which stood on the corner of the Rue Singer) the first lightning conductor seen in France.

In the Rue d'Ankara, between Rue Berton and the Seine, No. 17, now the *Turkish Embassy*, was once the residence of the Princesse de Lamballe, and later the private clinic of Dr Émile Blanche, where Maupassant died in 1893; Gérard de Nerval and Gounod had also sought treatment there.

Not far SW of Balzac's House (before reaching the *Maison de l'ORTF*; see p 213), the Rue des Vignes leads NW, where at No. 32 Gabriel Fauré (1845–1924) died; James Joyce lived at No. 34 during the latter period of his stay in Paris.

Other distinguished residents of Passy include Frances ('Fanny') Burney (Mme d'Arblay; 1752–1840), in 1802–12; Béranger, in 1833–35; and Maeterlinck, in 1897–1910. Others were Rossini, from 1857–68; Gossec, from 1822–29; and Joseph Proudhon, from 1861–65, who all died there.

The Rue des Vignes also leads to the Chaussée de la Muette and the E end of the **Jardin du Ranelagh** (Pl. 10;7), part of the ancient royal park of *La Muette*. It was designed to emulate its fashionable namesake in London, and just before the Revolution was a favourite resort. The first balloon ascent in France was made nearby in 1783 by Pilâtre de Rozier and the Marquis d'Arlandes.

The royal *Château de la Muette*, originally a hunting-lodge, improved by the Regent Orléans, and restored by Louis XV for Mme de Pompadour, has completely disappeared. It is also associated with Marie-Antoinette, who was welcomed here by Louis XVI on her arrival in Paris from Vienna in 1770. It also accommodated an establishment for spinning cotton under the direction of a manufacturer from Lancashire and under royal patronage. The Château was later occupied by Philippe-Égalité, who stood on the terrace watching the mob bringing Louis XVI from Versailles to the Tuileries in 1789. From 1820 to 1920 it belonged to the Erard family, piano manufacturers. The present mansion, just N of the *Jardin du Ranelagh* and E of the *Porte de la Muette*, was built by Baron Henri de Rothschild, and is now the property of the *Organisation for Economic Cooperation and Development*.

At No. 2 Rue Louis-Boilly, leading off the W side of the gardens, is the *MUSÉE MARMOTTAN (Pl. 10;5/7; MÉTRO: *La Muette*). It contains, apart from the *Monet donation* (see below), a number of interesting paintings, among which are works attributed to *Van der Weyden* and *Schongauer*. In October 1985 several paintings were stolen from the collection, including *Monet's* Portrait of Renoir, of Poly, the fisherman from Belle Isle, and Impression—Soleil levant, which gave the name to the Impressionists; and *Berthe Morisot*, Young girl at a ball.

Also displayed are portraits of Talma by *Riesener* and of A young woman by *Lawrence*; of Désirée Clary, by *Gerard*; and of the

Duchesse de Feltre and her children, by *François-Xavier Fabre*; also
works by *L. de France* (1735–1805), *Jean-Baptiste Mallet* (1759–
1835), *Carmontel* (1717–1806), *A.-I. Melling* (1763–1831), *Louis Boilly*
(1761–1845), and *Philibert-Louis Debucourt* (1755–1832), together
with drawings by *Fragonard* and *Hubert Robert*. There are also some
pleasant views of Schönbrunn, etc., by *Jean-Joseph-Xavier Bidault*
(1758–1846) and *Carle Vernet*, and of Rowing at Fontainebleau, by
Bidault and *Louis Boilly* (attributed).

In a gallery to the left of the entrance are works by *Claude Monet*
(1840–1926) and his friends, including *Carolus Duran*, Portrait of
Monet; of Monet and his wife by *Renoir*, and, by *Monet* himself,
Argenteuil in the snow, Vertheuil in the mist, A train in the snow, and
The beach at Trouville, together with sketches for his later canvases
and several caricatures; also displayed are characteristic works by
Caillebotte, Guillaumin, Jongkind, Berthe Morisot, Pissarro, Renoir,
and *Sisley*. The collection also contains drawings by *Constantin Guys,
Boudin*, and *Signac*, among others.

In November 1987 a new room was inaugurated to accommodate
the Duhem Donation of some 60 oil-paintings, watercolours, and
drawings. Notable are *Gauguin*, Bowl of Tahitian flowers; *Corot*, The
lake at Ville-d'Avray seen through trees; *Le Sidaner*, Daybreak at
Quimperlé; *Monet*, Walking near Argenteuil; *Sisley*, The Canal du
Loing in Spring; *Renoir*, Girl in a white hat (pastel); several works by
Guillaumin, and *Lebourg*, and examples of paintings by *Henri
Duhem* (1860–1941) himself.

The Museum also houses the notable **Wildenstein Collection** of
medieval illuminated miniatures, some 230 in all, assembled in one
room as they were when in private hands. They deserve a better
display, and some examples are also in need of restoration. Among
those of the Italian schools are several by *Lucchino Giovanni Belbello
da Pavia* (fl. 1430–62); and among the French, some by *Jean Colombe*
(fl. 1467–1529), *Jean Perreal* (1455–1530), *Jean Bourdichon* (c 1475–
1521), and *Jean Fouquet* (c 1420–77/81), together with a depiction of a
boar-hunt (late 15C); also some Flemish works of the period.

Stairs descend to an underground gallery built to house the
spectacular collection of *Monet's* colourful paintings of water-lilies,
wisteria, and other flower-pieces, the majority of them donated to the
museum in 1971 by the artist's son Michel Monet, and which form a
complementary collection to those displayed in the *Orangerie* (see
Rte 13).

In the residential district of **Auteuil**, to the S, Henri Bergson (1859–
1941) lived and died at No. 47 Blvd de Beauséjour, skirting the Jardin
du Ranelagh, and the Goncourt brothers (Edmond, 1822–96; and
Jules, 1830–70) lived and died at No. 67 Blvd de Montmorency ('le
Grenier'), its continuation S, where they entertained Huysmans, Zola,
Daudet, Maupassant et al. In parallel streets to the E of the latter lived
Dr Émile Blanche and his son, the artist Jacques-Émile Blanche (at 19
Rue Docteur-Blanche). At No. 10 Sq. Dr-Blanche is the *Le Corbusier
Foundation*, in a villa designed by *Le Corbusier* in 1923, which
may be visited. André Gide lived in the nearby Av. des Sycomores.—
Paul Dukas (1865–1935) died at No. 82 Rue du Ranelagh, leading E
from the Blvd de Beauséjour.

At the S end of the Blvd de Montmorency is the *Porte d'Auteuil*, the SE entrance
to the *Bois de Boulogne* (see below), and an approach to the A13 autoroute and
Blvd Périphérique. From the PL. DE LA PORTE D'AUTEUIL the BLVD EXELMANS
swings SE to reach the Seine at the *Pont du Garigliano*; the Rue d'Auteuil leads E

to *N.-D. d'Auteuil*, built in the Romanesque-Byzantine style (1877–88) on the site of the 12C parish church; in front is the tomb of the chancellor D'Aguesseau (died 1751) and his wife.

No. 59 Rue d'Auteuil was the home of Maurice Quentin Delatour (1770–72), and then of Mme Helvétius until her death in 1800. Sir Benjamin Thompson, Count von Rumford (1753–1814), lived here from 1808 until his death. Marcel Proust (1871–1922) was born at a house on the site of No. 96 Rue La Fontaine, a short distance to the N. François Mauriac lived at No. 38 Av. Théophile-Gautier for some 40 years until his death in 1970. Boileau, and probably Molière (in 1667) were also residents of Auteuil.

In the small **Cimetière d'Auteuil**, in the Rue Claude-Lorrain (S of and parallel to the Blvd Exelmans), lie Rumford (see above; whose original tombstone was shattered by a shell from Mont Valérien in 1871), Hubert Robert, Mme Helvétius, Carpeaux, Gavarni, and Gounod.

28 The Bois de Boulogne and Neuilly Musée National des Arts et des Traditions Populaires; Bagatelle

MÉTROS: Porte-d'Auteuil, Muette, Porte-Dauphine, Porte-Maillot, Les Sablons.

The **Bois de Boulogne** (Pl. 10;1–3), familiarly known as the 'Bois', lies immediately to the W of the 16th arrondissement of Paris (*Chaillot, Passy*, and *Auteuil*: see Rte 27), and was originally bounded on the E by part of the peripheral fortifications of the city. Now the BLVD PÉRIPHÉRIQUE tunnels below the E and S edges of the Bois, which is bounded on the N by *Neuilly*; the suburb of *Boulogne-Billancourt* to the S, and by the Seine to the W, on the far side of which rise the hills of Mont Valérien, St.-Cloud, Bellevue, and Meudon.

Although the châteaux of La Muette, Madrid, and Bagatelle, and the abbey of Longchamp were erected on its borders, the Bois was utterly neglected until the middle of the last century. Much timber was cut down for firewood during the Revolution, and a large part of the Allied army of occupation bivouacked there after Waterloo. It was the haunt of footpads and often the scene of suicides and duels.

In 1852 it was handed over by the State to the City, was transformed into an extensive park (863 hectares), and became a favourite promenade of the Parisians. The model was Hyde Park, which had so impressed Napoléon III. More trees were felled in 1870 to prevent them affording cover to the enemy. The equestrian scenes which were such a favourite subject of Constantin Guys (1805–92) often had the Bois in the background.

Carlyle condemned it as 'a dirty scrubby place', and in many respects it has little changed since. Visitors are strongly advised *not* to stray into the Bois at dusk or after dark.

There are four main entrances to the Bois from Paris, namely the *Porte Maillot* (at its NE corner); the *Porte Dauphine* (at the W end of the Av. Foch); the *Porte de la Muette* (at the S end of the Av. Victor-Hugo); and the *Porte d'Auteuil* (at its SE corner). Between the last two is the subsidiary *Porte de Passy*.

The usual approach to the Bois is by the imposingly wide, garden-flanked AV. FOCH (opened in 1855 as the Av. de l'Impératrice), leading W from the *Étoile* to the *Porte Dauphine*. It was later known as the Av. du Bois de Boulogne, in which George Du Maurier (1834–96), author of 'Trilby', who was born in Paris, attended a school in 1847–51. Note one of the original art-nouveau entrances to the *Métro* on the N side of the avenue here, designed by Hector Guimard.

Not far from the Étoile is a monument to Adolphe Alphand (1817–91), who laid out the Bois and many other parks in Paris in their present form.

At No. 59 Av. Foch, on the left, is the **Musée d'Ennery**, with a collection of oriental art formed by the dramatist Adolphe d'Ennery (Eugène Philippe; 1811–99); the building also houses a small museum of Armenian art.

Anatole France (1844–1924) died at No. 5 Villa Said, leading NW off the avenue. No. 80 Av. Foch was the home of Claude Debussy (1862–1918), who died at No. 24 Square de l'Av. Foch (off the NW end of the avenue). Nos 82–6 Av. Foch were the German counter-espionage HQ in Paris during 1940–44.

SW of the park entrance is a huge building (1955–59) constructed for NATO but now accommodating *Paris Université IX.*—Paul Claudel (1868–1955) died at No. 11 BLVD LANNES, skirting the Bois to the S; Supervielle lived from 1918 to 1943 at No. 47.

The direct approach to the *Porte de la Muette* from the *Étoile* may be made by following the Av. Victor-Hugo, in which Hugo (1802–85) died in a house on the site of No. 124. Lamartine (1790–1869) died near the square named after him off the S section of this avenue (house demolished), beyond the PL. VICTOR-HUGO.

At No. 24 Rue Copernic, just E of the Place, took place a deplorable bombing incident outside a Synagogue in 1980.

It was at the *Porte de la Muette* that Gén. Galliffet set up his HQ in 1871 and supervised the indiscriminate shooting of hundreds of Communards en route to Versailles. The **'Bois'** is divided diagonally by the long ALLÉE DE LONGCHAMP, leading SW from the Porte Maillot towards the CARREFOUR DE LONGCHAMP, and a popular equestrian rendez-vous. It is intersected by the ROUTE DE LA REINE MARGUERITE (from the CARREFOUR DE LA PORTE DE MADRID to the PORTE DE BOULOGNE, on the S side of the Bois).

Of particular interest in this N section of the Bois is the *MUSÉE NATIONAL DES ARTS ET DES TRADITIONS POPULAIRES (Pl. 10;2), easily approached from either *Porte Maillot* or *Porte Dauphine*, or, more directly, from the MÉTRO: *Les Sablons*. The Museum is housed in a not unattractive functional building by *Jean Dubuisson*, completed in 1966, standing just W of the CARREFOUR DES SABLONS.

Its contents are exceptionally well displayed on two floors. Several rooms are devoted to temporary exhibitions.

The GROUND FLOOR contains the 'Galerie Culturelle', laid out in a series of convoluted sections covering aspects of rural life in the pre-industrial period, in which some 5000 objects are seen in context or 'ecological groups', among which are those concerned with sheep and shepherding; baking; the smithy; stone-splitting; forms of rural transport; wood-turning, and furniture carving; viticulture; the fabrication of objects of horn and wood; the embellishment of metalwork; ceramic production; together with sections devoted to peasant costumes, coiffes, etc., with a charming painting of an Arlesienne (1858).

In the BASEMENT is the 'Galerie d'Étude', where similar objects are more systematically displayed in a series of nine parallel passages or 'rues'. By the entrance is a bell-forge.

Rue 1. Farming equipment: yokes, harnesses, traps, etc.—2. Harrows, hoes, rakes, flails, scythes and sickles, and viticultural implements.—3. Cowbells, branding-irons, protective collars, crooks; bee-keeping equipment; sheepshearing, and dairy implements.—4. Spinning, carding, rope-making, and basket-weaving; brick and tile manufacture; surveying equipment and carpenters' tools.—5. Lamps and candlesticks; andirons, jacks, and bedwarmers; kitchen utensils—jars, waffle-irons, butter-moulds, etc.; furniture and lacework.—6. Ritual costumes; rural medicine; cradles and early toys; regional and traditional costumes: capes and sabots, etc.—7. Games and pastimes: archery, tennis, skittles and *boules*, marbles and croquet. Musical instruments: rattles, hurdy-gurdies, flutes, and whistles; bagpipes, etc.—8. Fairs and circuses: puppets, marionettes, and silhouettes.—9. Graphic arts: metal and wood blocks; engraving and lithographic equipment: stencils, etc.

There are ' audio-visual cabins adjacent. The *Library* contains upward of 60,000 volumes and 2000 periodicals; the *Archives* over 80,000 old post-cards, 40,000 designs, almost 200,000 photographs, among numerous other specialised collections of ethnographical studies, etc.; the *Record collection*, some 50,000 recordings; an additional 70,000 objects may be seen on request, together with c 90,000 drawings, paintings, prints, and other illustrative material. The building also contains an auditorium, and laboratories, the whole comprising an important centre for the study of French ethnography.

NW of the museum is the *Jardin d'Acclimatation*, with a small-scale zoo (its former inmates eaten in 1870) and children's playground. To the W, near the *Porte de Madrid*, stood the *Château de Madrid*, built in 1528 by François I (who is said to have named it in memory of his captivity in Spain, after the Battle of Pavia). It was gradually demolished between 1793 and 1847.

Further W, skirted by the ROUTE DE SÈVRES À NEUILLY, are the walls of the **Parc de Bagatelle** (24 hectares), famous for its rose-garden, at its best in mid-June. The attractive *Bagatelle Gardens* are open to the public until dusk (fee); the restaurant is expensive. The elegant little *Château*, replacing an earlier residence, was built for a wager within 64 days by Bélanger for the Comte d'Artois, later Charles X, in 1779. The dome was added in 1852. It was acquired by the Ville de Paris in 1904.

Henry Swinburne observed that during the Revolution it had been turned into a tavern. It was later the residence of Sir Richard Wallace (1818–90), supposed natural son of the Marchioness of Hertford. Wallace had a town house at No. 25 Rue Taitbout where he accumulated art treasures (now in the *Wallace Collection*, London) in addition to those he had inherited from his half-brother the eccentric Richard Seymour Conway, 4th Marquis of Hertford (1800–70), who had bought the mansion in 1835 and died there. Hertford's brother, Lord Henry Seymour (1805–59), was founder of the exclusive 'Jockey Club'. Wallace was also a great benefactor of Paris, which he provided with drinking fountains, and helped to equip ambulances during the 1870–71 war. He founded the *Hertford British Hospital* in Paris (opened 1879), and built the Anglican church of *St. George* (1887–88; Rue Auguste-Vacquerie, off the Av. d'Iéna).

To the W are various sports grounds (including polo; *tiercé*, etc.); to the SW is the *Hippodrome de Longchamp*, opened in 1857. Here on 29 June 1871 the French 'army', responsible for the insensate massacre of thousands of Communards during previous weeks, was reviewed by MacMahon and Thiers. On the N side is a windmill (restored),

The Château in the Parc de Bagatelle, built within sixty-four days in 1779 by Bélanger for the Comte d'Artois

From the CARREFOUR DE LONGCHAMP (just E of the windmill), a road leads due E past the *Grande Cascade* (an artificial waterfall) to skirt the enclosure of the *Pré-Catelan* (named after the troubadour Arnaud Catelan, murdered here c 1300), with a huge copper beech, and a 'Jardin Shakespeare', said to contain specimens of all the plants and trees mentioned in his plays.

Further E are buildings of the *Racing Club de France*, flanking the W bank of the *Lac Inférieur*, with two linked islands. Boats may be hired on the E bank. Further S is the *Lac Supérieur*, beyond the CARREFOUR DES CASCADES; in the SE corner of the Bois, is the *Hippodrome d'Auteuil* (steeplechasing).

Just S of the Bois is the *Jardin Fleuriste* (municipal nursery gardens), with occasional flower-shows, just W of which is *Stade Roland Garros*, one of several sports grounds in the vicinity.

N.-D.-des-Menus, in the Av. J.-B. Clément, leading SW from the *Porte de*

Boulogne, although frequently restored (by Viollet-le-Duc among others), preserves a 14C nave. Beyond (right) are the *Jardins Albert Kahn* (including one laid out in the Japanese style), open daily April–November.

From the *Arc de Triomphe* (see Rte 25), the Av. de la Grande Armée slopes NW to the **Porte Maillot** (Pl. 10;2), the site of extensive works in recent years—and more are threatened—commanded on the N side by a complex of buildings comprising the *Palais des Congrès*, a hotel, shopping-centre, and one of the *Aérogares* (or air terminals) of Paris.

A short distance to the NW, near the PL. DU GÉN. KOENIG, or DE LA PORTE DES TERNES, stands *N.-D. de la Compassion*, a mausoleum in the Byzantine style .(1843) moved here from its original neighbouring site, where stood an inn at which Ferdinand, Duc d'Orléans, son of Louis-Philippe, died as the result of a carriage accident. As a travesty of taste it equals the Orléans mausoleum at *Dreux*.

Beyond the *Porte Maillot* and the wide Av. Charles-de-Gaulle (which bisects *Neuilly-sur-Seine*: see below), is the concrete jungle known as **La Défense** (named after a monument commemorating the defence of Paris in 1871), an aggressive example of high-rise building housing miscellaneous national and international companies. Few will appreciate its attractions, and those who may wish to do so at close hand will have to cross the *Pont de Neuilly* (or take the RER from *Étoile*). The stone bridge, by Perronet (1768–72, almost entirely rebuilt in 1935–39), replaced an earlier bridge erected in 1606 after Henri IV and Marie de Médicis were almost drowned here.

On the left beyond the bridge is the *Tour Nobel*, built on the site of the house in which Vincenzo Bellini died in 1835, while to the NW of this area is a large triangular-shaped domed edifice built to accommodate exhibitions, etc., and known as the CNIT building. Nearby is the *Fiat Tower*, and adjacent, the last 'stabile' by Calder. Also to the N of the main axis are the *Manhattan Tower* and *GAN Tower*, among others. A monumental 'picture-frame' arch-shaped erection, 105m high, and known as the *Arche de la Défense*, is under construction. It was designed by J.O. von Spreckelsen, who has since died.

W of La Défense lies *Nanterre*, the préfecture of the department of Hauts-de-Seine.

To the N of the *Île de Puteaux*, crossed by the *Pont de Neuilly*, is the *Île de la Grande Jatte*, painted by Seurat in 1884.

Neuilly itself, once the most fashionable suburb of Paris, was partially laid out in what was formerly the park of Louis-Philippe's château (built in 1740 and burnt down in 1848), and later developed as a colony of elegant villas, but the construction of blocks of flats has overwhelmed the distinctive character of the neighbourhood.

Its S half has the attraction of being adjacent to the *Bois de Boulogne*. At a house on the site of No. 33 Rue de Longchamp (leading S from near the bridge), Théophile Gautier died in 1872. Ossip Zadkine (1890–1967), the sculptor, also died at Neuilly. Further to the E, in the old cemetery, lie Anatole France and André Maurois.

In the **Cimetière de Lavallois-Perret**, the suburb N of Neuilly, lie Louise Michel (1830–1905), the revolutionary, and Maurice Ravel (1875–1937).

29   From the Place de la République to La Villette
The Hôpital St.-Louis; the Cité des Sciences et de l'Industrie; the Cité de la Musique; the Buttes-Chaumont; Belleville

MÉTROS: République, Colonel Fabien, Jaurès, Porte de la Villette, Porte de Pantin, Buttes-Chaumont, Jourdain, Télégraphe.

The Rue de Lancry, the first main turning right off the BLVD DE MAGENTA (leading N from the *Pl. de la République*), shortly crosses the *Canal St.-Martin*, beyond which the Rue Bichat leads right to the entrance of the ***Hôpital St.-Louis** (Pl. 9;6), founded by Henri IV and built by Claude Vellefaux in 1607–12. It is an excellent and now rare example of the Louis XIII style, and its Courtyards and *Chapel* may be visited on application at the porter's lodge; the chapel is normally open only on Sundays.

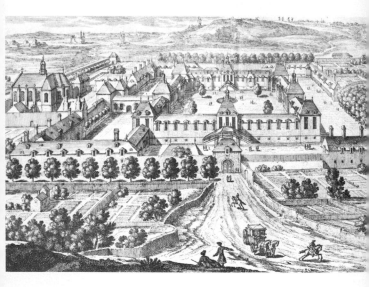

Late 17C view of the Hôpital St.-Louis

Follow the Rue de la Grange-aux-Belles (which skirts its N side), where to the N of the next crossroad stood a small Protestant cemetery, now built over, where in 1792 Paul Jones was buried (subsequently exhumed, and now at Annapolis). Nearby stood the *Gibet de Montfaucon*, the 'Tyburn' of Paris, set up in the 13C and finally removed in 1790.

The gallows proved fatal to three Surintendants des Finances: Enguerrand de Marigny, who erected it; Jean de Montaigu, who repaired it; and Semblançay, who tried to avoid it. Olivier le Daim, confidential barber to Louis XI (1484; cf. 'Quentin Durward'), was hanged here, and after the massacre of St. Bartholomew Coligny's headless body was exposed, hanging from the feet. In 1608 it was visited by Thomas Coryate, who thought it 'the fayrest Gallows that ever I saw...which consisteth of fourteene fair pillars of free-stone'.

Further to the N is the PL. DU COLONEL-FABIEN, from which the BLVD DE LA VILLETTE leads to the PL. DU STALINGRAD. Here, in the shadow of the overhead Métro line, on a small island site, stands the **Rotunda**, built as a toll-house by *Ledoux* in 1789, and now a repository for archaeological finds in the Paris area.

At No. 44 Rue de Flandre, leading NE from the N side of the Place, is a relic of the old *Portuguese Jewish Cemetery*, in use between 1780 and 1810.

The Rotonde de la Villette (1789) by Ledoux

The district of **La Villette** was distinguished until the early 1970s for its cattle-market and *Abattoirs*. Formerly an iron-foundry stood there, run by two English engineers, Davidson and Richardson, 'well-known for the beauty and precision of the machines which left their workshops'.

The ambitious project of converting the extensive site of some 55 hectares into a public park lying on both sides of the *Canal de l'Ourcq*, and the building of a science museum in its N half, has now been partly realised.

The S entrance to the park and the buildings within it is best approached from the MÉTRO *Porte de Pantin*, while the *Cité des*

Sciences (see below) is more conveniently reached from the MÉTRO Porte de la Villette.

The project should be completed by the end of 1989 or 1990 with the establishment of a **Cité de la Musique**.

This last will comprise a complex of modernistic buildings by Christian de Portzamparc laid out on either side of the S entrance to the park. On the W side of this entrance, at 211 Av. Jean-Jaurès, will be the new *Conservatoire National Supérieur de Musique*, formerly—since 1911—in the Rue de Madrid, near the Gare St.-Lazare, the site of which will be re-developed. It will contain practice studios and a small concert-hall. On the E side, with a student hostel, will be a large auditorium with a seating capacity of 2300, and a smaller rehearsal hall, etc. It is planned to house the formerly cramped *Musée Instrumental* in a *Galerie des Instruments*.

Although they will not be inaugurated until after this edition of the Guide is published, a brief history of the Conservatoire and a description of the present collection of musical instruments is given below.

The Conservatoire was founded in 1765 as the *Académie Royale de Chant*, amalgamated with the *École de Déclamation Dramatique* in 1786, and refounded in 1795. Among past directors have been Cherubini (1796–1842), Auber (1842–71), Ambroise Thomas (1871–96), the academic Théodore Dubois (1896–1905; during whose period the institution four times rejected Ravel's attempts to win the Prix de Rome), Gabriel Fauré (1905–20), Henri Rabaud (1920–40), and Marcel Dupré (1954–56). Among pupils were Berlioz (from 1826, taught by Lesueur and Reicha), Florent Schmitt, Charles Koechlin, Georges Enesco, and Paul Dukas.

The *****MUSÉE INSTRUMENTAL** originated in the Clapisson collection, and now contains over 4000 instruments. Of particular importance and interest are the collections of medieval, Renaissance, and 17C instruments, which have again come into their own. Among earlier items is a Bible-regal (16C German); a clavecin (Venice; 1543); a variety of lutes, viols, theorbos, basset-horns, spinets, harpsichords (outstanding amongst which is one of 1646 by *Andreas II Ruckers*), clavichords, virginals (including a fine example by Ruckers), square pianos, harps, finely decorated guitars, a curious one-stringed marine-trumpet, and a unique octobasse (c 1850), constructed by *J.-B. Vuillaume*. Also shown are representative brass, woodwind and percussion instruments of all periods, and examples of the *vielle à roue* or hurdy-gurdy. The collections of stringed instruments (some owned by Lully, Kreutzer, and Sarasate), include five violins by *Antonio Stradivari*, and others by *Amati* and *Guarneri*. Among pianos are examples manufactured by *Erard, Pleyel* (including Chopin's, and Bizet's), and *Longman and Broderip*. Other instruments of historic or artistic interest are Beethoven's clavichord (1786), Marie-Antoinette's harp, and Adolphe Sax's saxophone.

Since 1967 a department for the restoration of old instruments has flourished, and constructional plans of early examples can be bought. The *Library* contains an extensive collection of photographs of instruments, but the valuable series of scores, books on music, and MSS. (including Mozart's 'Don Giovanni'), are now preserved in the *Bibliothèque Nationale*.

Beyond an extensive paved forecourt three older buildings on the site have been retained, comprising two pavilions between which is the former *Grande Halle aux Boeufs*. Erected by Jules de Mérindol in 1867, it has been renovated and adapted by Bernard Reichen and Philippe Robert, and is now used for a variety of public performances and 'animations', exhibitions, trade fairs, etc. Its dimensions are 241m long, 86m wide, and 19m high. The pavilion to the W now contains a small *Theatre* for the production of contemporary plays.

An avenue of trees leads away from the E pavilion to the *Zénith*, a lightweight structure accommodating 6400 and designed specifically for pop concerts and similar spectacles.

A covered passageway parallel to the W side of the Grande Halle leads across the park and crosses the *Canal de l'Ourcq* (the S bank of which is skirted by another transverse passageway) to enter the N sector. The **Park** itself, designed by Bernard Tschumi, and yet to be completed, with the inclusion of a gardening house and greenhouse, an electronic-game gallery, and several other buildings, is already studded by a variety of 'Follies', conspicuous structures of bright red enamelled metal, and laid out on a grid pattern.

The N half of the park is dominated by the spherical *Géode* (see below), beyond which is the huge rectangular building of the *Cité des Sciences et de l'Industrie*, normally entered from the *Porte de la Villette* at 30 Av. Corentin-Cariou. Near this is a restored pavilion, formerly the rotunda of the Veterinary Surgeon, now housing a small museum devoted to the history of the abattoirs.

The impressive **CITÉ DES SCIENCES ET DE L'INDUSTRIE*, inaugurated in March 1986, and 270m long, 110m wide, and 47m high, stands on the site of the auction-hall of the slaughter-house, but the structure was never completed. This consisted of 20 reinforced concrete piers sustaining 16 lattice girders each 65m long, which formed the basis of the present building, radically adapted by Adrien Fainsilber, and employing several new technologies.

View of the Cité des Sciences with the Géode on the right

Among unusual innovative features are the three glazed sections of glass wall on its S side, each 32m square, rising to the roof and in fact forming conservatories or hot-houses; the two rotatable roof cupolas, each 18m in diameter; and—within the conservatories—the transparent lifts or elevators ascending within a stainless steel framework. The whole building is surrounded by a moat.

The *Cité des Sciences et de l'Industrie* is normally entered from the N, and most of the facilities and amenities, including a science bookshop, are grouped on the main entrance level. Opening times: Tuesday, Thursday, and Friday 10.00–18.00; Wednesday 12.00–21.00; Saturday, Sunday, and holidays 12.00–20.00; closed Monday. The *Géode* is open Tuesday and Thursday 10.00–18.00; Wednesday, Friday–Sunday 10.00–21.00; closed Monday, but is open daily during school holidays 10.00–21.00.

Details of the numerous sections of the Cité which may be visited are not given here, but a leaflet in English is available at information desks, specifying the whereabouts of the displays and exhibitions, permanent and temporary.

The main hall is 100m long and 40m high, below which are two levels from which the *Géode* is reached (see below), accommodating a multimedia library, a conference centre, etc. Escalators, with their mechanism visible, ascend to the upper three floors (on the second of which is the *Planetarium*) devoted to the permanent exhibitions, known as 'Explora', which occupy an area of 30,000m².

Although at present (early 1988) some 45 per cent of visitors are of school age, this should not imply that the exhibits are designed largely for them; anyone interested in any aspect of modern science and technology will find more than enough displayed and explained here to satisfy his curiosity.

Among the several scale models which may be entered are the latest *Nautilus*, which can plunge to a depth of 6000m; a nose cone of the third stage of the *Ariane* satellite launcher; and a mock-up cockpit of an A 320 airbus, which simulates take-off conditions etc.

Another section displays three-dimensional models of the 2500 atomic nuclei currently known to exist, together with a 'particle accelerator', with a transparent skin, which may facilitate a better understanding of nuclear reactions. Several different types of robots are shown, and another section is devoted to computers and other radical changes in communications technology, but these are only a few of the sciences touched on.

Immediately to the S of the main building is the **Géode*, a spherical dome of 36m diameter, its 630 tonne double shell composed of 6433 preformed triangular plates of polished stainless steel, with an inner framework of c 1600 triangles constructed with 2580 steel tubes linked by 835 assembly knots. The interior houses some 360 tiered seats facing an hemispheric cinema screen of 1000m² and 26m in diameter, on which a series of specially adapted films using the 'omnimax' technique are shown, projecting an image at an optical angle of 180°

From the PL. DU COLONEL-FABIEN the Av. Mathurin-Moreau leads to the W entrance of the **Parc des Buttes Chaumont**, one of the more picturesque, and least known, of Parisian parks (23 hectares) lying in the midst of the district of *Belleville* (which belies its name).

It was laid out under Haussmann's régime in 1866–67 by Alphand and Barillet on the bare hills ('*monts chauves*') which had long been used as a general rubbish-dump and slaughterhouse for horses, etc., its extensive gypsum ('plaster of Paris') quarries being ingeniously transformed into rock-scenery. These heights had been the scene of the 'Battle of Paris' in 1814, and in 1871 were held by the Communards until dislodged by bombardment from Montmartre, to the W.

From near the SE end of the park, the Rue Fessart leads E, crossing the Rue de la Villette, where at No. 51 the artist Georges Rouault

(1871–1958) was born, to Gothic-revival *St. Jean-Baptiste* (by Lassus, 1854–59).—From the S side of the church, the Rue de Belleville continues E, passing a developing area to the N, to the *Cimetière de Belleville*, the second highest point in Paris (128m).

An inscription to the right of the entrance in the Rue du Télégraphe records that Claude Chappe here experimented with the aerial telegraph that was to announce the victories of the French Revolutionary Wars. Originally called 'Tachygraphe', it was set up in 1792 on this site, and was the base of lines to Lille and Strasbourg.

In the Rue Haxo, parallel to the E, at No. 79 (right), is the *Chapelle des Otages*, built in 1936–39 on the site of the Villa des Otages, behind which (at the end of the passage just N of the chapel) 52 hostages held by the Communards were shot on 26 May 1871.

The return to the centre may be made from the MÉTRO: *Télégraphe*, via *République*.

30 Père-Lachaise

MÉTROS: Père-Lachaise, Alexandre-Dumas, Philippe-Auguste.

From the PL. DE LA RÉPUBLIQUE, the Av. de la République leads ESE across the BLVD RICHARD-LENOIR, built over the *Canal St.-Martin* in 1860 by Haussmann, to the NW corner of *Père-Lachaise*, the main entrance of which is in the BLVD DE MÉNILMONTANT.

The quarter of *Ménilmontant*, N of the cemetery, was the home of the philosophical fraternity of the Saint-Simoniens in the early 1830s.

The *Cimetière de l'Est*, better known as *PÈRE-LACHAISE, is the largest (47 hectares) and long the most 'fashionable' cemetery in Paris, and its tombs display the work of many 19C French sculptors, funerary and otherwise, several of which are of importance in themselves. Regrettably, a number of graves and statues have been vandalised or mutilated by graffiti.

Père François de La Chaise (1624–1709) was the confessor of Louis XIV, and lived in the Jesuit house rebuilt in 1682 on the site of a chapel. The property, situated on the side of a hill from which the king, during the Fronde, watched skirmishing between Condé and Turenne, was bought by the city in 1804 and laid out by Brongniart, and since extended.

The first interments were those of La Fontaine and Molière, whose remains were transferred there in 1804. The monument to Abélard and Héloïse, set up in 1779 at the abbey of the Paraclete (near *Nogent-sur-Seine*), was moved here in 1817, its canopy composed of fragments collected by Lenoir from the abbey of Nogent-sur-Seine.

In the E corner of the cemetery is the *Mur des Fédérés*, against which 147 Communards were shot in 1871 (28 May; see above also); and here also is a monument to the many thousand Frenchmen who died either in German concentration camps or during the Resistance of 1941–44.

Thousands of Parisians still converge on the cemetery on 1 and 2 November ('Jour de la Toussaint'—All Saints' Day—and 'Jour des Morts').

A guide-plan may be obtained for a nominal sum from the keeper's lodge at the main entrance, which will indicate the position of the tombs of a few of the illustrious dead interred here, which indeed make an impressive list.

Among *writers*: Beaumarchais, Victor Hugo, Béranger, Proust, Balzac, Benjamin Constant, Mme de Genlis, Gérard de Nerval, Alfred de Musset,

Daudet, Rémy de Gourmont, Anna de Noailles, Apollinaire, Henri de Régnier, Barbusse, Bernardin de Saint-Pierre, Villiers de L'Isle-Adam, Colette, Éluard, and Sartre.

Among *composers* and *musicians*: Méhul, Gossec, Grétry, Boieldieu, Hérold, Pleyel, Lesueur, Rossini (later removed to Florence), Cherubini, Bellini (removed to Catania), Bizet, Reynaldo Hahn, Chausson, Kreutzer, Chopin, Lalo, Gustave Charpentier, Auber, Poulenc, Dukas, and Georges Enesco; the librettist Scribe; Erard, the piano-maker, and the singer Adelina Patti.

Among *artists* and *sculptors*: David, David d'Angers, Pradier, Pissarro, Corot, Doré, Ingres, Gros, Daumier, Daubigny, Clésinger, Guillaume Coustou, Alfred Steven, Barye, Prud'hon, Delacroix, Géricault, Seurat, and Modigliani.

Among Napoléon's *marshals*: Davout, Kellermann, Lefèbvre, Masséna, Ney, Murat, Victor, Macdonald, Suchet, Gouvion-Saint-Cyr, Grouchy, and Augereau; and generals Foy, Junot, Reille, Savary, Marbot, and Baron Larrey.

Other famous names in their respective fields are: Mlle Mars, Rachel, Talma, Isadora Duncan, Sarah Bernhardt, and Yvette Guilbert; Marie Walewska; Manuel Godoy; De Sèze; Brillat-Savarin; Champollion; Parmentier; Blanqui; Baron Haussmann; Brongniart; René Lalique; the philosophers Saint-Simon, 'Alain', and Comte; Lammennais; Michelet; Arago; Félix Pyat; Reclus; Cuvier; Monge; Branly; Barras; Sieyès, Chambacérès; and Thiers (see below).

Also interred here are Oscar Wilde (1856–1900; but not moved here until nine years after his death; with a monument by Epstein); Sir William Keppel (1702–54), second Earl of Albemarle; Gen. Lord John Murray (1711–87); Adm. Sir Sidney Smith (1764–1840); Gen. Sir Charles Doyle (1770–1842); and Sir Richard Hertford-Wallace (1818–90), the connoisseur and benefactor of Paris (see p 223), and Mary Clarke (Mme Mohl; 1793–1883).

N of the Rue de la Roquette, opposite the main entrance of the cemetery, stood the *Prison de la Grande-Roquette*, itself on the site of the convent of the *Hospitalières de la Roquette*, founded in 1639, replaced in 1899 by the *Petite-Roquette* (for women). From 1853 to 1899 condemned prisoners were held at *La Roquette* while awaiting execution. Here in 1871 some 50-odd Commune hostages were shot, although c 130 were also released. Thiers' victorious government forces 'of law and order' then proceeded to round up thousands of Communards—both repentant and unrepentant—and in two days shot out-of-hand 1900 in retaliation, or 'in expiation'!

To the SE of the cemetery, approached by the BLVD DE CHARONNE (forking off the Blvd de Ménilmontant) and Rue de Bagnolet, stands **St.-Germain-de Charonne**, a rustic church of the 13–14C, restored in the 19th, retaining its village cemetery (the only other in Paris being *St.-Pierre-de-Montmartre*).—*St.-Jean-Bosco* (1937), of concrete, and with a lofty tower, stands a short distance SE of the junction of the Blvd de Charonne and the Rue de Bagnolet.

31 The Faubourg St.-Antoine

MÉTROS: Bastille, Nation, Gare de Lyon, Bércy.

From Père-Lachaise (see above), the BLVD DE MÉNILMONTANT, with its continuation S, the Av. Philippe-Auguste, leads SE to the *Pl. de la Nation*, also approached direct from the *Pl. de la Bastille* by Métro. The RUE DU FAUBOURG-ST.-ANTOINE leads ESE from the Pl. de la Bastille to the *Pl. de la Nation*, through an area memorable in the history of the Revolutions of 1789 and 1848. It was also the scene of skirmishing during the Fronde (1652), when Turenne defeated Condé.

Since the late 13C it has been a centre of cabinet-making, and many courtyards and passages still accommodate busy workshops behind 18C façades.

At No. 1 Rue du Faubourg-St.-Antoine, leading away from the Pl. de la Bastille (see Rte 21) and the new opera-house, Fieschi hatched the plot against Louis-Philippe (see Blvd du Temple). At No. 61 (left), at the corner of the Rue de Charonne, is the *Fontaine Trogneux* (1710). Further on (right) the SQ. TROUSSEAU occupies the site of the *Hospice des Enfants-Trouvés*, in the graveyard of which the Princesse de Lamballe was buried after her corpse had been paraded through the streets (1792).—In front of No. 151, Jean-Baptiste-Victor Baudin, representative of the people for the department of the Ain, was killed on a barricade while inciting the Parisians to protest against the coup d'état of Napoléon III (1851).

To the left, the Rue St.-Bernard leads to the church of *Ste.-Marguerite*, built in 1634 but many times altered since. Behind the high altar is a Pietà by *Girardon*. It is believed that the 10-year-old Louis XVII, who in all probability died at the *Temple*, was buried in the graveyard here, with other victims of the Revolution.

S of the Rue du Faubourg-St.-Antoine at this point is the *Hôpital St.-Antoine*, rebuilt in 1905 but retaining part of Lenoir's 18C building for the former *Abbaye de St.-Antoine-des-Champs*.

Several thoroughfares converge on the spacious **Pl. de la Nation**, at the hub of which is a colossal bronze group representing the 'Triumph of the Republic', by Dalou (1899). It was known formerly as the *Pl. du Trône* (named after the throne erected for Louis XIV's triumphal entry in 1660 with Maria Teresa); in 1794 no less than 1306 victims of the Terror were guillotined here. Between 1793 and 1880 it was known as the *Pl. du Trône-renversé*.

To the E of the 'circus' are two *Pavilions*, built as toll-houses by Ledoux in 1788, each surmounted by a Doric column 30·50m high; one with a statue of Philippe Auguste (by Dumont), the other, of Louis IX, by Étex.

The COURS DE VINCENNES (once the scene in Easter Week of the *Foire aux Pains d'épice*, a festival dating back to the 10C, when bread made with honey and aniseed was distributed by the monks of the Abbey of St.-Antoine) leads directly E from the *Pl. de la Nation* to the *Porte de Vincennes*, and beyond to the *Château de Vincennes* (see Rte 32), also reached direct by the Métro.

The Rue Fabre-d'Églantine leads S to the Rue de Picpus, where, at the end of the garden at No. 35, a convent of Augustinian nuns, is the little *Cimetière de Picpus* (open 14.00–16.00 or 18.00, except Monday), a private burial-ground for 'emigrés' and descendants of victims of the Revolution.

Among individuals interred there is La Fayette; among famous families, those of Chateaubriand, Crillon, Gontaut-Biron, Tascher de la Pagerie, Choiseul, La Rochefoucauld, Du Plessis, Montmorency, Talleyrand-Périgord, Rohan-Rochefort, Noailles, Quélen, and Salignac-Fénelon, and sixteen Carmelites of Compiègne martyred in 1794. In a second section are buried members of the house of Salm-Kyrbourg, and those guillotined in the *Pl. du Trône-renversé*, including André Chénier; see above.

A short distance SE of the PL. DE LA BASTILLE, in the Rue de Charenton, is the rebuilt *Hospice des Quinze-Vingts*, founded as an asylum for 300 blind people by Louis IX in 1260. The previous building was later—until 1775—the *Caserne des Mousquetaires-Noirs*.

Nos 40–60 in the street occupy the site of the *Couvent des Filles-Anglaises de la Conception*, which in 1634/5–55 accepted only daughters of English parents. It was suppressed in 1796, but later restored to its former owners. In 1817–20 George Sand was a boarder there.

The Rue de Lyon leads S from the PL. DE LA BASTILLE to the **Gare de Lyon** (Pl. 5;6), terminus of lines to Dijon, Grenoble, Lyon, the South of France and Italy; it preserves a fin-de-siècle buffet. The boarding-point for auto-couchettes is at No. 48 Blvd de Bercy, further SE.

Opposite the station once stood the *Mazas Prison*, where 400 Communards were
rounded up and massacred by Thiers' troops in 1871. Rimbaud had been briefly
held there, in August 1870, for travelling from Charleville to Paris without a
ticket.

On its S side the station is now overlooked by tower blocks, including the *Tour
Gamma A*, 195 Rue de Bercy, containing offices of the *Observatoire économique
de Paris* (Institut National de la Statistique et des Études Économiques), a mine
of such information.

Just E of the *Pont de Bercy* (1864) is the hexagonal **Palais Omnisports**, a
stunted pyramid topped by a tubular platform sustained by four cylindrical
towers. It was inaugurated in 1984, and accommodates 17,000 spectators.
Immediately to the N is the new building of the **Ministry of Finance**.

A photograph by Atget *in the former Entrepôt des Vins, Bercy*

The area to the SE is to be laid out as a park. Here stood the once extensive
Entrepôt des Vins, with bonded warehouses and cellars. This spirituous district
has been the subject of a number of calamities in the past, among them the floods
of 1817, 1833, 1836, and 1850 and the fires in 1820, 1823, 1853, 1859, and 1860.

The BLVD DIDEROT leads W from the *Gare de Lyon* to the *Pont
d'Austerlitz* (also approached direct from the *Pl. de la Bastille* by the
BLVD DE LA BASTILLE), built in 1802–07, rebuilt in stone in 1855, and
widened in 1884–86.

To the NW, the QUAI HENRI-IV occupies what was until c 1840 the
Île Louviers, now joined to the Right Bank.—To the SE, at No. 12 QUAI
DE LA RAPÉE is the *Institut Médico-Légal* (no admission), which
replaced the old *Morgue*, which stood at the S end of the *Île de la Cité*.
Just beyond it the Métro crosses the Seine on a single span of 140m.

Other bridges seen in this direction beyond the *Pont de Bercy* are
the *Pont de Tolbiac* (1879–84), *Pont National* (1852, enlarged in

1939–42), and the new bridge carrying the Périphérique. The *Porte de Bercy*, on the N Bank here, is the commencement of the A4 autoroute to the E.

The *Pont d'Austerlitz* crosses the Seine to the *Gare d'Austerlitz*, see Rte 6.

32 Vincennes

Approximately 2km E of the *Porte de Vincennes*, and reached directly from the centre by the MÉTRO (*Château de Vincennes*), stands the impressive bulk of the historic ***CHÂTEAU DE VINCENNES** ◇, rectangular in plan, and flanked by nine square towers. All except the entrance tower, the finest and largest, which lost only its statues, were reduced to the level of the walls in the 19C. Michelet called it 'the Windsor of the Valois'.

The present castle, succeeding an earlier hunting-lodge fortified by Louis IX, was begun by Philippe VI in 1337, and its fortification was completed by his grandson Charles V (1364–73), who also commenced work on the Chapel, which was not finished until 1552. Some idea of how it once looked may be gained from the illustration of December in the 'Très Riches Heures of the Duc de Berri', or Fouquet's panel of Étienne Chevalier. The foundations of the *Pavillons du Roi* and *de la Reine* (to the S) were laid in the 16C, but these buildings were not completed for nearly a century, when the château, then in Mazarin's possession, was altered and decorated by Le Vau.

With the completion of the palace at Versailles (c 1680), Vincennes was deserted by the court, and the château was occupied in turn by a porcelain factory (1745; transferred to Sèvres in 1756), a cadet school, and in 1757, a small-arms factory. Offered for sale in 1788, it found no purchaser, and in 1791 La Fayette rescued it from destruction by the Revolutionary mob. In 1808 Napoléon converted it into an arsenal, when the surviving 13C buildings were demolished. In 1840 it was made into a fortress, and much of Le Vau's decoration was destroyed or masked by casemates.

During the Second World War, German occupying forces had a supply depot here, and the *Pavillon de la Reine* was partially destroyed by an explosion in 1944 during their evacuation of the building. Restoration continues to be undertaken sporadically, but much work is still to be done.

The historical associations of Vincennes are numerous. Here died Jeanne de Navarre in 1305, Louis X in 1316, Charles IV in 1328, Charles IX in 1574, and Mazarin in 1661; and Charles V was born here in 1337. In 1326 the 'Auld Alliance', or treaty between France and Scotland, was signed here. Henry V of England died here in 1422, seven weeks before the death of Charles VI, whom he was to succeed as king of France.

During the reign of Louis XIII, the keep was used as a state prison; and among its inmates were the Grand Condé, Card. de Retz, Fouquet, Diderot (visited there by Rousseau in 1749), and Mirabeau (who here wrote his 'Essai sur les lettres de cachet' in 1784). A later prisoner was Jean Henry de Latude (1725–1805), who, for a fraudulent attempt to extract money from Mme de Pompadour, was incarcerated here (and elsewhere), untried, for 35 years.

In March 1804 the Duc d'Enghien (son of the Prince de Condé), arrested five days before on Napoléon's orders, was tried by court-martial and shot here the same night. Gén. Daumesnil was governor of the château from 1809 to 1814, during the Hundred Days, and from 1830 until his death in 1832. When summoned to surrender to the Allies in 1814, his answer was 'First give me back my leg' (which he had lost at Wagram). In 1830, when the mob broke into the building in search of some former ministers of Charles X, he dispersed them by threatening to blow up the powder-magazine. Mata Hari was shot here in 1917. In 1944, three days before evacuating the city, the Germans shot some 30 hostages against the interior of the ramparts.

Crossing the moat, the fortress is entered beneath the imposing *Tour du Village*, 48m high, passing between a range of tawdry buildings in military occupation to reach the central courtyard. The ***Keep**, 50m in height, a square tower flanked with round turrets, is enclosed in a separate turreted enceinte, and is the finest of its type in France (since the *Château de Coucy*—N of *Soissons*—was blown up by the Germans in 1917), and as such deserves further restoration. The two doors on the ground floor facing the postern came from the prison of Louis XVI in the Temple. A wide spiral stair ascends to the first and second floors (third floor closed), supported by vaults springing from a central column; the corbels at each corner of the first floor room symbolise the Evangelists. Note the oak beams between the ribs.

The SECOND FLOOR, a favourite residence of Charles V, contains a fine chimneypiece, and an oratory in the NW turret. Henry V (of England) and Charles IX died on this floor. 17C prisoners of state were lodged above. The roof commands a wide view of the area, with the main landmarks of central Paris easily discerned to the W. The kitchen, with its internal well, is shown on the ground floor.

The *Chapel opposite was founded by Charles V in 1379 and, retaining the Gothic style, was only completed in 1552. The Flamboyant *Façade* has a magnificent rose-window surmounted by an ornamental gable filled with tracery. The bare interior contains graceful vaulting, and at the E end, seven stained-glass windows by *Beaurain* (16C), restored after an explosion in 1870. A monument to the Duc d'Enghien (see above; by *Deseine*, 1816) may be seen in the oratory.

To the S, approached through a portico, lies the immense *Cour d'Honneur*, and beyond, the monumental *Tour du Bois*. To the right stands the *Pavillon du Roi* (now containing military archives), and opposite, the *Pavillon de la Reine*, where Mazarin died in 1661. Both were completed by Le Vau in 1654–60. The latter houses the *Musée de la Guerre de 1914–1918*.

Some 3·5km NE—as the crow flies—in the *Parc de Montreau* (to the E of *Montreuil*), at 31 Blvd Théophile Sueur, is the *Musée de l'Histoire Vivante*, largely devoted to the Socialist ethic and the history of the revolutions of 1830, and 1848, the Paris Commune, and other proletarian movements (closed Monday).

For *Champs*, see *Blue Guide France*, and also for other districts in the Eastern environs of Paris.

The. **Bois de Vincennes**, first enclosed in the 12C, was replanted in 1731 by Louis XV and converted into a park for the citizens of Paris. It was further enlarged in 1860. To the SE of the château are extensive *Floral Gardens*, and beyond are stadiums and sports grounds. Further E is the *Lac des Minimes*, a *Jardin Tropical*, and an *Indo-Chinese pagoda*.

Towards the SW end of the Bois, approached directly from the château by the Av. Daumesnil (S of which are University buildings), is the *Parc Zoölogique de Vincennes*, the main zoo of Paris. Beyond it is the *Lac Daumesnil*, S of which is a *Buddhist Temple*.

As the Avenue leaves the Bois near an underground section of the Blvd Périphérique, the Av. Ste.-Marie leads right, at No. 60 in which stands the *Musée des Transports Urbains*.

Slightly further to the W is the reformed ***MUSÉE NATIONAL DES ARTS AFRICAINS ET OCÉANIENS**, housed in a building erected in 1931 for a Colonial Exhibition, with an ornately sculpted façade. It also contains an *Aquarium*. Some arabic or islamic material has been transferred to the *Institut du Monde Arabe*, see Rte 6.

As its name implies, it concentrates on the *arts* of the ci-devant French colonies rather than their ethnography, for which see *Musée de l'Homme*, Rte 27.

GROUND FLOOR: left, the Oceanian Collection: masks, wooden drums, and statues from the New Hebrides: to the right, naïf bark paintings from Australia. FIRST FLOOR: left, arts of the W African coast, including gold figurines etc., from Akan; brass and gold powder figures from Ghana and the Ivory Coast; note also the carved wood woman and child from Kran (Liberia). To the right, work from the Niger and Congo basins, Yoruba (Nigeria), and the Cameroons; Benin bronzes; nail-studded magic statues from the Congo; Bembe figurines, masks, jewellery, and pottery.

SECOND FLOOR: left, Moroccan jewellery, including a fine necklace from Fez (16–17C); arms; and a section devoted to fabrics, brocades, embroidery, caftans, etc. To the right, the arts of Tunisia and Algeria, including bonnets, pendants, fibulas, etc.

The return to the centre may be made from the MÉTRO *Porte Dorée*, adjacent.

THE IMMEDIATE ENVIRONS
OF PARIS

See map on previous page.

33   From Paris to Versailles

BY ROAD. Versailles is approached rapidly by taking the A13
motorway and turning left at the first exit after passing through the
tunnel at St.-Cloud. A road leads SW towards the *Château of
Versailles* (parking in the *Pl. d'Armes*).

An alternative is the N10, bearing SW from the Porte de St.-Cloud
over the Pont de Sèvres, which our route follows.

BY RAIL. A convenient approach is the RER line running along the S
bank of the Seine, where the train may be boarded at, for example,
St.-Michel, Musée d'Orsay, Invalides, Champ-de-Mars, or *Javel.*
The terminus nearest the palace is **Versailles-Rive Gauche**. There
are also lines from the *Gare St.-Lazare* to *Versailles-Rive Droit,* and
from the *Gare Montparnasse* to *Versailles-Chantiers.*

Alternatively, take the métro to the *Pont de Sèvres,* then bus 171.

Note that the *Château* of Versailles (see Rte 34) is closed on *Mondays,*
although the Gardens are open every day until dusk.

The N10, on leaving the *Porte de St.-Cloud* (with fountains by
Landowski), traverses the suburb of *Boulogne-Billancourt* before
crossing the *Pont de Sèvres* (rebuilt 1963). **SÈVRES** itself is famous for
the Porcelain Factory founded in 1738; the *****Musée National de
Céramique** (4 Grande Rue) also displays ceramics and porcelain from
other factories and countries.

For guided tours of the adjacent *workshops* (no children under 16), telephone
45349905. The *Sale-room* is open 9.00–12.00; 13.30–18.00 from Monday to
Friday. MÉTRO *Pont-de-Sèvres.*

The factory was moved here from Vincennes in 1756 at the instance of
Mme de Pompadour, and since 1760 has been State-controlled. It was
visited in 1776 by Thomas Bentley, Josiah Wedgwood's partner, who
was impressed by its workshops, in which a dozen carvers or
modellers and almost one hundred painters were employed. Among
designers of Sèvres ware may be mentioned E.-M. Falconet (1716–
91), and J.-B. Pigalle (1714–85).

On the FIRST FLOOR are Islamic ceramics (8–15Cs), and from Anatolia (16–18Cs);
and historical collections, mostly from France; Italian majolica; Hispano-
Moresque ware, etc., from the Middle Ages to the 18C.—SECOND FLOOR: *N
Gallery*: Delft ware; faïence from Nevers; from Moustiers, Rouen, Strasbourg,
Marseille, and Sceaux; and copies of Oriental pieces manufactured at St.-Cloud,
Mennecy, Meissen, and Chantilly. *S Gallery*: Porcelain from Vincennes and
Sèvres, and Saxe, etc.

Lully, the composer, once resided in a nearby pavilion, named after him. Some
distance to the W, in the suburb of *Ville d'Avray*, the 'Villa des Jardies' was the
country retreat of Balzac in 1837–41. It was later the home of Léon Gambetta
(1838–82), who died there. The 18C church contains frescoes by Corot, who
often painted the lakes in the *Bois de Fausses Reposes*, further SW.

Immediately SE of Sèvres is **Meudon** (Celtic *Mellodunum*), the
benefice of which was enjoyed by Rabelais in 1551–52. Wagner
composed 'The Flying Dutchman' here in 1841, at 27 Av. du Château;
here too is the 'Villa des Brillants', once the home of Rodin (1840–
1918), with a collection of his casts, and his grave; and a *Museum* of
local history at 11 Rue des Pierres.

Further S is the *Observatoire d'Astronomie Physique*. The building, formerly the *Château Neuf*, was built for the Grand Dauphin ('Monseigneur', the son of Louis XIV), by Mansart, but a fire in 1870 reduced it to the single-storeyed building which it is today. The terrace commands an extensive view. The *Forêt de Meudon* extends to the S and W.

St.-Cloud, 2km N of Sèvres, was the site of a porcelain factory from 1695 until 1773, when it was destroyed in a fire. St.-Cloud was also the birthplace of Hilaire Belloc (1870–1953). The royal castle—in which Henri III was assassinated in 1589; and Philippe d'Orléans was born (1674); where Napoléon's second marriage, to Marie-Louise, was celebrated in 1810; and where Charles X signed his infamous 'Ordonnances' in 1830—was burned down during the German occupation in 1870, but its remains were not cleared away until 1891. The **Park** (392 hectares), with its cascades, fountains, and views over Paris—which Queen Victoria thought splendid—is open to the public.

At *Montretout*, the upper part of St.-Cloud, is the HQ of *Interpol*.

On a height some 3km N is seen the fort of *Mont Valérien* (1830), where Col. Henry, implicated in the Dreyfus Affair, committed suicide in 1898; and where during the years 1941–44 some 4500 members of the Resistance, among others, were murdered. Off the Blvd Washington is an *American Military Cemetery*.

From Sèvres, the N10 continues SW (through the suburbs of *Chaville* and *Viroflay*) to (c 8km) *Versailles*.

VERSAILLES (95,000 inhab.), *préfecture* of the department of Yvelines, lies in a low sandy plain between two lines of wooded hills. With its regular streets and its imposing avenues converging on the palace, it seeks to retain its royal cachet, although the château, with which the history of the town is inextricably entwined, quite overshadows it in interest; see Rte 34. Nevertheless, the town does contain a certain number of buildings of importance, which are described below. See map on p 255.

Versailles was the birthplace of Houdon (1741–1828), the sculptor, Marshal Berthier (1753–1815), Kreutzer (1766–1831), the violinist, Gén. Hoche (1768–97), and Ferdinand de Lesseps (1805–94; at 18 Rue des Réservoirs). The artist Georges Rouault (1871–1958) is buried in the St.-Louis cemetery. Sir Jonah Barrington (1760–1834), author of diverting 'Personal Sketches', and the art dealer Ambroise Vollard (1865–1939) died at Versailles.

At 7 Rue des Réservoirs, N of the château, is the *Hôtel des Réservoirs*, built by Lassurance for Mme de Pompadour (but much altered), still bearing the marquise's arms. The *Théâtre Montansier* (No. 13), founded by the actress Mlle Montansier, was built by Heurtier and Boulet in 1777, and since restored. La Bruyère (1645–96) lived and died at No. 22, the *Hôtel du Prince de Condé*.

A few minutes' walk to the NE is the *Musée Lambinet*, in a mid 18C mansion (at 54 *Blvd de la Reine*) containing sculptures by Houdon. The collection of early prints and views of Versailles is of interest. Among paintings are *Vigée-Lebrun*, Portrait of Mme du Barry; and works by *Corot, Le Sidaner*, and *Bonington*, among others. The painting of Lalande and Couperin sharing a ham, by *Robert Tournières* is now in the *réserve*.

A short distance SW of the museum stands *Nôtre-Dame*, by Jules Hardouin-Mansart (1684), with a pulpit of the period.

By the same architect is the *Grand-Commun*, immediately S of the Château, built to accommodate court functionaries, which retains several fine bas-reliefs. It was converted into a small-arms factory at the Revolution, and later used as a military hospital. Adjacent is the former *Hôtel de la Guerre* (1759), and *Hôtel de la Marine et des Affaires Étrangères* (1761), now the municipal library, with Louis XV decoration. The Marquis de Louvois (1641–91) died at No. 6 in the street, once the *Hôtel de la Surintendance*.

From here the Rue du Vieux-Versailles (left) leads to the **Jeu de Paume**, the royal tennis-court (1686), but of little interest in itself (admission on application to the Conservateur, Château de Versailles).

On 20 June 1789, the deputies of the Tiers-État, finding themselves locked out of the States-General, adjourned here, and with the astronomer Bailly as their president, swore not to separate until they had given France a proper constitution. It was later used as a studio by Gros and Horace Vernet.

To the S stands a rare but frigid example of a Louis XV church, **St.-Louis** (1742–54; by Jacques Mansart de Sagonne), designated a cathedral in 1802.

To the W is the former royal kitchen-garden, now a horticultural college (entrance No. 4 Rue du Potager).—To the SE is the Pl. du Marché-St.-Louis, with 18C houses. Further on, at No. 4 Rue St.-Médéric, was the *Parc-aux-Cerfs*, purchased in 1755 by Louis XV—when in rut—for the indulgence of his amours. Its first occupant was Marie-Louise Murphy (1737–1814), born at Rouen and the daughter of an Irish shoemaker.

In the Av. de Paris, leading directly E from the château, No. 3 occupies the *Hôtel de Mme du Barry* (1751; admission on application), preserving contemporary *boiseries*. Comte Robert de Montesquiou (1855–1921), on whom Proust based his 'Baron Charlus' and Huysmans his 'Jean des Esseintes' in 'À Rebours', lived at No. 53, where he entertained many writers and dilettantes. Further on at Nos 57–61, are the *Laiterie de Madame* and *Pavillon de Musique*, built by Chalgrin in 1781 in emulation of the 'hameau' at the Petit Trianon, for Joséphine-Louise de Savoie, Comtesse de Provence, wife of the future Louis XVIII.

34 The Château and Gardens of Versailles: The Trianons

The Château of Versailles. **Admission**. The Château is open every day from 9.45–17.00, **except** Mondays, but only the *Grands Appartements*, the *Galerie des Glaces*, and the *Appartements de la Reine* may be visited entirely without restriction. Regulations with regard to visiting the *Chapel*, the *Trianons*, and certain other galleries are liable to variation. Normally the *Opéra, Appartements du Roi, de Mme de Maintenon, Mme du Barry*, the *Petits Appartements de la Reine*, and the *Appartements du Dauphin et de la Dauphine, et des Mesdames* may only be visited with a guided group (some with an English-speaking guide). Enquire in the main entrance hall, to the right (N) of the Cour Royale. Guided tours of the Appartements du Roi normally leave from adjacent to a passage (R39 on Pl.) every ten minutes or so between 9.45–15.30.

Enquire in advance to the *Service éducatif* (Tel. 3950 0020) for details of rooms open to the public: certain sections may well be closed for restoration. Others may only be visited on making a special request to this department.

Note that the *Grand Trianon* is open from 9.45–12.00, and 14.00–17.00, and the *Petit Trianon* is only open from 14.00–17.00.

Near the main entrance are cloakrooms, bookstalls, an information desk and refreshment facilities.

Versailles emerged from obscurity in 1624, when Louis XIII built a hunting lodge here, which subsequently developed into a small château. But the real creator of Versailles was Louis XIV, who in 1661 conceived the idea of building a lasting monument to his reign—a trophy of self-glorification. Louis Le Vau was entrusted with the renovation and embellishment of the old building round the Cour de Marbre, while Le Nôtre laid out the park. After Le Vau's death in 1670 the work was continued by his pupil François d'Orbay, while the interior decoration was supervised by Charles Le Brun. In 1682 Louis XIV transferred here from St.-Germain, the court and seat of government. Jules Hardouin-Mansart, appointed chief architect in 1676, remodelled the main body of the château and built the two huge N and S wings, giving the immense façade (with its 375 windows) a total length of 580m. The chapel, begun by him, was finished by his brother-in-law Robert de Cotte in 1710.

More than 30,000 workmen were employed at one time on the building and in laying out and draining the grounds; the cost, impoverishing France, amounting to over 60 million livres. In 1687 Mansart started work on the *Grand Trianon*. Under Louis XV a series of royal apartments, decorated in the current style, were incorporated; and one of the colonnaded pavilions in the entrance court, the interior of the opera-house, and the *Petit Trianon* were built by Jacques-Ange Gabriel. Louis XVI redecorated a suite of apartments for Marie-Antoinette and built the 'rustic village' or *Hameau*.

Not all visitors from England were impressed by Versailles. The poet Thomas Gray, in 1739, wrote of it as 'a huge heap of littleness'; Dr Johnson was more interested by the menagerie than the palace; Smollett described it as a 'most fantastic composition of magnificence and littleness, taste and foppery'.

The independence of the United States was formally recognised by England, France, and Spain, at the Treaty of Versailles, signed in 1783. The meeting of the Assembly of the States-General was held in Versailles in 1789, where on 20 June the deputies of the Third Estate constituted themselves into the National Assembly. On 6 October the Paris mob, led by the women of the Halles, marched to Versailles, massacred the bodyguard, and conveyed the king and the royal family to the Tuileries. The place was then pillaged.

In 1792, when Richard Twiss visited Versailles, he found it almost bare: glasses, tapestries, and pictures removed. It had been uninhabited for over two years, and the Grand Canal—which Arthur Young in 1787 remarked 'was not in such good repair as a farmer's horsepond'—was quite dry. In 1814 the palace was occupied by Tsar Alexander I and Friedrich Wilhelm III of Prussia. Under the Restoration, the second colonnaded pavilion was completed by Dufour, but the building later deteriorated from neglect. Louis-Philippe did irreparable damage to the château in housing a pretentious museum there, containing few canvases of any importance, and reflecting his prodigious lack of taste.

In the Franco-Prussian War Versailles became the HQ of the German armies operating against Paris, who had met near St.-Germain-en-Laye, when encircling the capital. The château was used as a hospital, and Moltke occupied No. 38 Blvd de la Reine. On 18 January 1871, Wilhelm I of Prussia was crowned German Emperor in

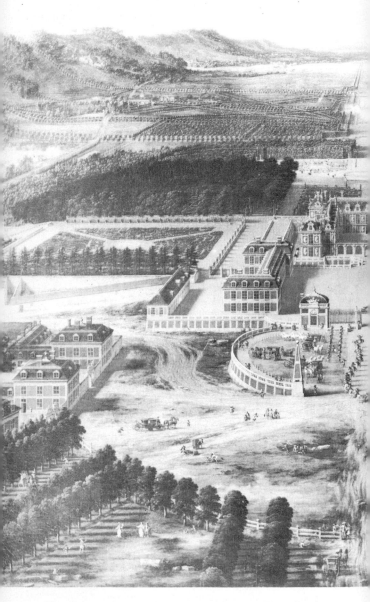

The Château de Versailles in 1668, painted by Pierre Patel

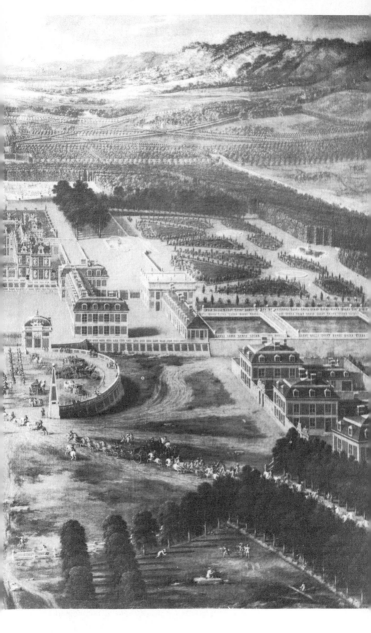

Early 18C view of the Château de Versailles from the East

the *Galerie des Glaces*; and on 26 January the peace preliminaries were signed at Bismarck's quarters at 20 Rue de Provence. In 1871–75 the National Assembly sat in the opera-house, and here the third Republic was confirmed on 25 February 1875. The general restoration of the complex began after the appointment of Pierre de Nolhac as curator in 1887.

During the First World War Versailles was the seat of the Allied War Council, and the Peace Treaty with Germany was signed in the *Galerie des Glaces* on 28 June 1919. Further extensive restorations were made in 1928–32, thanks largely to the donations of the Rockefeller Foundation, and were continued after the Second World War under the curatorship of Gerald van der Kemp. During that war, the Allied GHQ was at Versailles from September 1944 until the following May, and many buildings were requisitioned by the military, which hardly improved them.

The château was the birthplace of Louis XV (1710–74), Louis XVI (1754–93), Louis XVIII (1755–1824), and Charles X (1757–1836). Mme de Pompadour died in the château in 1764.

It is virtually physically impossible to visit *all* the galleries, the park, and the Trianons, in one day, although many attempt to do so.

The *Gardens* are described on p 254.

The wide Avenues de St.-Cloud, de Paris, and de Sceaux, converge on the *Pl. d'Armes*, E of the château, bounded to the E by the **Grandes Écuries** (S) and the **Petites Écuries** (N), the royal stables, built by Mansart in 1679–85, which once accommodated 2000 carriages and 2500 horses. Communards were incarcerated here in 1871.

Their façades have been restored recently, and the Petites Écuries are being converted into studios for the restoration of paintings in the national collections.

Flanking the gateway to the château, with *Mansart*'s original grille, are groups of sculpture: (right) France victorious over the Empire, by Marsy, and over Spain, by Girardon; and left, Peace, by Tuby, and Abundance, by Coysevox. The *Avant-Cour* or *Cour des Ministres* is flanked by detached wings once assigned to secretaries of state. Beyond the equestrian statue of Louis XIV (1837) is the *Cour Royale*, between two colonnaded pavilions dating from 1772 (right) and 1829.

In the time of Louis XIV, only those who possessed the honours of the Louvres—those called 'cousin' by the king, and who had the right to bring their coach or chair or liveried servants into the great Courtyard of the Louvre—could enter this court in a similar fashion.

The ****CHÂTEAU DE VERSAILLES**. The visitors' entrance is in the right-hand pavilion. Before entering, walk over to the *Cour de Marbre*, a deep, marble-paved recess at the end of the *Cour Royale*; this was the courtyard of Louis XIII's château and the nucleus of the whole, before being transformed by Le Vau and Mansart.

The information and ticket-offices, cloakroom (obligatory for umbrellas, parcels, etc.) and bookstalls are in the *Vestibule Gabriel* (**R23**).

Beyond this is the *Vestibule de la Chapelle*, which has handsome carved and gilded doors and contains a bas-relief by *Nicolas* and *Guillaume Coustou* of Louis XIV crossing the Rhine. To the right we get a view of the **Chapel** (open only for occasional services; enquire at the information desk), with its colonnade of Corinthian columns, begun by *Mansart* in 1699 and completed in 1710 by *Robert de Cotte*. The high altar is of marble and bronze, with sculptures by *Van Cleve* and *Guillaume Coustou*, above which is the organ. François Couperin was one of the great organists who played here. The central ceiling-painting is by *Antoine Coypel*, and above the royal pew is a Descent of the Holy Ghost, by *Jouvenet*.

From the vestibule one enters the **17C Gallery** (*Salles du Dixseptième Siècle*), with an impressive collection of portraits displayed in eleven rooms. **R2** *Rubens*, Marie de Médicis and her parents. **R3** Richelieu, by *Philippe de Champaigne*. **R4** is devoted to the Jansenists of Port-Royal, with perspectives and portraits, including *Philippe de Champaigne*, Angélique Arnauld, and the architect Lemercier. **R8** portraits of Racine, Molière, La Fontaine, et al. **R9** views of Versailles by *Pierre-Denis Martin* and others; and of sieges, by *Van der Meulen*, and a portrait of Mansart by *François de Troy*. **R11** portraits by *Beaubrun* of the royal family.

At the far end of this gallery is the *Foyer de l'Opéra*, retaining its 18C decoration by *Pajou*. Off the parallel *Galerie de Pierre*, to the right, are the *Salles des Croisades*, etc. (**RR17–21**), of very slight interest.

The **Opéra**, or *Salle de Spectacles*, was built for Louis XV by *Gabriel* in 1753–70, and first used on the occasion of the marriage of the Dauphin (Louis XVI) and Marie-Antoinette.

It was later repainted in the poor taste of the period of Louis-Philippe, and in 1855 was the scene of a banquet given in honour of Queen Victoria.

Modelled on the King of Sardinia's theatre in Turin, it is a perfect example of Louis XV decoration, having been skilfully restored (1955–57) by Japy, even the upholstery being copied from the original specifications. Seating 700 spectators and with a stage second in size only to the Paris *Opéra*, it is now reserved for rare gala performances.

Stairs ascend to **RR 93–84**, continuing the series of 17C portraits and busts. **R92** four battle scenes by *van der Meulen*, and equestrian portrait of Louis XIV by *Houasse*. **R91** views of palaces: St.-Germain and Vincennes by *J.-B. Martin*, Marly and Trianon by *P.-D. Martin*, and St.-Cloud by *Allegrain*. **R88** Mme de Maintenon by *Mignard*, and Fénelon by *Vivien*. **R87** *Rigaud*, Marquis de Dangeau. **R86** Princesses, including the Duchesse de Bourgogne in a red dress, by *Gobert*. **R85** *Benoist*, wax portrait of Louis XIV aged 68, with his own (?) wig. **R84** *Rigaud*, the Duchesse d'Orléans.

From the *Upper Vestibule* (**R83**), with figures of the Virtues by various sculptors, there is a striking view of the *Chapel* and *Royal Gallery*, the door of which has a chased lock by *Desjardins*.

The *Salon d'Hercule* (**R105**), was fitted up by Louis XV in the Louis XIV style. The elaborate decorations were sculpted by *Vassé* (1729–34). On the ceiling is the Apotheosis of Hercules by *François Lemoyne*; after three years' work (1733–36), he committed suicide on its completion. Swiss Guards used to be posted here to prevent the intrusion into the State Apartments of 'those freshly marked with smallpox, the shabbily dressed, petitioners, begging friars, and dogs'.

The *Salon de l'Abondance* (**R106**)—used as a refreshment room at royal receptions—is the first of the **King's State Apartments**, which, although they have lost their original furniture, have preserved their decorations of marble inlay, sculptured and gilded bronzes, carved doors and painted ceilings, executed under the supervision of *Charles Le Brun*. The ceiling-painting here is by *Houasse* (restored).

The *Salon de Vénus* (**R107**), named after its painted ceiling (also by *Houasse*), is noteworthy for its marble decorations in the early Louis XIV style. The carved doors are by *Caffieri*; above are bronze bas-reliefs. The mural decorations of this salon (and the succeeding one) are original. In the central alcove is a statue of Louis XIV in Roman costume *and wig*, by *Warin*: and on either side of the room are trompe-l'oeil paintings by *Jacques Rousseau*.

The *Salon de Diane* (**R108**), the former billiard room, has a ceiling by *Blanchard*, and contains a bust of Louis XIV by *Bernini* (1665).

The *Salon de Mars* (**R109**), once the *Salle des Gardes*, later a gaming-room and subsequently a ballroom and concert-room, has a ceiling by *Audran, Jouvenet* and *Houasse*. The dessus de portes are by *Simon Vouet*, and the portrait of Marie-Antoinette and her children by *Mme Vigée-Lebrun* (1787). The tapestries are the first of a series by *Le Brun*, illustrating 'The Life of the King', and are among the earliest works from the Gobelins factory (1668–72).

The *Salon de Mercure* (**R110**), a card-room under Louis XIV, and where after his death that monarch lay in state for eight days, has a ceiling by *J.-B. de Champaigne*. The Savonnerie carpet, and the clock (by *Morand*), should be noticed.

The *Salon d'Apollon* (**R111**), the former throne-room, is the last of the King's State Apartments. On the ceiling, by *Lafosse*, is Louis XIV (the 'Roi Soleil') as Apollo in a chariot escorted by the Seasons.

The three following rooms—the *Galerie des Glaces*, with its antechambers, the *Salons de la Guerre* and *de la Paix*—together form a grandiose decorative ensemble. The *Salon de la Guerre* (**R112**), completed in 1678, has preserved its original decoration of coloured marble and bronze, and contains six busts of Roman emperors, bequeathed by Mazarin. Over the mantlepiece is a stucco relief of Louis XIV on horseback, by *Coysevox*.

The ceiling-painting, the first of a series designed by *Charles Le Brun*, represents France victorious, with a thunderbolt in one hand and a laurel-wreathed portrait of Louis XIV in the other; in the lunettes appear Bellona in anger, and figures of defeated Germany, Holland, and Spain.

The ***Galerie des Glaces**, or *Grande Galerie* (**R113**), 73m long, 10·50m wide, and 12·30m high, is a masterpiece of the Louis XIV style. It was begun by *Mansart* in 1678, and its decoration, from designs by *Le Brun*, was completed in 1686. Among the artists employed were Caffieri, Coysevox, Le Comte, and Tuby, for the sculptures; *Cucci*, for the mirror frames; and *Ladoiseau*, for the trophies on the walls.

The gallery is lit by 17 windows looking on to the park, and facing these are as many bevelled mirrors of equal size. The red marble pilasters have bronze capitals decorated with cocks' heads, *fleurs-de-lys*, and suns. The cornice of

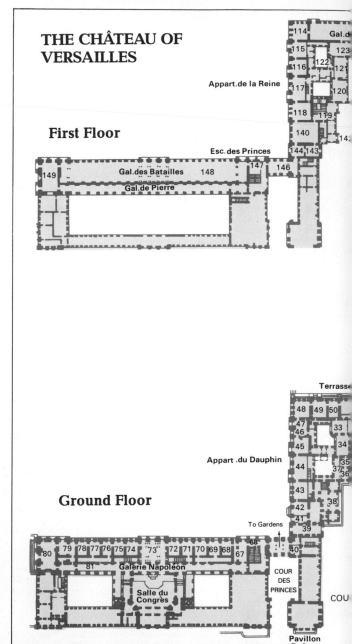

THE CHÂTEAU OF VERSAILLES

Appart.de la Reine

First Floor

Esc. des Princes

Gal.des Batailles   148

Gal.de Pierre

149

114   Gal.d

115   123

116   122   121

117   120

118   119

140

144 143

147   146

Appart .du Dauphin

Ground Floor

Terrass

48   49   50

47

46   33

45   34

44   35   37   36

43

42   38

41

39

40

To Gardens

68

80   79   78   77   76   75   74   "73"   72   71   70   69   68   67

81

Galerie Napoléon

Salle du Congrès

COUR DES PRINCES

COU

Pavillon Dufour

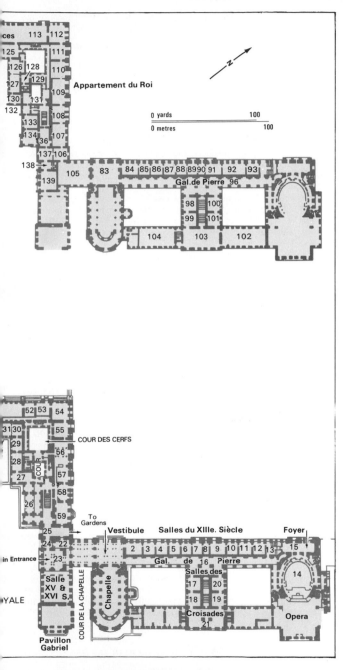

ces · 113 · 112

125 · 111

126 · 128 · 110

127 · 129

130 · 131 · 109

132

133 · 108

134 · 107

136

137 · 106

138 → 139 · 105 · 83 · 84 85 86 87 88 89 90 91 · 92 · 93

Appartement du Roi

0 yards · 100
0 metres · 100

Gal. de Pierre · 96

98 · 100
99 · 101

104 · 103 · 102

52 53 · 54

31 30 · 55

29

28 · 56

27 · COUR · 57

26 · 58

59

25

24 · 22

in Entrance · 23

COUR DES CERFS

To Gardens →

Vestibule · **Salles du XIIIe. Siècle** · **Foyer**

2 3 4 5 6 7 8 9 10 11 12 13 · 15

Gal. de 16 Pierre

Salles des

17 · 20

18 · 19

Croisades

21

Salle XV & XVI S.

YALE

Chapelle

COUR DE LA CHAPELLE

14

Opera

Pavillon Gabriel

gilded stucco is adorned with crowns and the collars of the Orders of the Saint-Esprit and St. Michael. The marble statues of Venus, Paris, Mercury, and Minerva in the niches are copies from the antique; some other statues are also copies of originals. Twenty silvered bronze and Bohemian glass chandeliers illuminate the gallery.

The central ceiling-painting represents Louis XIV omnipotent, while the numerous other paintings depict the subjection of Holland, Germany, and Spain, the Peace imposed by Louis on his enemies, his embassies abroad, the Protection of the Arts, and of the People, and the great Foundations established during his reign.

We now enter the *Salon de la Paix* (**R114**), the queen's card-room. The ceiling completes *Le Brun's* scheme, depicting France bringing the benefits of peace to Europe, etc. Over the chimneypiece (left unfinished by *Le Brun*) is a painting by *Lemoyne* (1729), showing Louis XV following his great-grandfather's example as the bringer of peace.

The *Chambre de la Reine* (**R115**), the first of the **Queen's State Apartments**, has been restored to its pre-Revolution appearance, the chimneypiece having been brought back from the Trianon and the silk hangings copied (at Lyon) from pieces of the original material. Here died Marie-Thérèse (1683) and Marie Leczinska (1768), and here took place the confinements of the queens of France. The jewel cabinet of Marie-Antoinette (by *Evalde*; 1770) was brought from the Château of St.-Cloud. Above the doors are allegorical paintings of the children of Louis XV by *Natoire* and *Jean-François de Troy*. The grisaille panels of the ceiling are by *Boucher*; the portrait of Marie-Antoinette is by *Mme Vigée-Lebrun*; and the unfinished pastel of the queen is by *Kucharski* (1792).

R116, the *Salon des Nobles* (or *Salon de la Reine*), was the queen's presence chamber. The ceiling is by *Michel Corneille* (died 1708); the busts are of Louis XVI by *Pajou*, and Marie-Antoinette by *Le Comte*.

In the *Antichambre* (**R117**), where the queen dined in public, are Gobelins tapestries, and busts of Louis XIV by *Coysevox* (1681), Louis XV by *Gois*, and Louis XVI by *Houdon*. The *Salle des Gardes de la Reine* (**R118**), with marble decoration of the period of Louis XIV, retains its ceiling by *Noël Coypel, the Elder*. It was here, on 6 October 1789, that the revolutionary mob burst in, and three of the Swiss Guards died in the queen's defence.

The *Chambre de la Reine* leads to the **Petits Appartements de la Reine* (**R122**), the small and cramped private suite of Marie-Antoinette, preserving its superb decoration. The *Boudoir* or *Petite Méridienne*, with its gilded woodwork and mirror-frames, and the *Library*, with imitation bookshelves, were designed by *Mique* (c 1781). In the *Small Library*, used by the ladies-in-waiting, is a marriage-chest of Marie-Antoinette. In the *Salon de la Reine*, with elaborate decoration by the brothers *Rousseau*, she received her intimate friends, and her musicians, Gluck and Grétry, and sat to Mme Vigée-Lebrun for her portraits. The last two rooms are the *Bath Room*, and the *Chambre de repos* or *Salon Jaune*.

To the left of R118 is the landing of the *Escalier de Marbre*, or *de la Reine*, built by *Le Vau* and *Mansart*, with an interesting perspective painting in the Italian style. Across the landing is a *Loggia* (**R119**) overlooking the *Cour de Marbre*, in which (right) a door admits to the *Apartments of Mme de Maintenon* (see below); to the left is the *Salle des Gardes du Roi* (see below).

It may be convenient to visit from this point **R140**, the *Salle du Sacre* (previously the *Grande Salle des Gardes*), restored since its mutilation by Louis-Philippe. The ceiling-painting is by *Callet* and the dessus de portes by *Gérard*; the walls are adorned by huge paintings depicting Napoléon presenting eagles in the Champ-de-Mars (1804), and his coronation at Notre-Dame, both by *David*; and Murat at the battle of Aboukir (1799) by *Gros*.

In the adjoining *Grand Cabinet* (**R143**), Racine's 'Esther' was played before the king, and in 1702 his 'Athalie' was presented by the princes and princesses.—**R144** leads to the *Salle de 1792* (**R146**), containing military portraits, and originally the 'Salon des Marchands', to which vendors of goods were admitted for the convenience of the inmates of the palace.—The *Escalier des Princes* (**R147**), by *Mansart*, gave access to the S wing, once reserved for the princes of the blood.

The series of rooms beyond this point are of little interest. The *Galerie des Batailles*, nearly 120m long, constructed under Louis-Philippe by combining most of the rooms on the first floor, displays a sad selection of huge canvases representing French military achievements—perhaps the only one of note being The Battle of Taillebourg, by *Delacroix*—Thackeray considered them among 'the worst pictures that eye ever looked on'.

On returning to **R119**, one may visit (right) the **Apartments of Mme de Maintenon** (**RR141–142**; shown on request), furnished by Louis XIV in 1682 for Mme de Maintenon, who became his second wife probably the following year. The *Antichambre*, and *Bedchamber* (where most of the business of state was transacted), now contain a fine **Collection of 16C portraits* by *Corneille de Lyon* and other artists of the School of Clouet.

The adjoining *Escalier de Stuc* (built under Louis-Philippe) ascends to the SECOND FLOOR. Here, in the **Attique de Chimay** (right) and **Attique du Midi**, are displayed an outstanding **Collection of Historical Paintings* illustrating the early Napoleonic period. Unfortunately, the galleries are not always open, and it is advisable to check beforehand.

In **R174** are displayed battle scenes of Arcole by *Gén. Bacler d'Albe*, and of Lodi, by *Gén. Louis-François Lejeune*; and other views by war-artists of the period including *Hippolyte Lecomte, Antoine-Alexandre Morel, Nicolas-Antoine Taunay, François-Henri Mulard, René-Théodore Berthon*, and *Didier Boguet*. Note also *Gros*, Napoléon at Arcole, and the impressive collection of scenes by *Giuseppe-Pietro Bagetti* (in display cases). In the small room to the right are sketches by *Carle Vernet* and others.—To the left is **R176**, dominated by *Lejeune*, Battle of the Pyramides (among other scenes of the Egyptian Campaign).—**R177** *Lejeune*, Battle of Marengo; *Antoine-Pierre Mongin*, Passage of the army through the defile of Albaredo; and *David*, Napoléon crossing the Alps.

R178 *Jean-François Hue*, Napoléon visiting the camp at Boulogne.—**R179** *Jean-Baptiste-François Desoria*, Portrait of Letourneur, member of the Directoire; *Gérard*, Joachim Murat; and miniatures by *Louis Gauffier*.—**R180** *Pierre-Julien Gilbert*, Combat between 'La Canonnière' and 'The Tremendous' (1806); *Hoppner*, copied by *George Healy*, Lord Nelson, and Lord St. Vincent; *Lawrence*, copied by *Healy*, William Pitt.—**R181**, the first of a series devoted to **Small portraits* by *François Gérard*.

R171 is dominated by *Gérard*, Napoléon as Emperor of the French, and 'Madame Mère'; *François-André Lethière*, Joséphine; *Vigée-*

Lebrun, Marie-Annunciade-Caroline Bonaparte, among other members of the Imperial family.—**R170** *François Kinson*, Bernadotte; *Charles Meynier*, Ney; and *Lejeune*, Napoléon visiting the bivouacs before Austerlitz.—**R169** *Robert Lefèvre*, Napoléon I, and Augereau.

R168 (Life in Paris): *Lefèvre*, Baron Denon; *Girodet*, Chateaubriand; *David*, Pope Pius VII.—**R167** *Adolphe Roehn*, Napoléon at Wagram (night scene).—**R166** *Mathieu-Ignace van Bree*, Launching of 'Le Friedland'; *Joseph Franque*, Marie-Louise and the King of Rome.

R165 (Peninsular War): *Lejeune*, Crossing the Somosierra; Assault on the monastery of Sta. Engracia, Zaragoza; and The Battle of Chiclana (Barrosa); *Nicolas-Antoine Taunay*, Crossing the Guadarrama; *François-Joseph Heim*, Defence of the castle at Burgos. The second half of this gallery is devoted to the Russian Campaign.

From the *Salle du Gardes du Roi* (**R120**) enter the **Appartements du Roi**, starting with **R121**, the *Antichambre du Roi*, in which Louis XIV dined in private on the rare occasions when he could do so.—**R123**, known as the *Oeil-de-boeuf* after its small 'bull's eye window', where scandalmongering courtiers used to wait for admission to the king's 'lever'. The decorations are original, including the stucco frieze showing children's games, on a gold background, by *van Cleve*, *Hurtrelle*, and *Flamen*. A curious picture by *Nocret* represents the royal family in mythological costume.

The lavishly restored **Chambre du Roi** (**R124**), Louis XIV's bedchamber (in which he died in 1715), overlooks the *Cour de Marbre*. Here took place the ceremonious '*lever*' and '*coucher*' of the king, who used to lunch daily at a little table placed before the middle window. It was from the balcony of this room that Marie-Antoinette and Louis XVI, at La Fayette's suggestion, showed themselves to the mob on 6 October 1789. The decorations of carved wood and the balustrade separating the (reconstructed) bed from the rest of the room have been regilded, but are in part original: most of the rich brocades and other fabrics are of recent manufacture, woven at Lyon, scrupulously copying the original materials. The sculpture of gilded stucco above is by *Nicolas Coustou*. The chimneypieces date from 1761, with bronzes by *Caffieri*; on one is a bust of Louis XIV; on the other, the Duchesse de Bourgogne, mother of Louis XV, both by *Coysevox*. Note the self-portrait by *Van Dyck*.

The adjacent *Cabinet du Conseil* (**R125**), dates in its present form from 1753, with *boiseries* by *Antoine Rousseau*. Note the two Sèvres vases, and the table on which the Treaty of Versailles was signed.

We now enter the *Cabinets du Roi* or *Petits Appartements du Roi* (**RR126–130**), a series of rooms constructed by Louis XV in 1738 to provide a retreat from the tedious etiquette of his court. These comprise (**R126**) the *Chambre de Louis XV*, his bedroom, in which he died of smallpox in 1774; with *boiseries* by *Verberckt*; **R127**, the *Cabinet de la Pendule*, deriving its name from *Passemant's* clock (1749), executed by *Dauthiau*, with chased designs by *Caffieri*, surmounted by a crystal globe marking the phases of the sun, moon, and planets: note also the barometer. The *Cabinet des Chiens* (**R128**), with a frieze of hunting scenes, and decorated with flower-paintings, was occupied by lackeys and the king's favourite hounds. On the staircase, Damiens attempted to assassinate Louis XV in 1757. Adjacent is a *Salle à Manger*, overlooking the much-altered Cour des Cerfs.

Returning through **R127** (in which also note the meridian line marked on the floor) enter **R130**, the *Cabinet de Travail*, with *boiseries* by *Verberckt* (1753), and a Savonnerie carpet; the ornate desk, the

Bureau du Roi, ordered by the king in 1760 for this room, was designed by *Oeben* and *Riesener* (1769), with bronzes by *Duplessis, Winant*, and *Hervieux*.

Adjoining is the *Cabinet de Mme Adélaïde* (**R132**), also with boiseries by *Verberckt*, where, in 1763, Mozart played before Mme Adélaïde (1732–1800), 4th daughter of Louis XV.—The *Bibliothèque de Louis XVI* (**R133**, with Louis-XV furniture) was decorated by *Antoine Rousseau*, with a chimneypiece by *Boizot* and *Gouthière*, and a candelabrum attributed to *Thomire*.

The *Salon des Porcelaines* (**R134**), with a desk by *Leleu*, was so called because of the annual sale of Sèvres ware arranged for the Court, which also occupied the two following rooms. These, the *Salle de Billiard* and *Salon des Jeux* (**RR136–137**), where Louis XIV's collections of paintings and gems were displayed, later became part of Mme Adélaïde's suite.

The adjoining staircase ascends to the **Apartments of Mme du Barry** on the second floor. The beautiful *boiseries* here have been restored and repainted in their original colours.—The attic floor contains the diminutive **Apartments of Mme de Pompadour**.

An uninspired flight of stairs descends to the ground floor, from which a passage leads to the gardens: see below.

From the corresponding passage (**B39**) on the far side of the courtyard, starts the guided tour of the **Apartements du Dauphin et de la Dauphine, et des Mesdames**, the restoration of which was completed in 1986. Looking out onto the gardens, they were occupied at various times by the Regent Orléans, and the sons and daughters of Louis XV, but they have been repeatedly altered, and much of the original decoration was spoiled—when not destroyed—by Louis-Philippe.

R42 contains *Rigaud*, Louis XV as a child; *Santerre*, The Regent Orléans; *Largillierre*, Louis-Urbain Le Pelletier; *Pierre-Denis Martin* (le Jeune), Departure of Louis XV from the Lit de Justice (12 September 1715), and The Consecration of Louis XV at Reims (26 October 1722); and *anon*. Portraits of the Regent Orléans, and of the Duc de Chartres.—**R43**. Several portraits by *Alexis Simon Belle*, among them Marie-Anne-Victoire (Maria-Anna-Victoria; Infanta of Spain, betrothed to Louis XV when she was three, who in 1729 married the future José of Portugal); attributed to *Pierre Gobert*, Peter the Great of Russia; *François Stiemart*, Marie Leczinska; *J.-B. van Loo* and *Parrocel*, Louis XV on horseback; *J.-L. Lemoyne*, Bust of Philippe, Duc d'Orléans.—**R44** *Jean-Baptiste van Loo*, Stanislas Leczinski, and Catherine Opalinska, Queen of Poland; *Belle*, Marie Leczinska and the Dauphin; *Rigaud*, Samuel Bernard the banker; *after Rigaud*, Cardinal Fleury; *School of Rigaud*, Philibert Orry; *Tocqué*, Marquis de Matignon.—**R45** Bedroom of the Dauphine, with a *lit au polonaise*, and containing a child's coach. Louis XVI, Louis XVIII, and Charles X were born in this room, which was also the bedroom of Marie-Antoinette on her arrival in France from Vienna.—**R46** (green decoration), with *Oudry*, The Seasons, and *Nattier*, Marie-Josèphe de Saxe.—**R47**, a small library, with *Joseph Vernet*, The times of day.

R48, at the corner of the building, has a splendid view of the gardens. Re-gilt, and with chairs by *Georges Jacob*, it contains portraits of the daughters of Louis XV by *Nattier*.—**R49** (also with green decoration), the Regent's Study, where he died in 1723, and later the Bedroom of the Dauphin Louis, son of Louis XV, with *Tocqué*, Marie-Thérèse-Antoinette-Raphaelle d'Espagne; *Louis-Michel van Loo*, Felipe V of Spain, and Elisabeth Farnese; *Nattier*,

Louise-Elisabeth de France (Duchess of Parma). Note the *boiseries* by Verberckt and the marble chimney-piece with figures by *Caffieri*, and *Nicolas Coustou*, Bust of Marie Leczinska.—**R50**, retaining traces of Louis XIV decoration; *Nattier*, Marie Leczinska, and Mme Adélaïde.—**R51**, the *Galerie Basse*, below the Galerie des Glaces, has been completely altered since the reign of Louis XIV, when Molière gave several of his plays here, including the first performance of 'Tartuffe' (1664); it has recently been remodelled, and contains several false arches.

R52 (once part of a suite of bathrooms) was later occupied by Mme de Montespan, Mme de Pompadour, and the daughters of Louis XV, and displays *Louis-Michel van Loo*, Duc de Choiseul, Duc de Penthièvre, and Portrait of Jean-Baptiste van Loo (his father); and *Tocqué*, Abel-France Poisson, Marquise de Marigny.—**R53**, with dessus-des-portes by *Oudry*, and containing a commode by *Riesener*.—**R54**, with a clavecin by Blanché.—**R55**, with good boiseries and furniture, and *Nattier*, Mme Adélaïde.—**R56A**, with a commode by *Foullet*.—**R56C**, with dessus-des-portes by *Jean Bernard Restout* of The Seasons.—**RR57–58** contains *Nattier*, Anne-Henriette, second daughter of Louis XV, playing a viola da gamba; a Gagliano violin belonging to Marie-Antoinette, and an organ.

From **R59**, with restored 'perspective' decoration, cross the foot of the staircase replacing the former Grand Escalier, a maquette of which is displayed, to enter an inner suite of rooms.—**R27B** contains a painting of Marie-Antoinette dancing at Schönbrunn, and a remarkable suite of mahogany 'Etruscan' chairs by *Georges Jacob*, formerly at Rambouillet.—**R28** *Roslin*, Portraits of the Dauphin, son of Louis XV, of Joseph-Marie Terray, and of the Marquis de Marigny; *Mengs*, copy of his portrait of Carlos III of Spain.—**R28B** *Duplessis*, copy of his portrait of Louis XVI.—**R29** Two Views of Versailles by *Hubert Robert*; *Gautier-Dagoty*, Marie-Thérèse at Versailles.—**R30** Portraits by *Vigée-Lebrun*, and *Labille Guiard*.

Passing through **R31** to **R32**, formerly a library, with its columns boxed in, and **R33B**, a Bathroom with aquatic decoration, we enter **R33A** containing *Duplessis*, Comte d'Angiviller de la Billarderie.—**R34** *Vigée-Lebrun*, Marie-Antoinette, and *Labille Guiard*, Prince de Bauffremont. (RR35–36 are still under restoration.)

The rooms on the ground floor of the S wing (**RR67–80**) are of only slight interest. They contain some paintings by *Gros*, and *Horace* and *Carle Vernet*, among others, and furnishings, made in the 1950s, reproducing original Napoleonic designs.

The *GARDENS OF VERSAILLES are conveniently approached by a passage (R25) just W of the main visitors' entrance.

André Le Nôtre (1613–1708), the celebrated landscape-gardener (responsible for Greenwich Park, London, and the Quirinal and Vatican gardens, Rome), designed the gardens for Louis XIV, although the fountains and hydraulic machinery were the work of *Jules Hardouin-Mansart* and the engineer *François Francini*, while the sculptural decoration was carried out under the supervision of *Le Brun* and *Mignard*.

The gardens were first laid out in 1661–68. The preliminary work of levelling and draining the site was prodigious, and thousands of trees were brought here from all parts. Inspired by Italian originals, interpreted with an amplitude and harmony hitherto unknown, Versailles is the masterpiece of French gardening. In their general lines and their 'classical' sculptural decoration, the gardens remain as they were planned, but it was not until the 18C that the planting of

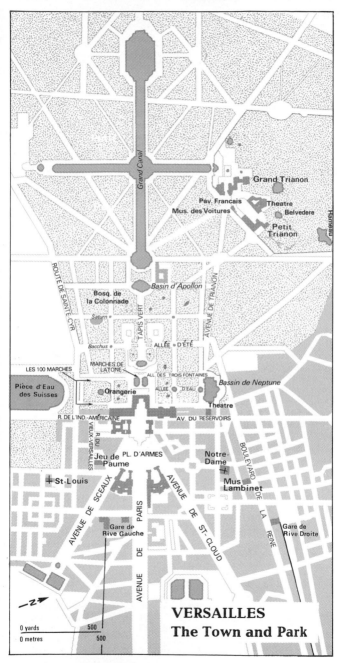

VERSAILLES
The Town and Park

trees was developed to its present extent, so that what we now see are basically the gardens of Louis XV and Louis XVI.

They are essentially formal, with their carefully planned vistas and straight tree-lined walks, their artificial lakes and ponds, arranged with geometrical precision, their groves and clumps of trees, lawns, and terraces, all interspersed with innumerable statues and vases of marble and bronze, and embellished with a variety of fountains.

Admission. The gardens and park are normally open all day to pedestrians (no picnics); cars are admitted to the park on payment, and to the Trianons (via the Blvd de la Reine, N of the château).

The *Fountains* play on certain Sundays in May–October only. For further information contact the Tourist Office, 7 Rue des Réservoirs, just N of the Château.

The most direct approach to the **Grand Trianon** for the pedestrian is to follow the *Allée d'Eau* (see below), leading N from the terrace behind the central block of the palace to the *Grille de Neptune*, then bearing NW along the Av. de Trianon, approximately 20 minutes' brisk walk. But by taking this route, one sees little of the main Gardens of Versailles, which merit exploration.

The central axis of the main *Terrace* commands splendid *Views*, and the terrace itself is adorned with bronze statues after the antique (some 'good enough to wish under cover', commented Arthur Young), and with marble vases of War, by *Coysevox*, and Peace, by *Tuby*. Beyond the *Parterres d'Eau*, two large ornamental pools decorated with bronzes (1690), are the *Marches de Latone*, monumental flights of steps, from which one may obtain an impressive view of the château, and, in the opposite direction, a famous vista of the gardens. Flanking these steps are the *Fontaines de Diane* (right) and *du Point-du-Jour* (Dawn). By the former are statues of Air, by *Le Hongre*, and Diana the Huntress, by *Desjardins*.

On the right of the Terrace extend the *Parterres du Nord*, where the original design of Le Nôtre has been largely respected. Just beyond is the *Fontaine de la Pyramide* (in lead), by *Girardon*, and among the sculptures in the cross-walk (left) is Winter, also by *Girardon*.—The *Allée d'Eau*, designed by *Perrault* and *Le Brun* (1676–88), with its groups of children, leads directly to the **Bassin de Neptune** (1740), the largest fountain-basin in the gardens. The *Allée des Trois Fontaines* (parallel to the *Allée d'Eau*), leads back to the main axis, passing (right) the *Bains d'Apollon*, within a grove laid out by *Hubert Robert* under Louis XVI, in a 'romantic' spirit very different from the formal symmetry of Le Nôtre.

The *Marches de Latone* (see above) descend to the oval *Bassin de Latone*. (Latona, or Leto, mother of Artemis and Apollo, insulted by Lycian peasants, had them turned into frogs by Zeus.) Further W is the so-called *Tapis Vert* (or *Allée Royale*), a lawn 330m long and 36m wide, lined with marble vases and statues, many of them copies from the antique. Note (on the left) Venus, by *Le Gros*, and Achilles at Scyros, by *Vigier*. Towards its far end (right) is the entrance to the *Bosquet des Dômes*, with several statues, including Acis and Galatea, by *Tuby*.

Almost opposite, on the far side of the *Tapis Vert*, in the *Bosquet de la Colonnade*, is a *Circle* of marble arches by *Mansart* (1685–88), in the centre of which is the Rape of Proserpine, by *Girardon*.

At the end of the *Tapis Vert* is the *Bassin d'Apollon*, in the centre of which is the impressive group of Apollo's Chariot, by *Tuby*. To the right is the *Petite Venise*, where Louis XIV's Venetian gondoliers were housed. Beyond the *Bassin d'Apollon*, and separated from the gardens by railings, is the *Petit Parc*, divided by the *Grand Canal*, 1650m long, and 62m wide, the scene of Louis XIV's boating parties. Almost at its central point it is crossed by a transverse arm (c 1070m), extending from the *Grand Trianon*, to the N, to the few remaining buildings of the former royal *Menagerie*.

To return to the château, cross the (so-called) '*Salle des Marronniers*', a chestnut grove behind the *Colonnade*, passing the *Bassin de Saturne* and *Bassin de Bacchus*, with sculptures by *Girardon* and *Marsy*, to reach the *Bosquet de la Reine*.

This glade was notorious as the scene of the court scandal known as the 'Affair of the Necklace' (Affaire du collier; 1784–85), in which the Card. de Rohan (seeking the favour of Marie-Antoinette by means of a costly gift) was duped by the Comtesse de la Motte.

The *Parterres du Midi* lead from here to the château. To the right two flights of steps, known as the *Cent Marches*, descend alongside the **Orangerie**, by *Mansart*, into which Communards were herded in 1871 prior to their imprisonment.

To the S, beyond the St.-Cyr road, is the *Pièce d'Eau des Suisses* (682m long, by 134m wide), excavated in 1678–82 by the Swiss Guards, many of whom are said to have died of malaria during the operation.

The ***GRAND TRIANON**, a miniature palace designed by Jules Hardouin-Mansart and *Robert de Cotte*, was built for Louis XIV in 1687 as a retreat from the formality of court life, yet retaining sumptuous marble decorations comparable with those of Versailles itself. It replaced a flimsy summer-house for picnics, tiled inside with blue and white Delftware, and known as the 'Porcelain Trianon', which had been erected on the site of the village of *Trianon*.

The building was occupied for a time by Mme de Maintenon. It was redecorated for Napoléon, who frequently stayed there, and the Empire furniture which he installed still remains. In 1818 the Duke of Wellington dined here with Louis XVIII. Louis-Philippe did his best to spoil the interior decoration in 1837. A restoration of both *Trianons* was carried out in 1925–27; the *Grand Trianon* (again) in 1963–66, and the *Petit Trianon* more recently.

The accurate work of reproduction of fabrics of the period, undertaken during the 1960s, is admirable, although the protective sheets of plastic detract from the splendid effect intended; however historically irreproachable the decoration may be, a little 'faded glory' would perhaps have been more becoming.

On the left of the courtyard, with the open colonnade or Péristyle ahead, is the visitors' entrance. Off the entrance vestibules (**RR1–2**) is **R3**, with Views of Versailles and Chambord by *Allegrain* and *Pierre-Denis Martin* respectively, and a console table by *Jacob-Desmalter*.—A corridor leads to a small *Boudoir* (**R8**), containing a gondola-shaped sofa, to the right of which is the splendidly mirrored *Salon des Glaces* (**R7**), furnished with a handsome set of white and gilt chairs covered with Beauvais tapestry.—**R6**, the *Salon des Colonnes*, with Napoléon's bed (1809) from the Tuileries, later broadened and radically altered by Louis-Philippe.—Beyond **RR5** and **4**, we cross the open Péristyle of Languedoc marble pillars to the RIGHT WING, first entering the circular *Drawing-Room* (**R9**), with paintings of American flowers and fruit, by *Desportes*.—**R10** (*Salon de Musique*): note the bronze table with Vosges granite top, two consoles by *Jacob-Desmalter*, and the Beauvais tapestry-covered set of chairs.—We are next conducted through the *Grand Salon* and *Malachite Room* (**R12**), the latter with a malachite bowl given to Alexander I of Russia after the Treaty of Tilsit, in 1807.—From the adjoining *Salon Frais*, with a painting of the view E from Versailles by *J.-B. Martin*, we turn left into the *Grande Galerie*, decorated by *Mansart*, with good views S over the terrace. It contains 24 allegorical views, almost all similarly

View of the West front of the château

framed, of the Gardens of Versailles and Trianon, 21 by *Jean Cotelle* (1645–1708), two by *Allegrain*, and one by *J.-B. Martin*. The suite of rooms beyond, known as the *Trianon-sous-Bois*, is not open to the public.

Return through the *Salon Frais* to reach the *Salon des Sources*, with Views of Versailles by *P.-D. Martin* (1663–1742) and *Charles Chastelain* (1672–1740) and turn right through a further series of tastefully furnished rooms, the *Apartments of Mme de Maintenon*, subsequently occupied by Stanislas Leczinski, former king of Poland (1741), Mme de Pompadour, and Napoléon and Marie-Louise.—The remaining rooms (**RR23–24**) were installed on the site of a theatre which stood here until 1703, and from 1845 they formed a suite of rooms for Louis-Philippe's daughter, Louise-Marie, and her husband, Leopold I of Belgium.

The gardens were laid out by Mansart and Le Nôtre. To the W is the *Buffet* (the main fountain), also designed by Mansart, with bas-reliefs and figures of Neptune and Amphitrite. A bridge leads from the *Jardin du Roi*, behind the palace, to the gardens of the *Petit Trianon*.

Between the *Grand* and *Petit Trianons* is the **Musée des Voitures**, containing among others the carriage used at the marriage of Napoléon and Marie-Louise (1810), the state coach used at the coronation of Charles X (1824) and the marriage of Napoléon III with the Empress Eugénie (1853); also *berlines* and *calèches* of the 18C.

To the E is the ***PETIT TRIANON** (1751–68) on two floors, unlike the Grand Trianon, built by Gabriel for Louis XV as a country retreat for himself and Mme de Pompadour, who did not survive its completion. Mme du Barry then occupied it. It was a favourite residence of Marie-Antoinette, and was subsequently occupied by Pauline Borghese, Napoléon's sister.

To the left of the courtyard is a derelict *Chapel*. The interior of the *Petit Trianon*, recently restored, contains an elegant suite of rooms on the first floor, many of them retaining their original decoration, including chimneypieces by *Guibert* in the *Dining Room* and *Grand*

Salon. In the dining room, traces of a trap-door, through which it was intended that tables would appear ready-laid, are still visible in the floor.

The **Gardens** of the *Petit Trianon* were originally a ménagerie and botanical garden laid out by Jussieu for Louis XV, but were altered for Marie-Antoinette in the English style (1774–86). Arthur Young visited it in 1787, and observed that there was 'more of Sir William Chambers here than of Mr [Capability] Brown, more effort than nature, and more expense than taste'. Here, so Thicknesse was told, the king 'had a little garden...where he often picks his own salad, makes his own soup, and enjoys the conversation of a few select friends, without the plague, impertinence, and above all, the parade that generally attends royalty'.

To the W of the main building is the *Pavillon Français*, built in 1751 by *Gabriel*, with a good view of the façade of the palace. To the N is the *Theatre* (1780), where Marie-Antoinette made her début in court theatricals, beyond which is the octagonal *Belvedere* (by Mique), with charming interior decoration, overlooking a small lake. The queen was resting in a grotto here, when on 5 October 1789, she was told the news that a rebellious mob had broken into Versailles.

Some few minutes' walk to the NE, on the far side of a larger lake, is the **Hameau**, a theatrical village built for Marie-Antoinette to gratify her taste for 'nature', as popularised by Rousseau, although, apart from churning butter, the queen left the work of the farm to real, not royal, peasants. It comprises a mill, the *Maison de la Reine* (with a dining-room, billiard-room, and card-room, with a kitchen or 'Réchauffoir' behind), and the 'Boudoir' on the right; a *Colombier*, with pigeon-cote and chicken-run; the *Dairy*; the 'Tour de Marlborough'; and farm-buildings.

One may return past the *Temple d'Amour*, with its Corinthian colonnade and Mouchy's copy (1780) of Bouchardon's statue of Love, to the courtyard of the *Petit Trianon*, and the exit.

35 From Paris to St.-Germain-en-Laye Malmaison; Bois-Préau; Musée des Antiquités Nationales; Musée du Prieuré; Maisons-Lafitte.

Malmaison may be approached either by road (N 13; 7·5km) from the *Pont de Neuilly*, or on the RER from *Auber* via *Étoile* to *La Défense*, there taking the 158A bus to within a few minutes' walk of the château.

The *CHÂTEAU DE MALMAISON, built in 1622 on the site of a leper colony dependent on the Abbey of St.-Denis, was the home of Joséphine Bonaparte after 1798, and was enlarged in 1800. It now contains collections of considerable historical interest, as does its annexe, the *Musée du Château de Bois-Préau*; see below.

At the height of her power, the empress held a literary and artistic salon at Malmaison, and after her divorce in 1809 she retired here and devoted herself to gardening, dying only five years later of a chill caught while doing the honours of the grounds to the allied sovereigns. Joséphine (Marie-Josèphe Rose) Tascher de La Pagerie (1763–1814), born in Martinique, had married Napoléon in 1796, two years after her first husband, the Vicomte de Beauharnais, had been guillotined. Napoléon spent five days here in 1815; between Waterloo and his departure for St. Helena.

Malmaison was later bought by María Cristina of Spain, and by Napoléon III in 1861. Despoiled of most of its contents, it was sold in 1896 to the philanthropist Daniel Osiris (1828–1907), who refurnished it and presented the château to the State as a Napoleonic Museum. Further appropriate acquisitions have been made since, and the rooms redecorated.

GROUND FLOOR. From the entrance vestibule, in Antique style, displaying busts of the Imperial family, we turn right into the *Billiard Room*, containing Napoléon's throne from Fontainebleau, his portrait in Gobelins tapestry, and a Savonnerie carpet with his insignia. The *Salon Doré*, with a chimneypiece given to Napoléon by Pope Pius VII (its decoration torn off by the Germans occupying Malmaison in 1871), contains *Girodet's* painting of Ossian welcoming the dead to Valhalla, a portrait of Joséphine by *Gérard*, and her embroidery frame, etc. The adjacent *Music Room*, restored to its original appearance, displays instruments which may have belonged to Joséphine, and her marble bust by *Chinard*.

Returning through these rooms, we enter the *Dining Room*, with its original frescoes of Pompeian dancers by *Lafitte*, restored, and the silver-gilt 'surtout' of table decorations presented by the city of Paris to the emperor on the occasion of his coronation. The *Council Chamber*, shaped like a tent, contains a yew-wood desk (gift of the city of Bordeaux), and a clock from the Tuileries. The adjoining *Library*, retaining its original decoration by *Percier* and *Fontaine*, accommodates a number of books from Napoléon's personal collection, which, previously widely dispersed, have been purchased and reassembled on their original shelves. Here also are Napoléon's bureau and armchair, and a clock made in 1791 for Louis XVI by *Janvier*, and purchased by Napoléon.

On the FIRST FLOOR landing is a Gobelins tapestry, *after Gérard*, of Joséphine at Malmaison.—*Salon de l'Empereur*, a reconstruction of Napoléon's bedroom at the Tuileries, with the original furniture and hangings, and a drawing by *Isabey* of Napoléon as First Consul at

CHÂTEAU DE BOIS-PRÉAU **261**

Malmaison. The three following rooms contain sumptuous services of Sèvres ware; the 'Table d'Austerlitz', decorated with portraits of Napoléon and his marshals; the silver-gilt ewer and basin used at his coronation, etc.—*Joséphine's Apartments:* Antechamber, with water-colours of Malmaison by *Garnerey*, of topographical interest; portraits of the empress, and personal souvenirs. In her *Bedroom* is the bed, designed by *Jacob-Desmalter*, in which she died, and other contemporary furniture, and a fine Sèvres clock. The silk-lined *Salle des Atours* contains a work-table (from *St.-Cloud*); the *Boudoir* is likewise hung with silk; and in the *Bathroom* are Joséphine's dressing-table and dressing-case by *Rémond*.

On the SECOND FLOOR is the *Salle de Ste.-Hélène*, hung with the brocade that covered the catafalque in which the emperor's remains were transported to his tomb. It contains the camp bed on which Napoléon died in 1821, his death-mask moulded by Antommarchi (his Corsican doctor), clothing, MSS and paintings. Other rooms are devoted to souvenirs of Queen Hortense (mother of Napoléon III) and Eugène de Beauharnais, Joséphine's children by her first marriage, etc.

The PARK, of which but 6 hectares remain of 200, contains a rose garden planted with the varieties of rose that were grown by Joséphine. The *Coach House*, to the right of the entrance lodge, contains the 'Opal', the state carriage in which Joséphine drove to Malmaison after her divorce, a gala coach (of the time of Louis XIV) used by Napoléon; his *'dormeuse'* used at Waterloo, and Blücher's *landau en berline*. Behind is the *Pavillon Osiris*, with collections of caricatures, medallions, and snuffboxes propagating the Napoleonic legend, and a portrait of Tsar Alexander I, by *Gérard*. Beyond the other side of the entrance drive is a *Summer-House* used as a study by Napoléon when First Consul.

A few minutes' walk to the E will take one to the **Musée du Château de Bois-Préau**, in the Av. de l'Impératrice Joséphine, admirably displayed in a building bought by Joséphine in 1810, and in 1926 bequeathed to the State by Edward Tuck, its American owner (see also Petit-Palais, Rte 25).

To the right of the entrance is a room containing portraits by *Gérard* of 'Madame Mère'; Joséphine in her coronation robes; Joseph Bonaparte as King of Spain, and his wife; and Napoléon's sister, Elisa.—To the left of the entrance is a series of rooms containing such souvenirs as a *surtout* or *épergne* given to the emperor by Carlos IV of Spain; a portrait of the King of Rome by *Georges Rouget*; the King of Rome's cradle by *Jacob-Desmalter*, and other mementoes; and Marie-Louise, by *Gérard*.—At the top of the stairs, turn right past a collection of sabres, Napoléon's grey coat and hat, flask, and nécessaire, his mantle (note bees); and Hortense's court dress. Other rooms display Murat's splendidly ornate bed, and sabre-legged *tabourets* or stools, and *Gérard's* portrait of Murat; Napoléon's hat and coat (and chairs) from St. Helena; *Marchand's* sketch of the dead emperor; and a book given to Napoléon by Lord Holland.

In the nearby church of *Rueil* (1584, with a W façade by Lemercier, of 1635), is the tomb of the Empress Joséphine, erected in 1825 by her children, Eugène and Hortense de Beauharnais. The tomb of Queen Hortense, in the chapel opposite, was erected in 1858 by her son, Napoléon III, who also donated the 15C Florentine organ-case, by *Baccio d'Agnolo*.

The N13 skirts the S bank of the Seine, passing at *Bougival*, with a

Romanesque church tower, the house where Bizet died (1875). Miss Elizabeth Harriet Howard (1823–65), mistress of the future Napoléon III, retired to *La Celle-St.-Cloud*, to the S, in 1853.

ST.-GERMAIN-EN-LAYE (40,800 inhab.), known as *Montagne-Bon-Air* during the Revolution, is easily reached from central Paris by the RER from Auber or Étoile (replacing the first railway constructed in France, in 1837).

By road, it may also be approached from the *Pont de Neuilly* by the N13 (taking in en route the *Château of Malmaison*, see above), or by the N190 branching right off the N13, which passes through the suburb of *Le Vésinet*.

Anthony Hamilton, the author of 'Mémoires du Comte de Grammont' (1703), who lived at St.-Germain in 1690–1720, was one of many Jacobites resident in the area during and after this period. Thickness rented a house here in 1766, and Henry Swinburne lived 5km N at *Les Mesnils* in 1786 and again in 1796. Claude Debussy (1862–1918) was born at St.-Germain.

The *Municipal Museum*, from which 'The Juggler', by Bosch, was robbed in 1978, is at present being reorganised. For the *Musée du Prieuré*, see below.

The strategically sited royal **Château**, dominating a bend of the Seine, was erected in the 12C by Louis VI, and completely rebuilt (except for the keep) by François I in 1539–48. The infant Mary Stuart lived here from October 1548 until her marriage to François II in April 1558. In 1862 Eugène Millet restored the castle after it had been used as a military prison for three decades, and it was adapted as a Musée Gallo-Romain.

The so-called *Château-Neuf*, below the original castle, constructed for Henri II and Henri IV, was demolished in 1776, except for the *Pavillon Henri IV* and the *Pavillon Sully*, at the foot of the steep slope E of the town, in the suburb of *Le Pecq*.

It was in this 'new' castle that Louis XIV was born in 1638, five years before the death of his father in the same building; and the royal family escaped there in January 1649 during the Fronde. It remained one of the principal seats of the French Court until the completion of Versailles in 1682. Large sums were spent on its improvement during the years 1664–80. Meanwhile, the Château-Neuf afforded refuge to Henrietta Maria of England (1644–48). After 1688 what was then called the 'Vieux Château' was the residence—and Court—of James II, who died there in 1701, as did his wife, Mary of Modena, in 1718. John Caryll was secretary of state to the exiled dynasty. During this period it was a focus of Jacobite intrigue. St.-Germain has been the scene of several international treaties, the last being in 1919—the territorial clauses in which provided for the dismemberment of Austria-Hungary—which has had its repercussions.

In 1962, a century after the setting-up of the earlier museum in the château, the *MUSÉE DES ANTIQUITÉS NATIONALES was installed here, and has more recently been tastefully reorganised to display its impressive collections in chronological order, which are well labelled and described.

Stairs ascend to **R1**, devoted to *Neolithic* finds.—**R2** *Bronze Age*, including (*Case 3*) swords and sword moulds, and (*Case 13*) torques, bracelets, and other gold objects.—**R3** *Hallstatt* period (1st Iron Age; 800–450 BC).—**R4** (across landing) *La Tène* culture (450–52 BC), with a good collection of bronze vessels and vases—note that in *Case 18*—and jewellery.—**R6** reconstituted chariot-burial from La Gorge-Meillet.—**R9**, with a model of the important fortified site of Alesia.

The series of rooms on the floor above concentrate on *Roman and Merovingian Gaul*. **R10** contains Celtic divinities; **R11**, divinities of the Graeco-Roman world, including some fine figures of Mercury;

ex-votos and their moulds; note the Venus in *Case 5*. Here is also an exemplary display of silver utensils, glassware, bronze lamps, scales, handles, keys, etc., and sigillate pottery.—Across the landing are rooms displaying small sculptured objects—birds, boars, horses, and human figures: note the charming couple in bed, with a dog at their feet, from Bordeaux (*Case 6*); a collection of jewellery, buckles, and fibulas; games, etc.—**R16** contains a large mosaic pavement (3C AD) from St.-Romain-en-Gal (adjacent to Vienne), showing a rustic calendar of the seasons, while various agricultural implements, etc.,

Gallo-Roman domestic scene, Musée des Antiquités Nationales

are also shown here.—Articles of jewellery, plaques, glassware, and buckles of the *Merovingian* period are displayed in the adjoining room. Other sections have been opened, devoted to the *Paleolithic* period and to comparative archaeology.

The adjacent *Chapel* of 1230–38, just predating the *Ste.-Chapelle* in Paris, also by *Pierre de Montreuil*, has been sadly disfigured over the years. It contains copies of tombs from the Aliscamp at Arles. Here were baptised François I, Claude de France (1499–1524; daughter of Louis XII, and the first wife of François I), and Louis XIV.

To the N of the château is the *Parterre*, originally a park laid out by Le Nôtre, beyond which is a *Jardin Anglais*. At its SE corner, at 21 Rue Thiers, is the *Pavillon Henri-IV* (see above), since 1836 a hotel: Dumas wrote 'The Three Musketeers' and 'Monte Cristo' here; and Thiers died here in 1877.

To the NE extends the *Terrace of St.-Germain* which commands a splendid *View of Paris (and particularly of *La Défense*): *Notre-Dame* itself is approximately 21km to the E. James II once compared the view (unfavourably) to that from the Terrace at Richmond. At the far end is the *Grille Royale*, the entrance to the *Forêt de St.-Germain*, the former royal hunting preserve, once over 4000 hectares in extent, and still retaining a number of pleasant drives and walks (see IGN map 419).

From behind the church of *St.-Louis* (opposite the château), containing the tomb of James II of England, erected at the request of George IV, and in which his partial remains were re-interred in 1824, the Rue au Pain leads SW. With its continuations, this approaches—after a few minutes' walk—the **Musée du Prieuré* (2 Rue Maurice-Denis).

A former royal hospital founded by Mme de Montespan in 1678, it was the home of Maurice Denis from 1914 until his death in 1943. The collection of his paintings bequeathed by his family, and those of the Symbolist School and the group of artists known as the Nabis ('Prophets' in Hebrew), was inaugurated in 1980. Denis had lived closed by from 1893, and had rented one of its larger rooms as a studio in 1905.

Maurice Denis, Self portrait, with the Prieuré in the background

Among the more important works are *Maurice Denis*, Self portrait (1921), with the Prieuré in the background; posthumous Portrait of Albert Besnard; Portrait of Paul Sérusier; The sewing lesson; Portrait of his mother; With Marthe, his first wife, in the garden at dusk; The ladder; Jacques Portelette aged four; and Mme Ranson and her cat. *Vuillard*, Dr Viau, the dentist; The reservoir; *Thérèse Debains* (1907–74), Self-portrait; *Paul Sérusier* (1864–1927), Portrait of his wife, Breton girl; *Félix Vallottan* (1865–1900), Bookshelves; *Georges Lacombe* (1868–1916), carved wood Bust of Maurice Denis; *Gauguin*, The patron's daughter (in fact a boy; 1886); *Louis Anquetin* (1861–1932), Self-portrait, and Woman in black; *Odilon Redon* (1840–1916), Portrait of Maurice Denis; and representative paintings by *Charles Filiger* (1863–1928).

Also displayed are several designs by Maurice Denis for wall-papers, and stained glass. Several pieces of furniture and examples of the decorative arts of the period are also shown, including ceramics by the *Daum brothers* of Nancy, etc.

The *Chapel* was decorated entirely by Maurice Denis with blue frescoes, and Stations of the Cross, and he also designed the glass with the exception of the round Visitation, by *Marcel Poncet*.

The adjacent Studio was built by *Auguste Perret* in 1912 for Maurice Denis when he was working on the frieze for the Théâtre des Champs-Élysées. It now displays his sketches for the decoration of the apse of St.-Paul de Genève, and is the venue of temporary exhibitions.

At *Chambourcy*, 4km W of *St.-Germain*, famous for its cheese since the 17C, are the tombs of the Chevalier d'Orsay and Marguerite Power, Countess of Blessington (1789–1849), author of 'The Idler in Italy', etc.

Some 4km S of *St.-Germain*, to the W of the N386, stood the royal château of *Marly* (its name preserved in the town of **Marly-le-Roi**), built in 1679–86 by Jules Hardouin-Mansart for Louis XIV, and a favourite retreat from the formality of Versailles: regular visits to Marly (and vice versa) were essential, to allow the palaces to be cleaned and aired.

The château was destroyed at the Revolution, although vestiges remain of the park, where stood the famous hydraulic *Machine de Marly*, originally constructed in 1681 to raise water from the Seine to the Marly aqueduct, which in turn carried it to Versailles. New machinery had been installed in 1855–59, taking its water from an underground source, but the whole was dismantled in 1967.

The church of *Marly-le-Roi* was also built by Mansart (1689), and contains some works originally in Versailles.

For other sites W, SW, and NW of St.-Germain, see *Blue Guide France*.

Some 4km N of St.-Germain-en-Laye is **Maisons-Laffitte** (23,900 inhab.), birthplace of Jean Cocteau (1889–1963). It possesses training-stables and a racecourse.

The town, its station known as 'Maisons-Lafitte' as early as 1843 (after a nephew of the financier, himself a railway entrepeneur) was officially so-named in 1882.

Its celebrated *__Château de Maisons__ ◊ was built for René de Longueil (1596–1677), first Marquis de Maisons, a Surintendant des Finances prior to Fouquet; the masterpiece of François Mansart (1642–51), it is also notable for its interior decoration.

The property was bought in 1777 by the Comte d'Artois, and partly redecorated by *Bellanger*. It was deserted at the Revolution and its contents dispersed. In 1804 it was acquired by Marshal Lannes, Duc de Montebello, who died there in 1809 from wounds received at Essling. His widow sold it in 1818 to Jacques

Laffitte (1767–1844), a banker and speculator who had profited out of
the Napoleonic Wars, who in 1833 demolished the stables and sold off
the estate. It later passed into the hands of Tilman Grommé, a Russian
artist, who further fragmented the property, cutting it up into building
plots. The shell of the château was saved from demolition in 1905,
being acquired by the State, and the whole was restored.

From the present entrance, formerly a chapel, a series of rooms on the
Ground Floor may be visited. These include the *Salles des Graveurs*,
with a trompe l'oeil ceiling, and collections of prints and plans; and
the *Salon des Captifs*, with a coffered ceiling, and a fireplace carved
by Gilles Guérin. Passing through the *Vestibule d'honneur*, with
reliefs by Jacques Sarrazin, the S wing is entered, redecorated by the
Comte d'Artois (later Charles X). The main *Staircase*, embellished
with putti executed by Philippe de Buyster, ascends to (left) the *Salon
d'Hercule*, hung with early 18C Gobelins tapestries of the Hunts of
Maximilian, among others, a musicians gallery, and another fireplace
by Guérin; the *Chambre du Roi*; the *Salon à l'italienne*, containing a
portrait by *Van Dyck* of the Countess of Bedford; and the domed
Cabinet aux miroirs, with a marquetry floor. In the S wing is the
former Queen's suite, transformed by Lannes.
    Voltaire wrote 'Marianne' when a guest here in 1723, and it is
claimed that he was dosed with 200 pints of lemonade to avoid death
by smallpox; he is also said to have set light to his bed. Later visitors
were La Fayette, and Benjamin Constant.

The N308 leads E towards *La Défense* (see Rte 28), and central *Paris*,
passing, after crossing the *Pont de Bezons* (S of *Colombes*), the site of
a château in which Henrietta Maria died in 1669.

36 St.-Denis

St.-Denis (91,300 inhab.) is best approached by car by turning off the
Al autoroute about 3km N of the *Porte de la Chapelle*; or by taking
the MÉTRO, recently extended to its terminus at **St.-Denis-Basilique**.

The Gothic **CATHEDRAL OF ST.-DENIS** ◇ stands in the centre of
St.-Denis (91,000 inhabit.), one of the more unattractive, and com-
munistic, of the northern suburbs of Paris, spreading beyond the site
of the celebrated 'Foire du Lendit' which was held here from
Dagobert's time until 1552. It was founded on the probable site of
Catolacus, where the missionary apostle of Lutetia was almost
certainly buried.
    The W front, although disfigured at the Revolution, retains one
good 12C tower with a low modern steeple. The transeptal portals,
each with a rose-window, are mid-13C work.
    It is overshadowed in interest by the *Tombs* it contains. Unfortu-
nately, these may not be studied in detail during the rapidly conducted tour (every 30 minutes from 10.00–17.30, except Sunday during
services): little has changed in this respect since Augustus Hare
complained that parties were 'hurried full gallop round the church
under the guardianship of a jabbering custode'!

The abbey of St.-Denis was founded c 475, perhaps at the instance of Ste.
Geneviève, and rebuilt in 630–38 by Dagobert, who also founded a monastery
for Benedictines. The first substantial church on the site was built by Abbot
Fulrad in 750–75, and here in 754 Pope Stephen III consecrated Pepin le Bref and
his wife and sons, thus establishing them securely on the throne. This church

was itself replaced by another built by Abbot Suger, of which the narthex (W porch) and apse (c 1136–44) survive, ranking among the most important examples of the earliest Gothic architecture. Recent excavations in the crypt, also of this period, and retaining the Romanesque arch, have brought to light Gallo-Roman Christian tombs, and remains of the earlier churches. The rest of the building dates from 1231–81, following the designs of *Pierre de Montreuil* (died 1267), while the chapels on the N side of the nave were added c 1375.

Most of the effigies of earlier kings were made during the reign of Louis IX (St. Louis; died 1270), when St.-Denis became recognised as a royal mausoleum; others were brought here during the Revolution. With the exception of Philippe I, Louis XI, Louis-Philippe, and Charles X, all the French kings since Hugues Capet are buried here. In 1422 the body of Henry V lay in state here on its way from Vincennes to Westminster, and seven years later Joan of Arc dedicated her armour here. In 1567 Condé's Huguenots captured the place, but he prevented them from despoiling the basilica: later in the year he was defeated in the plain to the S by Anne de Montmorency, who was himself mortally wounded. Henri IV abjured Protestantism here in 1593.

Henriette d'Angleterre, daughter of Charles I, was buried here in 1670, her funeral oration delivered by Bossuet. Her mother, Henrietta Maria, had been buried here the previous year.

It was visited in 1774 by Lady Mary Coke, who, on leaving, passed Louis XV's funeral cortège coming from Versailles: 'the Guards who follow'd the Coach gallop'd. The mob was very great & very indecent; so far from showing the least concern they hoop'd & hollow'd, as if they had been at a horse race instead of a funeral procession; never was a King less regretted'.

After injudicious alterations in the 18C, the abbey was suppressed at the Revolution, the church unroofed, its tombs rifled and their contents dispersed, but the best of the monuments were saved from destruction by Alexandre Lenoir, who preserved them in his *Musée des Petits-Augustins* (École des Beaux-Arts), from where they were later returned, and drastically restored. Restoration of the fabric of the basilica was taken in hand in 1813, but it was so incompetently carried out that the stability of the N tower was endangered, and in 1847 it had to be taken down. A subsequent 'restoration' by Viollet-le-Duc and Darcy went some way to repair the harm; but the explosion of a nearby bomb-dump in 1915 caused further damage.

INTERIOR. Only the more important tombs are listed. Smollett, who visited the abbey in October 1763, condemned the 'attitudes' of the sculptures as 'affected, unnatural, and desultory; and their draperies fantastic; or, as one of our English artists expressed himself, *they are all of a flutter'*.

The conducted tour begins in the *S Aisle*, with, among others, the tomb of *Louis d'Orléans* (died 1407; see p 185) and *Valentine de Milan* (died 1408), a fine Italian work of 1502–15, commissioned by their grandson, Louis XII. Opposite, against the SW pillar of the crossing, is the heart-tomb of *François II* (died 1560), by *Germain Pilon* and *Ponce Jacquiau*. Also in the S Aisle, the Urn (1549–55) by Bontemps, containing the heart of *François I*.

In the *S Transept*: the *Tomb of *François I* (died 1547) and *Claude de France* (died 1524), a masterpiece by *Philibert Delorme, Pierre Bontemps, Primaticcio*, and others, begun in 1548. The royal pair appear both recumbent and (above) kneeling with their children: reliefs depict the king's military exploits. On the E side of this transept are the tombs of *Charles V* (died 1380), by *André Beauneveu*, and *Charles VI* (died 1422) with their queens; and of *Bertrand Du Guesclin* (died 1380), one of the few commoners buried here (his heart is at Dinan; his entrails at Le Puy).

At the W end of the *Choir* are the tombs of *Philippe III*, le Hardi (died 1285), by *Pierre de Chelles* and *Jean d'Arras*, remarkable as being one of the earliest known French portrait-statues. The effigy of his queen, *Isabella of Aragón* (died 1271), is particularly fine. Also *Philippe IV*, le Bel (died 1314). Following the *Ambulatory*, we pass (to the left of the steps) the tomb of *Dagobert* (died 638), showing reliefs of the torment and redemption of the king's soul. and with a beautiful *Statue (13C) of *Queen Nanthilde*: the figures of Dagobert and his son are 19C restorations. We next pass the tomb of *Léon de Lusignan* (died 1393).

Note the 12–13C glass in the *Lady Chapel*, and adjacent chapels, including a Tree of Jesse. Turning W along the N side of the Ambulatory we pass (left) *Blanche* and *Jean* (both died 1243), children of Louis IX (from Royaumont), with fine enamelled plaques; *Frédégonde* (died 597), queen of Chilperic I, a remarkable slab in cloisonné mosaic (11C, from St.-Germain-des-Prés); and also from St.-Germain, *Childebert I* (died 558), a 12C statue. In the chapel at the top of the steps, draped statues of *Henri II* (died 1559) and *Catherine de Médicis* (died 1589) by *Germain Pilon* (1583). In the *Sanctuary* is the *Altar of the Relics* (by *Viollet-le-Duc*), on which are placed the reliquaries, given by Louis XVIII, of St. Denis and his fellow-martyrs.

In the *N Transept* is the splendid tomb of **Henri II* and *Catherine de Médicis*, designed by *Primaticcio* in 1560–73, with recumbent and kneeling effigies of the king and queen, and supporters and reliefs by *Germain Pilon* and other contemporary sculptors. The king and queen were formerly kneeling at a bronze prie-dieu, which was melted down at the Revolution. Here also are the tombs of *Philippe V* (died 1322), *Charles IV* (died 1328), *Philippe VI* (died 1350), and *Jean II* (died 1364, prisoner at the Savoy, London), the last two by *André Beauneveu*. Opposite (left, in the choir) are tombs of *Louis X* (died 1316) and his son *Jean I* (died 1316).

Tomb of Louis XII and Anne of Brittany, St.-Denis

In the *N Aisle*, the *Tomb of *Louis XII* (died 1515) and *Anne of Brittany* (died 1514), made by *Jean Juste* (Giovanni di Giusto) in

1516–32. The royal pair are depicted naked and recumbent on the tombstone, and kneeling on the canopy above (the conventional design for Renaissance tombs); bas-reliefs illustrate episodes in the king's career.

Lastly, among other 13–14C tombs, that of *Louis de France* (died 1260), the eldest son of Louis IX, with Henry III of England as one of the bearers.—Note, before entering the crypt, the *High Stalls* of the Ritual Choir (1501–07) from the chapel of the Château de Gaillon; the *Low Stalls* are 15C work from St.-Lucien, near Beauvais.

The *Crypt*, entered on either side of the choir, was constructed by Suger round the original Carolingian 'martyrium', the site of the grave of St. Denis and his companions, and retains some 12C capitals. Here are seen the sarcophagi of Louis XVI, Marie-Antoinette, Louis XVIII, among other 18–19C royal personages. The ossuary on the N side contains the bones that were thrown into a pit when the tombs were rifled in 1793, including those of Henrietta Maria and Maria of Modena, wives of Charles I and James II respectively. In a side chapel is a charming 12C Virgin, originally at the abbey of Longchamp.

To the S of the basilica are monastic dependencies, under restoration, rebuilt in the 18C by Robert de Cotte and Jacques Gabriel, and occupied after 1809 as a *Maison d'Éducation de la Légion d'Honneur*.

Some five minutes' walk further S, at 22 bis Rue Gabriel Péri, the **Musée d'Art et d'Histoire** is installed in a Carmelite monastery founded in 1625. The compartmented cupola of its chapel (1784), by Mique, built while Louise de France was in residence (1770–87), is notable. It preserves the reconstituted *Pharmacy* of the Hôtel-Dieu (demolished 1907), and the *Study* of the poet Paul Éluard (Eugène Grindel; 1895–1952), born in St.-Denis; an archaeological section of interest; rooms devoted to the Commune de Paris (1870–71); some 4000 engravings and lithographs by *Daumier*; and paintings and drawings by *Albert André, Cézanne, Léger*, and *Dufy*, among others.

Also in St.-Denis, but best approached from the MÉTRO: *Porte de Paris* and following the Blvd Anatole France to the SW across the Canal St.-Denis, and there turning right, is the **Musée Bouilhet-Christofle** (open 10.00–17.45 Monday to Friday). Here are replicas of historical interest and original pieces of the art of the *gold-* and *silversmith* produced by the Société Christofle since their establishment.

37 Écouen: Musée National de la Renaissance

Écouen can be approached by public transport (MÉTRO to *St.-Denis-Porte-de-Paris*, and then the 268C bus, direction Ezanville).

From the *Porte de la Chapelle*, take the N16 towards **St.-Denis** (see Rte 36), which may be by-passed. The road crosses a dreary dormitory area between (left) *Sarcelles*, with relics of a 12C church with a Gothic nave and Renaissance façade, and (right) *Villiers-le-Bel*, which belies its name, at 20km reaching (left) **Écouen**. The town is of slight interest in itself, although the church of *St.-Acceul* retains some *Stained-glass* attributed to *Jean Cousin* in its choir (1544).

The town is commanded by the magnificent Renaissance *CHÂTEAU D'ÉCOUEN, now housing the *MUSÉE NATIONAL DE LA RENAISSANCE**, inaugurated in 1976, and displaying a number of outstanding objects from this epoch long stored at the *Musée de Cluny*.

Its construction began c 1535 for the Constable Anne de Montmorency, and among artists employed were *Jean Goujon* and *Jean Bullant*, to whom is ascribed the interior portico of the S Wing (in the niches of which once stood Michelangelo's 'Chained Captives'). It was put to a variety of uses during the Revolutionary period, and in 1805 became a school for the daughters of members of the Légion d'Honneur, with Mme Campan as *directrice*. It later reverted to the Duc d'Aumale, who chose to remove a number of its embellishments to Chantilly, including an altar by Goujon from the chapel.

From the entrance turn left into the *Chapel* (**R1**), with painted ribbed vaulting and delicately carved stonework, before traversing a series of rooms on the ground floor ranged around the central courtyard.— **R2**, with a painted mantel-piece (one of six depicting biblical themes) in the style of the School of Fontainebleau, contains arms and armour. The mantel-piece of **R3** backs onto that of the adjoining room, in which is a collection of Renaissance woodcarving; **R5** preserves a number of leather panels.

A series of smaller rooms is devoted to collections of carved wood plaques (**R6**), and larger panels (**R7**), including some remarkable examples in ebony.—**R8** pear-wood and box-wood statuettes, mainly German or Flemish; coffers; a fine ivory flagon; bronze figurines, including fornicating fauns, by *Riccio*.—**R9** is devoted to metalwork, some damascened, cutlery, and a collection of Renaissance door-furniture. **RR10–11** contain mathematical instruments and watches, and work in precious metals.—**R12**, known as that of Catherine de Médicis, is crossed before reaching a room reserved for concerts and other functions, and another with collections of sculpture.

FIRST FLOOR. **R1** Furniture, some ebony; and tapestries of the 'Labours of Hercules'.—**R2** Chairs and *'caquetoires'*.—**R3**, with notable carved doors. In **RR4–7** are hung a remarkable series of tapestries entitled 'The story of David and Bathsheba' (Brussels; 16C). Note also the finely carved stone fireplaces in **R5** from Chalons-sur-Marne (1562), with reliefs of Christ and the Samaritan, and Actaeon surprising Diana in her bath.—**R6** contains a collection of enamelled plaques by *Pierre Courteys* (Limoges; 1559), and tile-pictures.—Beyond a carved wooden staircase, is **R8**, with a made-up marble chimney-piece, and a tiled pavement by *Masséot Abaquesne* (mid 16C). Beyond are rooms displaying glass panels of 1544–52, majolicas, including work by *Luca della Robbia*, furniture, embroideries, etc. Further rooms on the second floor are being opened progressively.

For a detailed description of the area N of Écouen, see *Blue Guide France*. For the excursion to **Chantilly**, see Rte 39.

38 Sceaux

The N20 leads S from the Porte d'Orléans to (10km) *Sceaux*, which may also be approached by the RER, stopping at *Sceaux* or *Bourg-la-Reine*.

We pass (left) 2km S of the Blvd Périphérique a double *Aqueduct* crossing the valley of the Bièvre, the lower part of which was built in 1613–24 by Marie de Médicis to supply the Luxembourg fountains; it was preceded by a Roman one, built in the 4C to bring water to the Palais des Thermes (see *Musée de Cluny*).

At 4·5km the broad Allée d'Honneur ascends W from the N20 to the entrance of the **Château de Sceaux**. A 19C building replaced the sumptuous 17C château built by Claude Perrault for Colbert, which, during the first half of the 18C, was the scene of the literary and artistic court of the ambitious Duchesse du Maine (1676–1753) as described by Mme de Launay, among others. Mme du Deffand was a frequent visitor, while Voltaire wrote 'Zadig' here; and works by Racine, Molière, and Lully were performed in the adjacent *Orangerie* (left), constructed by Jules Hardouin-Mansart (1684; restored).—To the right is the *Pavillon de l'Aurore*, also by Perrault.

Since 1937 the *MUSÉE DE l'ÎLE DE FRANCE* has been installed in the château. This illustrates the history and topography of the area now covered by the departments of Hauts-de-Seine, Seine-St.-Denis, Val-de-Marne, Essonne, Yvelines, and Val-d'Oise. It is well worth visiting, not only for its site, but for the wealth of interesting material depicting the appearance of, and life in, the environs of the capital in past centuries. The building also contains a reference library, open daily from 9.00–12.00; 14.00–18.00, except Sunday.

The majority of the rooms are devoted to specific regions. **R2** contains a model of the château, and **R3** portraits of Colbert attributed to *Lefebvre*, and of the Duchesse du Maine by *De Troy*.—**R4** (providing a charming view): Sceaux ceramics (1754–95).—**R5** Sèvres and St.-Cloud ware.—**R7** Views of St.-Cloud by *Dunouy*, *Fleury*, and others.—**R8** is devoted to Meudon. On the SECOND FLOOR, a series of rooms display views of the Machine de Marly; of St.-Germain by *James Basire* (1730–1802); of Mousseau, by *J.-M. Morel*, drawings, watercolours, and engravings by *Dunoyer de Segonzac* (1874–1946); two of Etry occupied by Cossacks in 1814, by *J. Randon*, and a number of views by *Paul Huet* (1803–69), among others of topographical value, including the Tower of Vincennes, by *Bonington*.

The extensive *Park*, laid out by *Le Nôtre*, forms one of the more attractive open spaces near Paris, and contains, S of the château, a series of cascades leading to the *Octagon*, to the W of which is the *Grand Canal*. From here we have a view of the *Pavillon de Hanovre*, moved here in 1832 from the Blvd des Capucines. It was built in 1760 with money extorted from the Hanoverians in the Seven Years War.

A short distance NW of the château, approached across the park, is the old churchyard of **Sceaux**, where the fabulist Florian (1755–94) is buried. The simple tombs of Pierre (1859–1906) and Marie Curie (née Sklodowska; 1867–1934), the discoverers of radium, may be found in the local cemetery. It was at the Lycée Lákanal at Sceaux that Alain-Fournier and Jacques Rivière first met.

Some 2.5km W is the restored residence (in 1807–18) of Chateaubriand, in the *Parc de la Vallée aux Loups*.

For the area S of Sceaux, see *Blue Guide France*.

EXCURSIONS FROM PARIS

The following two routes concisely describe two of the more important monuments and collections which may be conveniently visited
in day trips from Paris. For more detailed descriptions, and for more
information with regard to what m^ay be seen en route, see *Blue
Guide France*.

39 To Chantilly and Senlis

Distance from Paris 41km (25 miles) on the N16. *Chantilly* may also
be approached by the N17 and D924A, a very slightly longer route;
Senlis, 10km E of Chantilly, is also reached directly by the A1
motorway.

Two approaches to Chantilly are briefly described below.

The N16 skirts **Écouen** (see Rte 37), and 11km beyond, **Luzarches**,
with a mid 16C church of interest, preserving part of its 12C
predecessor.

A DETOUR may be made to **Royaumont**, 6.5km NW, with the
considerable remains of a great Cistercian abbey, founded in 1228,
in the dismantled church of which Louis IX was married in 1234; the
beautiful **Refectory*, its vaulting sustained by five monolithic
columns, contains the tomb by *Coysevox* of Henri of Lorraine (died
1666).—*Chantilly* is 8·5km NE; or 9km directly N of Luzarches.

The N17 leaves Paris by the *Porte de la Villette* and at 16km
passes (left) the old airport of *Le Bourget*, where the *Musée de l'Air*,
with a notable collection of 140 aircraft, largely from 1919, but
including earlier flying machines, has been installed. The first
regular flights between Le Bourget and London (Croydon airport)
commenced in 1919.—A short distance beyond, the modern airport
of *Charles de Gaulle* is passed to the right. At 18·5km the D924A
forks left for (9·5km) Chantilly, first crossing part of the *Fôret de
Chantilly* before reaching the *Château de Chantilly*; the right fork
leads 9·5km directly to *Senlis*; see below.

Chantilly (10,200 inhab.), formerly reputed for its silk-lace, and
porcelain, and the 'Newmarket' of France, where race-meetings
have been held since 1836, is famous principally for its château. This
is approached via the Rue du Connétable, passing (right) *Notre-
Dame* (1692), and the ***Grande-Écuries** (1740), which had room for
240 mounts. It has recently been restored, and houses an *Equestrian
museum*.

The ***Château de Chantilly** consists of two connected buildings
standing by a carp-stocked lake, and contains the ***MUSÉE
CONDÉ**, especially rich in French paintings and illuminations of the
15–16Cs.

It came into the possession of the Montmorency family in 1484 and passed to
the Grand Condé (1621–86) in 1632. The *Petit Château* was erected c 1560 for
the Constable Anne de Montmorency, probably by *Jean Bullant*. The *Grand
Château* was reconstructed by *Mansart* on the site of an earlier mansion (in
which Molière's 'Les Précieuses ridicules' was first performed in 1659), but
destroyed at the Revolution. It was entirely rebuilt by the Duc d'Aumale
(1822–97), who bequeathed the domain and his art collection to the Institut de
France.

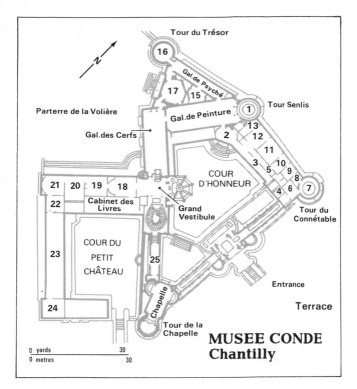

The *Galerie des Cerfs* is first traversed, hung with 17C Gobelins tapestries of hunting scenes, and then the *Galerie de Peintures*, with portraits of Mazarin and Richelieu by *Philippe de Champaigne*, and of Colbert by *Nanteuil*, to reach the *Rotunda*, with a mosaic from Herculaneum, and paintings by *Clouet, del Sarto, Annibale Carracci* and *Piero de Cosimo*.—Hence we turn into the *Galerie de Logis*, with a magnificent collection of French portrait drawings, many by *Corneille de Lyon*. From the *Rotonde de la Minerve* we return along an exterior gallery, with a series of rooms displaying Greek and Roman antiquities, and an interesting series of paintings to reach the *Salle Caroline*, containing works by *Greuze, Watteau*, and *Nattier*, among others, while in the adjoining rooms are more paintings, largely of the *Schools of Clouet* and *Corneille de Lyon*.

Re-crossing the Galerie de Peintures, the *Galerie de Psyche* is entered, with 42 sepia *Stained-glass windows* representing the Loves of Cupid and Psyche, probably designed in 1541 by *Michiel Coxie* for Écouen. On the walls are other portrait drawings, ascribed to *Clouet* or *Jean Perréal*. The adjacent *Santuario* contains *Raphael's* Madonna of the House of Orléans, and The three Graces, and reproductions of 40 miniatures from the *Book of Hours of Étienne Chevalier* (ascribed to *Jean Fouquet*, and executed in 1453–60). Beyond is the *Cabinet des Gemmes*.

The *Tribune* is then traversed, decorated with views of country seats of the Duc d'Aumale (including Twickenham), and a variety of good paintings, even if some of them are of doubtful attribution, to regain the Galerie des Cerfs.

The richly decorated and furnished apartments of the *Petit Château* are then visited, among them the *Salon des Singes*, with chinoiserie wall-panels by *Christophe Huet*. The long *Galerie des Actions* is devoted to scenes of battles fought by the Grand Condé (including Rocroi, Nördlingen, and Lens), painted by *Sauveur Lecomte* in 1686–96, together with portraits and busts.

Retracing our steps, the *Cabinet des Livres* or *Library* is next entered, preserving numerous remarkable bindings, and reproductions of the magnificently illuminated **Très Riches Heures du Duc de Berri*, executed c 1415 by *Pol de Limborg* and his brothers. The delicate originals (together with those of the above-mentioned Étienne Chevalier miniatures), although preserved here, are understandably no longer on general view.

On reaching the principal staircase, turn right along the *Galerie de la Chapelle*, with drawings by *Dürer, Domenichino, Piombo*, and *Raphael*, to enter the *Chapel*, many times rebuilt, in which is the mausoleum of Henri II de Condé (died 1662), with mid 16C *boiseries* and stained-glass brought from Écouen, together with an altar by *Jean Bullant* and *Jean Goujon*.

The **Park** was largely laid out for the Grand Condé by *Le Nôtre*, and is embellished by several buildings, including the *Maison de Sylvie* to the SE (the name being given by Théophile de Viau to Marie Félice Orsini, Duchesse de Montmorency, who hid the poet here when he was condemned to death in 1623 for his licentious verses). It was rebuilt in 1684, and was later the scene of a romantic affair between Mlle de Clermont and Louis de Melún, Duc de Joyeuse, who was killed in 'a hunting accident'. To the N is a '*Hameau*' (1776), and to the W, near the stables, the *Jeu de Paume* of 1757, containing carriages, etc.

The **Fôret de Chantilly**, of 2100 hectares, extending to the S and SE, is intersected by numerous roads or sandy tracks (in the interest of the training-stables), the latter being closed to cars. See IGN Map 404.

5·5km NW of Chantilly is the notable 12C **Church* of **St.-Leu-d'Esserent**.

The D924 leads E from Chantilly along the N bank of the Nonette to (10km) **SENLIS** (15,300 inhab.), which retains several attractive old alleys within the Gallo-Roman ramparts of the *Silvanectes*, and a cathedral of interest.

Probably built on the site of *Ratomagnus*, Senlis was a royal residence from the time of Clovis to Henri IV; Hugues Capet was elected 'Duc des Francs' here in 987; in 1358 it was the scene of a massacre of nobles by the Jacquerie. It was briefly in German hands in September 1914, when they set fire to some streets and plundered the town. It was also damaged in 1940.

A stretch of its medieval ramparts survives to the SE, while in the town centre is the *Hôtel de Ville*, rebuilt in 1495, from which the Rue du Châtel leads into the Gallo-Roman enceinte, of which 16 towers remain, although many are hidden by abutting houses. It approaches the *Hôtel des Trois-Pots*, first mentioned in 1292, but with a 16C façade, the entrance to the ruined castle, the *Priory of St.-Maurice* (14C), a *Hunting Museum*, and the cathedral.

The **Cathedral* was built in 1155–84 (almost coeval with St.-Denis, and Nôtre-Dame), its S tower surmounted by a 13C spire. The central door of the W façade is embellished with statues and reliefs.The transepts were rebuilt in the mid 16C after a fire, and display

Renaissance tendencies; the five E chapels and the side portals date from the same period.

The interior preserves a beautiful triforium gallery, and a splendid 16C vault in the E chapel of the S transept. The late 14C *Chapter-house*, with a remarkable central pillar, and the octagonal *Sacristy*, a relic of the original church, are both notable.

To the E is the former *Bishop's Palace*, behind which is the former church of *St.-Pierre* (now a market) with a Flamboyant façade of 1516, one tower with a dome of Renaissance date, and the other partly Romanesque, with a spire of 1432.

To the W of the town are the relics of a *Gallo-Roman amphitheatre.*—2·5km SE are the picturesque ruins of the *Abbaye de la Victoire*, founded by Philippe Auguste to commemorate the Battle of Bouvines (1214), and rebuilt in the 15–16C.

For areas beyond Chantilly and Senlis, see *Blue Guide France.*

40 To Fontainebleau

Distance from Paris, 65km (40 miles).

The A6 motorway provides a rapid route for the first 49km; then veer SE onto the N37. This skirts the W perimeter of *Orly Airport*, and bears SE past (left) *Évry* (29,600 inhab.), préfecture of the department of Essonne, and *Corbeil-Essonnes* (38,100 inhab.).—At 7km after leaving the motorway, a crossroad leads right 1km to the village of **Barbizon**, now the sophisticated resort of artists emulating the School of artists who made it their headquarters in the mid 19C, among them Millet, Théodore Rousseau, Corot, Diaz de la Peña, and Daubigny. The first two were buried at *Chailly-en-Bière*, just N of the main road, where Bazille, Monet, Renoir, Sisley, and Seurat also painted.

The N37 joins the N7 just beyond this crossroad, and traverses part of the *Fôret de Fontainebleau* (see below) to approach (8km) the town of **Fontainebleau** (18,800 Bellifontains). It takes its name from *Fons Blandi* or *Fontaine de Bland*, and is one of the pleasantest resorts in the neighbourhood of Paris, although one may quote Arthur Young, who visited the place in September 1787, and remarked that the landlord of the inn there 'thinks that royal palaces should not be seen for nothing; he made me pay 10 livres for a dinner which would have cost me not more than half the money at the Star and Garter at Richmond'.

It is mentioned as a royal hunting-seat in 1137, and was later fortified. Thomas Becket, then in exile, consecrated the chapel of *St.-Saturnin* in 1169. Although Philippe IV was born and died here, it was later deserted for the Loire. It owes its present form to François I, who assembled a group of Italian artists (among them Serlio, Rosso, Primaticcio, Vignola, and Nicolo dell'Abate) to rebuild and decorate the château, which continued during the reign of Henri IV, whose son Louis XIII was born here. Christina of Sweden retired here in 1657; here Louis XIV signed the Revocation of the Edict of Nantes (1685); and it was visited by Peter the Great in 1717 during the minority of Louis XV.

The château was restored by Napoléon, who confined Pope Pius VII here. Napoléon abdicated here in 6 April 1814, only to return (20 March 1815), via Grenoble from Elba, to review his guard before leading them to the Tuileries. Louis-Philippe likewise restored it, in his usual questionable taste. From 1941 it was the HQ of Von Brauchitsch, until liberated by Patton in August 1944, after which it became the HQ of the Allied powers in Europe for some years.

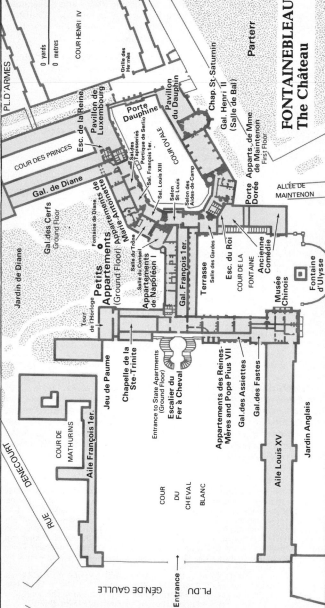

FONTAINEBLEAU
The Château

COUR HENRI IV

Grille des
Hermès

PL. D'ARMES

COUR DES PRINCES

Esc. de la Reine

Pavillon de
Luxembourg

Porte
Dauphine

Pavillon
du Dauphin

Chap. St-Saturnin

Gal. de Diane

Salle des
Pâtisseries

Portique de Serlio

COUR OVALE

Gal. Henri II
(Salle de Bal)

Apparts. de Mme
de Maintenon
First Floor

Parterr

Gal. des Cerfs
Ground Floor

Fontaine de Diane

Petits
Appartements
(Ground Floor)

Jardin de Diane

Sal. François 1er.

Sal. Louis XIII

Salon
St Louis

Salon des
Aides-de-Camp

Porte
Dorée

ALLÉE DE
MAINTENON

Appartements de
Marie-Antoinette

Salle du Conseil

Salle du Trône

Appartement
de Napoléon I

Salle du Trône

Gal. François 1er.

Terrasse

Salle des Gardes

Esc. du Roi

COUR DE LA
FONTAINE

Ancienne
Comédie

Musée Chinois

Fontaine
d'Ulysse

Etang des Carpes

Tour
de l'Horloge

Jeu de Paume

Chapelle de la
Ste-Trinité

Entrance to State Apartments
(Ground Floor)

Escalier du
Fer à Cheval

Appartements des Reines-
Mères and Pope Pius VII

Gal. des Assiettes

Gal. des Fastes

Aile Louis XV

Jardin Anglais

COUR
DU
CHEVAL
BLANC

DENECOURT

RUE

COUR DE
MATHURINS

Aile François 1er.

Entrance

PL. DU
GÉN. DE GAULLE

N

50
50
0 yards
0 metres

The Rue Royale (in which No. 15 contains a small military museum) and the Blvd Magenta converge on the *Pl. du Gén. de Gaulle*, facing the W front of the château, in which the doorway of the *Hôtel du Card. de Ferrare* is an authentic work by Serlio.

The exterior of the **CHÂTEAU DE FONTAINEBLEAU**, composed of many distinct buildings erected over the years, is plain compared with its richly decorated interior. The main entrance is approached via the *Cour des Adieux* (after Napoléon's farewell to the Old Guard on 20 April 1814), also known as that 'du Cheval Blanche', from the cast of a Roman equestrian statue which once stood by the horseshoe-shaped staircase by *Jean du Cerceau* (1634), ascending to the FIRST FLOOR. The interior is visited in groups.

To the left of the *Vestibule* is the *Chapelle de la Sainte-Trinité*, built by Philibert Delorme, in which Louis XV and Marie Leczinska were married in 1725.—To the right are the *Apartments of the Queens-Mother*, occupied by Catherine de Médicis, Anne of Austria, and Marie-Thérèse (and later by Pope Pius VII), among which the main bedroom; the *Galerie des Fastes*, with its carved foliage; and the *Galerie des Assiettes*, decorated with Sèvres plates, are notable.

Opposite the entrance is the 64m-long *Galerie François-Ier*, of 1528–44, one of the few rooms extant of that period. Beyond, we cross (right) the *Salle des Gardes* and *Escalier du Roi* (by *Gabriel*; 1749), the upper part once the bedroom of the Duchess d'Étampes, to reach the splendid *Salle de Bal*, by *Philibert Delorme*, in which the interlaced monograms and emblems of Henri II and Diane de Poitiers are ubiquitous. The mythological paintings were designed by *Primaticcio* and executed by *dell'Abate* (1552).

Returning to the Salle de Gardes, first traversing the *Salon de St. Louis*, in the original castle keep, a series of *Royal Apartments* on the N side of the *Cour Ovale* are visited, among the more interesting of which is the *Salon Louis XIII*, with paintings by *Ambroise Dubois* and facing N, the *Appartements de la Reine* (or de Marie-Antoinette, who chose the decorations), built between 1545 and 1565. Notable are the *Queen's Bedroom* and the *Salle du Trône* (previously the king's bedroom), with a ceiling of the time of Louis XIII and a copy of *Philippe de Champaigne's* portrait of that king.

The imposing *Salle du Conseil*, decorated by *Boucher* and *C. van Loo*, among others, with a bay added in 1773, is crossed before entering the *Apartments of Napoléon-I*, abutting the *Galerie François-I*, partly furnished in Empire style, and containing several Napoleonic relics.—On the floor below are the *Petits Appartements de Napoléon et de Joséphine*, preserving their Louis XV and Louis XVI decoration, and more Empire furniture and Napoleonic souvenirs.

Admission to other parts of the château is normally only granted on specific request to the conservateur.

The *Jardin de Diane* may be visited from the NE corner of the entrance courtyard, while to the SE of the main block of buildings extends the *Parterre*, and further W, the *Jardin Anglais*, laid out for Napoléon. Thomas Coryate, passing through Fontainebleau in 1605, was amazed to see ostriches running wild somewhere in these gardens! Beyond the parterre is the Park, with a canal dug for Henri II.

Some distance to the E beyond the walls, lies the suburb of **Avon**, with a 13–16C church in which are the tombs of Monaldeschi (Christina of Sweden's favourite, whose assassination she had ordered), Ambroise Dubois, the artist, and the naturalist Daubentin; while in the cemetery lies Katherine Mansfield (1888–1923), who died near here while under the malign influence of Gurdjieff.—At *Valvins* (1·5km NE of the railway-station), lived Mallarmé (1842–98) from 1884 until his death. He is buried in its cemetery.

The *Forest of Fontainebleau* surrounding the town, and approx. 17,000 hectares in extent, although traversed by a number of good roads, is best explored on foot. Its thick glades and picturesque wildernesses of rock interspersed by sandy clearings, make it a pleasant place for excursions. Two of the more attractive sites are the *Gorges de Franchard*, and *d'Apremont*, some 4km W and NW respectively of the *Carrefour de la Libération*. See IGN Map 401.

For **Melun** (18km N), **Vaux-le-Vicomte** (6km NE of Melun), and areas beyond Fontainebleau, see *Blue Guide France*.

INDEX OF THE PRINCIPAL FRENCH ARTISTS AND ARCHITECTS

This includes those whose works are frequently referred to in the text, together with their dates. It includes certain foreign artists working in Paris and its environs.

GENERAL INDEX

Topographical names in Paris are in Roman type; those in the envrions in **Bold**. The names of notable people are in *Italics*; see pp 279–81 for the principal French artists and architects.

Note that streets, etc. named after persons are known by and indexed under the full name: i.e. Rue Antoine-Bourdelle, not Rue Bourdelle, which can be confusing when the visitor is not aware of the Christian name in question. The names of Ministères are subject to change. These, together with Avenues, Bibliothèques, Boulevards, Cafés, Carrefours, Chapelleș, Châteaux, Cimetières, Collèges, Écoles, Fontaines, Forêts, Gares, Hôpitals, Hôtels (mansions), Instituts, Jardins, Ministères, Musées, Palais,Parcs, Places, Ponts, Portes, Prisons, Quais, Rues, Squares, Théâtres, and Tours, *in Paris* are indexed alphabetically in sub-groups under these headings, as are departments of the Musée du Louvre, etc.

Académie Française 87
ADMISSION, HOURS OF 45–8
AÉROGARES 105, 109, 225
Aigle d'Or, Auberge de l' 191
AIR SERVICES 33
Alain-Fournier 83, 205, 271
Alembert, Jean le Rond d' 65, 106, 155, 186, 196
Allée des Arbalétriers 185
Allée des Cygnes 116, 213–4
Allée de Longchamp 222
American church 109
American Embassy 204
Amphithéâtre de St.-Côme 89
Apollinaire, Guillaume 83, 108, 232
Arc de Triomphe 206
Arc de Triomphe du Carrousel 121
Archives Nationales 186
Arènes de Lutèce 78
ARRONDISSEMENTS 37–8
Arsenal, Quartier de l' 173
ART EXHIBITIONS 49
Arts et Métiers, Conservatoire Nat. des 189
Assemblée Nationale 105
Assumption, Church of the 155
Auber, Daniel-François 199, 228, 232
Auteuil 220
Automobile Club 117
Avenant, William d' 208
Avenue Bosquet 109
de Breteuil 113
des Champs-Elysées 117, 204, 206

Avenue (cont'd)
Charles de Gaulle 225
de Clichy 212
Corentin-Cariou 229
Daumesnil 236
Denfert-Rochereau 83, 84
Émile-Zola 114
Foch 221, 222
de Friedland 208
Frochot 202
Gabriel 204
du Gén.-Lemonnier 119, 120, 123
George-V 206, 213
des Gobelins 80, 81
de la Grande-Armée 207, 225
Hoche 209
d'Iéna 216
J.-B. Clément 224
Jean-Jaurès 228
de La Motte-Picquet 109
de Lowendal 113
Marceau 214
du Marigny 204
Mathurin-Moreau 230
Matignon 206, 208
de Messine 210
Montaigne 206, 213
de New York 213
de l'Observatoire 90
de l'Opéra 194, 195
Pierre-1er de Serbie 214
Philippe-Auguste 232
du Président-Kennedy 213
du Président-Wilson 214, 216
Rachel 202
René-Coty 84
de la République 231
Ste.-Marie 236
de Ségur 113
des Sycomores 220
Théophile-Gautier 221
de Tourville 113

Avenue (cont'd)
Velasquez 212
de Victor-Hugo 222
Victoria 169
de Villars 113
de Villiers 213
Winston-Churchill 204
Avon 277

Baccarat 199
Bagatelle 223
Bailly, Jean-Sylvain 56, 114, 169, 240
Balzac, Honoré de 83, 89, 92, 95, 173, 191, 195, 209, 219, 231, 238
BANKS 31
Banque de France 159
Barbizon 275
Barbusse, Henri 209, 232
Barrière de Clichy 201
Barrière d'Enfer 84
Barrington, Sir Jonah 239
Bastille 177–8
'Bateau-Lavoir' 204
Batignolles, Quartier des 212
Baudelaire, Charles 58, 83, 85, 88, 104, 172, 195, 202
Beardsley, Aubrey 107
Beaubourg, Centre 174–6
Beaumarchais, Pierre Caron de 92, 180, 185, 231
Beckett, Samuel 83
Bedford, John, Duke of 180, 186
Belleville 220–1
Bellini, Vincenzo 225, 232
Belloc, Hilaire 239
Bennett, Arnold 201
Béranger, Pierre-Jean de 198, 199, 219, 231
Bergson, Henri 71, 81, 220
Berkeley, George 74
Berlioz, Hector 110, 166,

<u>Restaurants</u>

Guy Savoy
18 Rue Troyon - main one? Cheaper opposite

Montmartrebus runs from S. side
of Pl. Pigalle every 10 - 15 mins - takes
about 1/2 hr. all the way round.
Paris Visite valid.

NOTES

NOTES

ATLAS CONTENTS

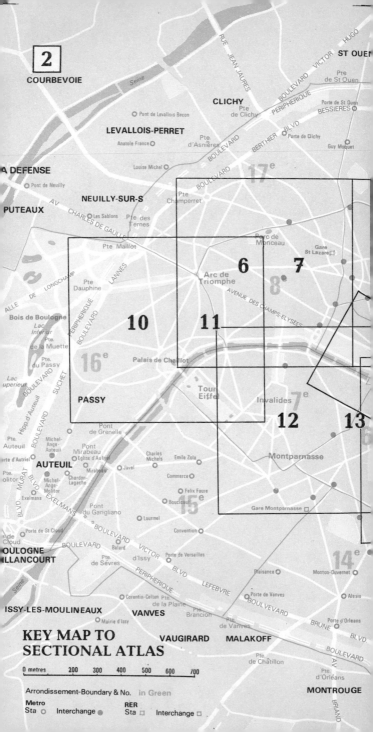

2

COURBEVOIE

ST OUEN

Seine

RUE JEAN JAURES

HUGO

Pont de Levallois Becon

CLICHY

Pte de Clichy

BOULEVARD VICTOR

Pte de St Ouen

PERIPHERIQUE

Porte de St Ouen

BESSIERES

LEVALLOIS-PERRET

Anatole France

Pte d'Asnières

BOULEVARD BERTHIER

BLVD

Porte de Clichy

Guy Moquet

Louise Michel

A DEFENSE

Pont de Neuilly

BOULEVARD

Pte
Champerret

17e

PUTEAUX

AV CHARLES DE GAULLE

NEUILLY-SUR-S

Les Sablons

Pte des
Ternes

Parc de
Monceau

Gare
St Lazare

ALLE DE LONGCHAMP

Pte Maillot

LANNES

Arc de
Triomphe

6

7

8

Pte
Dauphine

Bois de Boulogne

Lac
Inférieur

Pte
de la Muette

PERIPHERIQUE BOULEVARD SUCHET

10

11

AVENUE DES CHAMPS-ELYSÉES

16e

Pte
du Passy

Palais de Chaillot

Lac
Supérieur

BOULEVARD

PASSY

Tour
Eiffel

Invalides

7e

Pte
Auteuil

Hipp d'Auteuil

BOULEVARD

Pont
de Grenelle

12

13

rte d'Auteuil

MURAT

BLVD

Michel-
Ange-
Auteuil

Pont
Mirabeau

Charles
Michels

Emile Zola

Montparnasse

Pte
olitor

AUTEUIL

Eglise d'Auteuil

Mirabeau

Javel

Commerce

Michel-
Ange-
Molitor

EXELMANS

Exelmans

Chardon-
Lagache

Felix Faure

Pont
du Garigliano

Boucicaut

15

Gare Montparnasse

de
Cloud

Lourmel

BOULEVARD

Convention

OULOGNE
ILLANCOURT

VICTOR

14e

BOULEVARD

Balard

d'Issy

Porte de Versailles

Plaisance

Monton-Duvernet

Alesia

Seine

Pte
de Sèvres

BLVD

LEFEBVRE

PERIPHERIQUE

Porte de Vanves

Porte d'Orleans

BRUNE

BLVD

ISSY-LES-MOULINEAUX

Corentin-Celton Pte
de la Plaine

VANVES

Pte
Brancion

BOULEVARD

Pte
de Vanves

Mairie d'Issy

VAUGIRARD

MALAKOFF

BOULEVARD

KEY MAP TO
SECTIONAL ATLAS

Pte
de Châtillon

Pte
d'Orléans

MONTROUGE

BRIAND

0 metres   200   300   400   500   600   700

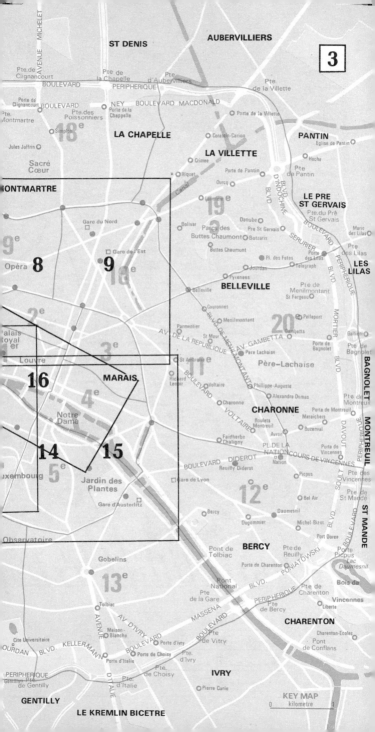

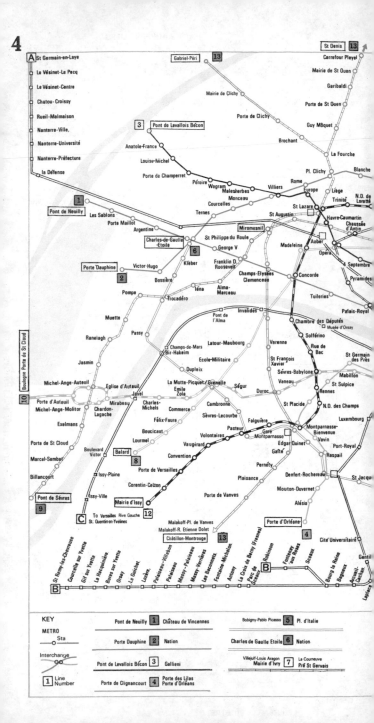

THE METRO and RER Systems

5

KEY
RER [A] [B] [C]
[] Sta
Interchange

[8] Balard — Créteil Préfecture Hôtel de Ville
[9] Pont de Sèvres — Mairie de Montreuil
[10] Boulogne J. Jaures — Gare d'Orléans Austerlitz
[11] Châtelet — Mairie des Lilas
[12] Porte de la Chapelle — Mairie d'Issy
[13] Châtillon-Montrouge — Gabriel-Péri St Denis

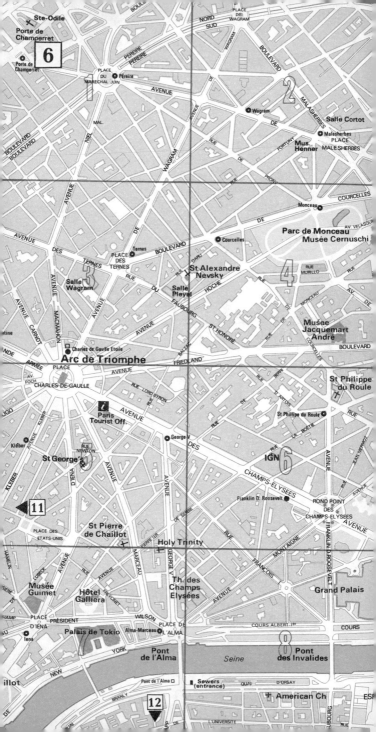

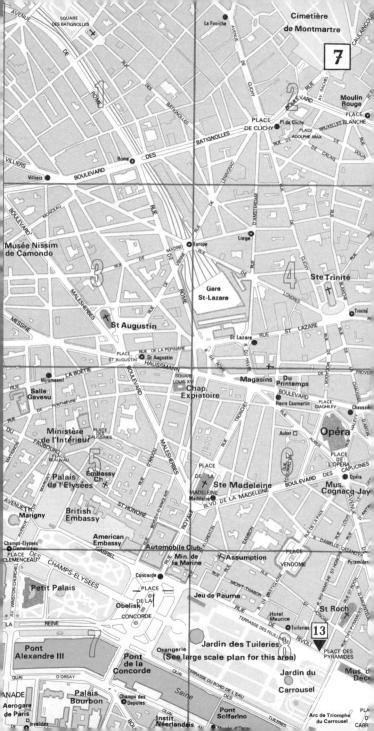

AVENUE
SQUARE
DES BATIGNOLLES
La Fourche
Cimetière
de Montmartre

7

RUE
DE
ROME
RUE
DES
BATIGNOLLES
DE CLICHY
BOULEVARD
Moulin
Rouge
PLACE
BLANCHE
BRUXELLES

VILLIERS
Rome
DES
PLACE
DE CLICHY
Pl. de Clichy
PLACE
ADOLPHE-MAX
DE
DOUAI
DE CALAIS

Villiers
BOULEVARD
BATIGNOLLES
LEGENDRE
RUE

BOULEVARD
MONCEAU
RUE
MADRID
DE
VIENNE
Europe
Liege
D'AMSTERDAM
RUE
CLICHY

Musée Nissim
de Camondo
3
DE
ROME
Ste Trinité

MALESHERBES
RUE
Gare
St-Lazare
4
Trinité
RUE
ST LAZARE
LONDRES

MESSINE
St Augustin
St Lazare
RUE
DE ROME
DE MOSCOU

St Augustin
PLACE
ST AUGUSTIN
RUE DE LA PEPINIERE
St Augustin
HAUSSMANN
RUE
DU HAVRE

Miromesnil
LA BOETIE
SQUARE
LOUIS XVI
Chap.
Expiatoire
**Magasins Du
Printemps**
BOULEVARD
PLACE
DIAGHILEV
Chaussée

Salle
Gaveau
DE
PENTHIEVRE
Havre Caumartin

Ministère
de l'Intérieur
PLACE DES
SAUSSAIES
PLACE
BEAUVAU
Auber
Opéra
HALEVY

Palais
de l'Elysée
5
Embassy
Ch
ST HONORE
PLACE
DE LA
MADELEINE
Madeleine
Ste Madeleine
BLVD. DE LA MADELEINE
PLACE
DE
L'OPERA
Opéra
BOULEVARD DES CAPUCINES
Mus.
Cognacq-Jay

AVENUE
Th.
Marigny
**British
Embassy**
ROYALE
DE LA PAIX

**American
Embassy**
GABRIEL
Automobile Club
DANIELE CASANOVA

Champs-Elysées
Clemenceau
PLACE
CLEMENCEAU
DES CHAMPS-ELYSEES
Concorde
Min. de
la Marine
Assumption
PLACE
VENDOME
Pyramides

Petit Palais
AV. WINSTON CHURCHILL
PLACE
DE LA
CONCORDE
MONT-THABOR
St Roch

Obelisk
Jeu de Paume
RUE
Hotel
Meurice
St Roch

LA
REINE
Tuileries
13
RIVOLI
PLACE DES
PYRAMIDES

**Pont
Alexandre III**
**Pont
de la
Concorde**
Orangerie
(See large scale plan for this area)
Jardin des Tuileries

TERRASSE DES FEUILLANTS
**Jardin du
Carrousel**
Mus. d'
Déc

ESPLANADE
Aerogare
de Paris
**Palais
Bourbon**
Champs des
Deputes
Seine
QUAI
Pont
Solferino
Arc de Triomphe
du Carrousel
PLA
D
CARR

Invalides
Instit.
Néerlandais
Musée d'Orsay

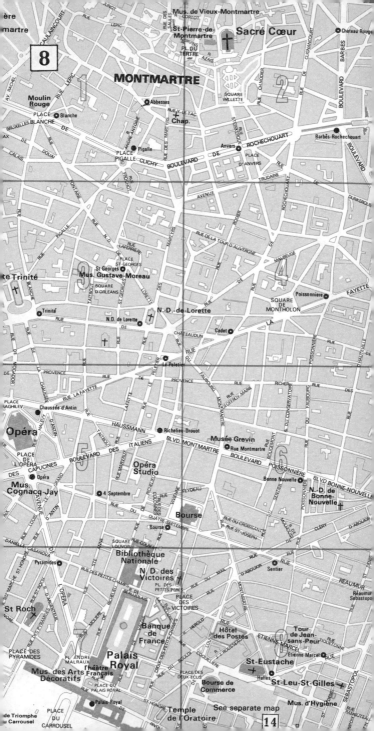

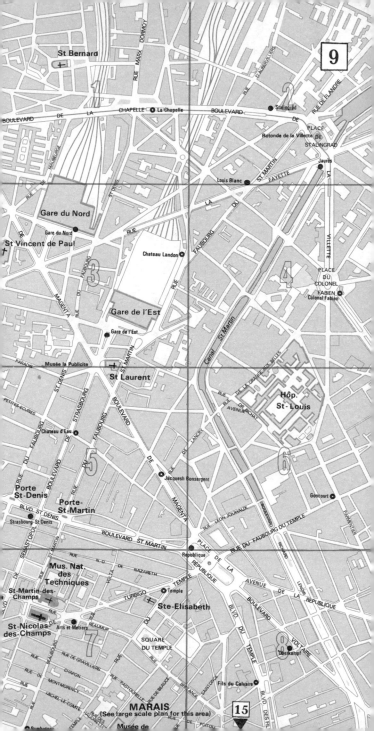

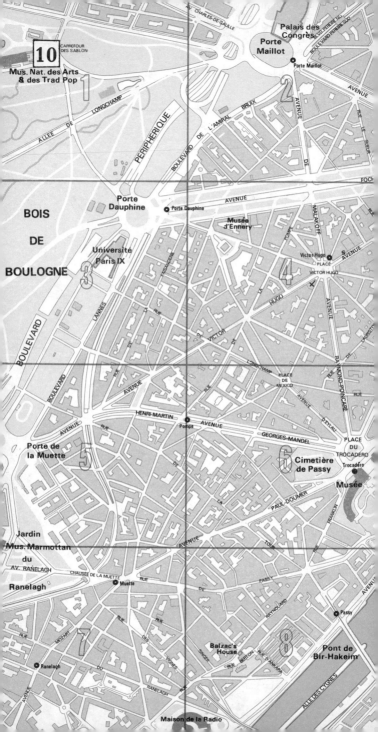

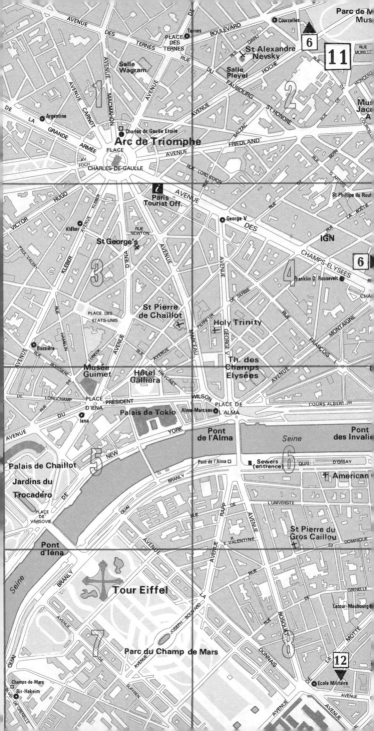

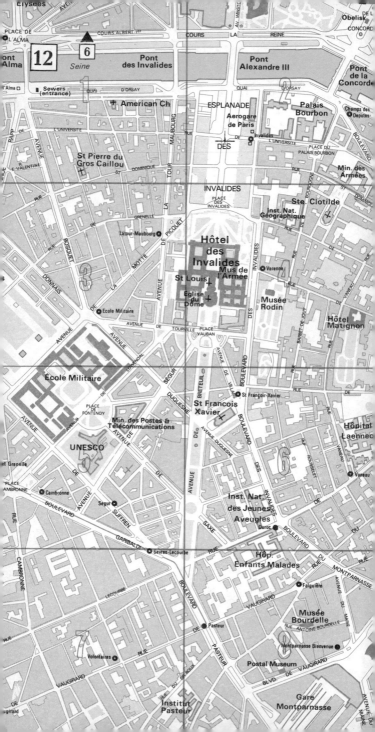

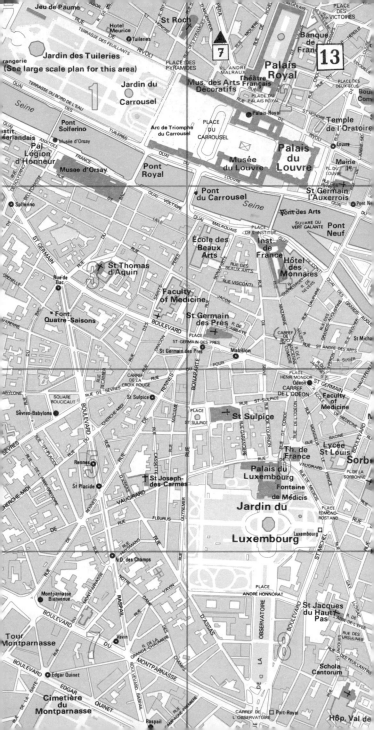

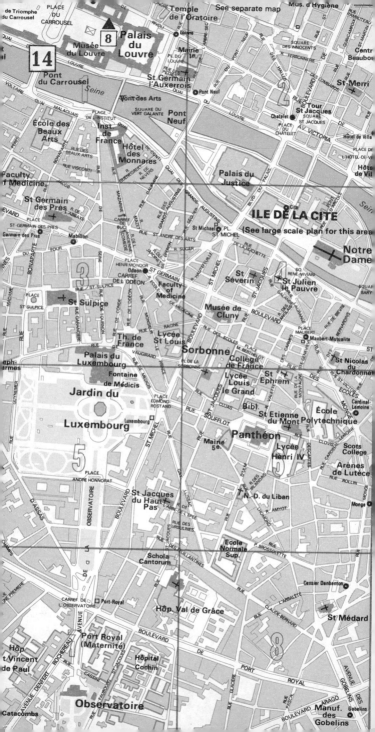

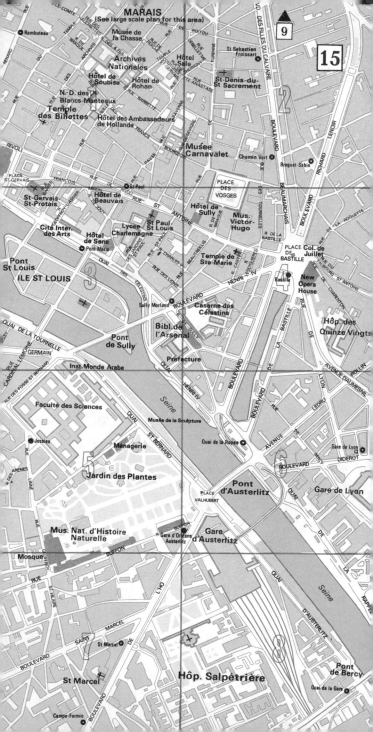

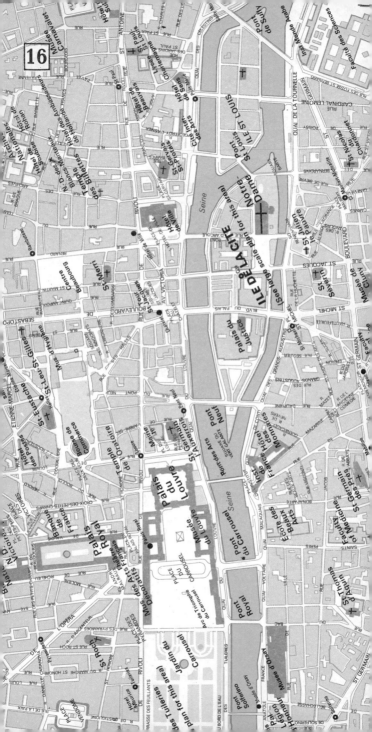